HEALTH FOR ALL
Cultural, Operational & Technological Influences

35th UIA/PHG International Seminar on Public Healthcare Facilities
Dalian, China. May 23-25, 2015

Proceedings
edited by Romano Del Nord

Conference organized by:

UIA/PHG International Union of Architects/ Public Health Group
GUPHA Global University Program in Healthcare Architecture

Published by
TESIS Inter-University Research Centre
Systems and Technologies for Social and Healthcare Facilities
University of Florence
Italy

Scientific Editor:
Prof. Romano Del Nord
Director of TESIS Inter-University Research Centre
University of Florence

Volume layout
Maria Grazia Giardinelli
Arch. PhD
University of Florence

Published by

TESIS Inter-University Research Centre "Systems and Technologies for Social and Healthcare Facilities"

Department of Architecture DIDA
University of Florence

Via San Niccolò 93
info@tesis.unifi.it
+ 39 055 275 5348
Florence 50125
Italy

ISBN 978-88-941518-1-7
First Print 2016

Cover photograph Sarah Brasilia Lago Norte, Brasilia

The texts have been faithfully reproduced as provided by the authors without any intervention by the editor, except for the necessary cuts and reductions of the text for layout purposes.

Index

TESIS Inter-University Research Centre "Systems and Technologies for Social and Healthcare Facilities"
University of Florence, Italy

Index

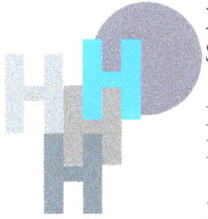

6

Foreword

by Romano Del Nord

As has already been noted at previous UIA-PHG annual conferences, at the Dalian event too the design problems addressed in the different sessions and in the individual papers presented concerned aspects of professional benefit and general interest that go beyond the specificities of the geographic and socio-economic contexts of the speakers.

The topic of the humanization of care spaces is confirmed as a central issue with respect to the objectives to be pursued in hospital intervention programmes, even if treated from angles and slants that highlight its close interdependence with behaviour models that vary in relation to the culture of the places, the varied forms of social interaction and the economic conditions of the different geographic areas. As regards the increasingly marked and widespread attention to the "patient centrality" requirements, the existence of very different design solutions was noted, which were particularly stimulating due to the understanding of the impact generated by "lifestyles" on the arrangement of the care environment. The differences found not only between experiences in different continents but also in different regions within the same continent are tangible evidence of this.

Particular attention was paid to problems deriving from the need for "integration", for which the hospital must ensure an adequate response given that users of different cultures tend to co-exist with similar health demands while their expectations over treatment methods often vary. The different solutions presented by the speakers represent a mosaic of compliant solutions, each of which can teach us something new.

Contributions concerning alternative approaches tested to ensure adequate assistance for the growing spread of chronic diseases and co-morbidity in elderly people are particular stimulating. This problem, in addition to enhancing awareness of the set up of the entire system of regional public health services for an ever broader range of users, raises some questions on the characterization of spaces where environmental logistical support prevails over the true function of care.

For the most part the discussions highlighted the close interdependence between the strategic planning of the future city and methods of managing public health. The relationship between the hospital and the city increasingly assumes strategic value in the reconfiguration of the public spaces destined for community use. The role of invisible technologies has a hand in seeing that the facilities that help to ensure the widespread well-being of citizens are interactive and interdependent.

As a result, the development of new technologies is increasingly considered an opportunity to recover the social value of healthcare facilities which technological innovation risks compromising.

The city thus becomes a fundamental place for triggering "health promotion" processes, not only through how socio-healthcare facilities are used but through the creation of structural opportunities that stimulate the development of healthier lifestyles.

Finally, the exchange of opinions and views on the requirements of a population considered to be "vulnerable", in the broadest sense of the word, further emphasized the importance of the patient-user centrality objective. The categories that come under this definition are rather broad and take into account the degree of autonomy and type of physical, mental, spatial and environmental conflicts that are generated in the use of the spaces and services under normal and exceptional conditions. Once again, aspects linked to the physical and mental conditions of citizens in critical situations bring to light the need to conceive of the design of the built environment as a design for the universal user.

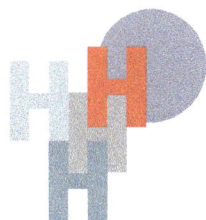

CULTURAL INFLUENCES ON HEALTHCARE DESIGN

Session introduction
Alessia Spirito
Eng., Research Fellow University of Florence

Reconciling the high international design standards of healthcare facilities with different cultural specificities is a highly topical issue.

The experiences shared in the sessions highlight how the use of criteria aimed at increasing the humanization of the spaces is essential in design that is ever more sensitive to Human-centered Design topics.

Moreover, it can be seen how the same functional and design quality of spaces is strongly linked to the intrinsic characteristics of the local culture. The full steps used to manage the development of planning and design decisions are revealed, seeking to integrate multiple disciplines through the participation of staff and consumers.

For the redevelopment of Sarah Hospitals in Brazil, an attempt was made to validate the effectiveness of the principles used in the design. Interesting conclusions emerged on the integration of the very principles of Evidence-based Design theories in the design and construction of healthcare facilities. The growing demand for adequate healthcare in China has led to questions about the effectiveness of a highly Westernized international model broadly used in its hospital facilities, identifying cultural preferences for organizational communication and assessing how they are reflected in the spatial configurations of the treatment units.

Local religious and cultural integration is a key aspect for architecture that acts as a model for the promotion of health and equality.

The case studies reported highlight differences in European architectural parameters with respect to those of the Arabic culture, particular characteristics being the humanization of some healthcare environments through religious culture.

There was also an attempt to provide criteria and indications useful for integrating the best practices and international standards with local traditions and specific requests concerning requirements.

For some cultures more than others, healthcare facilities must be a place for the healing of the body but also of the spirit. The study on integrating the requirements of Buddhism provides an illustrative framework of how to link spiritual requirements with the healthcare space.

Sometimes current trends need to be addressed, as in the case of Japan which has seen the demand for nursing rather than medical assistance increase for elderly people. This implies there is a demand to meet the new requirements and verify the appropriateness of the existing inpatient rooms, for example.

Finally, there was a look at integration between new technologies and medicine in an increasingly Smart hospital, in order to foster an improved user experience encouraging safety and integrating assisted monitoring activities for a better quality of care.

Designs by João Filgueiras Lima (Lelé) for Brazil's SARAH Network of Hospitals for Rehabilitation[1]

Gabriela Campagnol

campagnol@gmail.com
PhD. Arch., Department of Architecture at Texas A&M University in College Station, Texas

Mardelle McCuskey Shepley

DArch, FAIA, FACHA, EDAC, LEED AP,
College of Human Ecology at Cornell University, Ithaca, New York

João Filgueiras Lima, known as Lelé, has been a dominant figure in the 20th and 21st century Brazilian architecture and the architect of several rehabilitation facilities, in particular for the Sarah Network of Rehabilitation Hospitals. Architects in many parts of the world do not formally incorporate theories of evidence-based design, but there are multiple international examples of health facility designers that use nature and art to enhance the healing experience. The work of Lelé is a particularly salient example. Despite the lack of formal integration of evidence-based design in healthcare architecture in Latin America, many of the basic tenets generated from design research have been incorporated in Brazilian rehabilitation hospitals. As Campagnol & Shepley (2014) noticed, the use of positive distraction, an evidence-based design tenet, in the rehabilitation facilities of Lelé for Sarah hospitals is a clear example of this phenomenon and has served to inspire many current healthcare projects. Lelé's success is a demonstration of the critical role familiarity with medical treatment protocols and insights regarding human behavior play in creating an alignment between research and practitioner experience. This paper discusses the design principles (such as the use of positive distraction) in rehabilitation of the Sarah hospitals in Brazil designed by Lelé.

Keywords: *Rehabilitation Hospital, Healthcare design theory, Evidence-based design, Healing Environments, Brazil, João Filgueiras Lima (Lelé).*

1. *Portions of this paper first appeared in Campagnol, G. and Shepley, M. M. (2014). "Positive distraction and the rehabilitation hospitals of João Filgueiras Lima". In Health Environments Research & Design Journal, 8(1), pp.199-227. While the publication was under revision, the architect Lelé passed away on May 21, 2014 in the city of Salvador, Brazil. He leaves a legacy that synthesizes art, technology, and social responsibility. The hospitals for the Sarah Network are examples of conciseness, humanization, and how architecture can positively affect the healing process. Lelé's hospitals serve to inspire healthcare design worldwide. The authors wish to thank D. Kirk Hamilton, Jaynelle Stichler, Jennifer Crane, Sonia Bello, Lucia Willadino Braga, Adriana Filgueiras Lima, Hermínia Machry, Denise Menicucci, Hugo Segawa, Zhouzhou Su, and Heriberto Zazueta.*

INTRODUCTION

While many international healthcare architects do not formally address positive distraction - an evidence-based design tenet - as part of their design philosophy, there are multiple examples of health facility designers that incorporate nature, daylighting, art, and social interaction to enhance the healing experience.

The work of Brazilian architect João Filgueiras Lima, known more colloquially as "Lelé," is a particularly salient example. A collaborator of Oscar Niemeyer and Lina Bo Bardi, Lelé springs from a tradition of well-known and prolific Latin American architects.

He has been the designer of more than a dozen hospitals, focusing primarily on rehabilitation and children's facilities. Critical to Lelé's design strategies for healing environments are the incorporation of nature, water, daylight, art, color, sculpture and strong graphics. While Lelé does not mention positive distraction in his writings, interesting lessons can be learned from his work by those who embrace evidence-based design (EBD). Positive distraction, in the context of medical facilities, can be defined

Figure 1. Lelé and Oscar Niemeyer (Photo: Personal archive of Lelé)

as "the ability to allow the individual to shift focus from negative foci within the health environment to the more restorative aspects of the non-medical world" (Shepley, 2006, p. S34). There are several forms of positive distraction, the most common of which are art (music, entertainment), access to nature and presence of daylight. Social interaction can also serve as a form of positive distraction for staff, patients and families.

A rehabilitation hospital is normally defined as a facility for patients whose medical conditions are stable, but still require 24-hour care. In reviewing the literature, two main types of rehabilitation facilities are encountered – those that support physical and emotional trauma and those that address drug addition rehabilitation. The notion of rehabilitation hospitals is new relative to other healthcare specialties.

LELE'S ROLE IN BRAZILIAN HEALTHCARE ARCHITECTURE

Lelé was born in 1932 in Rio de Janeiro, Brazil. In 1957, two years after his graduation in architecture from the National School of Fine Arts in Rio de Janeiro, he moved to Brasília to assist in the construction of the new capital, where he collaborated with Oscar Niemeyer on several projects. Together with the anthropologist Darcy Ribeiro, Lelé participated in all the aspects of the construction of the University of Brasília, where he also taught for few years. Lelé distinguished himself as one of the most important architects in Brazil by working in pre-fabricated constructions, innovative results in ergonomics, daylighting and natural ventilation, and the "total design" for the Sarah Network of

14

Figure 2. Lelé: Taguatinga Hospital, Brasilia, 1968

Hospitals across the country.

Among his awards, he received the Grand Prize of the Biennale of Architecture and Engineering in Madrid (2000) for the Sarah Hospital in Salvador (Haidar 2001, p. 14).

In 1968, Lelé designed a hospital in an administrative region in the Federal District, which was the first in a series of healthcare facilities designed by him. The building was conceived according to the guidelines established by the Federal District Secretariat of Health and by the architect Oscar Niemeyer, aiming for flexibility and expandability of construction. This led to the use of pre-casting techniques for the structural system, which Lelé pioneered in Brazil. This was also the first collaboration between Lelé and the Brazilian painter and sculptor Athos Bulcão (1918-2008) in a healthcare facility.

In 1969, Lelé went in a business trip to Finland. While there, the high level of technology, the "human environment" of several hospitals, and a hospital furniture factory impressed him (Risselada 2012, p. 20). Thus, this experience might have a great influence in his later work, in particular for the Sarah Network.

The importance of Lelé in healthcare architecture in Brazil is synthesized by Oscar Niemeyer: "I love to talk about friends, and even more so when it is question of such an old and dear companion, as Lelé (…) In Brasilia, Lelé has built his first projects and a series of admirable houses and apartment blocks. (…) I Remember a conversation I had at the Rio de Janeiro Institute of Architects, and how I couldn't contain myself when the question of hospitals turned up, saying: 'Today, if somebody wants to plan an up-to-date hospital, he'll have to talk first with Lelé'" (Latorraca, 2000, p.11). Despite of Lelé's recognition in Brazil, his work has not gained international exposure.

15

TESIS

Figure 3. Lelé: Taguatinga Hospital. Wall panels by Athos Bulcão. Brasilia, 1968

BRAZILIAN REHABILITATION HOSPITALS: THE SARAH NETWORK AND THE CENTRO DE TECNOLOGIA DA REDE SARAH (CTRS)

The Sarah Kubitschek Network of Reha-bilitation Hospital, called "Rede Sarah" [Sarah Network], and the "Centro de Tecnologia da Rede Sarah" (CTRS) [Sarah Network Technological Center] are critical to a discussion of rehabilitation facilities in Brazil.

Considered one of the world largest neuro-rehabilitation and neuropsychology networks, the Sarah Network comprises 1,000 beds distributed through nine hospital units located in Brasilia (DF), with a hospital and a International Center for Research and Rehabilitation, Salvador (BA), São Luis (MA), Belo Horizonte (MG), Fortaleza (CE), Rio de Janeiro (RJ), Macapá (AP), and Belém (PA). In 2012, the Sarah Network had more than 1.5 million patient visits ("O paciente," n.d.)[2].

The Network is funded by the Brazilian government and managed by the Associação das Pioneiras Sociais (APS) [Social Pioneers Association], a nongovernmental organization established in 1991. Abundant airy spaces, solarium and gardens designed to "soften the hospital environment units," are hallmarks of the Sarah Network, which has medical treatment and post-treatment units as well as research, continuing education, and employee training facilities. The environments support patients with different medical and therapeutic needs, with swimming pools, gymnasiums for physical therapy, complementary diagnostic exam units, and operational service stations.

---

2. *In 2012, the Sarah Hospitals Network held a daily average of 6,197 calls, totaling this year more than 1,536,899 patient visits.*

The development of these facilities was largely an outcome of collaboration between Lelé and the orthopedic surgeon Aloysio Campos da Paz, Junior, co-founders of the Sarah Network of Rehabilitation Hospitals. Lelé and Campos da Paz jointly developed a concept where architectural and medical realms merge[3].

_____

3. *This integrative concept was also developed in collaboration with Eduardo Kertész (economist with expertise in health, and who was responsible for the creation of important national health and nutrition plans), and the anthropologist Roberto Pinho (who, together with the designer Alex Peirano, found the Equiphos, an organization in charge of designing and producing hospital equipment).*

The first collaboration between these two professionals came from Lelé's drawings on traction equipment that Campos da Paz used for training the nurses in the Sarinha in Brasília.

The Sarinha was initially conceived only for rehabilitation, but eventually evolved towards becoming a small hospital for "locomotor disease," driven by the ideals of Campos da Paz, who was trained in England and advocated an orthopedic method of minimal invasive surgery and intervention, which differed from what was commonly practiced in Brazil at that time. Thus, a small 60-bed hospital was established with operating rooms, laboratory, X-ray apparatus, and

17

Figure 4. Sarah Hospital Macapá (1998 – 2005). Pediatric rehabilitation center

was coupled with what was initially just a "classic rehabilitation center" (Pinho, 2012, p. 52). In 1974, the Sarinha functioned in a building designed in 1960 for another purpose.

However, the demand growth, community pressure, and lack of space in the building hampered its proper functioning. At this time, Campos da Paz presented a draft of a nationwide subsystem of rehabilitation healthcare to be headquartered in Brasília.

This initiative emphasized the functions of the rehabilitation center together with the facilities of a large hospital of 300 beds.

Lelé acknowledged the importance of Campos da Paz in the Sarah's design, in particular in the creation of the CTRS. In implementing the hospitals of the Sarah Network, doctor and architect focused on two main concepts: the pro-

gressive care system (i.e., the successive transfer of the patient to sites with specific features provided directly linked to their clinical status), and maximum use of available/local resources.

The history of the Sarah Network began in 1980, with the inauguration of the first rehabilitation hospital in Brasília. A crucial factor in the development of the hospital's program was to create suitable environments that would foster the healing process of patients who were immobilized in their beds. Lelé and Campos de Paz believed that this method of treatment would eliminate or mitigate the need to use complex and invasive equipment.

Areas previously occupied by this sophisticated equipment, which are necessarily confined places, could then become open areas. For this reason Lelé designed light beds similar to gurneys that could be reclined and circulated around the hospital, increasing the patients mobility throughout the building and their accessibility to gardens, open spaces, and interaction with other patients and family. This brings the possibility of moving patients to gardens and outdoor spaces providing opportunities for positive distraction.

In 1988, Lelé and Campos da Paz headed a plan for expanding that initiative through the construction of three hospitals, which would be located in Salvador, Curitiba, and São Luis.

In 1991, "thanks to Campos da Paz's determination," the Associação das Pioneiras Sociais, through a special law approved by the National Congress (n. 8.246, October 22, 1991), was given the task of managing the public patrimony of the Sarah network of rehabilitation hospitals.

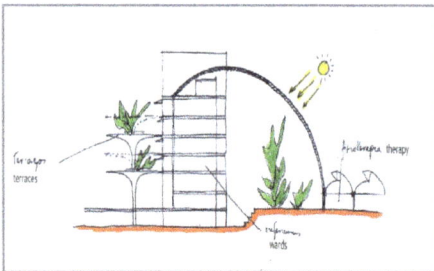

Figure 5. Access to nature

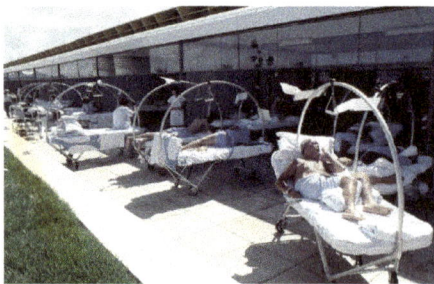

Figure 6. Social interaction for staff, patients, and families

Figure 7.   Sarah Rio de Janeiro Children Rehabilitation Center, Rio de Janeiro, RJ (2001-2002)

The Sarah Hospital in Salvador, Bahia, was the first unit to be built during the contract between the Associação das Pioneiras Sociais and the Federal Government. One of the goals in the contract was to extend the network's action over the national territory (construction of new rehabilitation hospitals). Thus, a technological center for the Sarah Network (CTRS) was established in 1993. Lelé's previous experience with pre-fabrication in the city and its central location in relation to new hospital locations favored this decision.

With a $17 million investment and a highly automatized production, the CTRS Factory was built nearby the future rehabilitation hospital. The new hospitals would be entirely produced in the CTRS and delivered to the assigned hospital location to be assembled.

As a result of the technology and design based on simple structural principles, the hospitals produced in the CTRS cost less than the rest of the hospitals made in Brazil (Toledo, 2002; Pinho, 2012)[4]. Three main concepts underlay the hospitals designed by Lelé and produced in

4. *According to Lelé, the unsuccessful experience in the hospital in São Luis, where a private firm was in charge of the construction, helped in the decision to create the CTRS. The hospital in São Luis cost R$ 70 millions, while the hospital in Salvador, which was built later by the CTRS, cost R$ 36 millions, after equipped.*

the CTRS[5]:

1. Horizontality of the design in relation to the program.

2. A system of natural light and ventilation.

3. Structural stability of the construction system.

___

5. Lelé summarized the CTRS's goals as following: "1. Design and execute buildings based on principles of industrialization, aiming economy, rapid construction, and creation of appropriate construction/structural integration across all units of the network; 2. Design and execute, interacting with medical and paramedical teams of the association, the equipment required for the development of new techniques in treatment introduced in hospitals of the network; 3. Design and produce conventional hospital equipment whenever observed qualitative or economic advantage over those offered by the market; 4. Perform the maintenance of buildings, equipment, and facilities of all units in the network; 5. Conduct training courses in the area of expertise through partnerships with universities and other institutions of its kind; and 6. Promote the dissemination of the work and technological exchanges with other institutions operating in the same field of research" (Risselada 2012, p.105).

Figure 8. Sarah Belém Pediatric Outpatient Center, Belém, PA (1998 – 2007)

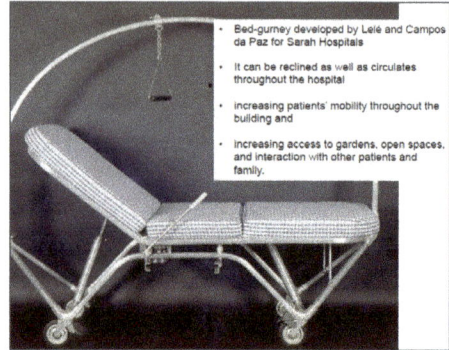

- Bed-gurney developed by Lelé and Campos da Paz for Sarah Hospitals
- It can be reclined as well as circulates throughout the hospital
- Increasing patients' mobility throughout the building and
- Increasing access to gardens, open spaces, and interaction with other patients and family.

Figure 9. Bed-gurney developed by Lelé and Campos da Paz for Sarah Hospitals

The horizontal arrangement of the hospital is critical for two reasons: the character of the construction and ventilation system, and by the fact that patients there frequently need help to dislocate.

The building is arranged over the top of underground galleries of one floor height, which serve as baseline for in the position of the ground floor, structural grid, and a shed system above. The sheds system allows the entry of natural light and extraction of air. Next to the opening of this galleries water sprays reduce the temperature of the air that is aspirated to the interior by fans.

The design was based on the following guidelines:

1. Suitable site: preferably in large and flat terrains, with higher altitude and prevailing breezes for the optimum operation of the natural ventilation system;

2. Construction system prefabricated in the CTRS;

3. Standard modulation of 625 mm (all the parts of the construction system produced by the CTRS should be based in modules of 625mm, which is derived from the international standards for panels. This module forms the base

20

for the layout and defines the position of the materials and components (Risselada 2012, p.110).

Lelé played a critical role in the design of the Sarah facilities and served on the director board of the CTRS from 1992 to 2009. As the main architect for these hospitals, he has left an indelible mark on the nature and spirit of rehabilitative environments. After the completion of the Sarah Hospital in Rio de Janeiro in May 2009, Lelé left the leadership of the CTRS, marking the end of a relatively long period in which high quality buildings and a series of components were developed. One of the reasons for his departure was the fact that the APS decided on not developing new projects, focusing primarily on the maintenance of the existent hospitals and centers of the Sarah Network.

THE USE OF POSITIVE DISTRACTION IN LELE'S HEALTHCARE FACILITIES

As Campagnol & Shepley (2014) notice, all Lelé's projects demonstrate the importance of the environment as a therapeutic factor. An analysis of the Sarah Network principles reveals a relationship to evidence-based design principles are summarized in table1.

THE SARAH NETWORK OF REHABILITATION HOSPITALS

As Campagnol & Shelpley (2014, p.) noticed, according to Sarah hospital administrators and the author's literature review, evaluation of the effectiveness of the design has not been analyzed through research: "This perhaps is the most significant shortcoming of the design process of the architects and the building owners." Below, we describe five of the Sarah hospitals and the way in which they incorporate positive distraction.

Sarah Hospital Brasília

This was the first hospital of the Sarah Network, which was driven by concept of flexibility, creation of green spaces and daylighting and natural ventilation. It was conceived as an urban hospital in a limited lot within a densely occupied district. The construction system allowed the insertion of terraces with views towards the city, for socialization and daily sunbath aimed at preventing cross-infection (Lima, 2012, p. 93).

The bed-gurneys allow the patients to be exposed to sunlight in the terraces and interact with family members and other patients there. Panels designed by Athos Bulcão decorated the public entrance.

As Lelé acknowledged, this project aimed to fulfill the basic function of "softening the wards spaces, decisively contributing to the psychological well-being of patients."

Furthermore, "the regular movement of patients to these terraces, fully vacating the wards, allows them to be cleaned and disinfected with the desired accuracy" (Lelé, 2012, p. 93).

Lelé designed the Brasília facility based on a pre-fabricated system of reinforced mortar and concrete, with 'Vierendeel' type beams and slab elements (115cm X 60cm) spanning variable spaces and which allowed for the creation of terraces, the passage of pipelines and the coupling of interchangeable parts for natural lighting and ventilation.

The general principles that guided the architectural concept were:

21

22

SARAH PRINCIPLES	EVIDENCE-BASED DESIGN PRINCIPLES
CREATE: a specialized health care center that treats the patient as a human being who is not merely the object upon which techniques are applied, but rather, is the agent of that action.	Related to research that suggests improved outcomes when patients have appropriate control/ choice (Entwistle, Sheldon, Sowden & Watt, 1998; Mills & Krantz, 1979).
LIVE: the reality of locomotor system medicine as a conglomeration of unified knowledge and techniques aimed at the restitution of the universal right to come and go in the physically challenged.	Related to research that suggests improved outcomes when patients have appropriate control/ choice (Entwistle, Sheldon, Sowden & Watt, 1998; Mills & Krantz, 1979).
PARTICIPATE: actively in society and work at the prevention of disability and deformity while at the same time combating prejudice against the physically disabled; after all, infinitely varied forms that change with time characterize life.	Related to preventive care and universal design (Brown & Gallant, 2006).
DEFEND: the principle that no human being should be discriminated against for being different in his/her physical form or way of performing an activity.	Related to positive impacts of patient empowerment (Anderson, Funnell, Butler, Arnold, Fitzgerald & Feste, 1995)
FREEDOM: from technological dependency by rejecting a passive attitude in the face of consumerism and imitation and by utilizing our culture's creative potential.	Related to positive distraction (Diette, Lechtzin, Haponik, Devrotes & Rubin, 2003; Eisen, Ulrich, Shepley, Varni & Sherman, 2008; Nanda, Eisen, Zadeh, & Owen, 2010).
DEVELOP: a critical attitude towards imported standards, be they techniques or conduct.	Related to culturally appropriate design (Betancourt, Green & Carrillo, 2000; DeVoe, 2009; Shepley, 2012).
SIMPLIFY: technique and procedures in order to adapt them to the genuine necessities born of Brazil's contrasting economies and regions. Simplification is the critical synthesis of the most complex systems and processes…	Related to culturally appropriate design (Betancourt, Green & Carrillo, 2000; DeVoe, 2009; Shepley, 2012).
APPRECIATE: innovative initiative and the exchange of experience, in education and research, stimulating the creativity of persons and groups; "the individual is the institution" and each person represents it, answers on its behalf, and dedicates his/her life to it.	Related to positive impacts of patient empowerment (Anderson, Funnell, Butler, Arnold, Fitzgerald & Feste, 1995).
LIVE: for health instead of merely surviving illness.	Related to positive distraction (Diette, Lechtzin, Haponik, Devrotes & Rubin, 2003; Eisen, Ulrich, Shepley, Varni & Sherman, 2008; Nanda, Eisen, Zadeh, & Owen, 2010).
TRANSFORM: each individual into an active agent responsible for his/her own health.	Related to research that suggests improved outcomes when patients have appropriate control/choice (Entwistle, Sheldon, Sowden & Watt, 1998; Mills & Krantz, 1979).
WORK: so that the UTOPIA of this hospital is educating for health until each individual, protected from illness, no longer needs it.	Related to providing opportunities for patient education (Planetree) (Cosgrove, 1994)

Table 1. Sarah Principles in relationship to evidence-based design principles (Campagnol & Shepley 2014).

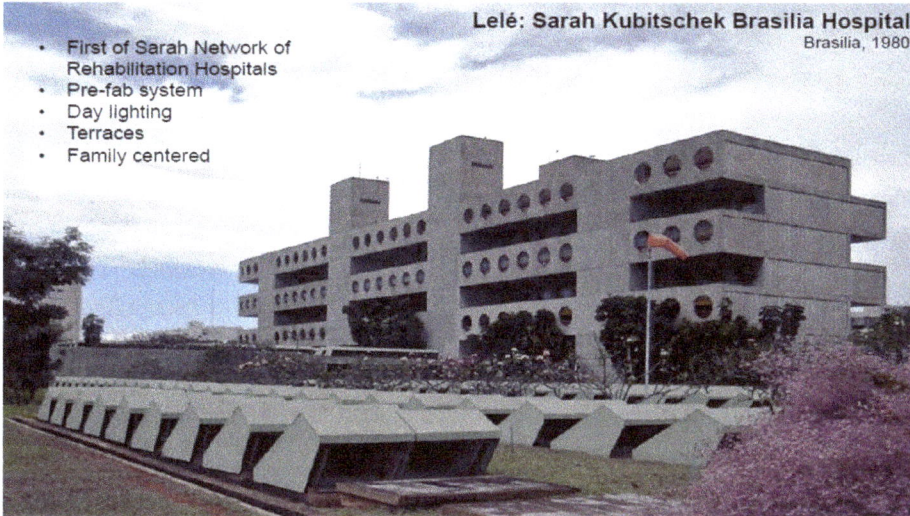

- First of Sarah Network of Rehabilitation Hospitals
- Pre-fab system
- Day lighting
- Terraces
- Family centered

Lelé: Sarah Kubitschek Brasilia Hospital
Brasilia, 1980

Figure 10. Lelé: Sarah Kubitschek Brasilia Hospital, Brasilia, 1980

1. flexibility and expandability of the building;
2. creation of green spaces;
3. Flexibility of the facilities;
4. natural lighting and the thermal comfort of the facilities, as Lelé believed that "the climate of Brasilia does not justify the generalized use of AC systems which unnecessarily affect the initial cost (…)" (Latorraca 2000, p. 126).

Sarah Hospital Salvador

This was the first hospital built by CTRS and served as a model for the subsequent hospitals. The design process was based on a combination of three departure points: the construction system based on pre-fabrication; spatial division (sectors), and a climate control system providing daylight ventilation.
From the public entrance, the inpatient wards and inpatient apartments comprise the left portion of the main building; on the right portion are located the

surgical center, outpatient, and waiting room with plenty access to gardens and outdoor areas.
Athos Bulcão designed the partition walls made of reinforced mortar, perforated and colorful, which allow visual connections, and, at the same time, mediate the interior and interior space.

The study center and doctor apartments are located in a detached building, which is connected to the main building through the central walkway.
Aspects of positive distraction are provided via water views from the rehabilitation rooms, access to gardens, use of color and art throughout the interior, and the pervasive use of daylight. The wards are visually and physically integrated to garden terraces.
The patients have full accessibility to the campus, due to the absence of architectural barriers, which allow them via tramcar/elevator to access a tropical forest located between the hospital and

23

24

Figure 11. Sarah Salvador Hospital & CTRS, Salvador, BA (1992)

the CTRS nearby; and via footbridge to public transportation and a large shopping mall located nearby.

Sarah Hospital Fortaleza

The facility is located far enough from the sea breeze to avoid deterioration of the construction, but with adequate wind to fully promote the ventilation system. The concept of this hospital was to mix the horizontal and vertical elements in order to minimize the site coverage. Preserving the wooded area nearby was a main concern.

This complex includes administrative and technical services on the lower floors, and wards and apartments on the four upper floors of the six-floor building. The inpatient areas are connected to four terraces/solarium in the form of discs; on the opposite side of this building, a translucent barrel vault structure with brise soleil from the top to the base, creates an indoor pubic space with gardens and pools that face the hydrotherapy room. Outpatient department and technical services are located on the first floor whereas the services and supplies are in the basement. There is also school for children with cerebral palsy disability, day nursery, and medical residence located in the wooded area.

Sarah Hospital Brasília Lago Norte - Rehabilitation Center

Sarah Hospital Lago Norte was built on a triangular site next to the lake due to the lack of surrounding parks/green areas in the previous Sarah Hospital in the city, which was conceived as an urban hospital.

As the urban facility would not provide suitable techniques for the treatment of seriously handicapped patients, a new facility was established in the north part of a lake district, in an area donated to the APS by the Government of the Federal District. This facility was designed with a dock, boats and sailboats designed by the CTRS, as boating and interacting with water may benefit patients. The site is landscaped to catch breezes off the lake and to filter the air and moderate humid conditions.

The facility is oriented to benefit from the solar conditions and has a roof design based on aerodynamic principles. The largest building, which is located on the waterfront, is divided in two parts: on one side, facing the water, are

25

Figure 12. Hospital Sarah Fortaleza, Fortaleza, CE (1996-2001)

26

Figure 13. Sarah Brasilia Lago Norte, Brasilia (2001-2002). Lake Rehabilitation center

the therapy rooms and semi-sheltered amphitheater, which are connected on the opposite direction to the clinic and waiting room that has access to a garden area; and the other part of the hospital, comprises the wards and apartments, is also facing the water.

The pediatric rehabilitation facility is located in a circular building with a translucent dome made of steel trusses for abundant daylighting and views towards the lake and surrounding terraces.

A pool, playground, and garden area are located in the center of the building. A veranda runs around the entire building offering access to an outdoor but still sheltered/shaded space.

The circular shape suggests ludic forms (e.g., circus, tent) or vernacular indigenous construction, and distinguishes it from the rest of the facility. The interior design was developed in collaboration with the artist Athos Bulcão, who designed the operable and colorful

Figure 14. Sarah Brasilia Lago Norte, Brasilia (2001-2002). Lake Rehabilitation center

wooden panels. The views to the lake, terraces, playgrounds areas, the mobility to indoor and outdoor gardens, and the colorful panels are important positive distraction components.

Sarah Hospital Rio de Janeiro

Inaugurated in 2009, this is the most recent facility of the Sarah Network, and one of the largest. An iconic roof marks the complex, which is located on a plain. The building is subdivided in two parts connected by a central corridor. Because of the climate, it was necessary to provide a conventional AC system, along with the usual system of natural ventilation. The horizontal stratification of the project is apparent in the construction logic and sequence of activities. The floor of the building is raised and made of reinforced mortar panels. In some parts of the buildings there is a flat ceil-

ing. In other parts, the ceiling is made of translucent operable components.

The translucent ceiling is curved above the wards, hydrotherapy areas, and public hall. This gives a sense of integration as well maintaining the intense presence of daylight. Reflective pools with native plants contour the facility.

A solarium/terrace of red metallic structure is attached to the inpatient sector, and contrasts with the curves and white finishing of the building. These terraces offer positive distractions through sunbathing opportunities, views towards the mountains, reflective pools and landscape design. The circular auditorium has an operable dome that opens in ten segments and eventually provides natural ventilation, day lighting and views to the sky. The mobility of the patient via gurneys offers the opportunity for interaction with the landscape design. The patients can freely experience the posi-

28

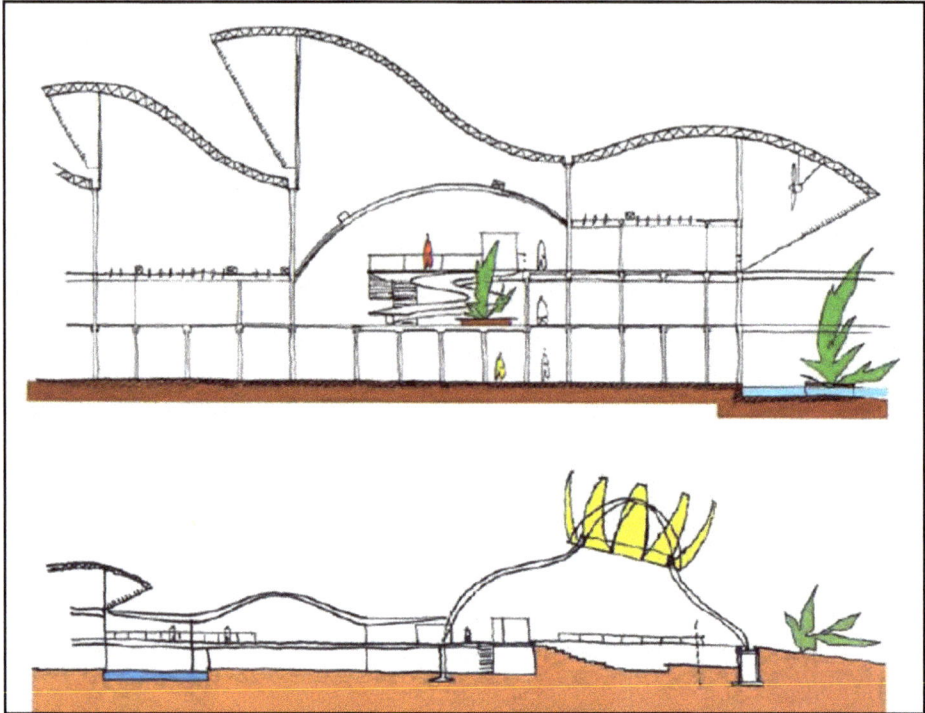

Figure 15. Sarah Rio Rehabilitation Hospital, Rio de Janeiro, RJ (2004-2009). Sarah Rio primarily treats neurological illnesses; patients seen at this Center have already been discharged from the hospitals where they had been admitted post-trauma

tive distractions brought by curvilinear ramps and walkways in the indoor and outdoor gardens. Indoor gardens and colorful perforated contrast with the luminous white and off-white background formed by walls, floor, and translucent ceiling. Patient artwork decorates the walls below a translucent operable ceiling.

FINAL CONSIDERATIONS

As Campagnol & Shepley (2014) observe, well before the dissemination of formal theories of evidence-based design (EBD), healthcare architects employed principles that would subsequently be endorsed by research. The potential positive outcomes of these design goals, such as the health-promoting impacts of views of nature, have been so profoundly obvious that architects have puzzled over the need to provide scientific evidence. However, corroboration of design goals is not just an academic exercise.

The amenities associated with evidence-based design may increase the cost of construction, so their financial or human justification needs to be empirically demonstrated.

In spite of the lack of formal integration of evidence-based design in healthcare architecture in Latin America, many of the basic tenets generated from design research have been incorporated in Brazilian rehabilitation hospitals.

According to Campagnol & Shepley (2014), the use of positive distraction in the rehabilitation facilities designed by Lelé is a clear example of this phenomenon and has served to inspire many current healthcare projects.

Lelé's success is a demonstration of the critical role familiarity with medical treatment options, and insights regarding human behavior play in creating an alignment between research and practitioner experience. The presence of nature, art and natural light and opportunities for social interaction in the Sarah hospitals serves as a model for evidence-based facilities throughout the world and presents a opportunity to measure the benefits of positive distraction on rehabilitation patient outcomes.

Implications for Practice

• Lelé provides multiple models for incorporating positive distraction in rehabilitation facilities. Terraces, gardens, sculpture, art, large open social spaces and views are among a few forms of distraction that recur in his buildings.

• For those conducting architectural practice in Latin America, it is useful to understand the status of evidence-based design. The presence of this approach appears to be appreciated by practitioners in South and Central America, but too new to be fully incorporated in design practice.

• Practitioner/researchers should consider site in South America for potential

29

Figure 16. Sarah Rio Rehabilitation Hospital, Rio de Janeiro, RJ (2004-2009). Sarah Rio primarily treats neurological illnesses; patients seen at this Center have already been discharged from the hospitals where they had been admitted post-trauma

Figure 17. Sarah Rio Rehabilitation Hospital, Rio de Janeiro, RJ (2004-2009). Sarah Rio primarily treats neurological illnesses; patients seen at this Center have already been discharged from the hospitals where they had been admitted post-trauma

studies. Potential topics might include cross-cultural comparisons regarding use of space by staff, patient satisfaction surveys, or interviews of Latin healthcare architects regarding the potential use of design research data.

• Most importantly, this study reminds the U.S. practitioner of the multiple excellent international examples of exemplary health facility design, regardless of their formal affiliation with evidence-based design.

REFERENCES

Appleton, J. (1996). *The experience of landscape* (2nd ed.). New York, NY: Wiley

Anderson, R. M., Funnell, M. M., Butler, P. M., Arnold, M. S., Fitzgerald, J. T., & Feste, C. C. (1995). *Patient empowerment: results of a randomized controlled trial*, in "Diabetes care", 18(7), 943–949

Betancourt, J., Green, A., & Carrillo, E. (2000). *The challenges of cross-cultural healthcare diversity, ethics and the medical encounter*, in "Bioethics Forum", 16(3), 27–32

Braga, L. W., Campos da Paz Jr, A., Brandão, M. C., & Aiko, M. (2008). *Método Sarah: Reabilitação baseada na família e no contexto da criança com lesão cerebral* [Portuguese]. São Paulo, Brazil: Editora Santos

Braga, L.W., & Campos da Paz Jr, A. (2006). *The child with traumatic brain injury or cerebral Palsy: A context-sensitive, family-based approach to development.* London, England: Taylor & Francis

Brown, K. K., & Gallant, D. (2006). *Impacting patient outcomes through design: Acuity adaptable care/universal room design*, in "Critical Care Nursing Quarterly", 29(4), 326–341

Campagnol, G. & Shepley, M. M. (2014). *Positive distraction and the rehabilitation hospitals of João Filgueiras Lima*, in "Health Environments Research & Design Journal", 8(1), 199-227

30

Campos da Paz Jr, A. (1995). *Remando contra a maré.* Salvador, Brazil: Sarah Letras

Campos da Paz Jr, A. (2002). *Tratando doentes e não doenças* [Treating patients and not disease]. Brasília: Sarah Letras

Cosgrove, T. L. (1994). *Planetree health information services: public access to the health information people want,* in "Bulletin of the Medical Library Association", 82(1), 57

DeVoe, J. (2009). *Measuring patients' perceptions of communication with healthcare Providers: Do differences in demographic and socioeconomic characteristics matter?,* in "Health Expectations", 12(1), 70

Diette, G. B., Lechtzin, N., Haponik, E., Devrotes, A. & Rubin, H. R. (2003). *Distraction therapy with nature sights and sounds reduces pain during flexible bronchoscopy,* in "Chest", 123(3), 941–948

Ekerman, S.K. (2005, September). *Um quebra-cabeça chamado Lelé,* in "Vitruvius", 06.064. Retrieved from www.vitruvius.com.br/revistas/read/arquitextos/06.064/423

Eisen, S. L., Ulrich, R. S., Shepley, M. M., Varni, J. W. & Sherman, S. (2008). *The stress-reducing effects of art in pediatric health care: art preferences of healthy children and hospitalized children,* in "Journal of Child Health Care", 12(3), 173–190

Entwistle, V. A., Sheldon, T. A., Sowden, A., & Watt, I. S. (1998). *Evidence-informed patient choice: practical issues of involving patients in decisions about health care technologies,* in "International Journal of Technology Assessment in Health Care", 14(02), 212–225

Estes são os princípios da Rede SARAH (n.d.). http://www.sarah.br.
Gesler, W. & Kearns, R. (2002). *Culture/place/health.* London, England: Routledge

Guenther, R., & Vittori, G. (2008). *Sustainable healthcare architecture.* Hoboken, NJ: Wiley

Haidar, S. (2001). Latin America 2001. In *"International Architecture Yearbook"*, vol. 7 (p. 14). Mulgrave, Australia: Images Publishing

Latorraca, G. (Ed.). (2000). *João Filgueiras Lima Lelé.* Lisbon, Portugal: Editorial Blau; São Paulo, SP, Brazil: Instituto Lina Bo e P.M. Bardi

Lima, J. F. (2012). *Arquitetura: Uma experiência na área da saúde.* São Paulo, SP, Brazil: Romano Guerra

Lima, J. F. (1995). *Muito além da máquina de curar,* in "Projeto", 187 (July), 78

Machry, H. S. (2010). *O impacto dos avanços da tecnologia nas transformações arquitetônicas dos edifícios hospitalares.* (Master Thesis) FAU, University of São Paulo, São Paulo

Mills, R. T., & Krantz, D. S. (1979). *Information, choice, and reactions to stress: A field experiment in a blood bank with laboratory analogue,* in "Journal of Personality and Social Psychology", 37(4)

31

Nanda, U., Eisen, S., Zadeh, R., & Owen, D. (2010). *Effect of visual art on patient anxiety and agitation in a mental health facility and implications for the business case*, in "Journal of Psychiatric and Mental Health Nursing". 18 (5), 386-393

Rede Sarah de Hospitals de Reabilitação. (n.d.). *O paciente*. Retrieved from http://www.sarah.br/Cvisual/SARAH/AA-Instituicao/po/p-02_O%20paciente.html

Pearson, C. A. (2000). *Brazil may be poised for an architectural comeback*, in "Architectural Record", 188(3), 49

Planetree. (2012). *Hospital Israelita Albert Einstein: Humanizing healthcare in Sao Paulo, Brazil*, in "Planetree case studies". Retrieved from http://planetree.org/?page_id=314

Pinho, R. (2012). *Lelé: Um arquiteto universal, in Risselada, M., & Latorraca, G. (eds.). "A arquitetura de Lelé: Fábrica e invenção"*. São Paulo, Brazil: Imprensa Oficial, Museu da Casa Brasileira, 46–55

Risério, A. (2012). *Um mestre da precisão e da delicadeza estética e social, in M. Risselada & G. Latorraca (Eds.),* "A arquitetura de Lelé: Fábrica e invenção". São Paulo, Brazil: Imprensa Oficial, Museu da Casa Brasileira

Risselada, M., & Latorraca, G. (Eds.). (2012). *A arquitetura de Lelé: Fábrica e invenção*. São Paulo, Brazil: Imprensa Oficial, Museu da Casa Brasileira

Ronconi, R., & Duarte, D. (2007). *Depoimentos: João Filgueiras Lima*. PÓS 21, 10-23

Santana Filho, J. (1994). *Luz e cor num hospital amigável (Light and color in a friendly hospital),* in "Design e Interiores", 41, 64-71

Segawa, H. (1995). *Tecnologia com sentido social,* in "Projeto" 187 (July), 60-77.

Segawa, H. (2012). Lelé: Tecnologia com sentido social, in M. Risselada & G. Latorraca (Eds.), *"A arquitetura de Lelé: Fábrica e invenção"*. São Paulo, Brazil: Imprensa Oficial, Museu da Casa Brasileira

Shepley, M. (2006). *The role of positive distraction in neonatal intensive care unit settings*, in "Journal of Perinatology", 26, S34–S37

Shepley, M. M. & Song, Y. (in press). *Design research and the globalization of healthcare environments*, in "Health Environments Research & Design Journal"

Toledo, L.C. (2002). *Feito para curar arquitetura hospitalar & processo projetual no Brasil.* (Master Thesis). FAU- UFRJ, Rio de Janeiro

Ulrich, R. S. (1997). *Pre-symposium workshop: A theory of supportive design for healthcare facilities,* in "Journal of Healthcare Design", 9, 3–7

Westphal, E. (2007). *A linguagem da arquitetura hospitalar de João Filgueiras Lima.* (Master thesis). Federal University of Rio Gande do Sul, Brazil

Behavioral Healthcare Development and Its Role in a Comprehensive Health Care Response: Driving Health Care Integration, Innovation and Value

Philip Patrick Sun

ppsun@aol.com
AIA, ACHA, NCARB

The "landscape" of the health care environment is changing. The requirement to provide mental health services is a crucial part of the Patient Protection and Affordable Care Act (otherwise known as ObamaCare) and all health care providers must now understand the implications of providing such services, integrating these services with physical health care and the intrinsic differences between traditional physical health services and mental health services; their care models, operations, environments, staff and patient types.

The focus is in Behavioral / Mental Health and the operations and design for this critical need. Key words in behavioral health are Hope, Strength and Resilience. Only 38% of those who need mental health care receive it in the USA. Worldwide it is worse. Low to middle income countries have a gap between 76-85% and high income countries only meet 35-50% of the need.

The measure of disability adjusted life years (DALYs) shows neuropsychiatric conditions cause losses that are higher than cardiovascular disease and cancer. Because of complex interactions and co-morbidity between mental health and physical health the disparities are believed to be even much higher by the World Health Organization (WHO). Additionally, almost one million people die due to suicide each year and this is the third leading cause of death among the young.

The "front line" and first priority on mental health care reported in WHO's "Mental Health Report 2001" is provision of mental health treatment through primary care.

Mental health is most devastating for the poor worldwide. Lessons learned include examples of positive and detrimental environments which are fundamentally different than physical health.

Because mental health fundamentally involves psychological and environmental perception the quality of the design or architecture for treatment is arguably more important than the "design" of other clinical care settings.

Interdisciplinary research, analysis, design and evaluation processes included physicians, therapists, case managers, patients (clients/consumer), researchers and health care planners/architects. Data, hypothesis, analysis of operational, physical/environmental conditions, patient interviews and surveys led to modeling and design approaches for healthier environments.

This paper includes the planning process and facilities which brings about innovation and improvement. This paper shows the integral steps used to manage the development of planning and design decisions and the incorporation of multiple disciplines, multi-level staff and consumer participation.

In addition the use and control of data, myth, logic and emotion and their role in planning and design are included. The process explores the mapping of clinical, administrative systems and financial systems to integrate sustainable clinical models for multiple funding environments including government funded programs, insurance, and private pay.

This paper focuses on planning, process mapping for outpatient facilities for this critical need and how this is much different than physical health operations and settings. The results are greater integration of health and wellness, innovation in care processes and value for patients and care providers. This findings suggest integrated approaches improves patient outcome and built environments.

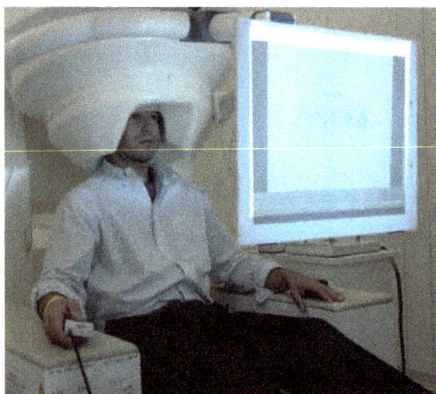

34

Figure 1. Neuroimaging

This paper is about a lesser known part of the health care map, behavioral health or mental health. While lesser known mental health is one of the most important issues worldwide.

"Health is a state of complete physical, mental and social well-being, and not merely the absence of disease or infirmity". World Health Organization, 1948
A sad soul can kill you quicker than a germ". John Steinbeck

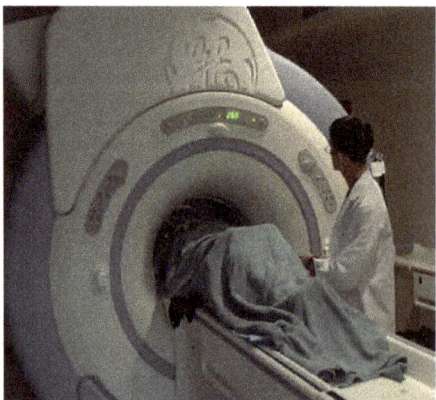

In the majority of health care (physical health) the problem is observable either by the naked eye or through technology. This is not the case with behavioral or mental health.

Science has changed what is observable. Neuroimaging has revealed how the brain works in ways never previously contemplated.

It is possible to distinguish between healthy and diseased brain structures.

The area of mental health is also known as Behavioral Health. In general in the

United States the practitioners are from three groups. These are as follows:
there are medical doctors who are psychiatrists – who provide therapy and are allowed to prescribe medications. There are psychologists who have doctorate degrees and provide therapy but do not prescribe medications. And there are Social Workers who are case managers and other licensed individuals who provide therapy and help affect the mental state through affecting the environment such as improvement in housing, access to transportation, and other services.

It has been shown through new imaging techniques that all three of these providers can affect and change the workings of the brain.

In addition the area of Genomics has also changed the frontier of understanding of mental and behavioral health through our genetic structure.

Today there are Smart Wristbands which can change color when certain moods or brain activity change, thus triggering the need for intervention.

In addition Mobile Technologies are becoming more common.

We are also seeing the introduction of highly accessible Mental Health Screening Clinics in high use retail centers.

In addition there is Tele Psychiatry where diagnosis and treatment is done remotely.

It may seem that there are multiple and adequate responses to this most important health issue but these approaches and technologies barely touch the significance of the problem.

Life expectancy for the seriously mentally ill is reportedly reduced by 15-25 years. And for those who smoke it is

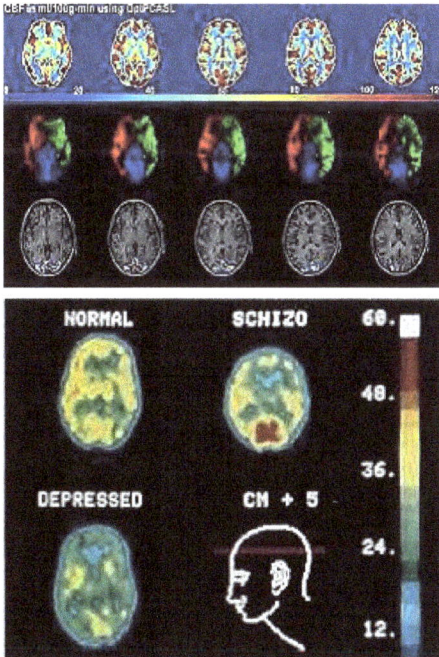

Figure 2.   Healthy and diseased brain structures

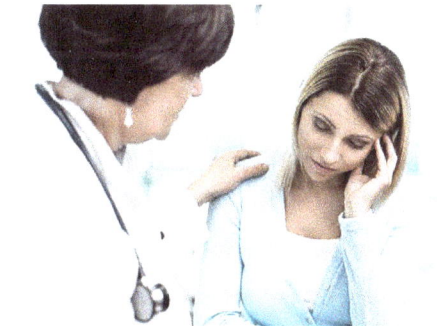

Figure 3.   Genomics

worse. But the problem is more than an individual one.

The following quotes offer the context of the global problem.

"It is becoming evident that when mental health services are available there may be reductions in the costs of physical health care, increases in productivity and reduced demands on other social services and the criminal justice system".

World Health Organization – 2003.

"Global spending on mental health is still less than US$3 per capita per year. In low income countries. Expenditure can be as little as US$ .25 per person per year".

World Health Organization – Mental Health Atlas 2011.

"Governments tend to spend most of their scarce mental health resources on long-term care at psychiatric hospitals.

Today, nearly 70 percent of mental health spending goes to mental institutions.

If countries spent more at the primary care level, they would be able to reach more people, and start to address problems early enough to reduce the need for expensive hospital care" -

Dr. Ala Alwan, World Health Organization.

"Almost half the world's population lives in a country where, on average, there is one psychiatrist (or less) to serve 200,000 people. Many low income countries have less than one mental health specialist per one million population"

Dr. Shekhar Saxena, World Health Organization – 2003.

In the United States the problem is also acute.

"One of the biggest untreated problems in the United States affecting everything from

Figure 4.   *Smart Wristbands*

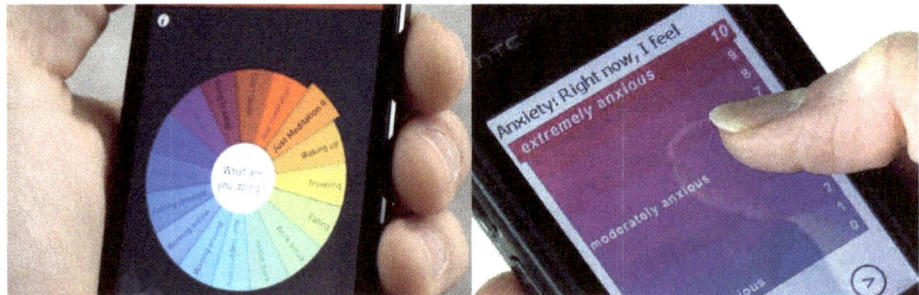

Figure 5.   *Mobile Technologies*

Figure 6. "Mental Health Screening Clinic"

social relationships to employment is mental health"

Chris Weiss, Langer Research Associates. "Around 25% of adults experience a mental health issue in a given year, yet less than 1 in 3 adults receives services"

Source: SAMHSA (Substance Abuse and Mental Health Services Administra-tion).

"The estimated impact in terms of loss of productivity in the workplace is around $63 billion." (in the USA).

Source: SAMHSA (Substance Abuse and Mental Health Services Administration)

"...only 38% of individuals with mental health issues have received appropriate services"

Source: SAMHSA (Substance Abuse and Mental Health Services Administration).

As shown in figures 9-10 the service use and treatment in the United States has not dramatically increased even as the problem has increased and the population has increased.

Notice in the figure 7 that Behavioral Health is only 7% of expenditures by payer in 2005.

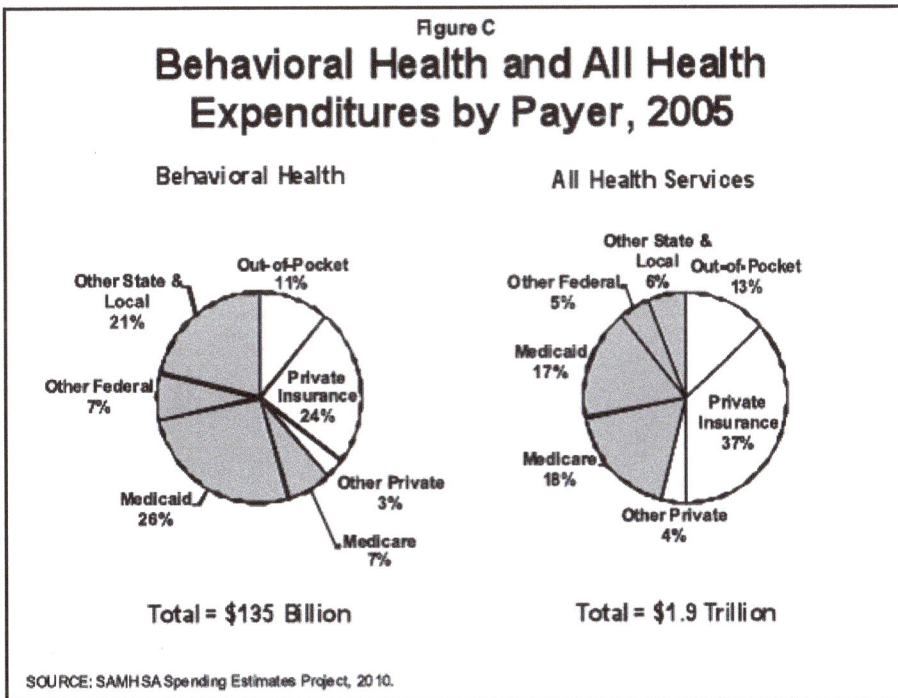

Figure 7. Behavioral Health and All Health Expenditures by Payer, 2005

38

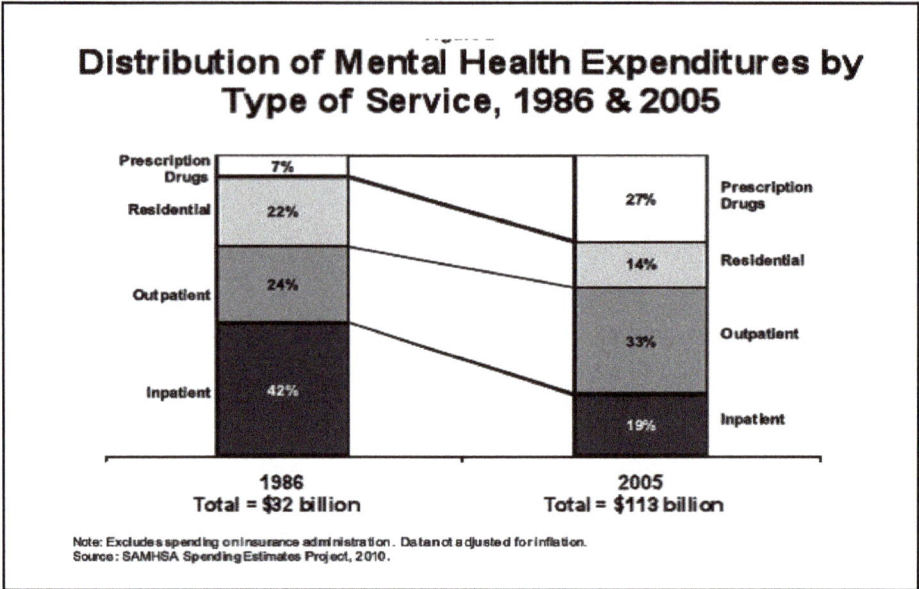

Distribution of Mental Health Expenditures by Type of Service, 1986 & 2005

Prescription Drugs — 7%
Residential — 22%
Outpatient — 24%
Inpatient — 42%

Prescription Drugs — 27%
Residential — 14%
Outpatient — 33%
Inpatient — 19%

1986
Total = $32 billion

2005
Total = $113 billion

Note: Excludes spending on insurance administration. Data not adjusted for inflation.
Source: SAMHSA Spending Estimates Project, 2010.

Figure 8. Distribution of Mental Health Expenditures by Type of Service, 1986 & 2005

And the distribution of expenditures has move from large scale impatient facilities to medication, residential programs, and increases in outpatient and community based programs.

Most recently the new health care law: Patient Protection and Affordable Care Act has made mental health a priority on the level of primary care.

Patient Protection and Affordable Care Act (P.L. 111 – 148)

"Essential health benefits (EHB): ambulatory services; emergency services; hospitalization; pre, peri-, and neonatal care; mental health and substance use disorder services; rehabilitative services; laboratory services; chronic disease management; and pediatric services"

Source: US Department of Health and Human Services.

While this is a very positive step the allocation of funds to this need has been less than minimal.

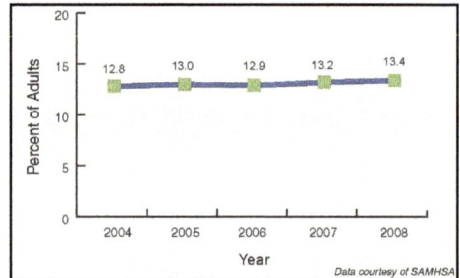

Figure 9. Mental Health Service Use/Treatment Among U.S. Adults (2004-2008)

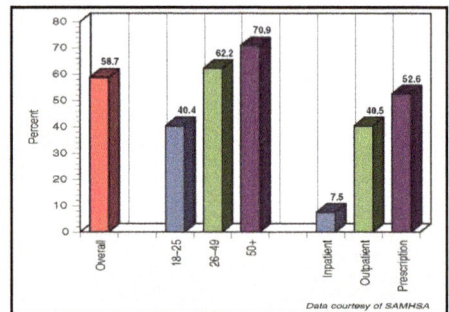

Figure 10. Service Use/Treatment of Serious Mental Illness Among U.S. Adults by Age and Type of Care (2008)

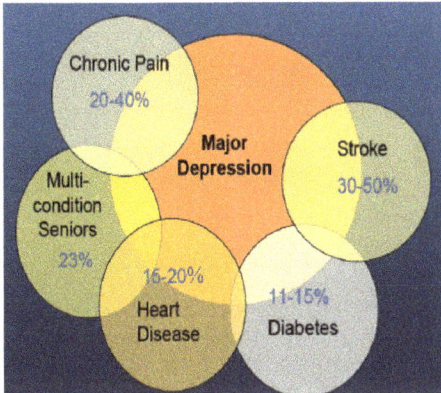

Figure 11. Context: comorbid conditions such as cardiovascular disease, diabetes, respiratory disease, or infectious diseases

"$50 million from the health care law will expand mental health and substance use disorder services in approximately 200 Community Health Centers nationwide (works out to $250,000 per CHC)"
Source: US Department of Health and Human Services
Still there is a positive picture.
"...with the implementation of the Patient Protection and Affordable Care Act (PPACA) access is now mandated and mental health is included ..."
Source: The Lewin Group
There is an interweaving of mental health and physical health issues. It is intuitive that those with mental health problems but the significance of the issue is now being understood.
Individuals with serious mental illness are at greater risk for complex physical health problems, may face more barriers in accessing Physical Health care, and on average die 25 years earlier.
Some premature deaths among individuals with serious mental illness are related to complex mental health issues, comorbid conditions such as cardiovas-

cular disease, diabetes, respiratory disease, or infectious diseases.
"The mental illness itself may interfere with individuals' ability to receive appropriate care"
Source: The Lewin Group.
The more progressive model today is an Integrated Care Model. This model combines physical health and mental health. In the United States there are two major agencies which are responsible for Federal programs in primary care (physical health) and mental health care. These are the following: Health Resources Services Administration (HRSA) and Substance Abuse and Mental Health Services Administration (SAMHSA). One of the new combined programs is called PRIMARY CARE INTEGRATION (PCI).
"...we cannot provide the most effective general medical care to older adults or control health care costs associated with hospitalization without taking mental health conditions into account."
"We must know when our patients have symptoms of depression and evidence of cognitive impairment and incorporate this knowledge into our discharge planning and ambulatory care processes. We need psychiatrists and other mental health experts working in general medical settings to directly assist in this work."
Robert P. Roca, MD, MPH, MBA, chair of the American Psychiatric Association's Council on Geriatric Psychiatry.

INTUITIVE AND COUNTER-INTUITIVE

What seems to be intuitively simple about blending care also begins to uncover attributes which set these two types of care apart, which in turns affects design criteria.

39

40

Relationship

"Patient vs. Client Why call them "clients"? Many experiments have confirmed that, when confronted by a "patient" or a "prospective patient," mental health professionals are less likely to diagnose actual disorders and are more likely to express unfounded opinions that match their training ... ".

"Patient vs. Client The label of "patient" should be used appropriately, as by its very nature it increases the power of the provider and weakens the person who is suffering. If there is an illness present, it is fair (though still problematic) to call that person a patient"

Eric Maisel, Ph.D.

Symptoms

In physical health the symptoms are usually "physically" apparent either through direct observation or tools.

In mental health experimenters concluded, *"Once an individual enters a therapist's office for consultation, he has labeled himself 'patient' ...*

The therapist's negative expectations in turn may affect the patient's own view of the situation, thereby possibly locking the interaction into a self-fulfilling gloomy prophecy".

- Eric Maisel, Ph.D.

Primary Care Objective

In physical health the treatment and cure are to eliminate the physical abnormality and allow the body heal or go back to a recognized state of normality. This may take a single or a few treatments but the "cure" is the objective.

Mental health objective

The treatment is not an occasion but a plan. The objective is stabilization and maintenance which is more likely than not long term ...

Frequency

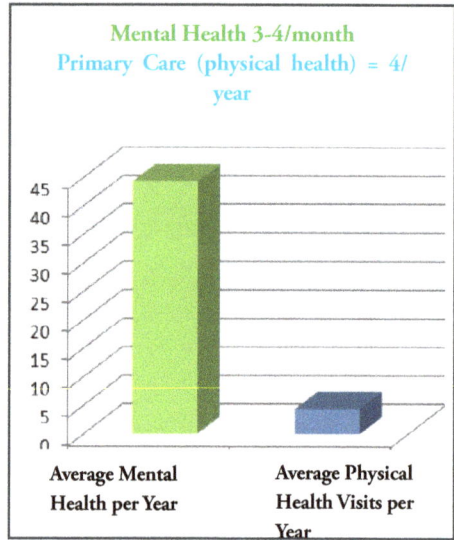

Figure 12. Frequency.

Provider volume

The critical point is that the expectation with the primary care model is that the "cure" can be achieved in a few visits. In mental health the preponderance of situations is that it is a matter of maintenance rather than cure.

Another major difference is the speed with which the medical /business model expects the patient to be seen. The expectation is built on financial metrics. The mental health model tends to address contact more than speed. As such the physical environment (aka the built

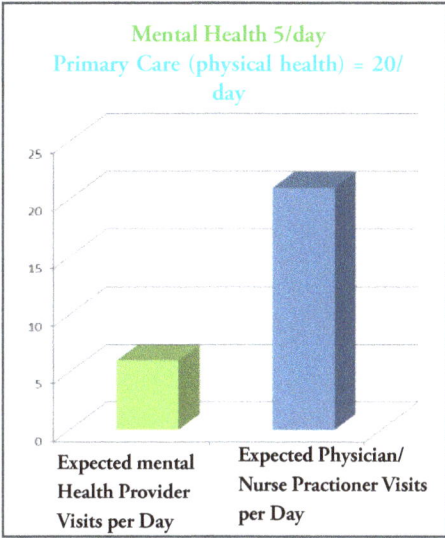

Mental Health 5/day
Primary Care (physical health) = 20/ day

Figure 13. Provider Volume

environment) has different design attributes for the different care models.

Speed vs Contact

Physical Health = Efficiency And Speed For Volume; which suggests the highest efficiency in patient care rooms with the best equipment. Clinical efficiency.
Mental Health = Patient Sensitivity (Neutral Colors, Small Patterns, Safety, Security) In this case it is a matter of building a relationship which is based on trust with the patients. As a result this aspect of the built environment is softer and the goal is to make the environment closer to residential setting.

Environment: natural light

Natural light is greatly desired in both mental health and physical health settings and in both settings it is considered a "healing" attribute.
The built environment is also defined by the furnishings and equipment in the environment. In his case the primary care environment is defined by clinical equipment and less on the feelings of the patient. The mental health environment is defined by the emotional quality of the space and the ability to offer security to the patient.

FURNISHINGS AND EQUIPMENT

41

Equipment vs Seating and Security.

The organization of the environment is also not random. There are two basic areas in the space called the treatment room, otherwise also known as the counseling room or sometimes the meeting room.

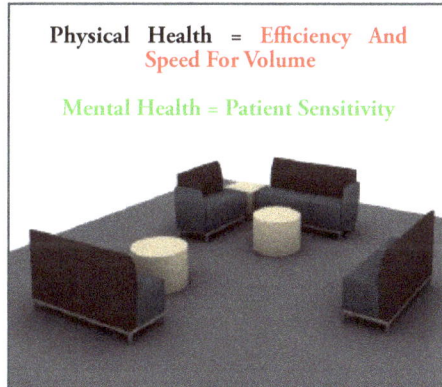

Physical Health = Efficiency And Speed For Volume

Mental Health = Patient Sensitivity

Figure 14. Speed vs Contact.

Figure 15. Natural Light

TESIS Inter-University Research Centre "Systems and Technologies for Social and Healthcare Facilities"
University of Florence, Italy

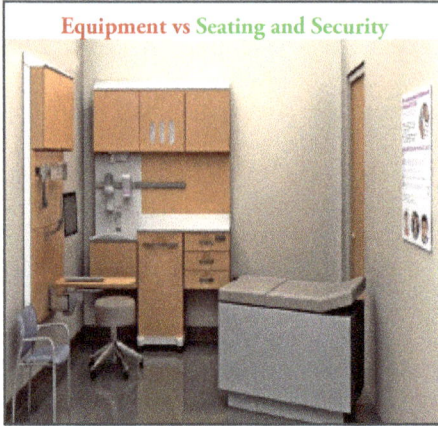

Figure 16. Equipment vs Seating and Security

Recent thoughts on the space have seen that treatment or counseling connotes the fact that there is something wrong with the patient and it may be better to use meeting so as not to create negative expectations. Within the space are a counseling area and an education area.

The advent of the electronic health record and the requirement of using electronic health records by the Patient Projection Affordable Care Act (ObamaCare) has also changed the nature of the engagement between the patient and the clinician. Eye contact and constant contact are being challenged by the monitor and the record system. This is not as great an issue as in primary care.

Electronic health record

Focus on The Computer Vs Focus on the Client

The essential Contact or Visit Time in primary care is a 20 minute period for the patient in primary care. In mental health it is generally a session which is 50 minutes.

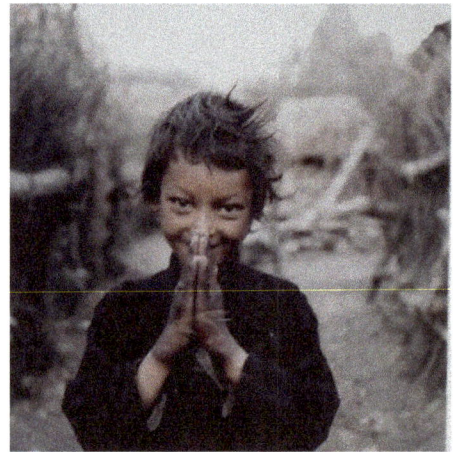

Figure 17. Images from other similar mental health centers which engage in stabilizing and maintaining the seriously mental ill in Asian communities

Visit/Contact time

But the actual contact time with the doctor or provider is also very different. In mental health the visit time is all with the provider. In primary care the provider is expected to see in excess of 18 patients a day. In many cases the number exceeds 30 per day. Thus the amount of time with a provider in mental health at 50 minutes is compared to 7.5 to 10 minutes in primary care.

42

Figure 18. Hanging tower of ceramic bowls

PROVIDER CONTACT TIME

ACMHS

These were some of the differences in primary care and mental health. As great as there is a need for mental health there is little attention given to The case study in this paper is ACMHS (Asian Community Mental Health Services).
ACMHS provides care to Asians in Oakland California. ACMHS provides are in over a dozen Asian languages through a staff of about 100.
The process used for planning and design centered on process mapping which followed "problem seeking" a book written by William Pena. In addition the principals help by other sources such as "Bioteaming" and "Toyota Way" were also principle.
Other facility lessons were learned. After planning the process the rooms were

also based on processes with the treatment space. One critical principal is the ability safety and security of the clinician when meeting with the seriously mentally ill. The clinician must have an alarm and also be able to escape the space and not be blocked. Some designs have not taken this into consideration.
This design does not meet safety precautions but is a model template.
This model is preferred.

The project is in construction and scheduled for completion is in a few weeks. Bridging the future and offering critically needed services is the goal of ACMHS.

Elements

Creating a welcoming and belonging environment for treatment where stabilization and maintenance is more likely than not long term.
In addition to art which helps create a feeling security and safety, projects such as engaging the patient community to a hanging tower of ceramic bowls helps the patients feel connected to the mental health center. Each bowl is made by patients and staff working with each other. Each is an original design and the interior has a gold glaze. Connectivity to the community is part of the therapy.
Space for other community activities is also critical to the healing and wellness process in mental health.

SUMMARY

1. Mental health is an important part of communities and health care. Mental health care is now equal to primary health care as defined by the new Patient

43

Protection and Affordable Care Act.

2. Mental health care operations and facilities are different than physical health or primary care and as such require different responses. The patient experience of the design environment is more challenging and arguable plays a greater role in mental health facilities.

44

3. Counseling and treatment space in mental health care facilities must be developed with a concentration on the behavioral health client and the security of the clinician.

4. Lean and integrated processes such as Problem Seeking and Bioteaming methodologies are well suited to the evaluation, analysis, and decision management which leads to effective planning and design of mental health facilities.

5. Interactive participation and transparency of all information by posting on the walls so that all parties can participate is important to durable decisions.

"Diseases of the soul are more dangerous and more numerous than those of the body." ~Cicero

How Culture Shapes Nursing Unit Design.
A Comparative Study on Chinese and American Nursing Unit Typologies

Hui Cai

huicai@ku.edu
Assistant Professor, Department of Architecture, The University of Kansas, Lawrence, Kansas

45

Craig Zimring

Craig.Zimring@mail.gatech.edu
Professor, Department of Architecture, Georgia Institute of Technology, Atlanta, Georgia

The rapid growth of economy and the increasing needs for better healthcare in China call for a higher quality healthcare design that is efficient and culturally appropriate. During the past few decades, Western model for healthcare design and construction has been widely adopted in China. This study aims to explore whether seemingly westernized Chinese nursing units still retained certain characteristics of Chinese socio-cultural preferences. It focuses on exploring the cultural preferences of organizational communication and how they are reflected in spatial configurations of Chinese nursing units.

Topic*: Cultural Influences on Health Facility Design*

Three main characteristics of Chinese national schema were identified from an extensive literature review on cross-cultural organizational studies and Confucianism: collectivism and the importance of maintaining social networks; the high "power distance", coupled with a tradition of respect for hierarchy; and the respect of "face." These national schema lead to a preference for high-context face-to-face communication, with differentiation of the in-group and out-group communication, and privacy for back-stage communication.

In order to find out whether and how cultural implications of space are manifest in Chinese nursing unit design, an in-depth comparative spatial analysis based on space syntax methodology was conducted on six Chinese and six matching U.S. nursing unit plans. Each pair of plans represents examples of one typical

46

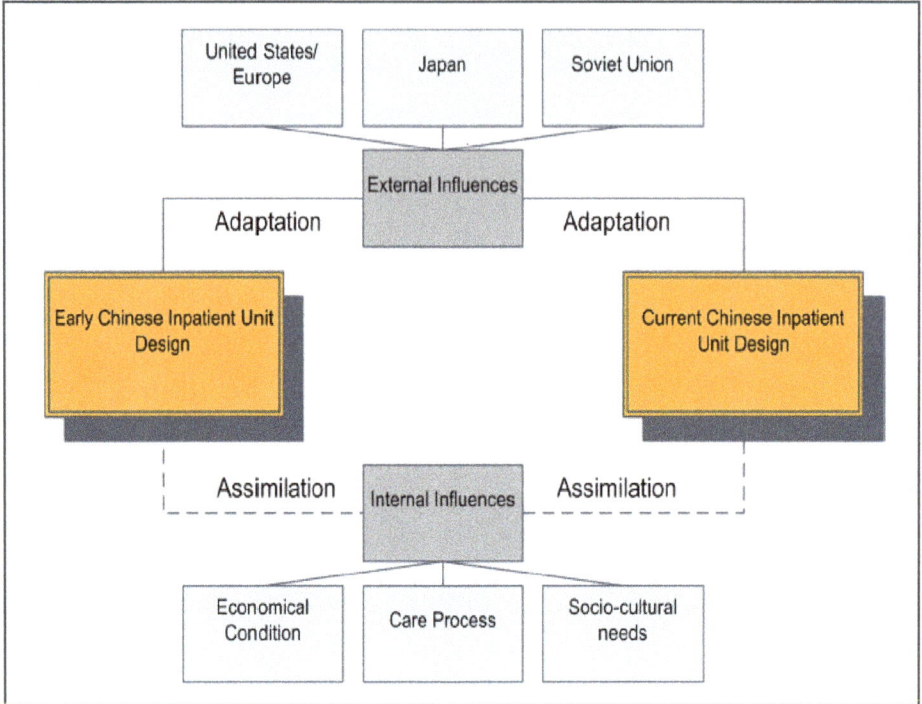

Figure 1. Modernization of Chinese Hospital. A Product of Adaptation and Assimilation

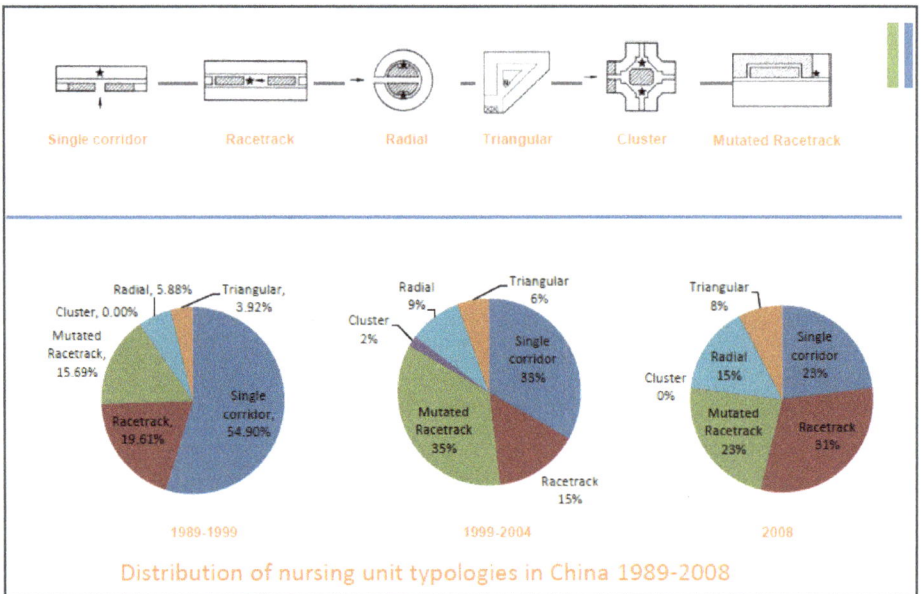

Figure 2. Evolution of Nursing Unit Typologies

National Schema	Communication	Space
Collectivism/ *Guanxi*	In-group and outside group distinction	Territoriality; Collocation of in-group members
High Power Distance/ *Dengji*	Respect for hierarchy	Hierarchy of space
Respect for face/*mianzi*	Privacy, High Context Communication	Backstage and fronstage , Accessibility

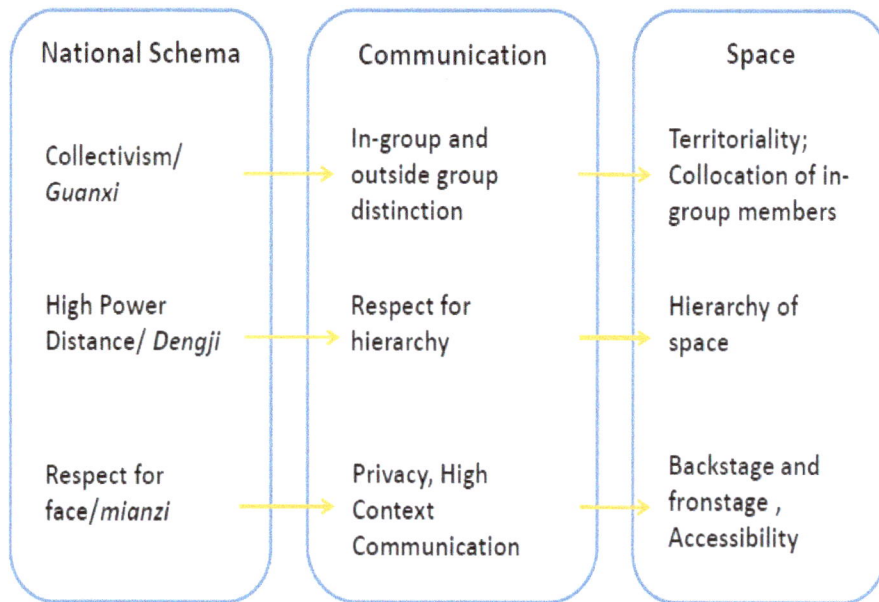

Figure 3. National Schema & Communication. Cultural needs of communication in Chinese nursing units

nursing unit typology. Comprehensive spatial analysis were conducted and several spatial metrics related to encounter, communication, territoriality, hierarchy, and privacy were evaluated.

The results of spatial analysis revealed significant national differences in the application of nursing unit typologies. The Chinese cases had significantly lower mean visual connectivity (p<0.05) and much lower mean visual integration values compared to the U.S. cases. However, with respect to physical accessibility, the Chinese cases had significantly higher mean connectivity (p<0.05), much higher mean integration, and a lower number of axial lines per space than the U.S. cases.

The results show dissimilar spatial strategies applied in the U.S. and Chinese nursing unit designs. The configurations of the Chinese cases were designed to better support movement and face-to-face communication, thus reflecting the collectivism and frame-based orientation of Chinese culture. Chinese nursing units also demonstrated that a stronger sense of territoriality and hierarchy. In addition, the Chinese cases had a clear demarcation of front-stage and back-stage space. Compared to their U.S. counterparts, the Chinese units had larger proportion of backstage space which supported the Chinese cultural preference of preserving "face."

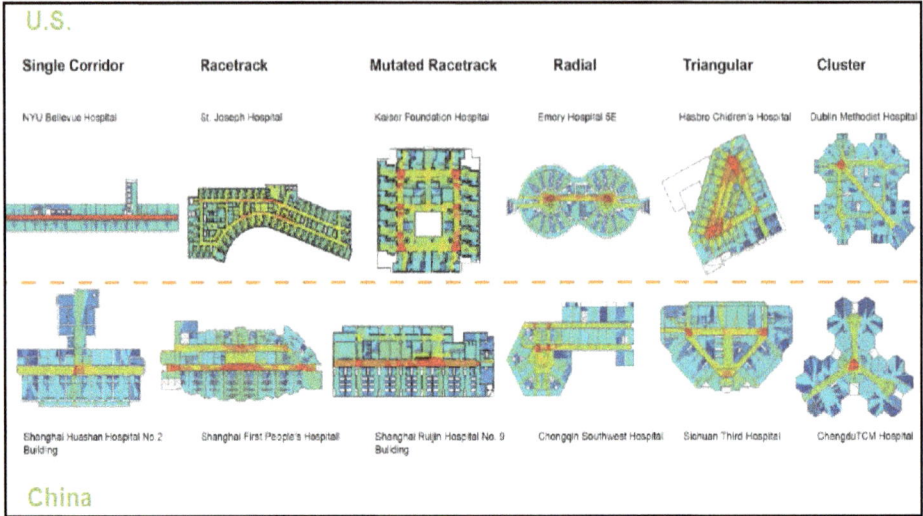

Figure 4. Comparative Case Studies. Comparative Study on Nursing Unit Typologies in China and the U.S. Visual Graph Analysis

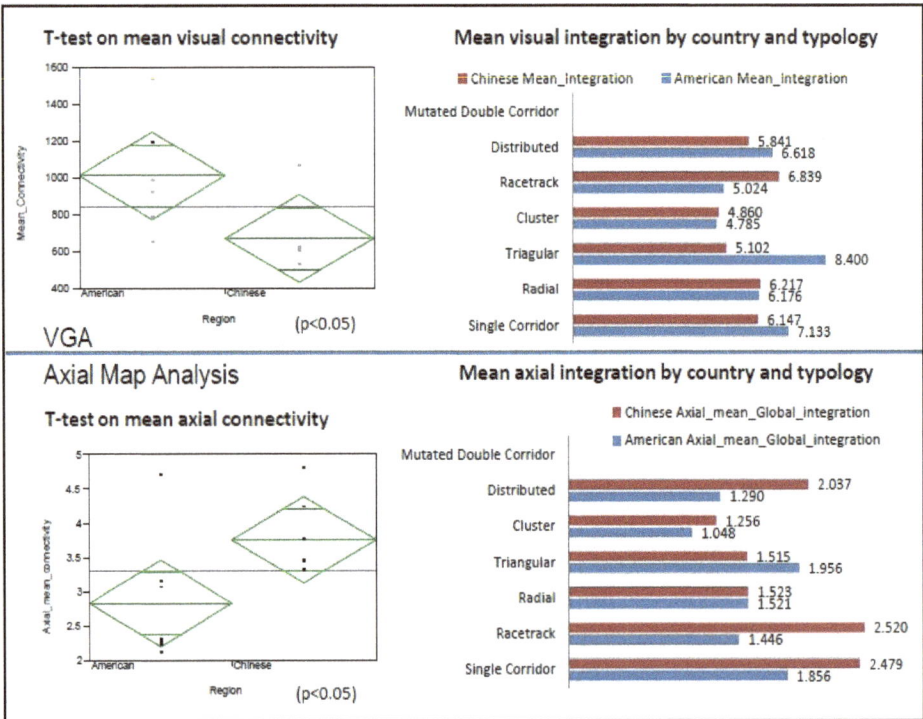

Figure 5. Finding: Chinese Layouts Are More Driven By The Needs For Face-to-face Communication

Skewness of visual integration by country and typology

■ Chinese_VGA_Integration_Skewness ■ American_VGA_Integration_Skewness

Typology	Chinese	American
Mutated Double Corridor		
Distributed	1.14	0.357
Racetrack	0.74	0.105
Cluster	1.218	0.899
Triagular	0.653	0.11
Radial	0.478	0.857
Single Corridor	1.068	1.074

Most Chinese case had larger skewness of the integration values than the U.S. counterparts with the same typology.

49

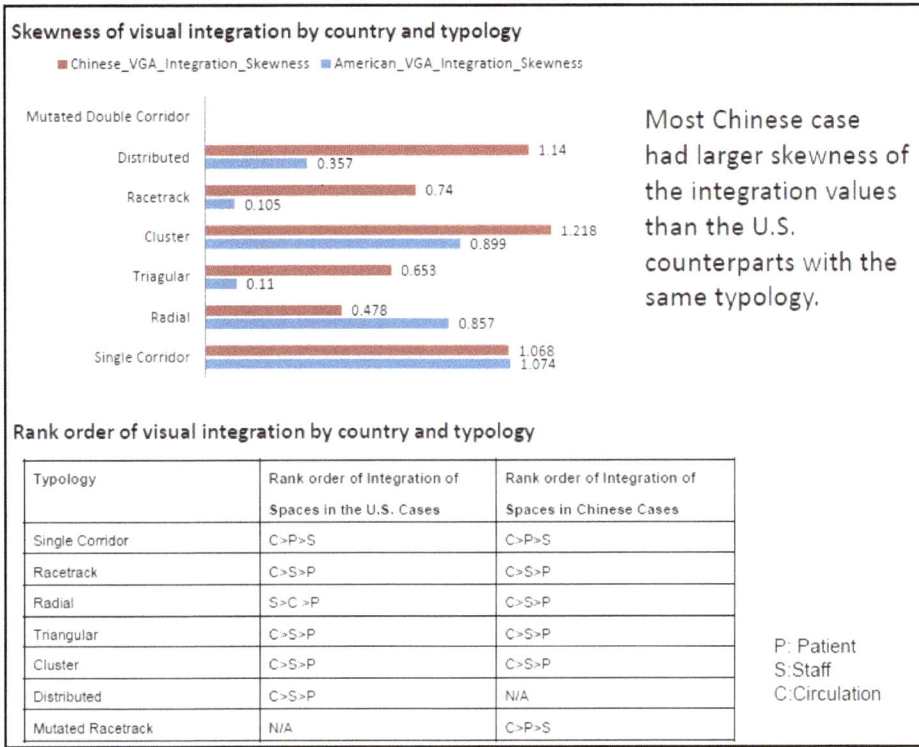

Rank order of visual integration by country and typology

Typology	Rank order of Integration of Spaces in the U.S. Cases	Rank order of Integration of Spaces in Chinese Cases
Single Corridor	C>P>S	C>P>S
Racetrack	C>S>P	C>S>P
Radial	S>C >P	C>S>P
Tnangular	C>S>P	C>S>P
Cluster	C>S>P	C>S>P
Distributed	C>S>P	N/A
Mutated Racetrack	N/A	C>P>S

P: Patient
S:Staff
C:Circulation

Figure 6. Finding: Chinese Layouts Have Stronger Sense of Hierarchy

EXISTING STUDIES ON NURSING UNITS DESIGN

- Space economy (Nuffield, 1955; James & Tatton Brown, 1986)

- Efficiency (James & Tatton Brown, 1986; Kobus et al., 2008; Thompson & Goldin, 1975)

- Single patient room vs Multiple patient room (Harris et al., 2006; Chaundhury, Mahmood & Valente, 2005)

- Same handed vs. Mirrored (Pati et al., 2010; Watkins et al., 2011)

- Centralized vs. decentralized nurse sta-

tion (Parker, Elsen & Bell, 2012; Cai & Zimring, 2010)

- Distribution and communication (Cai & Zimring, 2010; Lu & Zimring, 2012).

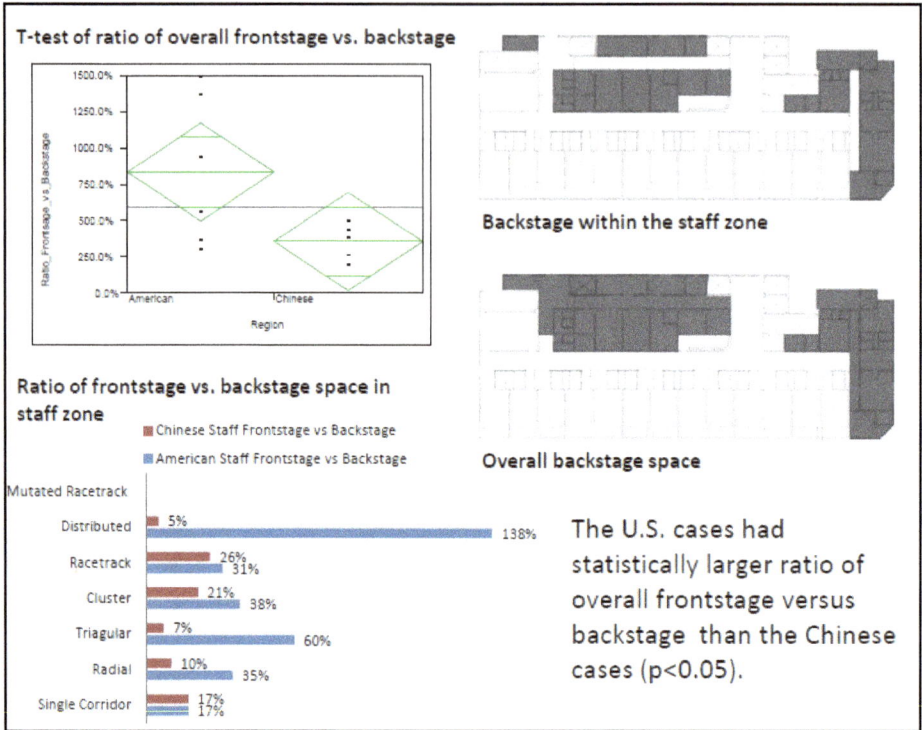

50

Figure 7. Finding: Chinese Layouts Have Larger Ratio of Backstage Space

Humanizing Healthcare Spaces through Culture: Design of Labour Delivery Room for the Malay-Muslim Community as Case Study

Norwina Mohd Nawawi

norwina@iium.edu.my
International Islamic University Malaysia

Zaiton Abdul Rahim

zaiton@iium.edu.my
International Islamic University Malaysia

Modern man and women have lived in the medicalised world from birth till death with the advent of modern sciences brought about into the healthcare environment. Culture as a way of life of an ordinary man suddenly stops as one enters the alien world of modern healthcare where certain expected behavioural standards are required. Many researches were made to humanize healthcare environment so as to soften this clashes of the environment. However, there are still very little inroads made to humanize the clinical areas of the healthcare environment apart from interior decoration and spatial layout.
Malaysia had awakened from its colonial days and had accepted the fact that traditional medicine lives in a separate stream from mainstream modern medicine as alternative choices. Birthing as a normal event, however has been brought into modern healthcare from its traditional setting to save lives of both mother and child. The objective of this research is to humanize the clinical spaces of the modern healthcare environment using labour delivery room as the case study and the Malay Muslim culture as the humanizing factor.

Keywords: *Humanizing, healthcare, culture, labour room design*

Introduction

The main stream birthing process is medicalized when a woman is moved from her home. The discipline is discussing who led the service; the consultant or the midwife. Santos (2010) in *"Challenges of a philosophy for the humanization of childbirth"* explained the challenges of childbirth over medicalization, and advocate to humanizing the process of childbirth by bringing back the soul, the mind and the body to the being in harmony.

Modern man and women have lived in the medicalised world from birth till death with the advent of modern sci-

TESIS

ences brought about into the healthcare environment for the betterment of mankind. Culture, as a way of life of an ordinary man that encapsulate humane environment suddenly stops as one enters the alien world of modern healthcare where certain expected behavioural standards are required. The motherhood stage as a natural event in the female's life has also entwined into the medical cycle. Realisation of these medicalised trends has lead to many reforms in maternity care with the growth of women-centred and family-centred birthing centres that facilitate the fulfilment of woman's choices as well as incorporating women's rights into maternity care. These are examples of the growing change towards getting the best outcomes for women, their babies, their marriage life and their position in society.

The World Health Organisation or WHO (1966) implied the practice of safe motherhood either delivered at home or at best in the hospital, without infringing the local customs. However, this intervention, especially in a hospital setting, causes abruption to the smooth flow of local traditions at the moment of birth, to the return of the mother and child from a local hospital after the birth. No traditions wish to endanger the lives of mother and child. It is, therefore, imperative when the life of both mother and child at childbirth are at stake, to find a bridge that fill the gap between humane and cultural requirements to the safe or clinical environment. This connection will support the mother and child well-being thus requires further research. The ability to give birth, in most cultures, gives a woman an identity that completes her well-being as a whole woman. Norwina (2015) suggests the model on linking medicalisation of

birth and normal female life cycle.

The significance of birth brought confidence to the father and gave strength to the family with a lineage or descendants. The importance of providing a birthing environment within a cultural context is best expressed by Laderman (1987):

"In a Malay women's own home, the Malay women give birth, but in the hospital, it is the obstetrician that delivers, not the Malay women."

"Humanization" in the context of this research is defined subtly by Merriam Webster's online dictionary (2008) as a process to make something or space "humane". Todres et al. (2009) define humanization through the conceptual framework of the dimension of humanization in healthcare as in Table 1. According to Todres et al. (2009), the person needs to attain the eight form of humanization values to feel humanize. Dehumanizing situation will occur if any one of the eight criteria is not balanced or subtracted. However, most of the reforms resulted from the studies were made to the areas of the healthcare facility such as the waiting areas, the in-

Form of humanization	Form of dehumanization
Insiderness	Objectification
Agency	Passivity
Uniqueness	Homogenization
Togetherness	Isolation
Sense-making	Loss of meaning
Personal journey	Loss of personal journey
Sense of place	Dislocation
Embodiment	Reductionist body

Table 1 - Dimension of humanization and dehumanization in healthcare (Source: Todres et. al., 2009)

OPTIMUM	USABILITY	MALAYSIANNESS
• Critical Determination	• Functionality, Efficiency,	• Characteristic that relate to
• Safety	• Effectiveness	the different
• Infection Control	• Satisfaction	• culture and
• Clinical procedure	• Ergonomics space	• mannerism /behavior of the
• Capacity	• Process/ sequence of activities	Malaysians of the Malays,
• Circulation	space	Chinese, Indians and other
	• Number of humans /occupancy	indigenous
	at peak period	
	• Equipment required	
	• Services required –water, light,	
	etc.	
	• Environmental requirements:	
	Privacy-noise, visual	

Table 2 - Definition of Balance Birthing Environment

patient accommodations and other public areas of the healthcare facility to be people friendly. However, review of the literature indicated there are still very little inroads made to humanize the clinical areas of the healthcare environment apart from touches made to the interior decoration and spatial layout.

The Malaysian essence, or values, in humanizing the birthing spaces of healthcare facilities, are expressed through its cultural factors conjoined with the needs of the modern or western environment (for clinical assistance) as a safety net (see table 2).

The "environment", is indeed an integral part of how living creatures function and develop. Therefore, there must be a conscious effort in the design community to give the new-born opportunity to be born naturally. That is to mean, to be born not only in the physically

and clinically safe as well as a secure environment but culturally appropriate to the people. The environment serves as a 'momentous' space for the rites of birth in the continuum of life. Aishah (2001) on maintaining traditional practices alongside western medicine in antenatal care in Malaysia, emphasised that a maternity care model needs to be user-friendly and also culturally appropriate while at the same time being safe and efficient. This quest concurred with WHO (2005)'s report.

The inclusion of cultural dimension in the healthcare spaces is important. Intangible elements such as shared beliefs, shared values, choices, acquired knowledge and skills through accepted traditions, although insignificant to particular worldviews, gave meanings to the individual, and the society in achieving

53

the 'ideal environment' including space for birth. The meaning that is tagged to the tradition made up the soul of these spaces that contained the tradition or culture.

Culture creates behavioural norms and, therefore, knowledge of cultural context allows one to predict, to some extent, the actions of those people in that culture (Geertz, 1973). The relationship between culture, behaviour and environment is intertwined.

Some authors suggest that culture and behaviour influence the environment while others argue the opposite. Many literature had indicated the link and relationship between behaviour and environment (Baker, 1968; Heimstra & McFarling, 1974); Pomeranz, 1980; Baron, Robert & Byrne, 1991; Betchtel, 1997; Rivlin, 2000; Wapner, Demick, Yamamoto & Minami, 2000). Understanding of the cultural context in providing an ideal environment is required to achieve a humane healthcare environment. Space, in architecture has many dimensions. Therefore, the space contains the essence of architecture as a reflection of conceptions of life, an environment to which our lives unfold (Barry, 1993).

ISSUES AND DISCUSSION

Malaysia has a long-standing tradition of professional midwifery – since 1923. Maternal mortality was reduced from more than 500 per 100 000 births in the early 1950s to around 250 in 1960. The country then gradually improved survival of mothers and newborns further by introducing a maternal and child health programme. A district health care system was introduced and midwifery care was stepped up through a network of "low-risk delivery centres", backed up by high-quality referral care, all with close and intensive quality assurance and on the initiative of the public sector authorities. This brought maternal mortality to below 100 per 100 000 by around 1975, and then to below 50 per 100 000 by the 1980s' (WHO, 2005).

Malaysia had awakened from its colonial days and had accepted the fact that traditional medicine lives in a separate stream from mainstream modern medicine as alternative choices. Birthing as a normal event, however, has been brought into modern healthcare from its traditional setting to save lives of both mother and child. In doing so, the cultural environment and shared values of celebrating new lives are taken away from the mother and the family to a sterile and clean environment where the mother is no longer in charge of her needs.

Figure 1 shows the evolution of Labour Delivery Room Design and Birthing Spatial Environment in Malaysia. Odent (1991) explained that in the privacy of a home, a birthing woman adopts instinctual behaviors, which cannot be learned in a class or from hospital personnel. Moreover, thus to attempt to teach a woman how to give birth, is, in his view, to attempt to control her. He said that all one could do is to "create the best of conditions" (Odent, 1991).

Recognition of the way the environment is being designed and facilitates the birth event is integral to optimal functioning of the healthcare setting including understanding the role of maternity care that provides the optimal environments for childbirth. To improve maternity care, Millennium Development Goals

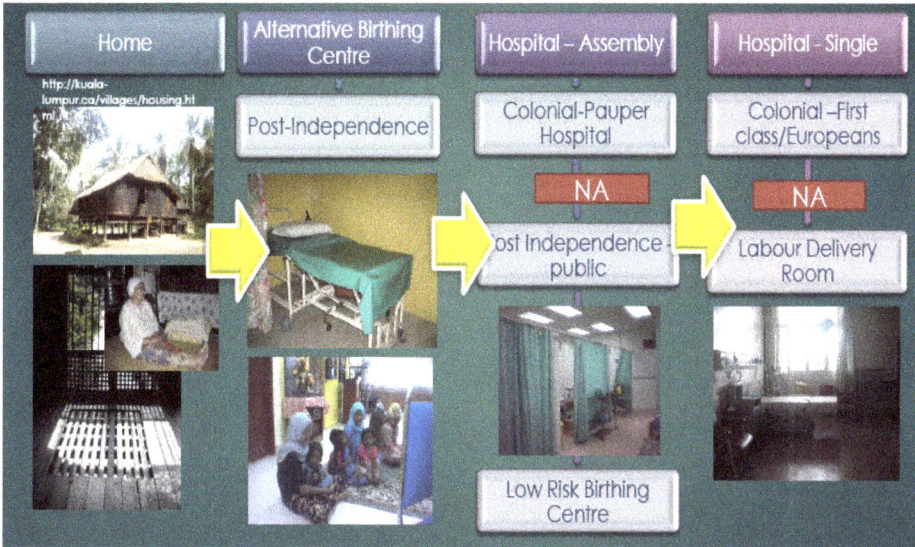

Figure 1. Evolution of Labour Delivery Room Design and Birthing Spatial Environment in Malaysia

(MDG) 5 Risk Approach in Maternal Health Care Advocate community education through various means recognition that socio-cultural and traditional environment of the family and community are inextricably linked. To ease the birth process, this study is in the opinion that the future birthing spaces should be designed to integrate the cultural dimension of the mother as part of essential design requirements. It is still imperative, however, for this research to take stock of current practices in the Malaysian hospitals and assessed the existing birth spaces and practices. Table 4 illustrates the advantages and disadvantages of home and hospital birth. Table 3 and 4 explain the Ministry of Health policies on Labour delivery unit in Malaysian hospitals.

Malaysia is a multi-culture country. Religions correlates strongly with ethnicity, with Muslims are mostly Malay, Hindus are mostly Indians and Buddhists are mostly Chinese. Although the culture is ethnic bound, a religion that is inculcated in the people's way of life plays a role in determining the culture of the ethnic that professed it obliviously. Characteristic of birth and birth spaces relate to the different cultures, religion and mannerism /behavior of the people.

The Malays made up over 60% of the population and currently the primary user of the public healthcare facility apart from being the most fertile of the ethnic groups.

In Malaysia, by virtue of Islam being a constitutional religion, Islam is, therefore, the official religion of the country and thus are assimilated in the official procedures and inculcated in all public facilities. However, as Islam is not ethnic based but universal in its practices, any ethnic related cultures that do not contravene Islamic believes are allowed to continue. This culture includes birth. Literature and findings on a site visit to

Excerpts (O&G1990)	Spaces proposed for labour unit
▪ Staffing and Equipment to be considered as Unit ▪ Centralized Labour Unit for 1st, 2nd and 3rd Class patients. i.e., classless ▪ Individual rooms to suit different cases e.g.pre- eclampsia. ▪ No separate 1st Stage. ▪ All patient in Labour to be admitted directly to Labour Unit and stay till delivery. ▪ Husbands encouraged to accompany	▪ Individual rooms for privacy minimum 10' x 13.' ▪ Two(2) rooms to share toilets One (1) room for every 600 deliveries Max deliveries per hospital 10,000/year ▪ One(1) room to be reserved for special care of ill patients that requires close monitoring and ventilators

Table 3 - MoH Policies on LDUs in hospital

HOME	HOSPITAL
ADVANTAGE ▪ As the queen of the house, i.e. able to deman and command comfort level ▪ Able to choose space and position of birth ▪ Able to continue taking care of other children before and after birth ▪ Need not move from one place to another ▪ Able to immediately continue the tradition of massage and heat reatment ▪ Baby are taken care of in between feedings ▪ Able to take up traditional medicine and appropriate food ▪ Able to have close relatives in privacy of her own space **DISADVANTAGE** ▪ Life risk if complication	**ADVANTAGE** ▪ Safe and sterile ▪ Less pain due to available pain killer **DISADVANTAGE** ▪ No freedom for mothers to choose the position comfortable for birth ▪ Need to listen to those in authority i.e. nurses, midwives, doctors on the dos and don'ts ▪ Move from one place to another based on stages of labour ▪ Loss importance; by being just one of the many patients. Not special anymore ▪ Relatives can only be around during visiting hours ▪ Need to take care of the baby herself

Table 4 - Home birth hospital birth in traditional upbringing (Zulkifli, 2001)

facilities showed similar usage pattern of public facilities by the Malays, the Indians and the Chinese in that order (figure 2). The Chinese, due to tradition since the colonial era, are used to having their own maternity hospital and has more purchasing power to choose private hospitals as other option. Based on the discussion presented, the study focuses on

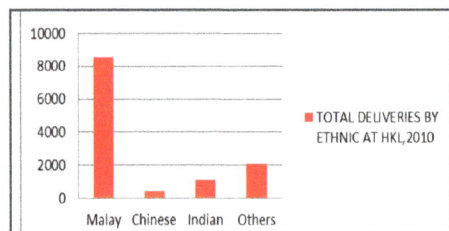

Figure 2. Total deliveries by ethnic, KL General Hospital, 2010

Department brief of LDU	Room space brief of LDR (birthing space)
▪ Functional Description ▪ Operational policies ▪ Workload ▪ Planning concept ▪ Manpower and staffing organization ▪ Space requirements and functions	▪ The LDU will consist of 4 delivery units/ LDR. Two delivery units will share one (1) en-suite of separated cubicles of toilet and shower, with a vanity outside the cubicles. ▪ Four (40 delivery rooms are required. ▪ The patient will be admitted into the room and go through the process of labour and delivery. ▪ As much as possible, the room should have a non-clinical atmosphere and husband friendly so as to encourage the husband, or a relative be with the patient during the entire delivery process. ▪ The necessary clinical items for delivery should be kept on delivery trolley inside the room (1 for each room) ▪ Two (2) rooms shall be sharing an ensuite toilet. This toilet shall be provided in the anteroom and toilet. ▪ Space should allow for at least two (2) staff managing the delivery, a bassinet, a cardiotocograph, a maneuvering trolley and one(1) visitor chair, a resuscitation equipment in case of urgent resuscitation is required. Or else resuscitation is done at the resuscitation bay.

Table 5 - Generic medical brief of requirement of labour delivery unit and labour delivery room of public non-specialist hospital in Malaysia

the design of Labour Delivery Room for the Malay-Muslim Community as Case Study.

OBJECTIVE OF THE STUDY

Based on the issue and discussion presented, the objectives of the study are:
1. To examine the spaces and practices of birthing conformation to the critical dimension of a functional entity as envisaged by current Ministry of Health Malaysia's standards or the Private Healthcare Facilities and Services Act 1998 in relation to the Malay-Muslim culture.
2. To examine whether the spaces and practices for birthing had accounted culturally for an enhance and satisfying birthing experience for the patients.

RESEARCH METHODOLOGY

The method adopted for the research is both qualitative and quantitative. Ex-

plorative and experimental designs using empirical data gathered from primary and secondary sources were made based on findings and comparative analysis of the existing environment to test the hypothesis of the culturally integrated labour delivery room design. Case study of design of Labour Delivery Room in nine hospitals in relation to the Malay-Muslim Community was used to demonstrate the importance of understanding the subject matter - the Mother, the culture surrounded her, the comfort and support she expects so that she can bear the process of child bearing, and succeed in her motherly effort. Interviews and observation used for the study supported by sketches, photographs and notation during visits to facilities. Sketches and information on the sequence of movements in definite space were redrawn in Autocad (Figure 3).

The use of space and sequence of activity and behavioural activity within space were observed and coded.

TESIS Inter-University Research Centre "Systems and Technologies for Social and Healthcare Facilities"
University of Florence, Italy

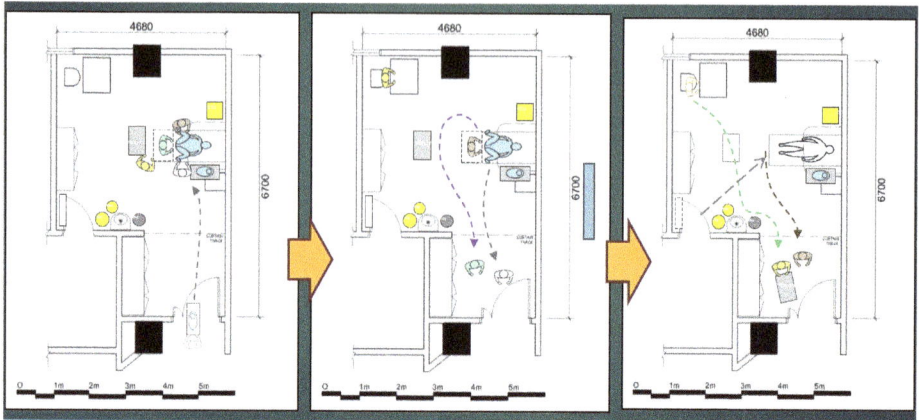

Figure 3. Drawing out sketches to Autocad

The interview includes both unstructured and structured with the consultant and staff in-charge of LDU. The interview covers on general information, flow, policies of visiting spouse, emergency and non-emergency flow, patients post labour. Room/ space (3 D) including Grid and Area. The physical measurement of room size, equipment, placement of furniture and building services were recorded and coded. Standard equipment and furniture required in the LDR at various stages were recorded and listed. Photos on the process were taken where possible.

For the purpose of this study, although birthing space is an individual experience, in providing a public facility for mass use, a form of standards, based on commonality of usage and physical needs, is ensued. For this reason, Minimum standards and guidelines are imposed to ensure the public are provided with the optimum birthing facility.

The selected standards and guidelines from respective health authorities from countries and WHO whom Malaysian architects infer for their projects were analysed. The selected guidelines discussed are from the Department of Health (DH) and the National Health Service (NHS) of England in the United Kingdom (UK); Australasian Health Facility Guidelines of Australia; and the Healthcare Facilities Guidelines from the United States of America (USA), summarised in Table 6. The selected Malaysian Hospitals LDUs and LDRs spaces were analysed based on the summary. Determination of the critical dimension through overlapping of images on circulation and equipment and activities conducted in the space gridded

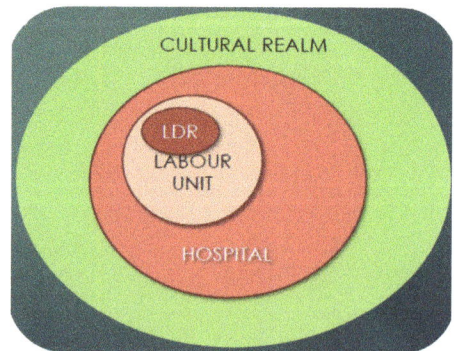

Figure 4. The limitation of the study

Reference	Terminology of Birthing Space	Critical Dimension (Space Configuration)	Optimum Area	Remarks
UK	Single/Twin Birthing space/ Room	4.9 x 4.2-4.65 m	20.58-34.8sq.m	Nett space
Australia	Birthing Room (LDR)	4.4 x5.55 m	28 sq.m	Nett Space
USA	LDR, LDRP	13-15ft. (3.96-4.57m) x 26.15-13.33 ft. (7.922-4.06 m)	200-340sq.ft (18.58-31.57sq. m)	Nett space
Average	LDR/Birthing Room	Not less than 3.96 m and not more than 7.922m (4 x 5-8)	Not less than 18.48 sq. m. not more than 34.8 sq. m	Nett space

Table 6 - Summary of Birthing Space Critical Dimension and Optimum Area (nett space) from the UK, Australia and the USA

to a dimension.

The study is limited within a hospital context, on entry to the labour unit (LU) Labour Delivery Unit (LDU), through to labour delivery room (LDR) prior discharge to Maternity Ward or home in terms of circulation, cultural practices of the birthing mother & relatives (figure 4).

FINDING AND DISCUSSION

The literature review on the detailed account of birthing in Malay culture is very much limited. The account by Laderman (1987) is entrenched in animistic belief and ritual that is not parallel to Islam. There is no discussion on the exact location where the birth took place in the traditional Malay house. However, discussion and interviews with elderly women and village folks that birthing can take place anywhere in the house that could be improvised to allow for privacy. Findings indicate the following space requirements for birthing:

i. adequate privacy from prying eyes;
ii. adequate space for 3-5 persons i.e.

the birthing mother, the mother or close female relative of the mother, the traditional birth attendant (TBA), a female relative or immediate neighbor as runner and lastly the spouse for strength;

iii. a one stop space for birth, hygiene, bath, sleep, massage and other activities after birth;

iv. near to kitchen for food and heat to ease the blood circulation.

Figure 5 illustrates the aspects of traditional Malay house in relation to the birthing process.

Based on the traditional birthing requirement, there is no particular space or rites in the Malay-Muslim birth practices. Privacy is paramount but life and death matter most in the Islamic law (Shariah) that the presence of another sex as a doctor is permitted at the crucial moment only. If there is a choice, preference for a female doctor is deemed. Culturally the birthing mother needs another female relatives more, so the birthing mother's own mother to be at her side. The presence of the spouse is only required when the strength to as-

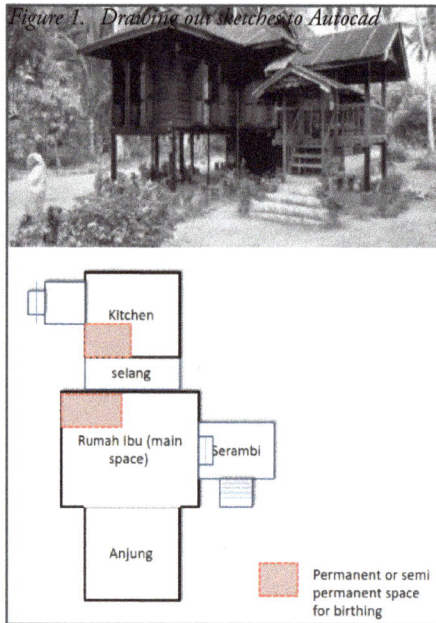

Figure 1. Drawing out sketches to Autocad

Kitchen

selang

Rumah Ibu (main space)

Serambi

Anjung

Permanent or semi permanent space for birthing

Figure 5. Aspects of traditional Malay house in relation to birthing process

sist the birth is required. Islam does not make any prescription to the process as it is on a natural accord. What Islam precedes is for the birthing mother to cite in her heart and whisper remembrance of Allah through 'zikir' and verses of the Al Quran especially at the peak of the labour pain. Spiritually the practice eases the pain as each pain is a pardon for the sins that we may done in the lifetime and birthing is like a process of cleansing. Upon the birth, the baby is whispered in both left and right ear, the call of prayer and the name of Allah as a reminder of the child's promise in heaven to know only Him as creator and that he/she will return to Him chaste and clean in the hereafter. The reading to ear is best done by the father or the grandfather. In the absence, the mother or the Muslim medical staff can perform.

The placenta upon delivery is returned to the family for proper burial as a human part. Although culturally the Malays conduct a similar ritual to the placenta as the Hindus due to previous faith embedded in the culture, the tradition, if contravening the *Shariah*, will be discontinued.

CRITICAL DIMENSION OF A FUNCTIONAL ENTITY OF SELECTED LDR IN CURRENT LDU

Analysis for cultural and critical dimension from standard brief and standard typical design of birth space in the case studies indicates the following findings:

1. Cultural dimension:
Evaluation on standard brief indicates cultural dimension is only evident in passing as a statement for the request for consideration of the presence of spouse or relative for design but no guideline provided or imposed as a mandatory requirement. Cultural dimension in standard/ typical design is evident only in the compliance of the following aspects:
i. in the orientation of labour bed away from direct visual view;
ii. presence of curtain tracks for privacy;
iii. presence of a chair for spouse/relative.
There is no tool or guideline to evaluate the presence of cultural consideration in both forms to ensure the provision in compliance.

2. Critical Dimension:
Evaluation on critical dimension indicates descriptive requirement of procedures taking place within the space and referring to other standards. No dimensions were provided that leaves the design professionals to refer to the Schedule of Accommodation (SOA) if

available or refer other standards. SOA does not provide the right configuration required. Findings indicate that for critical dimension, the design, as drawn, becomes the lingua franca/ communication between the designers/implementers and the user-clients. The drawings showed necessary placement of equipment, loose and fixed furniture, M&E services and basic dimension of width and length of the birth space (mostly at centre to centre dimension), with gross floor area only of the room to meet the SOA requirement. There are foreign standards and Malaysian Private Healthcare Facilities and Services Standards for licensing to ensure optimum compliance. However, this is done only after the project agrees in the process of compliance. The room by room discussion and mock-up of prior room construc-

tion will allow refinement of the birth space design. However, the issues will remain unless the user-client understands the drawings and designers know what he/ she is designing. For both cultural and critical dimension, a tool to check compliance is essential.

Table 7 shows the summary of evaluation in case study 2.

CONSIDERATION IN THE SPACES AND PRACTICES FOR BIRTHING FOR ENHANCING AND SATISFYING BIRTHING EXPERIENCE FOR THE PATIENTS IN RELAZTION TO MALAY - MUSLIM BIRTH

Findings indicate that a good Malay-Muslim birth environment should reflect and support the Cultural Dimension, defined by linkage to family and Critical Dimension for clinical and safe-

61

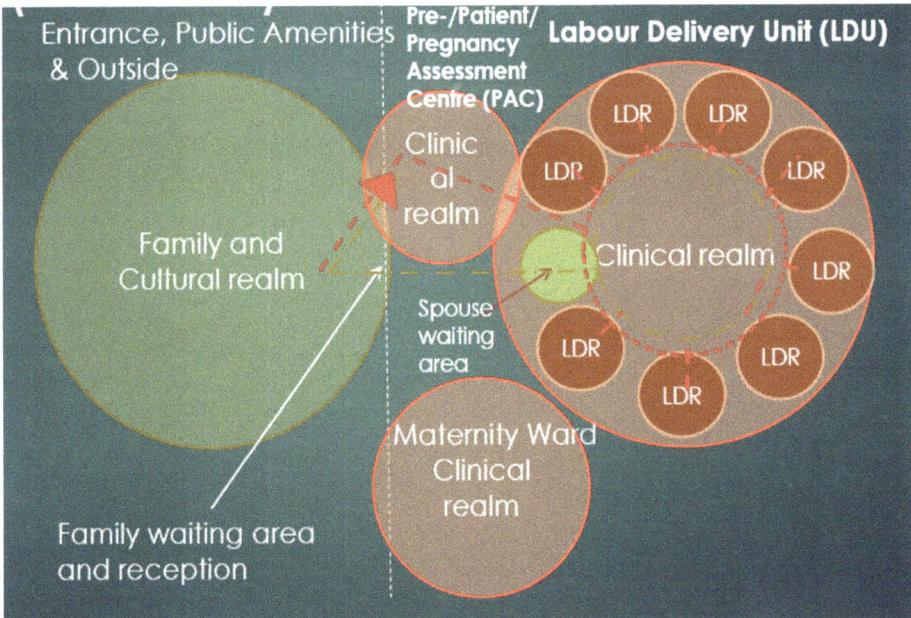

Figure 6. Relation and flow of family as linkage

ty consideration. Designing the birthing space or LDR only, do not make a holistic support to the cultural dimension of birth environment, as both spouse and patient-mother has to pass through the clinical areas of the hospital from admission to maternity ward. Waiting relatives have to wait at the main entrance outside LDU.

For safety and travel distance, after birth patient-mother are trolleyed or wheelchair by staff through dedicated routes to the wards. They seldom appear at the waiting area in front of the Patient

Assessment Centre (PAC) for a family celebration of a newborn prior to admission to the maternity ward. Findings indicate that in selected hospitals where all dealing with public or families are located outside the mother's cultural realm, both patient and spouse had to pass through clinical areas to enter a private domain (LDR) where they can be together for support without the next of kin or other family members familiar in a traditional setting. Families on hospital ground waited in the crowded waiting room or visitor's hall for the news of baby's arrival. The journey to the clinical

Configuration	4.2m x 4.8m	4.6m x 8 m
LDR	20.1sq.m	30.8sq.m
*Mirror image arrangement of LDR did not leave much space for cultural intervention		
Critical Dimension	Did not meet the requirement but manageable. Space adequacy for emergency is not met in configuration	Acceptable. Placement of fixed items to be clear of the critical area
Cultural Dimension	Spatially adequate Access for spouse is through clinical/ internal corridor Apart from SOP, others are discreet	Spatially adequate Access for spouse is through clinical/ internal corridor Apart from SOP, others are discreet
Remarks	Satisfy the requirement for area Configuration did not meet the requirement especially along the length of the bed for ease of intubation (head area), birth (foot area) and maneuverings to OT if need be (Foot area) Requires distract in case of prolong birth	Satisfy the requirement for area Configuration did not meet the requirement especially along the length of the bed for ease of intubation (head area), birth (foot area) and maneuverings to OT if need be (Foot area) Requires distract in case of prolong birth

Table 7 - Summary of evaluation in case study 2

Space	Cultural Dimension	Critical Dimension
LDU	• First impression of LDU • The reception and registration • Wheelchair, trolley • Friendly staff • Waiting area for relative and children playground • Away from mortuary	• Ease of bringing and handling of equipment • Consistency in surveillance / monitoring • Infection control • Space planning – next to MOT, SCN, maternity ward
LDR	• First impression of LDR • The constant presence of a spouse/ immediate family members for motivation/ moral support • Privacy (pre and post birth) • Female doctor/ nurse • Position and placement of labour bed, prayer space, family sittings, other children • Personal belonging • Spiritual condition (able to say prayers and *azan*) • *E*ase for ablution • Labour bed – comfort, safety, secure • Comfortable room size • Ease of toilet • Food • Ease of taking back placenta • Clock, view • Flexible	• Position and placement • Arrangement of bed • Consistency in surveillance/ monitoring • Infection control • Space planning – next to MOT, SCN, maternity ward • Easy access to medical gas and socket outlet • Female doctors, nurses/ trainees/ houseman (capacity) • Good lighting • Structural grid 7.5m x7.5m – 8.1m x 8.1m • Square shape 3.7m – 4.2m x 4.9m (600mm at head end and 2100mm at foot end) clear space • Ergonomic/ anthropometric • Flexible

Table 8 - Summary of criteria for an integrated- Muslim birth space (LDU and LDR)

realm is long and subjected to other patient's privacy and staff routine activities (Figure 6).

CONCLUTION

The search for criteria to humanize the birth environment through culture and belief system that encompass the way of life of Malaysians, with the Malay Muslim practices used as the case study, was initiated and found. To humanize the birth spaces, although the siting is within the clinical realm, it is important to be connected to the culture through family members not only within the birth space but all along the route from labour onset at home to the birth space. Adequate existing space can accommodate the requirements while others may have to scale the scope. The reorganisation of LDU for new LDU is, therefore,

eminent if it is to be a holistic endeavour. However, the findings and recommendations of the study does not an end here, but set forth to opens more avenues towards realisation that the future journey will no doubt brings bountiful gain and confidence in using own data and own method with understanding of the transient /intangible culture to give 'the space' a meaningful dimension.

Adaptation may have to be made to existing LDUs if policy makers are willing to Malaysianise the healthcare spaces and celebrates the new Malaysians with the value that culture brings into the modern healthcare environment. The outcomes require the reorganisation of the Labour Delivery Unit layout altogether and not just the labour delivery room in addressing the birthing culture. Malaysia is multi-culture. The study shows similarities in the birth event in

63

the cultures. Further studies on other cultures in Malaysia will provide a more conclusive finding to providing a culturally sensitive and humanized LDU design.

REFERENCES

Abidin, W.B.W. (1981). *The Malay House: Rationale and Change*. M. Arch. Thesis. Cambridge, Massachussetts Institute of Technology

Abdul Hadi Nawawi and Natasha Khalil (2008). *Post occupancy evaluation correlated with building occupants' satisfaction: An approach to performance evaluation of government and public buildings*, in "Journal of Building Appraisal" (2008). Vol.4, pp. 59-69

Abdullah Ahmad. (2006). *Rites of Passage*, in Hood Salleh (ed.) (2006), "Peoples and Traditions. Encyclopedia of Malaysia". Kuala Lumpur. Architecture Pelago Press, Chapter Malay festivals and celebrations, p. 41

Aida Kesuma Azmin. (2007). *A Discourse on Housing Based on Cultural Meanings in Malaysia*, Chp 3, in "Malay defined, characteristics, identity and tradition", pp. 4555. Unpublished Doctoral Dissertation. University of Heriot-Watt, Scotland

Aishah Ali. (2001). *Antenatal care in Malaysia: Maintaining traditional practices alongside western medicine*. Unpublished Doctoral Dissertation. New Zealand University of Otago

AmirHosein GhaffarianHoseini, and Nur Dalilah Dahlan (2012). *The Essence of Malay Vernacular Houses: Towards Understanding the Socio-cultural and Environmental Values*, in "Journal of the International Society for the Study of Vernacular Settlements", Vol. 2, no. 2, March 2012. pp. 53-73

Antonovsky, A. (1996). *The Salutogenic Model As a Theory to Guide Health Promotion*, in "Oxford Journals, Medicine, Health Promotion International", Oxford University Press, Vol. 11, Issue 1, Pp. 11-18. Retrieved 12 Nov 2011 at http://www.salutare.ee/files/ettekanded/Salutogenees.pdf

Barker, R. G. (1968). *Ecological Psychology. Concepts and Methods for Studying the Environment of Human Behavior*. California: Stanford University Press

Baron, R. A., and Byrne, D. (1991). *Social Psychology – Understanding Human Interaction* (2nd ed). London: Allyn and Bacon

Barry, A.J. (Ed). (1993). *As Space- How To Look at Architecture*. New York. De Capo

Bechtel, R. B., Marans, R. W., and Michelson, W. (Eds) (1990). *Methods in Environmental and Behavioral Research*. Florida: Robert E. Krieger Publishing Company

Betancourt, H. and Lopez, S.R. (1993). *The study of culture, ethnicity, and race*, in "American psychology". Am Psychol. 1993; 48: 629–37

Betancourt, H., et al. *Health Educ. Res.* (2010) 25 (6): 991-1007. doi: 10.1093/her/cyq052. First published online: September 23, 2010

Byford, J. (1998, December 1). *Childbirth and Authoritative Knowledge: Cross Cultural Perspectives (Review), in "The Australian Journal of Anthropology"*. Retrieved from http://www.questia.com

Chen, P.C.Y. (1975). *Medical Systems in Malaysia: Cultural Bases and Differential Use,* in "Social Science and Medicine Journal", Vol.9, Gt.Britain.Pergamon Press, pp. 171-180

Department of Statistics, Malaysia. (2011). *Vital Statistic, Malaysia, 2010.* Putrajaya. Encyclopedia Britannica Ready Reference (2002)

Foureur, M.J. et al. (2010). Midwifery: *The relationship between birth unit design and safe, satisfying birth: Developing a hypothetical model.* Vol. 26, Issue 5, pp 520-525, October 2010.

Geertz, C. (1973). T*he Interpretation of Cultures: Selected Essays*. New York: Basic Books

Heimstra, N. W., and McFarling, L. H. (1974). *Environmental Psychology.* California: Brooks/Cole

Laderman, C. (1987). *Wives and Midwives Childbirth and Nutrition in Rural Malaysia.* USA. University of California Press

MDG 5: *Improve Maternal Health. At* http://www.epu.gov.my/c/document_library, Retrieved 05May2015

Merriam Webster's online dictionary (2008)

Merli, C. (2011) *Patrescence in Southern Thailand: cosmological and social dimensions of fatherhood among the Malay-Muslims,* in "Culture, health sexuality", 13 (S2). S235-S248. Retrieved 20 March 2015 at http://dro.dur.ac.uk/7906/1/7906.pdf

Norwina Mohd Nawawi. (2006b). *Local Influence in the Dimensions of Designing Birthing Spaces for the Malay-Muslim Malaysians.* Presentation at IAPS 2006,11-16th September 2006, Bibliotheca Alexandrina, Alexandria, Egypt

Norwina Mohd Nawawi. (2007). *Inculcating Traditional Values in the Design of Healthcare Facilities for Sustainability - A Malaysian scenario.* Paper presented at the 27th International UIA-PHG Seminar, 1-6th July 2007, Beijing Friendship Hotel, Beijing, China

Norwina Mohd Nawawi, *Cultural Dimension of Birthing Spaces in the Malaysian Public Healthcare System. The Malay-Muslim Practices* (Ph.D. Thesis, International Islamic University Malaysia, 2015)

Norwina Mohd Nawawi. (2003). *Inducing Culture Into The Design Of Healthcare Architecture in the South East Asian Environment,* Poster Presentation for 3rd World Congress and Exhibition in Design and Health 2003 in Montreal, Canada 25-29th June 2003

Pomeranz, D. (1980). *Environmental Psychology,* in L. Krasner. (Ed). "Environmental Design and Human Behavior: A Psychology of the Individual in Society". New York: Pergamon Press. pp. 66-78.

65

Odent, M. (1991), *Home Birth for High-Risk Mothers (2004)*, in "Mothering Magazine", Gale Group

Odent, M. (2009). *The Masculinisation of the Birth Environment.* Academic Journal Article from "Journal of Prenatal & Perinatal Psychology & Health", Vol. 23, No. 3

Rivlin, R. G. (2000). *Reflections on the Assumptions and Foundations of Work in Environmental Psychology,* in S. Wapner, J. Demick, T. Yamamoto, & H. Minami (Eds). "Theoretical Perspectives in Environment-Behavior Research: Underlying Assumptions, Research Problems, and Methodology". New York: Kluwer Academic/Plenum Publishers. pp. 51-60

Science Museum: *Brought to Life: Exploring the History of Medicine. A natural process? Women, men and the medicalisation of childbirth.* Retrieved 25th April 2015 at http://www.sciencemuseum.org.uk/broughttolife/themes/birthanddeath/childbirthandmedicine.aspx

Todres, L., Galvin, K.T., & Holloway, I. (2009). *The Humanization of Healthcare: A Value Framework for Qualitative Research,* in "International Journal of Qualitative Studies on Health and Well-Being". (2009); Vol.4: pp. 68-77

Wapner, S., Demick, J., Yamamoto, T., and Minami, H. (Eds). (2000). *Theoretical Perspectives in Environment-Behavior Research: Underlying Assumptions, Research Problems, and Methodology.* New York: Kluwer Academic/Plenum Publishers

WHO. (2005). *Make Every Mother and Child Count. The World Health Report* 2005. http://www.who.int/whr/2005/whr2005_en.pdf

WHO. (1999). *Care in Normal Birth: A practical guide.* Safe Motherhood Report of a technical working group. Department of Reproductive Health and Research. Geneva. World Health Organisation. Retrieved 11Nov2011 at https://apps.who.int/rht/documents/MSM96-24/msm9624.htm

Zaiton Abdul Rahim. (2007). *Privacy and Modification of Terrace Housing among Malay Family Occupants in Klang Valley, Malaysia.* Unpublished PhD thesis, University Putra Malaysia.

The Study of the Relationship between Patient Care Level and Bathroom Proximity

Ruka Kosuge

kosuge@niph.go.jp
Research Associate, Ph.D., Architect
Dept. of Environmental Design, Kobe Design University

The aging phenomenon in Japan is a very severe problem. Aging is a major challenge not only among the non-admitted individuals but also among the terminal elderly patients admitted to a hospital. According to the Ministry of Health, Labour and Welfare, 80% of the elderly people die in hospitals and clinics, and not at their homes.

The need for nursing care is more than medical care in these aging wards, particularly in cases of dementia and those requiring excretion help.

Most of the hospital wards in Japan consist of rooms with 4 beds and rooms with a single bed. Sometimes, the weak elderly patients in 4-bed rooms use the portable toilet provided at their bedside with a curtain as a partition between neighbors as they are physically incapable go to a distant toilet.

OBJECTIVE AND METHOD

This study aims to clarify how the location of toilets in wards influences the patients' toilet routines and nurses' support with excretion.

The comparison survey was conducted in 4 wards. The locations included the med and surge wards in the old YMK hospital with a centralized arranged toilet area as well as med and surge wards in the new YMK hospital with a decentralized toilet in each room after renovation. YMK hospital is located at Kanagawa Pref., Japan.

Before its renovation, the old med ward had 59 beds and the old surge ward had 71 beds per a unit. The new med ward has 33 beds and the new surge ward has 34 beds per a unit.

New ward changes:
1) Open Staff Station (Counter-less);
2) High ratio of single bed rooms: 33% (15 rooms/44 beds);
3) Decentralized toilet – wheelchair accessible;
4) Built-in shelves for PPE; 5) Electronic medical chart.

The survey in old wards conducted from 11/19/2012 to 12/13/2012, and the survey in new wards conducted from 6/3/2013 to 6/30/2013.

The following were considered as survey parameters: 1) patient's bed location; 2) patient's elimination procedure; and

Figure 1. Old Med. Ward and Old Surg. Ward in YMK Hospital

3) patient's level of need for nursing care (there is standard measuring method in Japan).

The patients' elimination procedure was only focused on the excretion of urine at 14:00 each day.

The procedures were categorized into 7 classes as below to make complex procedures simplified for analysis:

1) walking;
2) walking with assistance;
3) wheelchair;
4) wheelchair with assistance;
5) portable toilet at bedside;
6) portable toilet at bedside with assistance;
7) diaper.

RESULTS

a) In case of old wards with a centralized toilet, nurses often took the patients to the toilet on a wheelchair. However, patients often had to wait for their turn in the corridor in front of the toilet area, because they could not know whether the toilet was vacant unless they checked. Sometimes patients who could not wait went back to their room and used the portable toilet at their bedside. Once a patient used a portable toilet, the nurses had to dispose the waste, wash the pan, and bring it back.

This increased the nurses' job. Patients who needed toilet care got admitted around a nursing station for more efficient nursing.

b) In case of the new wards with a decentralized toilet in each room, some patients could use it by themselves because of its close proximity.

c) The percentage of independent patients for the elimination procedure increased from 46% to 54% in the med ward and from 52% to 59% in the surge ward. The use of the portable toilet decreased from 7% to 4% in the med ward and from 6% to 2% in the surge ward. The percentage of patients using diapers remained constant at around 20%.

d) To check the patients' bodily waste elimination procedure against their

	# of Beds per unit (Average # of Patients)		# of Nurses	
	Old	New	Old	New
Surg. Ward	70 beds (57.8)	34 beds (28.3)	34	22
Med. Ward	59 beds (54.9)	33 beds (30.8)	35	21

Figure 3. YMK: Beds per unit

score level of need for nursing care, the elimination procedure of the patients on from level 2 to 7 was changed by changing the location of their toilet.

CONCLUSION

This study indicated that the decentralized toilet in each room encouraged patient's enhanced recovery. It was found to be effective at improving nursing support efficiency.

In the aging society, in order to maintain a good environment, it is very important to prolong patient ability of independent excretion to respect his/her dignity.

Figure 2. New Med. and Surg. Ward in YMK Hospital

Figure 4. Staff station of new hospital ward

69

70

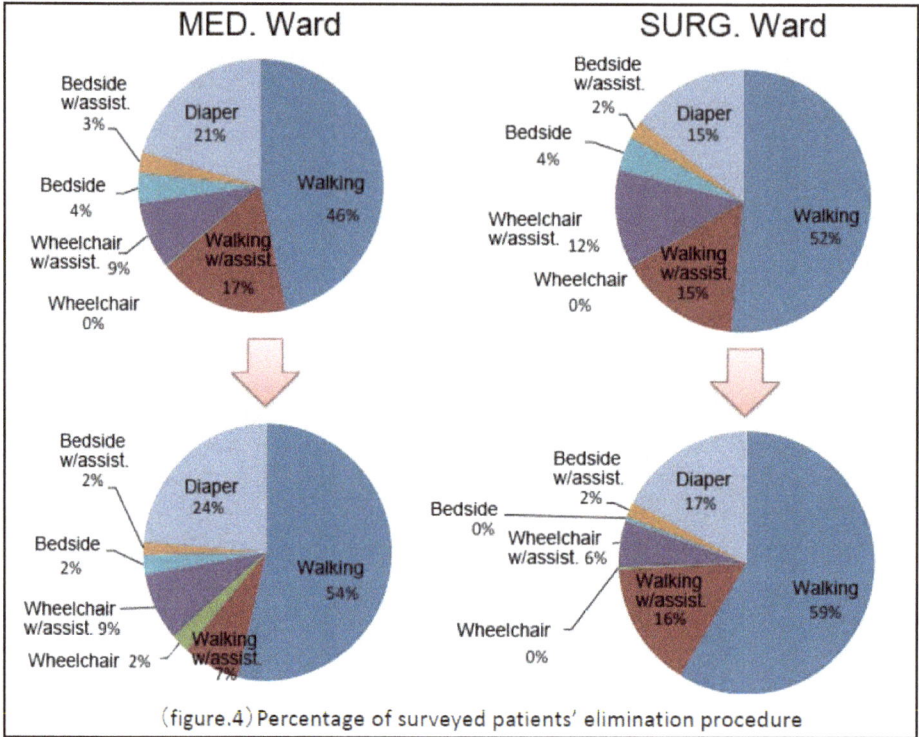

(figure.4) Percentage of surveyed patients' elimination procedure

Figure 5. Percentage of surveyed patients' elimination procedure

Transforming Hospital Design. Promoting Better User Experience from YongLin X Lab

Wynn Huey-Wen Yien

hwyiin@gmail.com
M.D., Ph.D., EMBA, CEO
YongLin X Lab, YongLin Healthcare Foundation, Taiwan (R.O.C)

Phoebe Ting Chuang
Cross-Field Innovation Designer

Lydia Wei-Cheng Weng
Managing Director

"First we shape our buildings, thereafter they shape us". Winston Churchill
To clinicians, design failure of a hospital is just like the genetic defects of a body. We want to make a difference in designing next generation smart hospital with the integration of medicine and technology. Like world-class medical centers, YongLin X Lab, a place to talk about user experience, lean management, research and technology, focuses on user experience to improve patient safety and quality of care.

OVERVIEW

About YongLin X Lab

Since 1982, cancer (malignant) has been the major diseases in the first place of the ten leading causes of death in Taiwan. Seeing cancer patient population is on the increase and the inadequacy of the medical services provided in Taiwan, Terry Gou, President of Foxconn Technology Group, donated a 500-bed cancer center with a proton therapy center to National Taiwan University (NTU) and founded YongLin Healthcare Foundation which was placed in charge of National Taiwan University Cancer Center (NTUCC, Figure 1) donation project in 2007.

YongLin X Lab is a R&D-oriented department in YongLin Healthcare Foundation and we cooperate with HKS Architects to join NTUCC design. We started from the donation project of NTUCC and dedicated to hospital design and innovation.

Take Center for Integration of Medicine and Innovative Technology (CIMIT) in Massachusetts General Hospital (MGH) and Center for Innovation (CFI) in Mayo Clinic as our model, we expect to build a brand new cancer center with NTU and make it as the first-tier comprehensive cancer center in Asia.

72

Figure 1. Diagram of NTUCC

YongLin X Lab, X means unknown in a function and it also stands for inter-disciplinary cooperation, experience and express design here. We emphasis on users- centered design and propose hospital design should invite people who live and work in the environment, like doctors, nurses, medical staffs, patients, family and so on, to join and discuss instead of purely raising 2D floor plans by architects. Based on users' involvement and experience, we further combine evidence-based medicine and problem-based learning methods in hospital design, cultivate knowledge in healing environment, evidence-based design and scenario-based design and converge then feedback to users in the end.

What We Do

YongLin X Lab, a multidisciplinary-developed platform which integrates Service, Management, Architecture, Research and Technology, conducts health-care planning, design and total-solution research in NTUCC and specific departments in cooperated hospitals such as outpatient clinics, inpatient wards, emergency room, etc.

User experience and lean management are core values in YongLin X Lab, we put them into hospital design in order to match smart service and management trends in the future and further elevate medical quality. We dedicate to build up the desirable space, work flow and process in healthcare environment, expect to derive more values of products and platforms from them and ultimately create a patient-centered healing environment which can bring senses of safe, respect and comfort to both patients and medical staffs.

In order to share and expand our experience in NTUCC project, Yong-

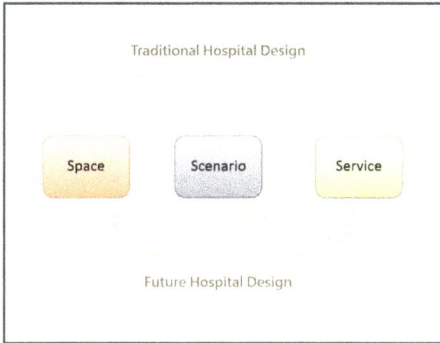

Figure 2. Traditional and future hospital design patterns

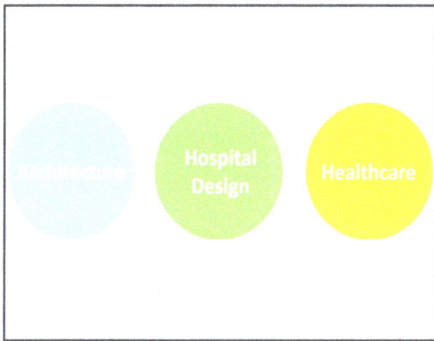

Figure 3. Multidisciplinary professionals in hospital design field

Lin X Lab not only trains biomedical and interdisciplinary students, but also promotes our design concept by prototyping and virtual reality exhibitions. Furthermore, we invite medical professionals from Asia to form a communication and knowledge sharing platform and forge an alliance with international experts to broaden the importance.

In YongLin X Lab, we care, and we share.

DESIGN CONCEPT

Background and Positioning

In traditional hospital design, the space in hospital will be build first then users have to compromise or adjust their daily work scenario and service patterns to fit the space which did not put users' requirements into consideration.

YongLin X Lab finds we should change the design sequences in future hospital design. To construct work and service flow first, then to think the scenarios inside the space and finally make suitable design to assist hospital daily operation (Figure 2).

YongLin X Lab found it is possible to build a perfect and fully-achieved users' demand hospital only when both professionals from healthcare and architecture join the design process (figure 3).

However, there is a huge gap between architects and medical staffs, so they are unable to understand professional culture and language between each other. For example, the medical staffs do not know how to read the 2D layout, and the architects and designers do not know how to put the clinical demand into the planning and design on the other side (figure 4).

Therefore, YongLin X Lab, a team consists of medical, architectural and con-

73

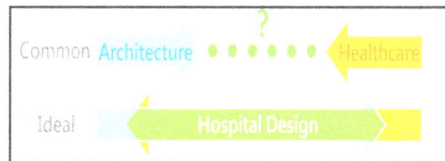

Figure 4. Common and ideal situation in hospital design

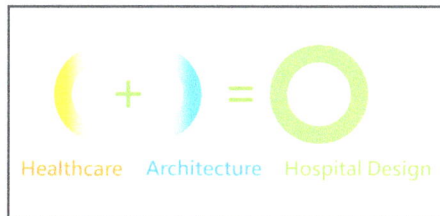

Figure 5. Expertise integration

structional professionals, tries to become the hospital design intermediary. The more YongLin X Lab involves in both professional fields, the more successful chance to make perfect hospital and healthcare planning and design (fig. 5).

Methodology and S.M.A.R.T. Features

In hospital predesign, our methodology could be mainly divided into three phases as follows (Figure 6).
X Journey, X TRIP (Teammate Rapid Improvement of Process) and X Mockup will be used in each phase and ends with Proof of Concept (POC). Those designs pass POC will be defined detail specifications and conducted; on the other hand, those fail will be sent back to prior phase to recheck and develop.
Through inviting users to join design process, we hope to put users' ideas into consideration from the beginning in order to truly fulfill user-centered design and desirable planning which could meet users' requirements and elevate working efficiency. Under three-phase model, YongLin X Lab further integrates past experience and proposes five features, Service, Management, Architecture, Research and Technology (S.M.A.R.T.) in our interdisciplinary design. That is to fuse Service and Management concepts into our design principles then combined with evidence-based Research and emerging Technology to build a user-centered Architecture and healing healthcare environment.

CASE STUDY: NATIONAL TAIWAN UNIVERSITY CANCER CENTER

In order to help bring a better quality of care to the increasing number of cancer

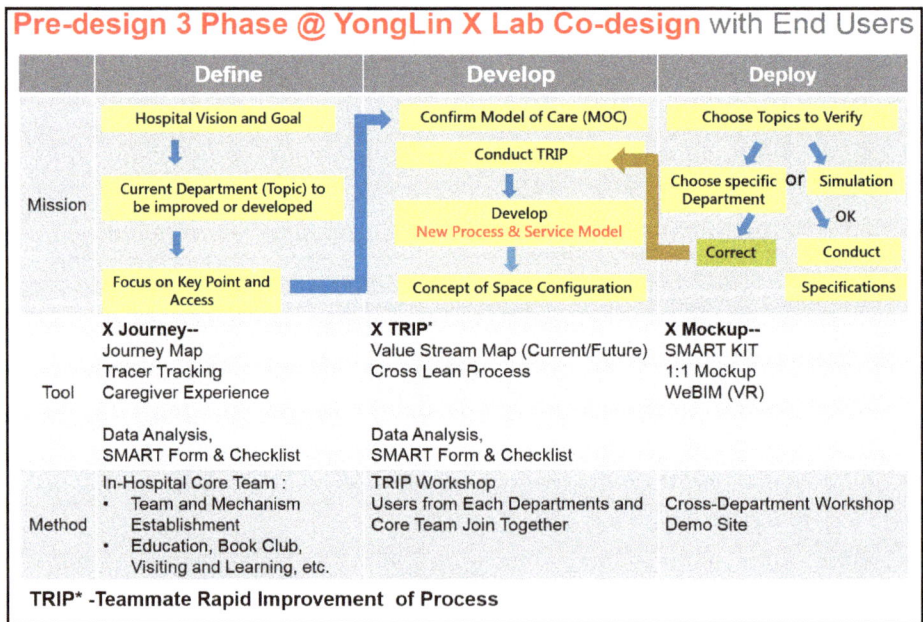

Figure 6. Three-phase model in hospital pre-design

patients in Taiwan, YongLin X Lab collaborated with NTU to simulate a system of design and communication tools for the development of NTUCC.

These tools were deemed necessary to reduce the pressures of the current healthcare system caused by medical workflow patterns as well as user demands.

By assembling a professional interdisciplinary team of specialists spanning the fields of medicine, architecture, electrical engineering and computer science, ergonomics, and industrial design, it is believed that a practical and systematic solution with reduced design flaws may be produced.

The research team visited many different international institutes to study the methodology by learning from the experiences of similar successful projects. To avoid the miscommunication, the hospital users and the architects discussed and worked together in the mock-up room to come out the best design scheme. By using the mini prototype, the hospital users could get the overall view of the space and design concepts and help them to visualize the operation processes and circulations. Furthermore, the full-size simulation would provide the realistic experience of the scale and the size of the space.

Discussions and workshops on key design issues held among these experts would allow for a review of prototype ideas in order to ensure that they would meet the end users' demands. By tailoring prototype designs for the end users' experience, we believed that a better patient-centered healing environment and revolutionary cancer hospital could be developed.

Since 2009, the first and second phases have already been completed, and the third phase addressing medical operation processes optimization with digital device application was accomplished in 2013. The fourth phase, user experience design, is currently in progress and all the details and outcomes in each phases will be stated below.

Phase I: Evidence-Based Design of Clinical Space
(Duration: 2009)

Objective and Methods:
Used a prototype simulation to inspect whether clinical space design met the practical needs, and conducted key issues' research based on evidence-based design concept to boost the quality of medical care.

Hardware Setup:
Seven clinical units had been selected to demonstrate, including outpatient chemotherapy area, double room, single room, nurse station of ward, bone marrow transplantation ward, intensive care unit (ICU) and outpatient clinic.

In each simulation, the walls, ceiling, and cabinets were constructed for validation of the facility structure and to allow efficient space adjustment if necessary. These construction materials are for simulation purposes only and are not intended for use in the final hospital structure. The wall switches, electrical sockets, gas outlets, call buttons, etc. were simulated using Velcro and Post-It notes in order to allow position readjustment at any point during simulation scenarios. Real utility were setup in the bathroom simulation to visualize practical operating space.

75

Discussion:
After data collecting and clinical practicing, we concluded that top four evidence-based design topics were privacy, infection control, efficacy and safety, and the proportion of each topic was varied in different units.

Therefore, when it comes to dilemma of space design, we adopted criteria of evidence-based design, besides professional judgment of medicine and architecture, to evaluate various solutions in order to elevate the objectivity of decision-making.

Phase II: Full-Sized Mockup
(Duration: May 2010 – October 2010)

A. Scenario-Based Simulation of Lobby Floor Space and Flow

Objective and Methods:
By performing common scenarios of lobby and outpatient clinics in a 1:50 mini prototype (Figure 7), users were encouraged to raise problems regarding space and flow. Then, all the problems were classified into four categories, Main entrance, Hoping Minaret (name of a Public Square in lobby), Cuiwei Life Street (name of Main Street in lobby) and Outpatient clinics, to evaluate and develop solutions by interdisciplinary research team.

In the full-size simulation workshop (figure 8), staffs introduced the origin, steps and topics to be discussed, and then participants started their practical operation and verified the solutions.

Hardware Setup:
The full-size simulation was built on the NTUCC construction site, and the research area around 68,870 square feet

(total area of lobby floor was 134,900 square feet). Each space was clearly stated by a standing wooden sign. Paint was used to mark borders of each area and walls were constructed by light steel frame and laminated plywood.

Pillars were made from light steel frame and movable wooden door frame were set to stand for windbreak room at main entrance. Tailor-made wooden stair with wheels to represent the stairs at Hoping Minaret and clinics' module were separated by construction fences in order to adjust easily. The workshop lasted for two weeks and total 320 participants involved.

Discussion:
All the problems were classified into four categories, Main entrance, Hoping Minaret, Cuiwei Life Street and Outpatient clinics, so participants were able to choose appropriate solution by practice

Figure 7. Panorama of 1:50 mini lobby prototype

Figure 8. Panorama of full-size simulation

in person. Each simulation has showed its strengths in specific scenarios and the radar diagram (figure 9) was used to present results by different research model.

1. Main Entrance - Investigate the wheelchair supply station and lane configuration

In 2-D floor plans, discussion was focused on quantity of wheelchair, lane traffic and configuration; in mini (1:50) prototype, research team found out it would cause a traffic jam to put wheelchair supply station, shuttle bus waiting station and regular vehicles all together in main entrance. Finally the solution was come out to a multi-function station including wheelchair supply, guard and volunteer service in full-size simulation (Figure 10).

2. Hoping Minaret – Direction of stairs

In 2-D floor plans and mini prototype, research team found out people would get stuck in Hoping Minaret to wait for admission and elevator, so architects proposed to add stairs. By full-size simulation, the stairs was finally confirmed to put on right-hand side for smooth routes and widen view compared with left-hand side (figure 11).

3. Cuiwei Life Street – Configuration of X-ray, Clinical Laboratory, Cashier and Pharmacy.

In 2-D floor plans, research team preferred to put all these units in the main street, named Cuiwei Life Street, to reduce walking distance but promptly noticed that people would get stuck here due to no satellite counter and waiting area in mini prototype. Moreover, the routes to cashier and pharmacy were contrast which would make crowd

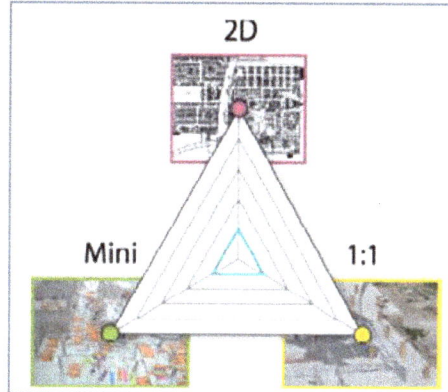

Figure 9. Radar diagram was used to analyze the effect of different tools on a specific topic

77

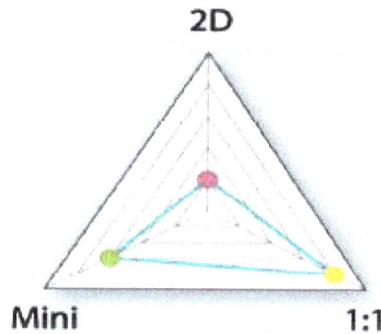

Figure 10. Full-size simulation was the most effective tool in Main Entrance topic

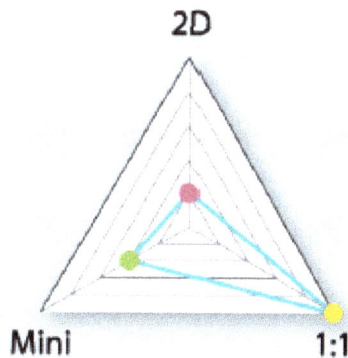

Figure 11. The content and results of discussion in full-size simulation was significant higher than others in Hoping Minaret topic

jammed more seriously. In full-size simulation, research team conducted a scenario that a patient with wheelchair was accompanied by family to clinic, blood collection room, cashier and pharmacy to inspect if the width of main street and moving distance were appropriate (Figure 12).

4. Outpatient Clinics – New trend of multidisciplinary clinic design

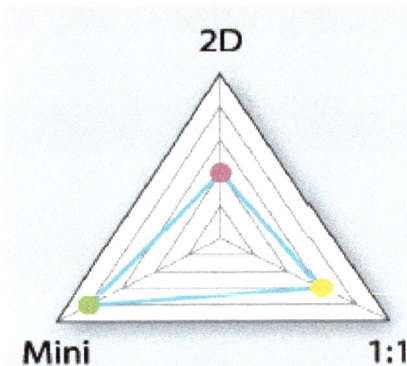

Figure 12. Mini prototype provided research team to inspect in aerial view and focused on the top priority, route issue, in Cuiwei Life Street topic

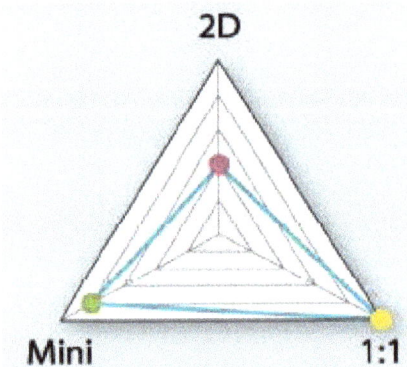

Figure 13. Mini prototype was used to discuss route issue and full-size simulation was focused on space and privacy in outpatient clinics topic

In 2-D floor plans, outpatient waiting area was arranged near windows, and clinics were concentrated in the central block with linked hallway behind each clinic to meet the trend of cancer multidisciplinary consultation.

However, in mini prototype, research team found the original design, a long strip of waiting area next to windows, was lack of privacy and patients would gather in front of clinics.

Also, the hallway-connected clinics were still not concentrated enough. To solve these problems, the architects designed a new outpatient clinics module and conducted visual and spatial validation in full-size simulation.

Not only did new module design increase patients' privacy but conformed to usual practice and past experience. More importantly, it facilitated more efficient medical service and reserve outdoor view of waiting area (Figure 13).

B. Emergency Drills

Objective and Methods:
This emergency drills were planned by National Taiwan University Hospital (NTUH) Department of Emergency Medicine and YongLin X Lab and mainly divided into two events – intra-hospital fire evacuation and a multiple casualty incident. Prior to full-size emergency drill, research team practiced emergency drills based on past hospital emergency experience in Taiwan on 2-D floor plans and 1:50 mini prototypes and concluded that lobby floor was the most important area to be investigated in space and routes design.

Two independent scenarios were set as below.

1. Fire was induced by a short circuit of an electric appliance in the ward on an autumn rainy night, so evacuation was conducted due to heavy smoke.

2. Major disaster created a multiple causality incident with large number of causalities in a near community. Lots of patients were sent to hospital even though cancer center was not duty hospital.

Hardware Setup:

Research team built full-size lobby simulation and marked key facilities and exits on the ground to let participants easily understand. The space was divided into nine area - triage area, critical patient area, minor patient area, observation area, family reception and waiting area, media area, command center and ambulance pickup area.

All personnel were separated into three groups. The first group was patients with difference severity showed on their vests. The second group was emergency response team. All the second group performers were actually taking the same responsibility in hospital. The third group was in charge of record and evaluation (Figure 14). Frequent-used medical

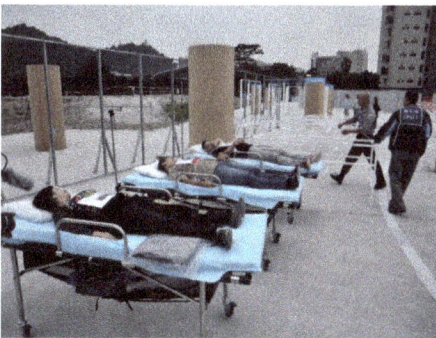

Figure 14. Patients and medical team were played by staffs to simulate real situation and staff workflow. Actual simulations were important in achieving the most realistic effects

equipment especially those with big size were set on the scene.

Discussion:

Unlike traditional drill, the goal of emergency drills this time was focused on space, routes and environment, instead of processes.

During the drills, all personnel were allowed to express their feeling on the scene and architects and supervisors were responsible for details confirmation such as light, electrical power, water, medical gas and suction equipment. By two scenarios, research team investigated if the design of lobby floor was sufficient to respond to emergency and key findings were listed in Figure 15.

Phase III: Digital Technology Transformation and Integration (Duration: 2012 – 2013)

Objective and Methods:

In response to the coming of digital era, the healthcare processes and management is evolving to become more paperless and efficient in order to reduce healthcare workers' workload.

Focused on optimizing the design of hospital lobby, outpatient clinics, inpatient wards, ICUs, outpatient chemotherapy rooms and the command center, we help the caregivers to optimize digital device applications in the medical operation processes and hospital management by using mock-up and scenario simulation as tools.

YongLin X Lab seeks to carry out a digital operation processes transformation in order to integrate new technologies into the NTUCC and create a "Hospital for the Second Century" (H2C).

79

Phase / Topic	2-D Floor Plan	1:50 Mini Prototype	1:1 Full-size Simulation
Internal Communication Channel	**Communication System:** It was a necessary measure to have handheld transceiver (walkie-talkie) as a backup or outdoor contact since phone or mobile may not be connected in an emergency.	**Communication System:** Agree with previous discussion. **Smooth Command System Channel:** Locations of commander and command center needed to be carefully considered and should be able to control the scene, in case the decision timing was missed by unconnected phone.	Agree with previous discussion.
Way to Convey Messages	**Original Way:** The original way such as handwriting was still very good when IT system shut down temporarily.	**Original Way:** Agree with previous discussion. **Patient Status:** Sometimes there was no alternative but speak directly.	Agree with previous discussion.
Stairs Location	**On-Site Control Point:** It should be closed to stairs to command and control evacuation.	Agree with previous discussion.	**On-Site Control Point:** It may locate on second floor of Hoping Minaret for conducting overall command in aerial view. **Direction of Stairs:** On the right-hand side of entrance would be better than left-hand side. Also, commander could see arriving patients from main entrance and elevators.
Emergency Patient-receiving	No related discussion.	Both Cuiwei Life Street and Hoping Minaret were available because of commodious space.	Hoping Minaret would be the best place due to nature light was available when power shut down and high-ceiling design provided commander on second floor a widen view.
Quantity and Direction of Beds	**Quantity:** It was difficult to estimate space needed by caregivers.	**Direction:** Put headboards near the center of Hoping Minaret.	**Quantity:** Total 30 to 50 beds were estimated by caregivers based on past experience, and additional beds could be placed on Cuiwei Life Street. **Direction:** Put headboards against the wall of Hoping Minaret because beds were easily to make U-turn on aisles in this way. Also, it was more convenient for caregivers to care patients and for designers to setup electricity, gas, suction equipment, etc. on the wall.
Configuration of Electricity, Gas, Suction	No related discussion.	**Priority:** Based on urgency and influence, the first priority is electricity, followed by gas, suction and water. **Piping Layout:** Chose mobile power supply or set piping in the ground or on the wall.	**Piping Layout:** Electricity, gas, suction and water piping should set in multiple places so that caregivers were able to connect to medical equipment easily.
Rescued Routes and Patient Classification	No related discussion.	**Rescued Routes:** Patients were evacuated from upstairs, so the whole area should not be far away from the stairs. Besides, patients were transferred from ambulance exits instead of main entrance in case there were too many people.	**Patient Classification:** Critical patient area was close to the emergency center, and ICU was located on the second floor near the stairs for evacuation and further treatment. **Rescued Routes:** Ambulances stood by for further transfer.
Media and Family Reception	No related discussion.	**Media Area:** Set up media area for photographing, but it could not affect emergency care or patients' privacy. **Family Reception Area:** Provided essential information for	**Media Area:** After confirming Hoping Minaret as emergency area, the relative location of media area could be recognized. **Family Reception Area:** Could be refitted from original front

Figure 15. Key findings of Phase II emergency drills

Hardware Setup:
The full-size prototypes, including in-patient ward (figure 16), outpatient chemotherapy area (figure 17), clinic and waiting area /figure 18), were built by light steel frame compartments.
Furniture inside the units was made of blank template such as foam board, cardboard cases, etc. Besides, a 1:50 mini lobby prototype and a 1:20 chemotherapy area prototype were used to inspect personnel's route and digital device applications.

Discussion:
Research team starts with design details reconfirmation and then investigates users' behaviors. High-lighted topics are as follows.

Outpatient Area – Screen applications
Screens have been extensively used in various place, even hospitals have adopted screen-related applications to provide efficient service. In this phase, research team conducts an ergonomic research on the distance and relative location of screens in outpatient area. Then, research goals will move on to achieve multidisciplinary clinic, shorten waiting time and provide healing environment with privacy by screen-related equipment and technology.

Inpatient Wards – Bathroom design
Wheelchairs, family and servants need to be taken into consideration when it comes to bathroom design.
After evaluated by user experience and ergonomics study, shift-in shower, a shower with a fixed seat and patient needs to move from wheelchair to fixed seat, was recommended in inpatient wards (figure 19). Handrails should be

installed on both sides of toilet, sink and fixed seat, and at least a moveable hand-rail in one side of toilet (sink side was recommended) (Figure 20).

Outpatient Chemotherapy Rooms Care process and bed arrangement
In NTUCC, chemotherapy area was divided into several modules for man-

81

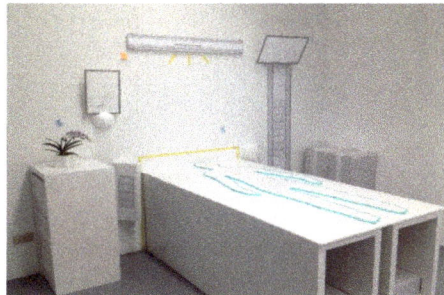

Figure 16. Full-size prototype of inpatient ward

Figure 17. Full-size prototype of outpatient chemotherapy area

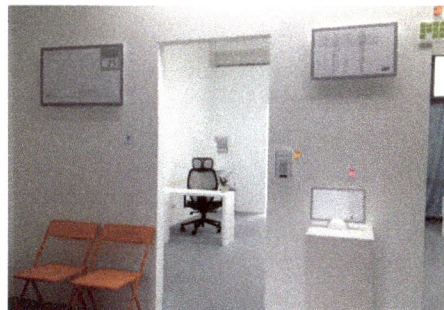

Figure 18. Full-size prototype of clinic and waiting area

Figure 19. Shift-in shower in full-size prototype of inpatient ward

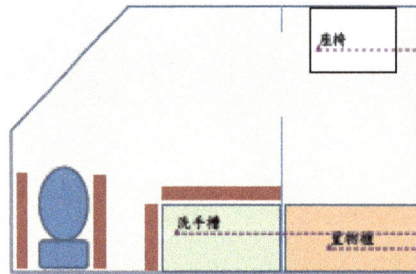

Figure 20. Bathroom configuration in inpatient wards

power and process allocation, and each module was further separated into 8 to 10 rooms to protect patients' privacy.

First, research team discussed treatment process in aerial view by 1:20 mini prototype. Then, experienced caregivers proposed common problem and architects and designers would moderate or revise the design. For example, each patient had different artificial vessel place but all beds were in the same direction; therefore, nurses had to treat patient in an uncomfortable posture due to space limitation. Research team now takes this kind of situation and related hardware such as patient digital entertainment system and caregivers' smart service into consideration and expects to build a cozy and efficient chemotherapy environment.

Phase IV: User Experience Design
(Duration: 2014 – Now)

Objective:
In Phase IV, we conduct research on patients' in-hospital activities during therapies based on human-centered belief and the study was held by YongLin X Lab, NTUH and NTU iNSIGHT (the Center of iNnovation and Synergy for IntelliGent Home and living Technology). To analysis current in-hospital activities by both qualitative and quantitative research then develop new service concept through design to build a reference model for NTUCC. We divide the study into two parts that are "User Experience Research" and "Innovative Service Design" and conduct by research and design team respectively.

A. User Experience Research

Methods:
Research team invited 6 medical professionals, including doctors, nurses and case managers, from oncology department in NTUH to conducted one-to-one interview to understand their thought and concepts regarding oncology patients' anxiety.
Next, 12 patients were selected by oncology doctors to start "Contextual Inquiry" by researcher and designer. Various conditions, behaviors and feelings during therapies were collected through patients' shadowing.
Researchers and stakeholders would join workshops to reestablish therapy process together through photos, videos and storytelling after each contextual inquiry. Features of patients' behavior would be analyzed bottom up and col-

Figure 21. Part of future hospital experience vision drawing

83

Figure 22. PVDI structure

Figure 23. Structure of job story

lected values and goals behind patients' user experience through affinity diagram workshops.

Discussion:
450 patient features were found from affinity diagram workshop then further converged to 6 key experience which are Comfortable, Efficient, Reliable, Commanded, Supportive and Valued.
12 patients' customer journey map in NTUH was drawn as reference to review current problem and discuss innovative service concept.
Transforming patient features to 40 parameters of behaviors and attitudes then generalizing 4 kinds of user model, that is people who are Dependent, Assertive, Dedicated and Leave their fate to god, via quantitative research. Currently, research team choose Dependent user

model to develop 4 kinds of future hospital experience vision and present the scenarios by drawing (figure 21)

B. Innovative Service Design

Methods:
Combining academic papers, investigation reports, medicine-related case studies and other second-handed information with first-handed user experience data from research team, design team translated it into Problem Value Chain (figure 22), PVDI structure, and marshaled 26 classifications, 90 problem and 80 design requirements as a foundation to problem space.
After that, we put PVDI structure and above-mentioned 12 patients' customer journey map together to build 160 Job Story in order to make complicated

84

problem which include both requirement and value simplify to single design topic (figure 23).

Design team invited research team and stakeholders to join design workshops to converge different Problem Awareness among everyone and built consensus. 160 Job Story were put into Problem Pool and finally generalized 20 Problem Space.

Discussion:
6 main Problem Space were proposed in this stage which stood for oncology patients felt Confused, Stuck, Agitated, Afraid, Complicated and Cold. Besides name, each Problem Space were also stated its spirits, problem features, reasons and other elements.

Currently, design team choose Confused and Stuck to conduct concept development and invite case managers, nurses, doctors and research team to join design workshops and produce 120 design ideas.

Same as Problem Space to Problem Pool in earlier stage, design team converge Service Concept from Idea Pool based on 120 design ideas. 5 Service Concepts, including 37 primary design, are proposed which are Kindly Cared, Safely Protected, Properly Introduced, Warmly Recognized and Clearly Understood and storyboard is used to express its brand-new experience visions.

As the fourth phase is currently still in progress, more workshop sessions are expected to be conducted in order to yield a well-researched and detailed design. The resulting prototype would then be tested in various simulations to study the patterns of behavior in these user-technology interfaces, hopefully establishing a better link between humanity, science, and technology to increase the standards of cancer care.

CONCLUSION

YongLin X Lab beliefs that State of Life is consist of body, mind and spirit, and that is the reason why we dedicate to build a desirable future hospital via Service, Management, Architecture, Research and Technology dimensions.

YongLin X Lab expect ourselves to express the way to guide hospital and medical service design by innovative thinking.

With management and science-based methodologies, we transform concepts to realities, eliminate barriers among professionals from various fields through simulation, collect information to balance their demands and further conduct innovative design.

In the future, we hope to create a design ecology of healing environment and prosper related industries in order to elevate healthcare design and planning level in Taiwan and Asia.

Comparison of Healing Architectural Parameters in European and Arab Countries

Christine Nickl-Weller

c.nickl-weller@nickl-partner.com
Dipl.-Ing. Architect - Berlin University of Technology / Nickl & Partner Architekten AG

85

Stefanie Matthys

Dipl.-Ing. Architect - Berlin University of Technology / Nickl & Partner Architekten AG

The study aims to identify similarities and differences in European and Arab architectural parameters to improve the quality of hospitals. The focus will be set on master plans and medical cities. Through comparing 4 different cases in European and GCC countries the specific requirements and solutions for planning and building healthcare facilities will be identified.

INTRODUCTION

The built healthcare environment is changing due to social, technical and political developments. The digital revolution, trends in medicine and public health as well as technical innovations are reflected in the design of hospitals and medical cities. Patient-centered care, prevention-orientated models and sustainable concepts are being discussed throughout all disciplines related to the building of healthcare infrastructure. All these innovations are strongly linked to various cultural backgrounds and local conditions.

DESCRIPTION

The 10 theses on Healing Architecture describe relevant criteria for the improved planning of hospitals. They reflect the many different aspects of healthcare architecture, focusing not just on function, but describing a brought spectrum of parameters, such as political, technical, societal and human conditions. These 10 theses have been developed in a European context. In the Arab World other parameters have to be considered.

The study aims to identify similarities and differences in European and Arab

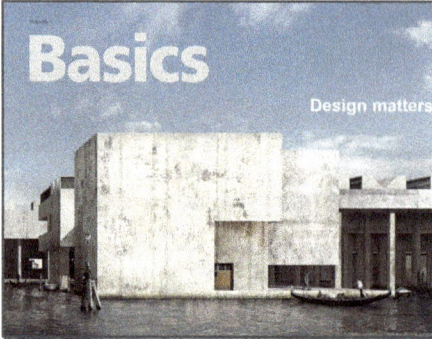

THESIS 1: BASICS

Architecture can shape the way in which we use our senses to perceive the world around us, and it can bring people together. The role of the architect is to create spaces that appeal not just to our eyes, but to all our senses.

THESIS 2: IDENTITY

The visual quality of a city is defined by its clarity and legibility. Its various areas and elements must be easily identifiable, and buildings must have simple, logical structures if their purpose is to be recognized by the general public.

THESIS 3: SOCIAL JUSTICE AND FUNCTIONALITY

The quality of architecture and planning is a major factor when deciding how to create healthy, liveable core areas that meet people's cultural and aesthetic needs. Architecture must provide answers to the demands expressed by society, including social cohesion and communal achievement based on personal wellbeing.

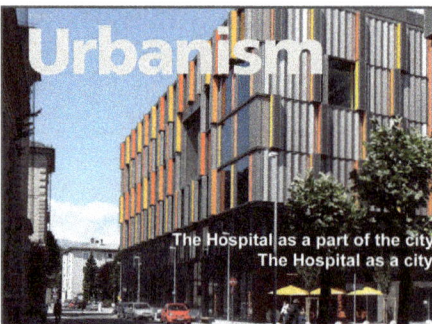

THESIS 4: URBANISM

Every city has a basic framework of buildings and public spaces that gives it shape and helps people to find their way around and identify with it. This forms part of the city's social and cultural capital, and any new projects must harmonise with it. Buildings must interlock and interact with their environment if they are to add functional and aesthetic value.

86

THESIS 5: URBANISM

Some changes, both good and bad, are the result of politics and the culture of building. If architecture and planning are to keep pace with social and demographic change, they must create sustainable structures that maximise the wellbeing of individuals and society. They can do this if they receive positive support from politicians who see the sustainability as an opportunity to make an important contribution to society.

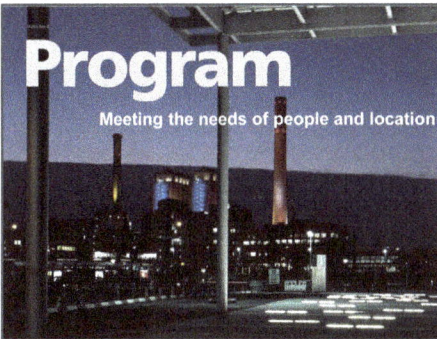

THESIS 6: PROGRAMME

People-centred architecture must strike a constant balance between form and function. The solution lies neither in formalism that creates buildings with no regard for their surroundings or for society's needs, nor in functionalism. Buildings will satisfy everyone only if they respect the history and circumstances of the area, and comply with urban plans.

THESIS 7: CHANGE

Social and technological change demands that the capacity for alteration and expansion be built in from the outset. This flexibility is an illusion, and we must create open-ended designs capable of responding to future needs while remaining cost-effective. If subsequent generations can see the connections between buildings and the underlying urban plans, they will continue the trends that we have set in motion.

THESIS 8: SPACE

Architecture creates and shapes space, and gives it structure. Some spaces are clearly defined beforehand, but others that connect them may not be set in stone. These make them particularly suitable for human interaction, so architecture can turn a purely functional space into an experience.

88

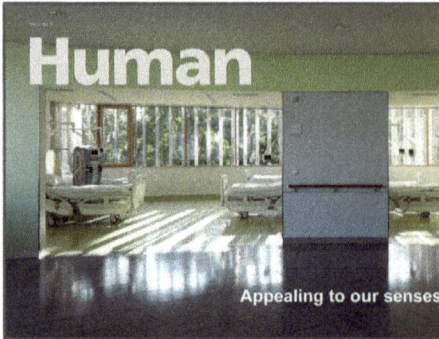

THESIS 9: HUMAN

Architecture is never anonymous, always personal, created by people for people. It interacts with us by appealing to our senses and creating positive or negative perceptions. Buildings are effective only if they are suitable for people, so architecture plays a key role in the social and cultural face of the community.

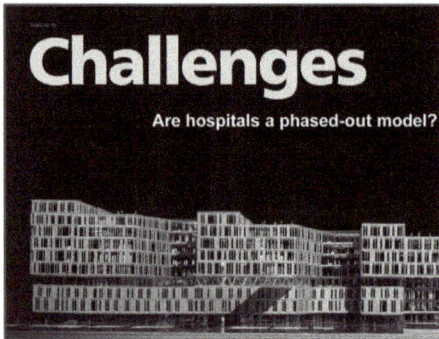

THESIS 10: CHALLENGES

Tomorrow's world will be affected by the quality of today's architecture, and this quality is dependent on the challenges of competition. Only by competing to find the best solutions to tasks can we show that architecture is relevant and innovative, and that it provides the best basis for the concepts and perspectives of the future. [...]

Figure 1. 10 Theses on Healing Architecture

architectural parameters to improve the quality of hospitals. The focus will be set on master plans and medical cities. Through comparing 4 different cases in European and GCC countries the specific requirements and solutions for planning and building healthcare facilities will be identified.

METHOD

A "Healing Architecture experts' meeting" was organized in Dubai the 27th of January 2015. The meeting brought together international experts in the field of architecture & health. They discussed trends in healthcare & health facilities by means of presenting existing and newly conceived projects in the GCC and European countries.

After introducing words from Christine Nickl-Weller and the Parliamentary State Secretary at the Federal Ministry of Health, Annette Widmann-Mauz, the conference was divided into three parts:
• Part 1 – Medical impacts to healthcare design.
• Part 2 – Societal impacts to healthcare design.
• Part 3 - Case presentations.

In part 3 Four exemplary projects were presented, two in European countries and two in GCC countries:
• Inselspital Bern, Switzerland
• Klinikum der Universität München, Germany.
• Hamad bin Khalifa Medical City, Qatar.
• Health Vision 2050 (including Sultan

FOUR COUNTRIES
FOUR CASES

89

Figure 2. Four countries, four cases

Qaboos Medical City & International Medical City) Oman. The eight speakers covered expertise in the fields of: Architecture & Planning, Medicine, Healthcare Management, Health policy and Medical Technology.

The sessions were followed by a discussion including the approximately 50 participants and by a concluding address of Christine Nickl-Weller.

Object of the conference was the comparison and discussion of trends in healthcare in European and GCC countries, the impact on actual healthcare projects in order to shed light on the following questions:

1. Shed light on the background and local conditions for healthcare design and planning in European and GCC countries – pointing out similarities and differences.

2. Deduce recommendations for design & planning of healthcare facilities. Recommendations with respect to local conditions as well as internationally valid recommendations.

The lectures and discussions were recorded and transcribed. Key-statements and concepts were summarized from these transcriptions. They delivered re-

sults in the following categories:

A) Results concerning background to healthcare facility planning:
• Demographic, societal and health trends
• Medical trends & Health system
• Economic trends & economic impact of healthcare design

B) Results concerning trends in Healthcare architecture & Planning:

RESULTS/OUTCOME

A) Background
Demographic trends

Today, GCC countries have a very young population, the average age is around 28 in Oman, and here only around 3% are over 60years old. Population in GCC countries is growing rapidly due to better health & healthcare conditions and to influx of expatriates.

Europe on the other hand is confronted with an ageing population. In Switzerland for example the life span increased over the last forty years of around 40 %. The demographic trend promotes the increasing use of healthcare facilities respectively nursing days.

90

Figure 3. Four countries, four cases

Health trends

Worldwide the main burden of disease lies within cardio-vascular diseases (stroke & myocardial infarction) and cancer diseases. In Switzerland for example these two categories represented 55 % of the overall death causes. Furthermore, depressions are a worldwide upcoming topic.

Diseases in GCC countries are developing similar to trends in Europe and worldwide trends. Non-communicable diseases and injuries caused by road traffic increase while communicable diseases are decreasing.

In GCC countries, the lack of mobility promoted by a very car-depended society, results in diabetes (25% of the population in the GCC region) and in obesity. Genealogical abnormalities are overrepresented in the region.

Social trends

A general lack of mobility is attributed to a very car-loving population. The preferred use of cars is creating problems in the transportation systems and the infrastructure. Issues of how car spaces can be integrated in the planning arise.

The working society in GCC countries is shaped by a large percentage of foreign workers in general as well as in the healthcare sector. But, there is a trend to train the local population especially the nursing personal. In Oman for example the "Omanization" of nurses has achieved the number of 60-70% in the last years due to a national training program. The "Omanization level" for doctors instead is still low.

Especially for doctors a "battle for talent" is to be noted in order to attract medical personal. This applies to European

Figure 4.   Four countries, four cases

clinics but to a larger extend to GCC countries who recruit a large percentage of doctors from foreign countries.

Worldwide the working environment or quality of work life has become an important competitor. This applies especially for the medical world because of the future shortage of medical personnel. This trend is considered important in European as well as GCC countries.

Health systems

Health systems of Oman and Qatar are formed after the international valid model of primary, secondary and tertiary care levels.

Currently, major initiatives in Oman and Qatar are in progress. They shall meet the demands of the growing population and the rapidly developing cities. Furthermore, these projects are meant to adapt the overcharged and outdated infrastructure to international healthcare levels.

In Oman the primary care system is considered as one of the best worldwide (number eight in an international ranking). The tertiary care level on the

91

other hand lacks behind, a tendency which is reported to be similar in Qatar. Both countries meet this perceived deficit with plans for the construction of medical cities. Those medical cities are considered to promote research, training and highly specialized care.

The aim to become a hub of tertiary care including high level research and training programs is a primary goal in both countries.

No such lack of the tertiary care level is reported from European countries. Modern medicine with research and education are already available. Here the focus lies on the reorganization and optimization of the health system in assuring continuous quality, innovation and the translation of research.

Translational research is mentioned as a future field of development in European as well as Arab context.

Generally, it is stated that individual care levels of the health system are perceived much more by the population than the collective system quality and public health quality although the impact of those levels are much more important.

A movement of health care provision from the public domain into private sector is predicted by several speakers.

Medical trends

Frank Christ reported general worldwide trends in medical knowledge and treatment. He highlighted rapidly changing medical knowledge, a shift towards specialization, the individualization of care and both artificial organ and replacement therapy. Changes in the delivery of care were emphasized especially by the European contributions:

- Interaction of therapy
- Change from separate clinic organization to networking of specialists
- Cross-linked clinics, interdisciplinary centers
- Patient-oriented organization of treatment (a "patient-first" concept)

The European speakers saw further trends influencing the spatial organization of health in the rising need of diagnostic and screening, in imaging as a central part of care and in the impact of information technology.

Economic impact

The economic impact of healthcare facility design and planning decisions was one of the major topics throughout the specialist's talks. Different aspects within this topics were addressed including the economic impact of campus reorganizations, the participation of private investment in healthcare facilities and the added values of hospital real estate. A movement of health care provision from the public domain into private sector is predicted by several speakers.

The project Inselspital Bern illustrated a trend towards inefficiency caused by outdated facilities and consequently

Figure 5. Attractive work environment

92

increased costs per case. The reorganization based on data assessments promise future economy. The Munich case pursues similar goals. Here, a return on investment for currently executed constructions is expected within ten years.

In Oman private investment is welcome in future healthcare projects. 50 % of costs are covered by public investment, 50% is expected to be covered by the private sector. Private investment is expected in rehabilitation, imaging and diagnostic centers.

Healthcare innovations are triggered by increasing healthcare expenses. The demographic development towards an aging population and consequently the increased demand for care delivery will raise healthcare expenses. The solution for this problem is proposed in the concept of value-adding design in hospital real estate with focus on accommodation.

Nine added values have been identified for hospital real estate based on interviews with CEOs and real estate project leaders in 15 Dutch hospitals:

User value (rated high)
• innovation and organizational culture
• patient satisfaction &healing environment
• employee satisfaction

Production value
• reduce accommodation costs
• increase productivity
• use flexibility

Future value
• support image
• reduce risk and increase financial possibilities
• sustainability

B) Healthcare design & planning trends.
Merging medical treatment & prevention strategies

A beneficial trend in merging strategies of medical treatment (based on crisis management) with prevention strategies based on environmental design for healthy cities) has been observed by Wagenaar in Europe the last years. The prevention strategy includes fighting urban problems like indoor and outdoor pollution, health-threatening life-styles and the depletion of global resources.

Award- winning design recommendations

The presentation of Khoo Tec Puat Hospital in Singapore delivered a broad set of design recommendations. The building is considered as one of the best in Singapore and was awarded 14 national and international prizes for its design. Ruzica Bozovic Stamenovic analyzed its architecture and deduced the following design recommendations:
• Knowledge: planning is based on current state of knowledge
• Vision: the hospital gives back to environment and society
• Value: hospital rises economic and social capital of the community
• Promote the connection between the inside (hospital) and the outside (public) world;
• Branding: a "green brand" is supported by gardens, healthy food, plants etc;
• Thrill: patients should be thrilled by their surroundings;
• Growth should be possible after completion of the construction;
• Forgiveness-factor: when the over-

93

all concept of a hospital is perceived as good, little problems which might occur don't change this positive perception.

4 cases – 2 different challenges

Four current healthcare projects were presented at the conference: Inselspital Bern, Klinikum der Universität Munich, Hamad bin Khalifa Medical City and Sultan Qaboos Medical City.

The European projects (Munich and Bern) represent existing healthcare facilities as they can be found all over Europe. These campus structures grew over several centuries and consist today of a very heterogenic and often outdated building stock.
The challenge for these buildings lies in the reorganization, the restauration, the adaption to new interlinked, patient-centered and disease-oriented processes in the delivery of healthcare.

The building stock is perceived as dysfunctional and outdated. As an example a specific building of the 70s at Munich Großhadern is mentioned.
It is perceived as "factory-like" and as an unattractive working environment although good quality in terms of interdisciplinary processes is attributed to this building.

The situation in the GCC region, represented by examples in Oman (Sultan Qaboos Medical City) and Qatar (Hamad bin Khalifa Medical City), differs considerably from the European setting. Here, next to renovating and extending the existing outdated building stock, the main focus lies in the fast construction of new facilities in order to catch up with

demographic developments. Gaps in the healthcare delivery (e.g. rehabilitations centers in Oman) have to be filled.

European trends for healthcare facilities

In addition to this specific issue Cor Wagenaar mentioned general trends in European Healthcare design:

• Distribution: top-down and bottom-up strategies of developing core-hospitals on the one hand and decentralized healthcare facilities of small size on the other hand;
• Support in the individual experience of healthcare, as manifested in the concept of Maggie's Cancer Caring Centres, is recognized in the medical world as important;
• In specialized facilities translational working methods rearrange the delivery of care around patients' paths and diseases;
• "Mean & Lean" is still a very important concept in hospital architecture;
• Care Path & Patient empowerment inside and outside the hospital will experience major developments due to new communication technologies;
• Merging of medical treatment & environmental design can have a beneficial effect on public health.

International best practice

Project leaders in the GCC region are very open for international trends. Oman representatives have visited international medical centers in order to find best practice models. European projects tend to build on the national acquired expertise.

Attractive work environment

Creation of high-quality working places in order to meet the staff's needs and to attract qualified staff is a very important issue both in Europe and GCC.
All presenters of the four cases emphasized this topic. Patient-centered care was used more for organizational description than for built environment description.

EBD – Master Planning

The projects in Bern and Munich used data assessments for the reorganization of their facilities. The example of Inselspital Bern was explained in detail.

Inselspital used hospital information system data, summarized in a "data cube" to align its infrastructure with the strategic development of the service portfolio. They visualized patient flows with interactive charts. The visualizations helped them to plan for a campus set-up with significantly reduced patient movements. The visualizations helped them to convince stakeholders in the decision process.

The Masterplan data cube can:
• show complete transfers between clinics;
• show selected clinics and their interrelations, for example the emergency ward;
• filter attributes, for example all transfers of patients with an acute myocardial infarct;
• zoom into a clinic to see more details;
• show in a 3d-Modell the transfers over the campus before and after optimization of processes.

DISCUSSION

Although demographic situations in Europe and the GCC region differ considerably there are fewer differences in the public health situation in both regions than it seems on first view.
Globalization of medical knowledge and assimilation of health systems tend to compensate existing differences.
Both regions will have to deal with the same burden of diseases in the future, the GCC reaching similar problems as European countries face today only with a time shift of about 20 years.
And health systems of both regions are facing significant pressure even if the reasons are different. On the European side aging population and consequently rising healthcare costs and on the other side the fast growth of population.

Problems of a car-dependent population and general lack of mobility have reached the GCC region. These problems have long since been in the focus of research for "healthy city" concepts promoting for example active transportation and healthy food environment. This promotion of preventive strategies must be supported and developed in a holistic approach of healthcare in Europe and GCC countries.
Here, moreover, the level of awareness about preventive urban planning solutions seems to be low.

The four healthcare projects presented at the conference (Inselspital Bern, Klinikum der Universität München, Hamad bin Khalifa Medical City and Sultan Qaboos Medical City) start with very different points of departure. Both institutions in Munich and Bern grew over

95

96

several centuries, the main tasks today lay in the renovation and restructuration of the facilities. The projects in Qatar and Oman on the other hand manifest the need for fast development of new and bigger facilities in order to respond to the fast growing population. In this respect the four projects can be considered a representative selection of building activity in the healthcare sector in European and GCC countries. Although the comparison of the four projects allowed getting relevant information of design trends, it did not allow coming to an exhaustive overview.

Both in European and GCC context, much importance is given to the attractive work environment in order to attract qualified doctors. This is considered to have a great economic impact for the hospital. The quality of the work environments seems to be rated even more important than the patient's experience of the building. Patients' needs in terms of healing environment were less in the focus of the presented project. Here a shift from the health perspective towards the economic perspective can be observed.

Healing environment research was originally triggered by the belief that the healing process could be positively influenced by the built environment. The staff's experience of the building was looked at from the perspective of risk prevention, reduction of stress level and improvement of efficiency. These aspects seem to be neglected when the benefit of an attractive work environment is considered purely as success factor in the attraction of qualified personnel.
Both medical experts and designers de-

scribed a major trend in modern medicine which will have great impact on future healthcare facility design and master planning: the new way of interlinked treatment organized around the patient.

This tendency was made clear especially in the two European projects, Munich and Bern. The former organizational structure was formed by clinics specialized in one specific field of medicine. Today this organizational structure is perceived as inefficient because it hampers trans- and interdisciplinary treatment and exchange of professionals.

The new trend goes towards spatial reorganization of medical care in interdisciplinary concepts and treatment arranged around the patient's needs, respectively around the disease.
This trend inspires the master plans of Munich and Bern.

Master planning on evidence-based assessments is common practice by now in European projects.

It allows informed decisions about reorganization of the build infrastructure and helps to optimize economic inefficiency linked to the spatial organization of clinics and medical cities by reducing paths for patients and personal and by creating above mentioned inter-disciplinary working environments.
Nevertheless, the presented assessments build exclusively on data concerning hard quantity facts like medical performance, financial performance, localization and process data.
They neglect quality facts in relation to the perceived environment.

CONCLUSION

The Healing Architecture experts' conference in Dubai pursued the goal to shed light on the background and local conditions for healthcare design and planning in European as well as GCC countries and to deduce recommendations. The speakers and participants were invited to report on current medical, societal and design trends in order to find out about similarities and differences in the two regions.

The results of the conference could contribute in several senses to these goals delivering results on demographic, societal and health trends as well as economic aspects and of healthcare design aspects. The importance of the dialog initiated by the conference was highlighted by several participants.

Nevertheless, the expert's meeting Dubai can only be seen as a starting point. Length and program of the meeting allowed a short overview over relevant topics and general trends but couldn't provide into-depth inside in specific projects and subjects.

Further exchange of knowledge and experiences is needed on the way to fully determine the specific local conditions and potentials for improvements in European and GCC countries. This especially considering that international expertise, partnership and knowledge is highly welcome in the GCC region.

Up-coming exchanges and events should include a broader range of disciplines such as experts in climatic conditions, building technology, energy efficiency, communication technology, urban planning and sociology and it should include more countries of both regions.

The conference highlighted healing architecture and human-centered design especially in the context of creating attractive work environments.

This is seen as an economic advantage because it attracts highly qualified personnel.

Considering that private investment will play a growing role in healthcare provision and projects in the GCC region (as it was pointed out by the Oman representative) recommendations concerning healing architecture measures should be directed especially to private investors in this region.

Connecting interest of the hospital staff with interests of hospital management and investors is a win-win situation. The conviction that healing environments for patients and visitors can lead to equally economic advantages seems to be less developed in decision makers strategies.

Here more research could contribute to solidify the conviction that healing environments for patients and visitors can contribute to the overall economic success of healthcare facilities.

Nevertheless it should not lead to neglecting the importance of healing environments in situations where the economic impact is less visible, for example to minimize the negative effects of stress for patients and visitors.

Urban planning and preventive urban solution should be considered as a relevant topic when it comes to innovative healthcare solutions, both in Europe and the GCC regions.

Although the tendency to promote urban healthy planning (for example promoting walkability or healthy food environments) is already strong in Europe, there is still a lack of awareness in the GCC region.

98

All projects in urban context, Doha, Munich and Bern, demonstrated the strong alliance between the hospital and its city.

Healthcare buildings are among the most significant urban components. This can be traced back to the 15th century and the Ospedale Maggiore in Milan or the Hôpital Lariboisière in Paris in the 19th century and it is still valid today.

The societal and cultural contribution of the hospital to the city remains the overall goal of hospital planning in urban context.

This must be considered a chance for future projects which can be achieved by design decisions on three levels: firstly the master planning level (distribution of healthcare buildings in the city) secondly the building's design level (open and closed spaces/public and private spaces) and thirdly the façade level (opening of the basements towards public spaces).

All three levels can contribute to the rightful placement of healthcare buildings in the center of society.

Perinatal Centers in Central Asia and Southern Africa: Using International Design Standards for different Cultural and Religious Groups – Case Study and Lessons Learned

Henning Lensch

h.lensch@rrp-international.com
RRP International, Singapore – Germany

Having the fortunate situation of being awarded with two concurrent design projects for Neonatal, Obstetrics and Gynaecology Tertiary Level Services in very different environments, we could face similar yet different cultural and religious challenges for international best medical practise facilities. Mauritius is a multi-cultural / ethnic environment in Southern Africa while Kyrgryz Republic is a formal UdSSR country and since 1991 independent Central Asian country with Muslim tradition. In both projects, we could successfully combine different requirements and conditions yet with small "specialities" to fulfil local procedures and expectations. The results is not in contradiction with international best practice yet adapting local traditions and specific requirements / conditions. There is a need for stronger discussion of "international standards" against "local cultural and religious integration" and formulate recommendation for the main global standards such as NHS HTM, AIA, AHFG and coming integration of EU standards.

Keywords: *Mother & Child Health Planning, Perinatal Centres, International Planning Standards*

WOMEN'S INSTITUTE IN MAURITIUS

The new 'Institute for Women's Health' shall offer the possibility of a new center for the provision of excellent health care for Mauritian women but also for a new approach to planning women's health care services 'from cradle to grave' and there is an urgent need to focus on the current provision and outcomes related to Obstetrics and Gynecology.

This project provides an overall and unique opportunity to develop a higher tertiary service for women's' health care in Mauritius, to improve health outcomes by improving the quality of care they receive and provide much needed training opportunities for doctors, specialists, midwives and ancillary staff.

PERINATAL CENTRE IN BISHKEK, KYRGYZ REPUBLIC

In terms of the longstanding engagement of German (Financial) Development Cooperation in the Kyrgyz Re-

100

public the Perinatal Centre Programme, which comprises components IV and V of the German bilateral "Mother and Child Care" Programme, consequently builds upon previous measures and efforts. The Perinatal Centre Programme is a landmark intervention in the Kyrgyz health sector reform and in the improvement of mother and child care throughout the country.

The "unique" status of the project can be summarized as follows:

- It is the establishment of the 1st tertiary care level facility for the adequate treatment of pregnant women and critically ill new-borns.

- It provides the "missing link" to previous efforts and interventions and is a crucial complementary measure for the overall functioning of the decentralized system of mother and child health care.

- It may thus serve as a sort of "blueprint" for further Perinatal Centres in the country that are currently planned and will be constructed in the future.

METHOD ANALYSIS

We had to decide about the design standards in relation to the cultural and religious conditions. The applied design standards and also results from Evidence Based Design have both to integrate latest medical studies e.g. about the impact of noise for the newborn recovery process, the impact of rooming-in concepts and the specific cultural and religious background of the countries.

We had to compare especially NHS HTM (UK), Australasian AHFG, formal UdSSR and adapted to Kyrgyz Republic planning regulations, RKI Robert Koch Institute and DIN guidelines (Germany), EU regulations and AIA (US) standards. Finally, the discussion with the medical advisory team, end-user in both countries and experts and advisers on the side of the donors were taken into strong consideration. The final design is taking the technical viability into account and is trying to create a healing environment matching the spe-

Figure 1. Women's Institute in Mauritius

cial local religious, cultural and climatical conditions.

Here, the existing international standards have partly too high requirements that could be adjusted in the direct discussion with medical advisors who work daily in their hospitals and could advise for the necessary design features while many international standards are partly static and too high for countries with lower budgets.

Our challenge was the integration of all aspects – international standards, local regulations and finally the opinion and recommendations of the local and international teams.

101

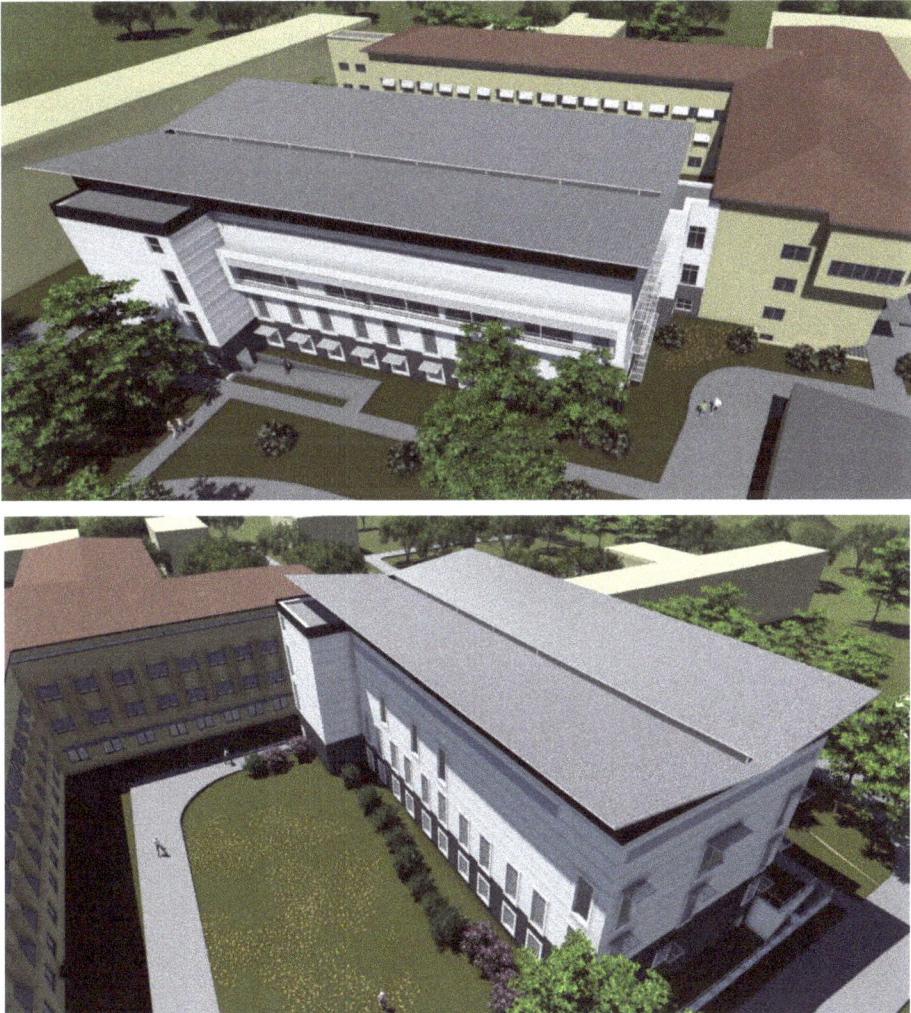

Figure 2. National Perinatal Center Bishkek

TESIS Inter-University Research Centre "Systems and Technologies for Social and Healthcare Facilities"
University of Florence, Italy

International Planning Standards

We had to compare especially NHS HTM (UK), Australasian AHFG, formal UdSSR and adapted to Kyrgyz Republic planning regulations, RKI Robert Koch Institute and DIN guidelines (Germany), EU regulations and AIA (US) standards.

Standards for Design in the Perinatal Centres in Kyrgyz Republic and Mauritius

We had to compare especially NHS HTM (UK), Australasian AHFG, formal UdSSR and adapted to Kyrgyz Republic planning regulations, RKI Robert Koch Institute and DIN guidelines (Germany), EU regulations and AIA (US) standards. The building is designed to meet local and international standard requirement. Here, it must be understood that the Kyrgyz Republic is still using the formal Soviet Union standards

and regulations that have not been updated since decades. For the so-called "international standard", the consultant is using both German and Australasian standards.

Both standards are very close to each other yet the Australasian standard is available in English and well documented while the German Hospital Standards are divided into many sub-chapters and organisations which makes it difficult to refer to only "one German hospital planning standard".

The local regulation used is based on "Hygienic requirements for accommodation, facilities, equipment and operation of hospitals, nursing homes and other health care hospitals" by the Ministry of Health of the Kyrgyz Republic 2004.

As for the international standards, our design is in line with the following standards:

1. RKI Robert Koch Institute Germany

102

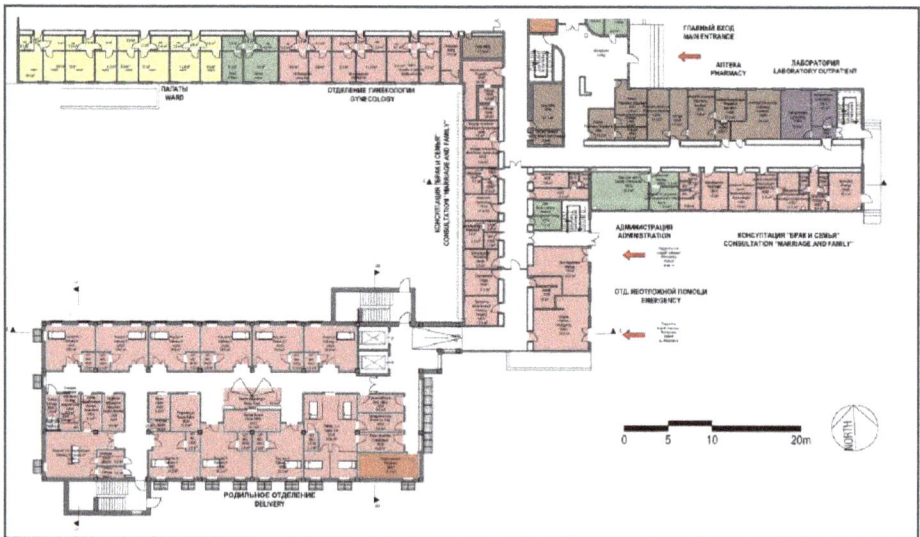

Figure 3.   National Perinatal Center Bishkek. Floor plan enlarge – First floor

Figure 4.   National Perinatal Center Bishkek. Floor plan enlarge – Second floor

Figure 5.   National Perinatal Center Bishkek. Floor plan enlarge – Third floor

"Richtlinie für Krankenhaushygiene und Infektionsprävention"

2. German DIN for all hospital related planning (e.g. materials, ventilation system and electrical power supply etc.)

3. Bavarian Building Regulation ByBauO 2014

4. Australasian Health Facility Guidelines (AusHFG).

Since the actual regulation "Hygienic requirements for accommodation, facilities, equipment and operation of hospitals, nursing homes and other health care hospitals" by the Ministry of Health of the Kyrgyz Republic 2004 is still valid and mandatory for the successful ap-

104

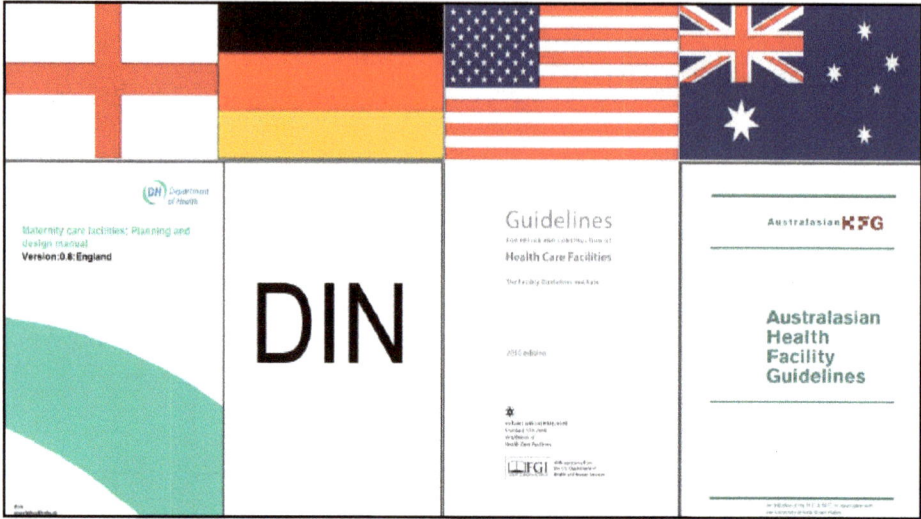

Figure 6. Standards NHS, DIN, NHS and Australasian HFG

proval, we needed to fulfil all applicable standards.

The following table is giving a comparison and is indicating fulfilment or amendment to international standards.

For the Women's Institute in Mauritius, we had to comply with NHS HTM. In developing the 'Concept Design' international guidelines have been used to determine the size of individual clinical and non-clinical departments and the resulting indicative Outline Functional Content for the new 'Institute of Women's Health' is almost 28,000m2.

Special Conditions to be fulfilled to work successfully as a Perinatal Centre

• Medical equipment must be properly maintained. As a precondition, the organization of spare parts, repair works and maintenance schedules must be set up and the staff trained accordingly. The medical staff must also been trained and guided in the correct usage of the medi-

cal equipment devices / availability of manuals and explanation of the manuals.

• Well functioning and maintained equipment is a precondition for the successful reduction of mortality. Without fulfilling this precondition, any further approaches for regionalization or increased number of neonatal intensive care units will not lead to any sufficient change of the existing condition.

• Hence, it is necessary to build up a well working system / organization to allocate and manage the financial resources for the regular maintenance, supply of spare parts and training of staff.

• Recruitment and training of staff (to be) qualified for advanced perinatal services.

In the course of reducing the mortality rate, patients will stay longer, which will then lead to and require regionalization and centralization. Then the transport system will have to be introduced and the demand for intensive and intermediate care beds will increase.

This will also require more qualified personal / staff and medical equipment. To summarize: improved quality and better regionalization will lead to increased need and utilization of intensive and intermediate care beds and at the same time increased need for medical equipment, specialized medicines and qualified staff.

With only one component of the system not working, the whole system may fail, e.g. in case of missing funds for spare part or when medical equipment is not working properly. In this scenario, there will be less beds required and regionalization will be more or less useless. The same scenario appears in the event of missing not appropriately trained personal, unavailable medications or not functioning building infrastructure (power supply, medical gas etc.).

CONCLUSIONS

In both projects, we could successfully combine different requirements and conditions yet with small "specialities" to fulfil local procedures and expectations. The results is not in contradiction with international best practice yet adapting local traditions and specific requirements / conditions. We need certainly more professional discussions about the following:

• Worldwide best practise and medical technology to combine with cultural and religious practises and conditions.
• Opening up healthcare planning standards for adaptations to cultural and religious conditions.

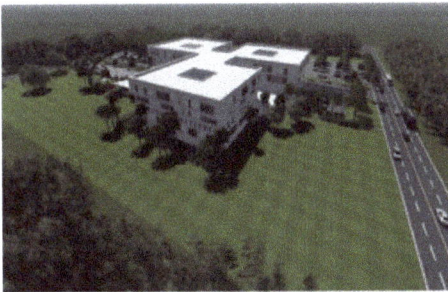

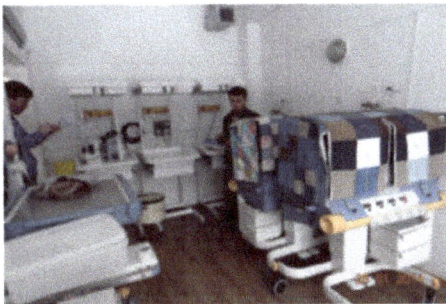

105

Figure 7. Perinatal Centers in Central Asia and Southern Africa

TESIS Inter-University Research Centre "Systems and Technologies for Social and Healthcare Facilities"
University of Florence, Italy

• Team members for the integrated planning, the role of the architect.
• Need for stronger discussion of "international standards" against "local cultural and religious integration" and formulate recommendation for the main global standards such as NHS HTM, AIA, AHFG and coming integration of EU standards.
• How can the UIA play a stronger role in the moderation.

106

AKNOWLEDGMENTS

Medical Advisory Team for the Perinatal Centre, Dr. med. Hans Kössel, Dr. med. Hans-Walter Vollert, Dr. med. Arunas Liubsys, Dr. med. Dr.-Ing. Andreas Roth, Technical Advisor Dipl.-Ing. MBA Lillian Lim.

Design for Spiritual Design in Healthcare Environment

Dave Tran

dltram@ku.edu
University of Kansas

Hui Cai

huicai@ku.edu
Assistant Professor, Department of Architecture, The University of Kansas, Lawrence, Kansas

This research aims to explore the protocols for religious practices in a hospital setting and implementing new guides to accommodate a various cultures in our societies and bring them to design. This research will narrow down the many religions practice today and focus, for a thorough study, a single religion I will be focusing on, the religion of Buddhism. However, this research can be conducted for many other spiritual groups.
What are the protocols for religious practices in a hospital setting and how can we implement new guides to accommodate the various cultures in our societies? We want to design for everyone, every medium, and every concern. Healthcare facilities should be a welcoming place of healing of both body and spirit.
All religions and cultures have different beliefs and practical procedures. The design of healthcare facilities should be based on a good understanding of patient's demographic and religious background. This study provides a framework of how to link spiritual needs with healthcare space in the Buddhist religion, which can be applied to other religions and cultures.

Spirituality is sometimes related to religion, but one can be spiritual without claiming a religion. Religion has always been a controversial topic in any conversation because of the varying beliefs and views.

With such a breadth of differences of opinions and faith, discussions may often lead to arguments and heated debates, sometimes even violence. In years past and present, religion was the instigator of many battles but, as a contrast, to most individuals, religion can be a savior.

This research is not about the "correct" religion but about respecting and embracing the freedom for each individual to practice their faith. Most importantly we need to look at the psychological benefits of faith for a person who is healing.

It provides an escape to the hardship and difficulties that a person is facing. It is important to understand that it eve-

TESIS

108

ryone has a right to freely express and practice their religion and faith. It is on us to respect everyone's beliefs, traditions, and customs.

Very little attention is given to one's spirituality in health facilities. There are hardly any guidelines to accommodate a person's spiritual and religious affinity in most facilities.

Healthcare centers have a duty to aspire and to kindle the culture of various religions and open the conversation to integrate the many different types of practices that are supported worldwide. Create a healing environment, not only of the physical but of the mental, is important for the well being of the patients and of the practitioners. A strong system of mental support aids greatly in the physical recovery of the body. There has been many research about the incorporation of spiritual design in the heal care field. This paper's goal is synthesizing these researches into a comprehensive design of a patient centered design.

What are the protocols for religious practices in a hospital setting and is it possible to implement new guides to accommodate the various cultures in today's society? The spirit of designing for a healing institute is to design for everyone, every medium, and every concern. Health facilities should be a welcoming place for healing of both the body and the spirit.

Patients want to be distracted from their troubles and one of the ways they overcome the fear is to turn to faith. The comfort afforded to a patient derived from faith is something that can not be overstated. It is a comfort not given by any medical procedure.

Faith can take a person to a place less fearful; a place of acceptance. However, a problem arises due to the multitude of religions and, from that multitude, religious inequality surfaces. There needs to be a discussion about religious equality in healthcare. Obtaining religious equality means that any religious associations given to any hospitals entirely will be eliminated. There will be no religious bias. A hospital is a place for healing the wounded and, by directly allowing itself to be dictated specifically for one religion and catering to only those of its flock, the hospital not only ignores the fundamental rights of patient's religious freedom but its fundamental purpose. Putting an association to a hospital only caters a certain type of religious demography and doing so can create a barrier and discomfort for those that are not of the same religion.

United States is a unique country compromised of various cultural ethnicities and provides a unique opportunity to integrate all religious traditions. Such diversity needs oversight. And luckily, it is written within the Constitution, that an individual has the freedom to practice their religion. Therefore there are no restrictions to what one can practice, only that it does no harm to another person's being and it does not discriminate. With this religious freedom ingrained into the very fabric of this country, many Americans feel safe in practicing their faith. A series of Gallup polls that surveyed 327,244 referenced in Koenig polled 78 percent of Americans identified as Christians, 16 percent Jewish, 0.5 percent Muslim, and 2.4 percent other non-Christian (Koenig, 2013).

A good state of mind would help patient heal quicker. Faith provides that steadiness to an enormous amount of people. While I am not advocating the absurd notion that medical professionals ignore medical treatments completely in lieu of faith, I believe that accommodating a patient's practices while treating them provides for a better care. Through research and understanding of different religious practices, I have come up with simple adjustments for healthcare to make their patients happier. The happier the patient, the less financial trouble the hospital or any healthcare facility will face.

STUDY PARAMETERS

This research's initiative is to convey how incorporation and accommodation of a patient's faith into healthcare design in minor and simple ways would not affect critical care but assist in recovery.

A parameter of this research is to disregard the conflict between religion and science, but what the science and religion can do to assist on the recovery of a person.

I have investigated what policies major hospitals have implemented in regards all the prominent religious practices.

Learning from the practices of major religions, I then exported these customs into practical design for healthcare facilities so that they may accommodate the practices. Some religious beliefs do come into conflict with the treatment but in this research I am focusing on the beneficial effects of the environment of faith in health care facilities.

The main idea of the research is to focus and to respect the religious cultural practice and how it aids in healthcare.

LITERATURE REVIEW

In this portion of this paper, we are going to take a look at the rituals and customs of the major religions of the world. Since there are numerous faiths, we are narrowing down to the seven major ones. These religious communities we are investigating are Christianity and its Denomination, Judaism, Islam, Hinduism, Buddhism, Sikhism.

Some of the unfortunate religions we will not discuss are the native spiritual ones, which emphasized comfort in their spiritual designs for their inhabitants. The major application of spiritual design

109

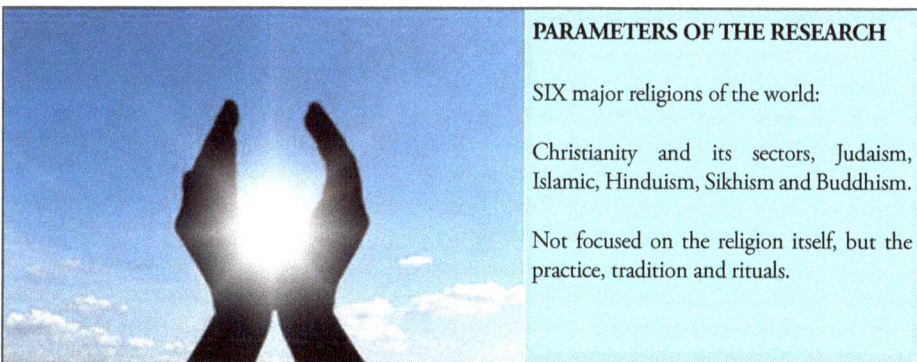

PARAMETERS OF THE RESEARCH

SIX major religions of the world:

Christianity and its sectors, Judaism, Islamic, Hinduism, Sikhism and Buddhism.

Not focused on the religion itself, but the practice, tradition and rituals.

Figure 1. Study the religion

*TESIS Inter-University Research Centre "Systems and Technologies for Social and Healthcare Facilities"
University of Florence, Italy*

110

upon which we focus are ones which centers on the departing of a loved one such as in a hospice environment and each religion differs in their rituals.

INVESTIGATING CATHOLICISM AND ITS DENOMINATION

The history of Catholicism influence in the medical field is lengthy. In the western world, like that of the United States, Christianity is the dominate religion. This dominance permeates through everything, even healthcare design.

For example, the chapel has been incorporated in the building fabric of most hospitals in the western world, with a space named after a sacred symbol: The Crucifix. However, the ways in which Christianity incorporates a spiritual space for their community is something to be commended and will be discussed further.

A focus of their design centers on their worshiping rituals and that can be the key to design for all other designs.

When examining the acute and near death experience of Christians, it is wholly religious affair. A priest is re- quested and stands on constant vigil and prayer. It is a ceremonial event, address- ing sins past and forgiveness so that in death, the soul of the deceased may en- ter Heaven. In this way, faith provides comfort, almost like a blanket. It calms the patient and sends them off peace- fully.

ISLAM

The rituals of the Islamic faith are a unique exploration. For the Muslim community, religious rituals play a vital role in their lives. Prayer is an important element for the community, allowing them to practice their faith in Allah. Be- fore and after the worship rituals, they perform an intense cleansing of their vis- ible body, washing their face, ears, fore- head, feet, ankles, hands, arms to elbows, the sniffing of water up to the nose, and washing out the mouth and hands. Wet hands are rubbed through hair to re- move dust. This idea of cleansing one's body before entering a holy place can be incorporated into a patient's room. Hos- pitals are notorious for ironically being unclean. By placing a water bowl at the

TAKE AWAYS

- Focus on the religious symbols
- Reading of the Bible Prayer
- Place for Services

Figure 2. Christianity (Digital image. Http://gasparian.stblogs.org/. N.p., n.d. Web. 20 May 2015 <http://www.yvonneortega.com/wpcontent/uploads/2012/02/Bible.jpghttp://gasparian.stblogs.org/small%20chapel%20ii.jpg>)

TAKE AWAYS

- Before and After prayer, wash themselves from a wash bowl
- Direct themselves toward Ka'bah in Makkah

Figure 3. Islam. Prefer a carpet matt to kneel and prey (Digital image. Http://www.dreamstime.com/, n.d. Web. 20 May 2015. <http://thumbs.dreamstime.com/x/islamic-prayer-done-muslim-sheikh-24553922. jpg>)

entrance of an Islamic patient's room, it shows respect and may ease the mind of the patient.

Due to the vast majority of physicians being of the Muslim faith, they may be more open to the idea of designing a room to cater to Muslim patients such as orientation of the room to face Khalla, including space for prayers, or projecting images of spiritual leaders and symbol on the walls.

In the Islamic faith they desire to be cremated quickly. After death, a group of family members will do a prayer before the cremation.

READING OF THE JUDAISM RITUALS AND WORSHIP ROUTINE

Among the two things of importance for worshippers of Judaism are the Sabbath, which lasts from Friday evening sunset to Saturday evening sunset, and the Passover. Sabbath should be viewed as the day of rest.

During this day of rest, followers are not able to touch any electronics devices or handle any money.

When associated with the near death situations, the Jewish community believes they should never be left alone. After death, and especially during Sabbath, the body should not be moved. A saying of prayer for the deceased may be spoken. And finally, the people from the Holly Brotherhood will take charge of the body.

HINDU

There are many spirits and Gods that the guide the worshippers of this ancient religion. Rituals for these deities are elaborate and play an enormous role in the lives of Hindus. Unsurprisingly, as in life, rituals for the deceased are just as intricate and complex. Many of Hindu's customs consists of a ceremonial task around a shrine. Their practice of worshiping includes wailing chants, bells being rung, and incense burning. Currently these practices are not welcome in a hospital, for they may be disruptive of the quiet. During birth, the rituals are to speak madras to the baby's ear, and placing honey and ghee on the baby's tongue. Similar to the Muslims, washing is an important ritual before worshiping.

111

TESIS Inter-University Research Centre "Systems and Technologies for Social and Healthcare Facilities" University of Florence, Italy

TESIS

112

NOTES

- At Sabbath they are not able to use any electronically devices and handle any money.
- Sabbath starts at sunset on Fridays till sunet of Saturday.
- They also would love to cleanse themselves before prayer.

Figure 4. Judaism. Woman praying (Digital image. Myjewishlearning. N.p., n.d. Web. 20 May 2015. <http://www.myjewishlearning.com/wp-content/uploads/2015/04/woman-lighting-candles.jpg>)

THE SIKH

The fourth largest religious community in the world is the Sikh. They are distinguished by five distinct visual traits: Uncut hair, comb, short dagger, steel bagel, white pants. For devout Sikhs prayer is everything.

One needs to have privacy for them to speak with their spirits. Washing is important and water with a bedpan near a toilet is required.

Information regarding their after death rituals are sparse. The followers of this religion enjoys privacy during prayer. However, they do have rituals which are performed for those whose life are fading.

During their last moments the group wants a family member or religious member by their side. It is also important to have their five symbolic traits place on their bodies and not be disrupted.

The tradition of this tribe for the body is cremation.

THE BUDDHISTS

The last group we want to explore are the Buddhists. This religion believes in karma and reincarnation. The worship rituals in this faith consist of speaking the madras and burning incenses. Prayers are essential and as is meditation. Meditation can be used in different scenarios. There are those who practice meditation in peace and others feel that meditation is a tool to deal with chaos of the material world.

There is a different process for the followers of Buddhism regarding death. When a person leaves this earth, the body must remain untouched for a certain amount of time (usually eight hours) allowing the soul to leave the body. There is an intricate ceremony including three days of prayer, burning of incense, and with monks blessing the body before it is cremated. Then the family of the deceased attends evening prayers for seven weekends.

The concept of spirituality and faith has always been followed with skepticism and an analytical eye, all with reasonable objections. Faith in a God or Gods opposes the view of an empirical world in which viable proof trumps necessitates evidence. Regardless of scrutiny, spirituality remains a significant aspect of a majority of people's lives. Koenig (2003), in the opening pages of his book, listed the need for spirituality as such:

"Many patients are religious or spiritual, have spiritual needs related to illness, and want their health professional to know about them.

Religion influences the patient's ability to cope with illness.

Patients when hospitalized are often isolated from their religious communities.

Religious involvement is associated with both mental and physical health, and likely affects the patient's response to medical and surgical treatments.

Failure to address patients' spiritual needs increase health care cost."

SURVEY

For this project, a survey was conducted and the subjects were a sample of the universal group of people around the area of Kansas. Thirty-one participants were gracious enough to have answered the survey questions.

The type of questions asked was to gauge people's interest in religion or spirituality intertwining with the health care environment.

DESIGN IMPLICATION

Lessons I have learned in my research become strategies that can be adapted to design. For example, a simple change of bed arrangements is one tool of accommodating a patient's faith. Through the studying of various religious cultures, we can create patient focused designs and easily apply them to healthcare facilities. This section will be examining the multiple faiths and how we can create a universal design for application in healthcare facilities willing accommodate such a request.

113

NOTES

THEY LOVE TO CHANT THEIR PRAYERS

-They also would love to cleanse themselves before prayer.
-They prefer privacy

Figure 5. Hinduism. Elderly praying (Digital image. Shipbright. .wordpress.com, n.d. Web. 20 May 2015. <https://shipbright.wordpress.com/2010/02/08/holywater-holy-river-the-ganges-the-goddess-of-purity-is-not-well-tibetan-plateau-series-4/>)

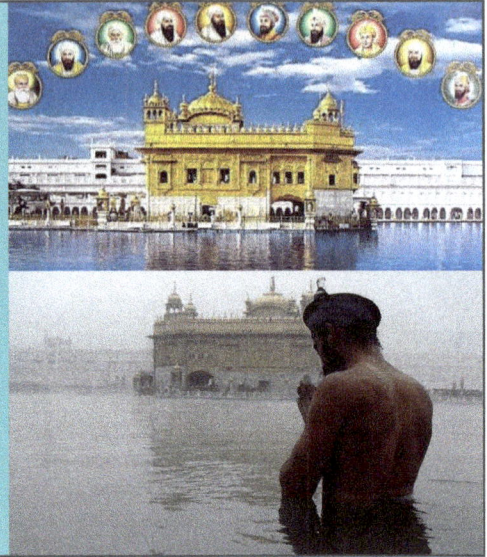

NOTES

-This group also would like to   cleanse themselves before prayer.
-They have seven symbols that are with them at all times.
-Prefer privacy and gender.

Figure 6. Sikhism. Privacy when praying (Digital image. Digital image. N.p., n.d. Web. 20 May 2015. <http://i45.tinypic.com/f9e538.jpg>)

An example of simple adjustments to accommodate faith is the previously mentioned arrangement of beds facing a certain direction. Muslims, during prayer, needs to turn to the direction towards the Mecca. If beds are adjustable or easily transportable, patients can shift their beds to face Mecca and pray without concern of disrespect. The design conundrum is how to use space to help patients easily cope with their stay in hospitals, therapy, etc.

A problem Jewish patients may face is their inability to directly use anything electric during Sabbath. They are prohibited from physically activating anything electric. So, to solve this conundrum, especially in a hospital, the patient either is at the mercy of their medical staff or automatic lights sensors can be installed into their room. As they are not able to use the electronics, the room can automatically do that for them. Having voice command can also allow patients to maintain control without violating any part of their faith.

We now look at the religion of the Buddhist and how meditation plays an important part in their worship and how we can address designs for Buddhist patients. The process of meditation focuses the mind, steadies breathing, and blocks out worldly concerns.

Like prayers, this relieves stress, alleviates the mind, and reduces fear. It provides control to the worshipper; control over their own emotions and uncertainty. And anything that reduces stress on the body reduces complications and makes treatments easier. Having a space to meditate and practice the words of the scripts is important for Buddhists. Hospital rooms can provide a small space for meditation. It does not have to be large but just big enough for the patient to sit and meditate. The rooms can also display the Buddha on the walls via posters or have a led screen to project and change different projections.

With the Hinduism there is a need to be more family interaction with the patient during hospital stays.

Throughout many religious practices, cleanliness has always been essential.

As science and technology advances, I can envision a space designed for the individual. Many even creating a virtual room where we can project a virtual world where we can create an environment that fits the patient's needs.

Using technology like Google Glass and incorporating that with a virtual world is also option of design. Maybe they can have a peace of mind before they pass. Maybe they can see a loved one that passed away before they join them.

DISCUSSION AND CONCLUSION

By understanding religion and the affects it has on culture, we can get a good notion of designing religion specific accommodations and to reduce any hindrance of medical treatments. As we advanced towards a more patient focus design, understanding the demography is important for the designs and for serving the community and its every need. A presence of spirituality is important in healthcare due to the stressful environment, uncertainty, and fear.

When dealing with a situation that maybe life threatening, measurements of reassurance can help comfort a person, keep them at ease, and put less stress on their body, which in turns boosts immunity and reduces heart complications. Some people feel that religion is a drug or that it is a disease. But when presented with death, it is natural to gravitate towards concepts of an afterlife or reincarnation. Patients desire privacy when praying so they can attain atonement about their situation or have a resolution from their inner self to either accept or fight their medical issues. It is the comfort that there is something more to life what is given. It is about dedication of belief and how hospitals can utilize that as a tool of healing. Hospitals and other healthcare facilities, especially a hospice, deal with life or death situations daily. A minute makes all the difference. And maybe a prayer does too.

115

NOTES

- Likes to Pray in front of a Depiction
- Sometimes Chants when Prayng
- Likes quiteness to mediate

Figure 7. Buddhism (Digital image. Digital image. Www.jsri.jp, n.d. Web. 20 May 2015. <http://www.jsri.jp/English/ojo/2008/ntu/chaplainteam.jpg>)

Figure 8. Integration to design

According to the survey, people do have an interest in uniting the practice of major religions and design to create something that is respectful of all cultures. The survey indicates that a majority of the surveyed respected other religions and agreed that tailoring a patient's hospital stay is beneficial. With such a large mix of people and the individuals making an impact, we want to make it more welcoming for those in the minority; make them feel as if they are just important as the majority. Everyone practices their spirituality in a different manner. What is important is the having privacy and space for their faith and acknowledging that it part of their lives especially during moments of life and death.

REFERENCES

Betancourt, J. R., Green, A. R., & Carrillo, J. E. (2002). *Cultural competence in health care: emerging frameworks and practical approaches* (Vol. 576): Commonwealth Fund, Quality of Care for Underserved Populations

Burton, L. A., & Bosek, M. S. D. (2000). *When religion may be an ethical issue,* in "Journal of religion and health", 39(2), 97-106

Cobb, M., Puchalski, C. M., & Rumbold, B. (2012). *Oxford textbook of spirituality in healthcare:* Oxford University Press

Dein, S., Cook, C. C., Powell, A., & Eagger, S. (2010). *Religion, spirituality and mental health,* in "The Psychiatrist", 34(2), 63-64

Johnstone, B., Glass, B. A., & Oliver, R. E. (2007). *Religion and disability: Clinical, research and training considerations for rehabilitation professionals,* in "Disability & Rehabilitation", 29(15), 1153-1163

Kirkwood, N. A. (2005). *Hospital Handbook on Multiculturalism & Religion:* Church Publishing, Inc.

Koenig, H. G. (1998). *Handbook of religion and mental health:* Elsevier

Koenig, H. G. (2013). *Spirituality in patient care: Why, how, when, and what:* Templeton Foundation Press

Puchalski, C., & Ferrell, B. (2011). *Making health care whole: Integrating spirituality into patient care:* Templeton Foundation Press

Testerman, J. K. (1997). Spirituality vs religion: Implications for healthcare. Loma Linda University

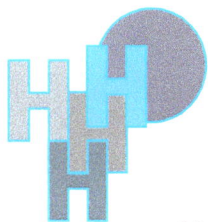

HEALTHCARE DESIGN FOR THE FUTURE
Session introduction
Maria Grazia Giardinelli
PhD. Arch., Research Fellow University of Florence

Hospital building is characterized by high organizational and technological complexity heavily influenced by innovations brought about by renewed forms of needs relating to health, protection, environmental sustainability and the reduction of energy consumption.

In parallel, we are witnessing an increasingly rapid revolution in healthcare delivery through innovative care methods supported by the latest generation technologies (from robotics to big-data, modelling & simulation, etc.). Hospital design must take into account continuous technology and IT developments, which are necessary to best meet the healthcare needs of people and of the community, ensuring technological integration, the digitisation of functions and the flexibility of the environments.

This is the topic addressed in the "Facility Design of the Future" session, namely the need for healthcare facilities to know how to adapt to new social trends and technological innovations, and to contain a great variety of services and functions that continuously evolve.

New technologies, social networks, the use of digital applications and new computerized forms for patient care tend to reduce (if not eliminate) the relationships that these environments generate, that is all those forms of community life that the traditional hospital, albeit with many limitations, managed to ensure. The design of a hospital cannot therefore be limited to merely respecting a functional programme and new technological trends, but rather it must also deliver a high level of humanization and environmental quality, according to a shared social programme. It is therefore necessary to pursue greater humanization in the hospital environment, recreating spaces for community life and increasingly blurring the characteristic elements of places of care in favour of a more familiar setting.

Another aspect to take into consideration in the design of the hospitals of the future is the necessary integration with the city and the cultural context of reference. A hospital in the Smart Cities era represents a hub in the network of territorial services through which the patient's journey develops, providing highly specialized and immensely complex services.

The move towards the decentralization and dehospitalization of the hospital requires, at the same time, the strengthening of interior-exterior connection capacities and a different form of grouping the various healthcare production units, which no longer interact with a closed environment (the traditional hospital) but rather with a virtually infinite number of other experiences that are closely linked to the city and community.

The hospital of the future must therefore generate value both internally, through the quality of the spaces, the humanization of the environments and integration between functions and technologies, and externally in dialogue with the city and the cultural and identity context in which it is located.

Finally, the hospital of the future must be capable of continuously adapting to the transformation of healthcare programmes in respect of the economic context of reference, environmental sustainability principles, and reducing energy consumption to a minimum.

Evolution of Hospital Architectural Morphology

Huang Xiqiu

huangxiqiu@ippr.net
Chief Architect, Chinese member of UIA PHG, Member of Architectural Society of China,
China IPPR International, Engineering Co,Ltd

119

Hospital architecture are broadly related to the humanities and sociology, deeply influenced by scientific and technologies, also involved in biological environment in many fields. Because of their specific characteristic, the evolution and development of hospital architectural morphology are concerned by hospital architects and researchers.

Keywords: *Evolution, Morphology, Hospital Architecture*

THE SIGNIFICANCE OF HOSPITAL ARCHITECTURAL MORPHOLOGY STUDY

Since 21th century the intention of building a better hospital was to humanize its healing environment, to find a rationalization approach of health facilities, to meet the requirement of their safety and reliable, to find the way of economy to build and run, as well as their sustainable development requirement have reach to a highly level.

The research and study on health facilities including comprehensive general hospital and various specific hospital are never stop. Healthcare facilities especially the large size hospital are usually not revealed as a monoblock building. Instead of that, a comprehensive teaching hospital has become an architectural building complex with variation of architectural form. Their architectural expression reveal the changing and evolution of hospital contents. Progress and evolution of healthcare architecture morphology have got many concern by so many healthcare facility planner and researcher.

FACTORS WHICH INFLUENCED THE MORPHOLOGY OF HOSPITAL ARCHITECTURE

There are quite a number of factors which influenced the forming of hospital morphology. The main factors could be summarized as below:

Consist of quiet a number of departments, the complexity of various flows, the stick requirement on hygienic segregation.

More than 30 to 40 departments with different function are very common within a large size comprehensive hospital. There are high frequency communication rate among them. They cover various people flows, logistic flows and information flows. Adding with the clearly segregation of clean and polluted flows and zones for hygienic control reason. All of above, forming the complexity of a hospital organic composition.

The evolution and progressive of healthcare service system.

In order to make the best use of limited health resources, improve the efficient of healthcare delivery, provide patients with available, affordable and equal health care.

An healthcare system with different level healthcare facilities are set up. An efficient patient transfer systems are introduced.

In China the changing of drug supply system, the promotion of day care unit, day surgery service are encouraged for instance.

The progressive of related sciences and techniques

The phenomena of cross disciplines, cross relation among different disciplines are clearly presented. In health care facilities. the effect are evident.

This include also the hospital planning and design.

Figure 2. The evolution and progressive of healthcare service system

Figure 1. Healthcare facilities are usually not revealed as a monoblock building

120

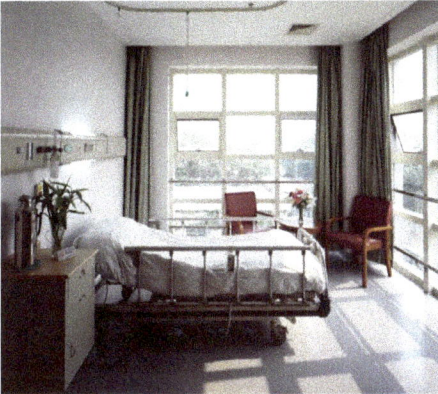

Figure 3. The awareness of humanization of hospital service

An example is the development of medical sciences and advanced medical apparatus and equipment have led to the popular of interventional surgery.

The integration of MRI or CT with OR Suite have forming the development of hybrid OT Suite. Information technology, internet, cloud computing have accelerated the application of electronic records. The digitalization hospital with no or less paper and film work are coming. 3D printing provide the orthopedic surgery with 3D printing prosthesis leg or arm, assist dental technique with artificial false teeth etc.

Besides, bioclean ventilation technique, various logistic transportation system were widely adopted in hospital complex. All of above are potentially affected the morphology of healthcare architecture.

The awareness of humanization of hospital service

Healthcare facilities have broadly contact with whole society.

They have special public and social char-

acter. Almost related to every citizen, no matter what ethnic he or she is, poor or rich , high or low level social status who stand on, no matter male or female, young or old, every one receives healthcare service from various health facilities during their whole life.

The image of hospital, space layout and planning, the planning of medical process would influence the feeling of patients and their accompany person.

The realization of moving from mono bio medicine model toward sociopsychological and biomedicine model the concept of people center or patient center have been widely spreaded and accepted by the whole society.

121

Higher requirement on resources saving low carbon release and environmental friendly — a sustainable development solution

We have enter to a post industrial age. People aware about the impact on biological nature. Artificial made environment has violet and destroy the bio balance on our earth. Back to nature, harmony with our nature are fully agree and accept by the whole world.

Hospital building related to so many points: noise control and protection, radiation protection and prevention, electric frequency wave protection, bio medical waste collection and management, polluted water treatment and drainage etc. They are all related to environmental friendly policy.

The consumer of hospital service also special. They are different from healthy people, patients are usually week or low immunity level.

They require special care either body or psychological aspect. And several ad-

TESIS Inter-University Research Centre "Systems and Technologies for Social and Healthcare Facilities"
University of Florence, Italy

TESIS

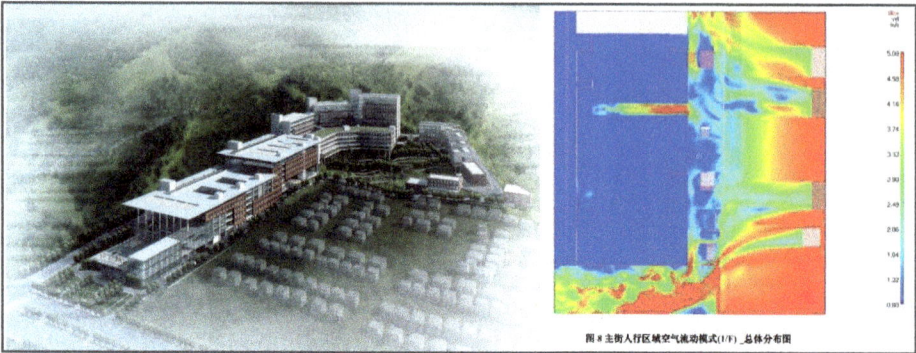

Figure 4. Higher requirement on resources saving low carbon release and environmental friendly

122

vanced and high tech medical equipment require work in a critical level of artificial indoor environment etc.

Those techniques and supporting system consume large amount of energy.
So far, hospitals are belong to high rank group of energy consumption.
How to select an appropriate morphology to reach the goal of resource saving, low carbon release and environmental friendly is critical issues. It has the specific meaning for exploring a sustainable approach for future hospital.
In general, the impacts which influenced the hospital morphology come from different fields.
Neither large size comprehensive hospital or smaller size specific hospital, they are becoming a high tech and high energy consuming institution.
Besides, the running of those institution need to engage high level healthcare professionals and workers. The willing for building the best inner nature and good outer image hospital. To build a pleasant space for whom to stay in or work also very import. They are forming the force to push the evolution and progressive of hospital too.

THE EVOLUTION OF HOSPITAL ARCHITECTURAL MORPHOLOGY IN DIFFERENT COUNTRIES

Since the past century, many research institutes quite a number of professor and researcher have paid attention to hospital architectural morphology.
They collected information, make analysis and compiled diagram. Following diagrams are some of the examples.

Anne Petillot AP-HP Paris France

The diagram showing the evolution of hospital architecture in France, especial in Paris capital area. As early as the beginning of 13th century, the hospital was revealed as a hall form. During the past centuries chechque board type, cluster type was adopted and then mono block on podium. Multi blocks on podium solution is gradually accept as the developing model for future.

Derec Stow. A compiled drawings for hospital built in the past decades U.K

The diagram showing the evolution of hospital morphology in U.K. By time

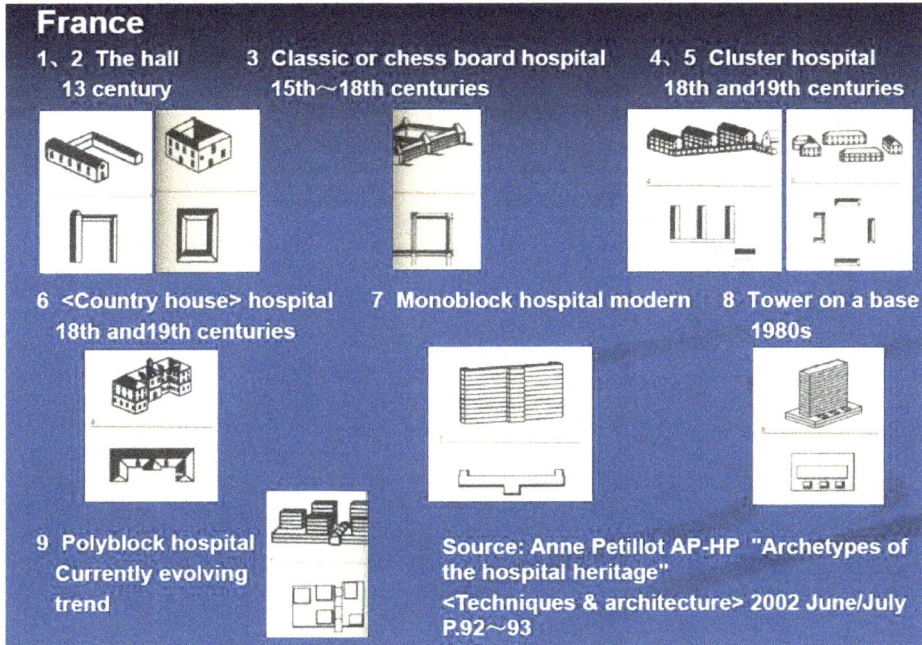

Figure 5. France (Source: Anne Petillot AP-HP "Archetypes of the hospital heritage"<Techniques & architecture> 2002 June/July, P.92-93)

sequences, before 1945 British hospital were greatly influent by Nightingale's concept. After the second world war, in 1948, NHS was set up. They make great effort to rebuilt old facilities and built the new institution. After several experimental practices, they promote Best buy system, Harness and nucleus system. The solution are highly depend on modular standardization approach.

Prof. Jan Delrue - KUL Belgium

He developed an evolution diagram also. In his evolution diagram, he reveal the hospital development of the past. Starting from Nightingale pavilion solution to high rise mono block and then highly integrated solution forming a Big structure given the name of "Titanic type".

Hospital became a healing machine and then toward the village type showing the trend of providing more better healing environment and create hospital with appropriate human scale.

Robbert Huijsman - The Netherland

He compiled a diagram illustrated the evolution of hospital in the Netherland. The drawings explain the development of hospitals during the past decades. From 1950s to year 2000, the hospitals morphology have changed from H T structure to Breitfuss and then the fabrics type in recent years.

The evolution diagram of China

The development of Chinese hospital

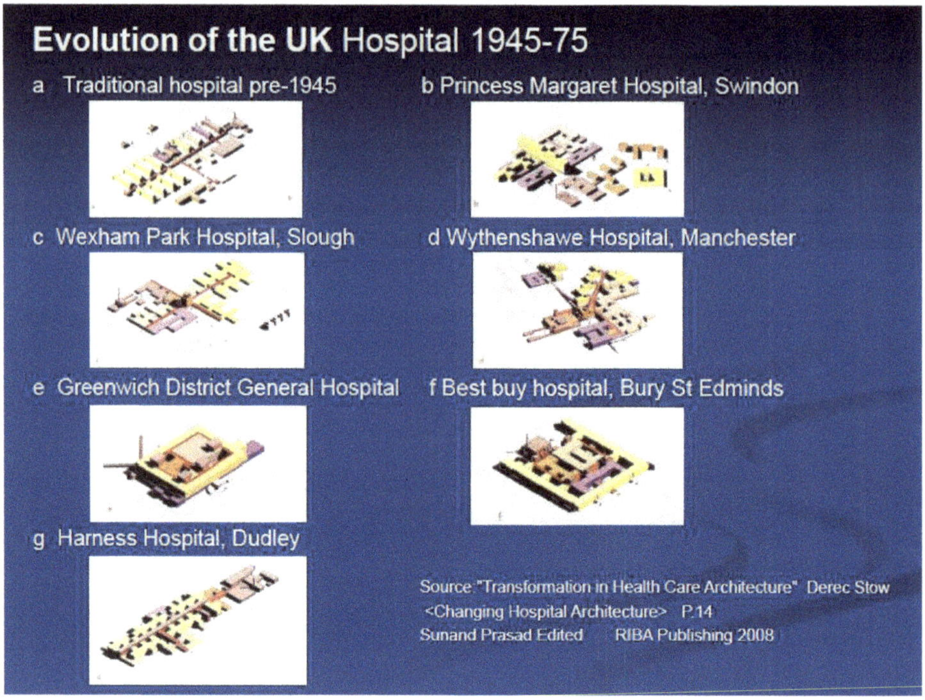

124

Figure 6. Evolution of the UK Hospital 1945-75 (Source:"Transformation in Health Care Architecture" Derec Stow <Changing Hospital Architecture> p.14 Sunand Prasad Edited RIBA Publishing 2008)

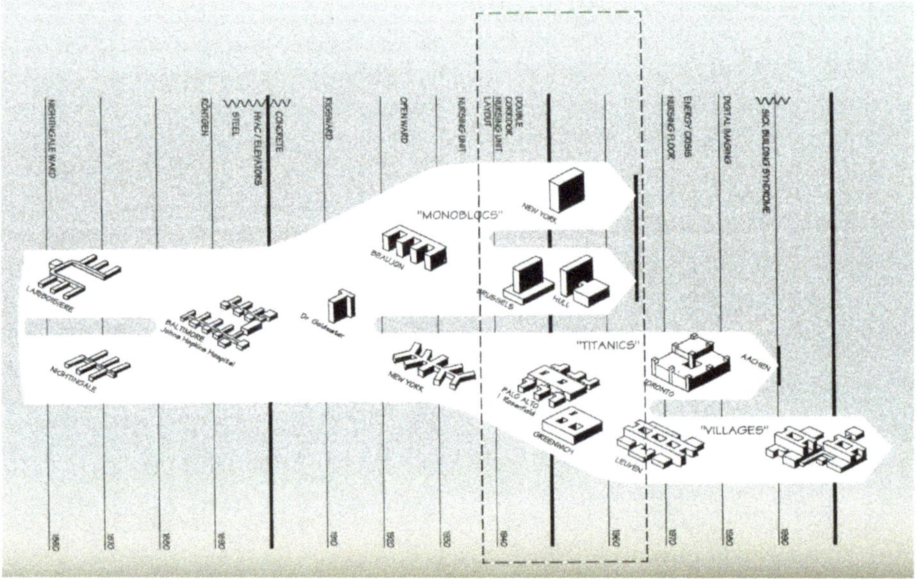

Figure 7. Prof. Jan Delrue's diagram (Source: Prof. Jan Delrue Lecture paper Catholic University of Leuven, Belgium 1990)

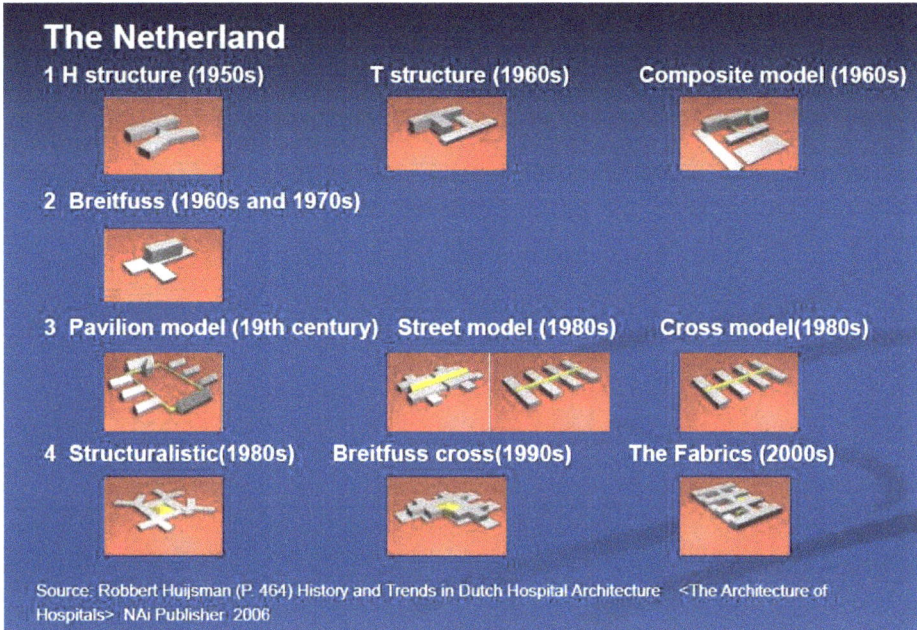

Figure 8. The Netherland (Source: Robbert Huijsman, p. 464 History and Trends in Dutch Hospital Architecture <The Architecture of Hospitals> NAi Publisher 2006)

was deeply affected by Pilitacal situation. Since the beginning of last century, several hospital were built by Religion charities.

The plan adopted concept which similar to western world. After 1949, hospital design and planning concept were deeply influent by Previous Soviet style. However they are some projects were excluded.

The new development reveal the plural trend are happened ahter year 1978 the adoption of "Open Policy".

CLASSIFICATION OF HOSPITAL COMPLEX TYPOLOGY

Based on the various morphological of hospital architecture, we could probably classify them in more abstract groups. They could summarize as several typical

types. Based the dense of building complex.

For instance, they could be divided into highly compacted type, semi compacted type and dispersed type—three basic types the advantage and disadvantage of them are compared as below.

Highly Compacted Type

Save the land, with tight link for flows, more dark space highly depend on artificial lighting and ventilation, provide good view for rooms which located on block.

Semi Compacted Type

Consume moderate amount of land, with appropriate links for flows make the best use of natural ventilation and

TESIS Inter-University Research Centre "Systems and Technologies for Social and Healthcare Facilities"
University of Florence, Italy

125

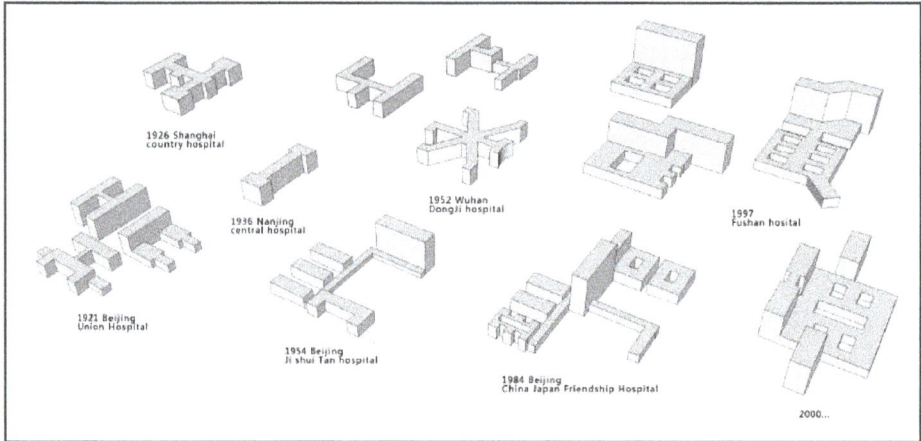

Figure 9. Evolution of Hospital Morphology in China (Source: Huang Xiqiu China IPPR International Engineering Co, Ltd)

126

light, provide good view for most of the rooms, provide potential possibility for low carbon release, energy saving solution.

Dispersed Type

Occupied more land, longer links for flows, could be made the best use of natural lighting and ventilation, more close to nature, provide more possibility tor energy saving and environmental friendly.

ANALYSIS ON ONE PRACTICAL PROJECT

Xiamen Cardiac Vascular Disease Center, Fujian Province China.
It is a newly built hospital with 600 bed. The campus is limited to 23 thousand sq.m. Building space 80,000 sq.m.
The proposal which is arranged a wide hospital street it link 5 storey outpatient Department, 4 story emergency department & medical support department as well as 12 storey inpatient ward block.
In OPD, consulting and examination

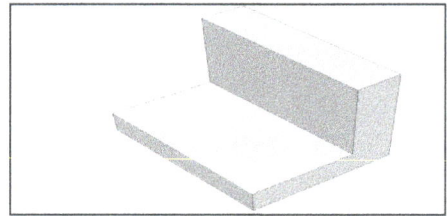

Figure 10. Highly Compacted Type

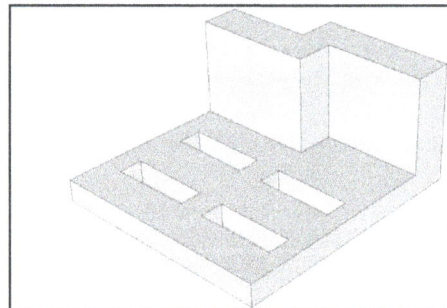

Figure 11. Semi Compacted Type

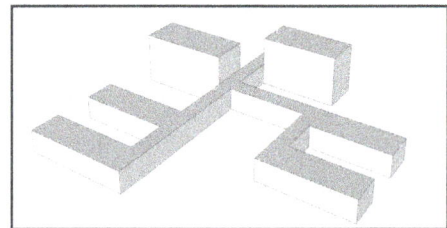

Figure 12. Dispersed Type

Figure 13. Xiamen Cardiac Vascular Disease Center, bird eye's view

127

rooms were clustered into four wings. They are divided with inner courtyards, central atria and link by wide bright street.

Emergency department put in the center at ground floor. Fast track concept was adopted and provide easy route for walking patient and patients who carried by ambulance.

A easy route for connecting to upper interventional Surgery and Operating department are well arrange. On three floor, 6 DSA rooms plus 2 hybrid operating rooms are directly link with 2 group of CCU.

On fourth floor, 6 Operating suites was directly connected with 2 group of ICU. All of them have direct and easy route to inpatient wards.

The basic concept of this new project is to provide patient with shortest medical process, find the best way to improve the efficiency and also pay attention to the safety and comfort for patients.

All the building complex was forming a concise form. Sunken plaza, inner courtyard Atria was inserted among their different department, wide and bright street which link all key area not only provide ease of flows, also become an key element for creating a pleasant healing environment for the user.

Figure 14. Xiamen Cardiac Vascular Disease Center, Master Plan

128

Figure 15. Xiamen Cardiac Vascular Disease Center, prespective

Design of a Cancer Radiation Therapy Center

Prosperidad C. Luis
Rogelio L. Luis,
Samuel P. Aguirre
Mariel C. Cruz

luis_associates@yahoo.com
LUIS and Associates, Architects & Environmental Planners, Philippines

Radiation therapy is a cancer treatment modality that uses high-energy radiation to shrink and kill cancer cells by damaging their DNA. However, this modality can also damage the DNA of normal cells, making it important for the treatment to be carefully planned to minimize what may be referred to as "collateral damage" incurred by the treatment.

The frantic search for cure for the dreaded disease, cancer, has caused the very fast pace of the progress of technologies such that new treatment protocols had become available to doctors and their patients at an equally fast pace, giving hope to patients now where they may have given up in the past. This fast pace, on the other hand, has made it more difficult for facilities planners and designers to produce functional spaces, forms and architecture, in general, that can accommodate with flexibility the requirement of fast change. The fearsome nature of treatment protocols delivered through the use of fearsome-looking huge equipment has also made it more difficult for facilities planners and designers to create spaces that somehow would help assuage the fear and give comfort to patients already heavily stressed by their illness.

This paper is a sequel to a paper presented by the principal author in the UIA Healthcare Forum 2013 in Toronto, Canada, entitled "The Design of a Breast Cancer Center" which discussed the human aspect of planning and designing a Breast Cancer Center containing an Infusion Unit that delivers a treatment modality, chemotherapy. While discussing the highly technical nature of the topic, this paper will also discuss the human-centeredness and patient-centeredness of the design of a facility for another treatment modality, radiotherapy.

INTRODUCTION

Radiation therapy is a cancer treatment modality that uses high-energy radiation to shrink and kill cancer cells by damaging their DNA.

However, this modality can also damage the DNA of normal cells, making it important for the treatment to be carefully planned to minimize what may be referred to as "collateral damage" incurred by the treatment.

The fearsome nature of treatment protocols delivered mostly through the use of fearsome-looking huge equipment has made it more difficult for facilities planners and designers to create spaces that somehow would help assuage the fear and give comfort to patients already heavily stressed by their illness.

Being ill is an occurrence in people's lives that is inevitable, as Susan Sontag, eminent critical essayist, novelist and film-maker, herself a breast cancer survivor, said in her work entitled "Illness as Metaphor":

"Illness is the night-side of life, a more onerous citizenship. Everyone who is born holds dual citizenship, in the kingdom of the well and in the kingdom of the sick.
Although we all prefer to use only the good passport, sooner or later, each of us is obliged, at least for a spell, to identify ourselves as citizens of that other place."

June Goodfield, British historian, scientist and writer, and author of "The Siege of Cancer" said:

"Cancer begins and ends with people. In the midst of scientific abstraction, it is sometimes possible to forget this one basic fact …

Doctors treat diseases, but they also treat people, and this precondition of their professional existence sometimes pulls them in two directions at once."

In using Sontag's passport in the kingdom of the sick, there can be reprieve from suffering from Goodfield's doctors who treat people of their cancer. Likewise, there can be reprieve from the environment of a cancer facility that is patient-centered and people-centered in general.

This paper will focus on the patient-centeredness and people-centeredness of the physical environment for patient-doctor interaction.

OBJECTIVES

The General Objective of this Paper is to present planning and design solutions that can soften for people the harsh experience of going through cancer treatment protocols involving radiation therapy.

The Specific Objectives are:
1. to quote from the innermost thoughts and feelings of patients, family and caregivers with regards to radiation therapy;
2. to distill from these thoughts and feelings some considerations for the design of a patient-centered radiation therapy center;
3. to describe the translation of the above considerations to planning and design.

UNDERSTANDING THE PATIENT

A patient-centered facility must have patients at the core of its planning and design. An understanding of the psychological and emotional state of patients results in a design which is receptive to their delicate condition.

Once diagnosed with this dreaded disease, the patient experiences a progression of emotion – what is commonly known as the seven stages of grief – shock, denial, bargaining, fear, anger, despair – and finally, acceptance – but not until after the patient has plummeted first into the labyrinth of the previous stages. The following are excerpts taken from patients' diaries and notes from interviews of patients and caregivers, which document some of the innermost feelings of a cancer patient.

Patient's Thoughts and Feelings:

- My shaking hands kept me from finishing the half a slice of sandwich I was trying to eat. Fear, uncertainty and doubt kept my lips from finishing a cup of tea. The morning after, hunger pangs and weakness due to lack of food made me see truth. It is not cancer that had made me lose my appetite.
It is the pain in my heart and my hopelessness that had stolen my desire to nourish my body with food.

- I do not know if it is part of the effects of radiotherapy but for some reason, my jaw snaps involuntarily when eating and even when sleeping. I often bite my tongue which has caused wounds on it. To prevent further accidental bites, I secure my jaw when I sleep by propping it with a pillow to keep it from hanging lose and snapping close when I sleep, or I rest it against my arms or hands so that it stays shut.

- Radiotherapy has affected my salivary glands. Lack of saliva has impeded my ability to talk at length.

This is disheartening – it is sad not to be able to say the words to thank people and answer their questions on how I am or how I feel. It is sad not to be able to talk to my mom, my loved ones, my friends, and everyone around me. It is hard, and even harder not to be sorry for myself.

- I have been coming to this place so many times that it seems it has started to become my home. The patient waiting area has become my living room; the patient changing my dressing room; that big room with the sign "Treatment Room 1", my great bedroom; and the metal moving bed, my bed. It is not a water bed, but I have pillows that prop me up and a sleeping mask that that had been designed for me alone.

- Radiotherapy has damaged the skin of my neck and left it with a darkened color and rough texture of itchy scabs all over. I do not want to endure the pain experienced by other cancer survivors who revealed that people moved away from them upon seeing their damaged skin. I have bought myself turtle-necked shirts to wear to conceal my neck.

- Ask for God's strength, love and healing. And when you do, make sure your hands are open to receive it. There is no way you can receive it if you do not even believe He has His hands out with the thing you asked for right there in front of you.

- This snapped the last knots of doubt that tied me back from allowing God to proceed with His plans in my life. Impatience left me when I accepted that it would take a few more months of

131

chemotherapy, a few more days of radio-therapy, and a few more years of regular check-up. God is in command.

He knows what He is doing. I don't.

Family and Caregivers' Notes and Observations:

132

- I wait in an area close to the Treatment Room. I should be alert to immediately lend assistance in physically supporting my patient because he feels very weak after each radiotherapy session.

Because the drop-off and the pick-up areas are far, I manage to break our travel by bringing him to sit for a while in the several waiting areas between the Treatment Room and the exit door.

- My patient is so despondent that he had expressed his desire to die. Fearing that he might jump off the balcony of the condominium unit we are occupying, I locked the door to the balcony and made it a point to be watchful of him for any attempt on his part to end his life.

THE NATURE OF RADIATION THERAPY

Radiation therapy is given in doses measured in a unit called a gray (Gy) which is a measure of the amount of radiation energy absorbed by 1 kilogram of human tissue.

Different doses of radiation are used for different types of cancer cells. A part of a human body can only receive a dose of up to a maximum safe lifetime dose of radiation and so, treatment protocols consider heavily this safety limitation.

Radiation therapy may be used:

a) as a primary treatment to destroy cancer cells;

b) in combination with other treatments to stop the growth of cancer cells;

c) before another treatment to shrink a tumor;

d) after another treatment to stop the growth of any remaining cancer cells;

e) to relieve symptoms of advanced cancer.

Radiation therapy may be delivered through the following methods:

1. External-beam radiation therapy directs radiation from a machine outside the body onto cancerous cells within the body, thru various technologies such as:

- 3-dimensional conformal radiation therapy (3D-CRT) uses computer software to deliver radiation to very precisely shaped target areas.

- Intensity-Modulated Radiation Therapy (IMRT) uses hundreds of tiny radiation beam-shaping devices, called collimators, which allow for modulation of dose for different areas of a tumor. The goal is to increase radiation dose to the areas that need it and reduce radiation exposure to specific sensitive areas of surrounding normal tissues.

- Image-Guided Radiation Therapy (IGRT) uses repeated scans to determine changes in the tumor's size and location due to treatment. Radiation dose and the position of the patient may be adjusted, eventually reducing the area of exposure of normal tissues.

- Tomotherapy is a type of image-guided intensity-modulated radiation therapy (combined IGRT and IMRT). It is a hybrid between a CT-scan and an external beam radiation therapy machine. The part of the machine that delivers radiation completely rotates around the patient like a CT-scan.

- Stereotactic Radiosurgery (SRS) delivers one or more high doses of radiation to a small tumor through an extremely accurate image-guided tumor targeting and patient positioning, resulting to minimal damage to normal tissues.

This is mostly used for brain or spinal tumors and brain metastases. SRS requires the use of a head frame or other device to immobilize the patient during treatment to ensure that the high dose of radiation is delivered accurately.

- Stereotactic Body Radiation Therapy (SBRT) uses smaller radiation fields and higher doses and treats tumors mostly outside the brain and spinal cord, especially small isolated tumors in the lung and liver. Many doctors refer to SBRT systems by their brand names such as the CyberKnife.

2. Internal radiation therapy or brachytherapy delivers radiation from radioactive material sources placed inside the body. Radioactive isotopes are sealed in tiny pellets or "seeds" which are delivered to the inside of the body by devices such as needles, catheters, or other types of carriers. As the isotopes decay, they give off radiation that damages the cancer cells nearby.

Brachytherapy can be given at a low-dose rate in which cancer cells receive continuous low-dose radiation from the source over a period of time; or at a high-dose rate for a shorter period.

Brachytherapy is delivered depending on the type of cancer:

- Interstitial brachytherapy is used for prostate tumor by placing the radiation source within the tumor tissue.

- Intracavitary brachytherapy is used for tumors that have developed within a cavity of the body. The radiation source is placed within the cavity near the tumor.

- Episcleral brachytherapy is used to treat melanoma inside the eye by attaching the radiation source to the eye.

Brachytherapy may be permanent (usually low-dose rate), in which the radioactive materials are permanently sealed within the body through surgery and left there even after all of the radiation has been given off, without causing any discomfort or harm to the patient.

On the other hand, brachytherapy may also be temporary (usually high-dose rate), in which radiation sources are removed after treatment.

- Systemic radiation therapy delivers radiation through a radioactive substance swallowed or injected by the patient, which travels through the blood to locate and destroy cancerous cells. An example of a type of cancer that is effectively treated by this type of radiation therapy is thyroid cancer.

Radiation therapy is a highly individualized treatment since different cancer types require different approaches. Radiation therapy may be delivered alone

Figure 1. AHMC Façade

TESIS Inter-University Research Centre "Systems and Technologies for Social and Healthcare Facilities"
University of Florence, Italy

133

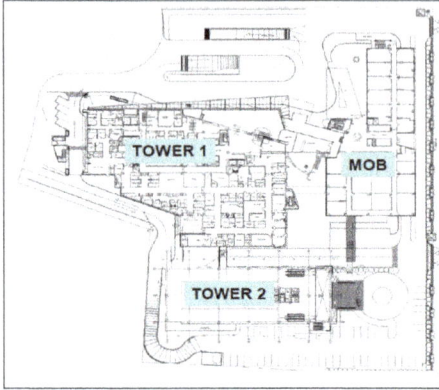

Figure 2. Structures within the AHMC Complex

134

Cancer treatment is an envisioned area of excellence of AHMC and a Cancer Center is progressively being built to attain this vision. The Breast Cancer Unit and Infusion (Chemotherapy) Unit was constructed at the fourth floor of Tower 2 in 2012 and 2013; and the construction of the Radiation Therapy Unit followed immediately after in 2014.

PLANNING AND DESIGNING THE FACILITY

Location of the Radiation Therapy Unit

The Radiation Therapy Unit would have as its site or location the available areas in Tower 2 and the adjoining open area that would be called Tower 2 Annex.

Prioritization and Phasing

The planning, design and construction of a Cancer Radiotherapy Unit has demanding requirements and conditions:
a) very high capital outlay;
b) availability of specialists;and
c) availability of huge spaces for bunkers to contain equipment.

The initial plan was to procure:
a) for diagnosis: 1-PET-CT Scan;
b) for simulation: 1- CT-Simulation;
c) for therapeutic functions: 1-Cyberknife and 2-Tomotherapy equipment.

The initial floor plan to accommodate these huge equipment is shown in Figure 3. However, the very high capital outlay for the procurement of all five equipment made it prudent for AHMC to consider the phasing of equipment procurement and construction.

as the only treatment modality, or it can be used in combination with other modalities such as surgery, chemotherapy, hormone therapy and immunotherapy.

THE ASIAN HOSPITAL AND MEDICAL CENTER (AHMC)

The facility that will be used to demonstrate the translation of the planning and design considerations for a Radiotherapy Unit is the Asian Hospital and Medical Center.
 It is a private hospital in Muntinlupa, Manila founded in 2002. It has a capacity of 310 beds.
AHMC sits on an area of 1.7 hectares and has 3 structures in its complex: Tower 1 and Tower 2 that house the hospital; and the Medical Office Building (MOB) that houses the doctors' clinics. Tower 1 rises up to 10 storeys; Tower 2 to 11 storeys; and the MOB to 7 stories.
AHMC currently offers cancer treatment services in the following areas: breast cancer, chemotherapy, colon cancer, leukemia, lung cancer, melanoma, ovarian cancer, prostate cancer, cervical cancer and lymphoma.

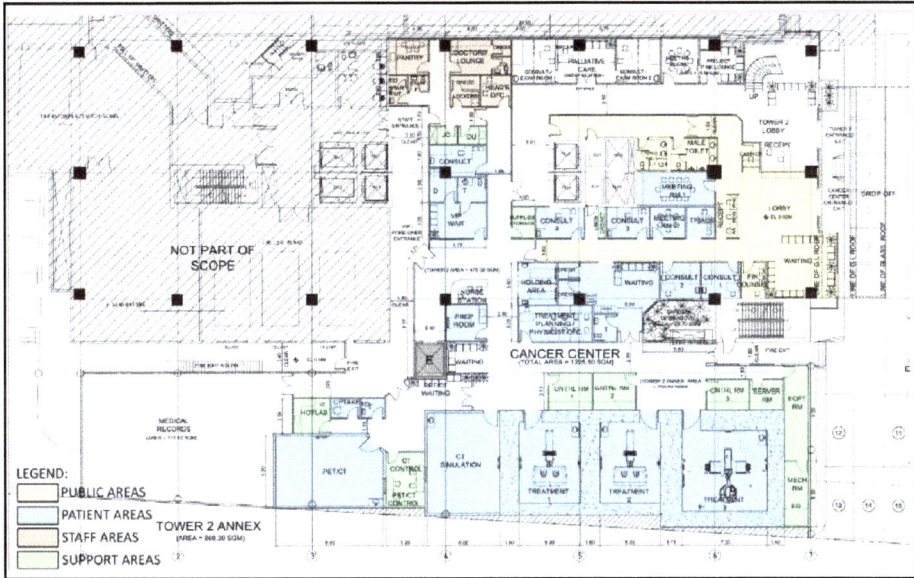

Figure 3. Lower Ground Floor Plan (Original Design)

135

Thus, the design was revised to consider phasing, prioritizing the procurement of 1-Cyberknife and 1-Tomotherapy equipment, both external-beam radiation therapy equipment.

It was decided that in the meantime, diagnosis would be carried out in the existing Imaging Department of the hospital and simulation and treatment both be done on the two equipment that would be procured.

Later, during the construction phase, it was also decided that an internal radiation equipment or brachytherapy equipment was necessary and so, the procurement of the Cyberknife was deferred. Instead, a Brachytherapy equipment would be procured and installed temporarily in the Cyberknife Treatment Room.

The spaces provided in the above Reduced Design are partially listed in figure 5.

Legibility of Design

To ease tension or stress of patients and companions, the design of the facility should be easy to understand.

There are two aspects that contribute to legibility: an organized zoning and a traffic flow that is straightforward and not crisscrossing.

The areas contained in the facility are zoned so that rooms are properly grouped under four different main blocks: public areas (colored yellow), patient areas (colored blue), staff areas (colored orange) and support areas (colored green). Areas of the same color had been grouped, zoned or blocked to assure that flow of traffic by end-users are simple and not crisscrossing.

Please refer to Figure 4.

The most important traffic flow is that which is generated by patients.

General Traffic Flow of Patients is as follows: Please refer to Figure 4.

136

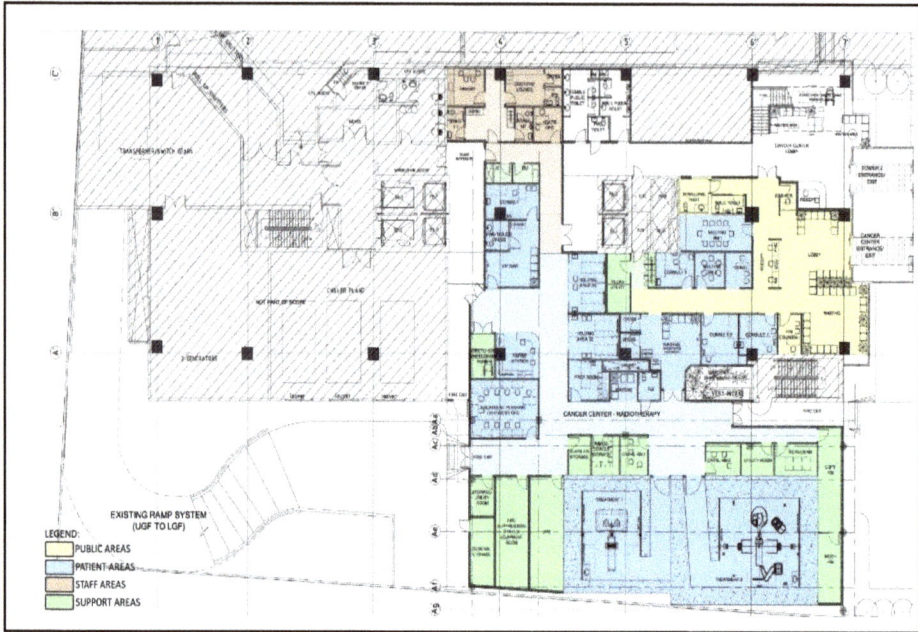

Figure 4. Lower Ground Floor Plan (Reduced Design)

Patient arrives at the Radiotherapy Center at the drop-off point and Main Entrance at the Lower Ground Floor.

1. Patient who is usually accompanied, approaches Reception where a form to be filled is given.

2. Patient or companion fills up the form.

3. Patient submits the form and is given a number.

4. Patient is seen and examined by doctor at one of the Consultation Rooms.

5. Patient enters the patients' area while companion waits in the Main Waiting Area. (Depending on the condition of the patient, companion may be allowed to accompany the patient even in the patient area).

6. Patient changes in one of the Dressing Cubicles, leaves street clothes in the locker, and uses the Toilet if necessary.

7. Patient waits number to be called in the Patient's Waiting Lounge, watches television or reads in the meantime.

8. Patient proceeds to and is serviced in the appropriate procedure room:

a. For simulation at the start of the treatment, patient is fitted with molds and masks and intensity of dose and direction of beams are determined.

b. For radiation, patient undergoes the therapy per the treatment plan and simulation. It can continue for several days as required.

9. After therapy, Patient may sit in the Patient Waiting Lounge or lie in bed at the Holding Area, depending on need after treatment.

10. Patient changes to street clothes in the Dressing Room.

11. Patient drops by Main Waiting Lounge to join companion.

12. Patient and companion leave the Radiotherapy Unit.

Space or Room	Qty	Unit Area	Total Area	Notes
Public Areas				
Reception	1.0	8.60	8.60	2-receptionists; provide counter
Cashier	1.0	3.25	3.25	1-cashier; provide secure cage
Financial Counsel	1.0	3.25	3.25	Small meeting table for 4
Entrance				
General Waiting/ Lobby	1.0	69.50	69.50	For general public not allowed entry to patient areas
Toilets				
Male	1.0	7.00	7.00	1-WC, 1-LAV, 1-URINAL
Female/PWD	1.0	4.40	4.40	1-WC, 1-LAV
Sub-Total			**96.00**	
Staff Areas				
Head's Office	1.0	6.90	6.90	Office table, guest chair
Meeting Rooms				
Meeting Room 1	1.0	18.40	18.40	For 10 people
Meeting Room 2	1.0	7.40	7.40	For 6 people
Staff Lounge and Pantry	1.0	10.00	10.00	For staff lounging and dining
Doctors' Lounge, Toilet, Dressing	1.0	14.90	14.90	For doctors exclusive use
Staff Lockers	1.0	2.00	2.00	For staff personal effects
Staff Toilet				
- Male	1.0	1.30	1.30	1-WC. 1-LAV
- Female	1.0	4.26	4.26	1-WC, 2-LAV
Sub-Total			**65.16**	

137

Figure 5. The spaces provided in the Reduced Design are partially listed in this tabulation

TESIS Inter-University Research Centre "Systems and Technologies for Social and Healthcare Facilities"
University of Florence, Italy

Design that is Kind to Patients

Radiation therapy takes a long a time. Patient returns to the facility every day for several days, even for a month or longer, depending on the type and advancement of the cancer.

Thus, the facility should evoke an atmosphere that is welcoming, warm, and comfortable, evoking pleasant feelings.

Radiation equipment are contained in bunkers of reinforced concrete poured monolithically, with wall thickness as much as 1.60 meters and roof thickness as much as 1.50 meters.

No window or any punctures are allowed for the assurance of proper shielding. Entrance to the Treatment Room is through a maze to contain the radioactive rays.

As such, it can evoke the atmosphere of a prison if interior design is not properly handled. The radiation therapy equipment are huge and fearsome.

Entrance into a Radiation Therapy Treatment Room is a fearsome experience. The patient is confronted by a huge machine that fills the room. The therapy procedure is long and repetitive. Thus, the interior design of the treatment room should be a great concern to ease the suffering of the patient and provide a reprieve to him/her.

The following photos are some of the design features that have been conceptualized or implemented as wall and ceiling features for treatment rooms.

While patient is being exposed to radiation, positive distraction may also be provided by music that is familiar to the patient. The patient may even be encouraged to bring his or her favorite music to be played while treatment is on-going.

COUNTERACTING PSYCHOLOGICAL ATTACK ON PATIENTS

Cancer Radiotherapy Treatment Units are known to be one of the most fearsome facility in hospitals. The fierce psychological attack on people can definite-

Figure 6. Soft, comfortable, home-like furniture

Figure 7. Pleasant, airy, welcoming lobby

Figure 8. Cheerful, pleasant Patients' Waiting Lounge

138

Figure 9. Reinforcing bars of bunkers

Figure 10. Thick concrete walls of bunkers

ly be assuaged by patient-centeredness in physical facilities planning and design.

REFERENCES

Alviso, Roscoe. Blog. http://coxisacancersurvivor.blogspot.sg/

Asian Hospital and Medical Center. *Various documents for the planning, design and construction of the Radiotherapy Unitl.*

Luis and Associates. *Construction Documents for the Asian Hospital and Medical Center Radiotherapy Unit.* 2014

Radiological Society of North America. *Information on Various Radiation Therapy Technologies.* 2013

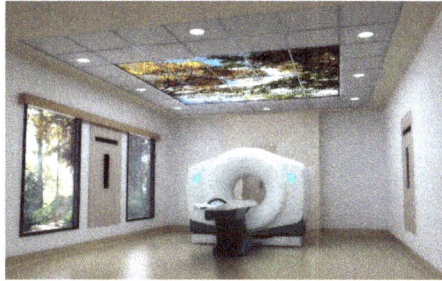

Figure 11. Simulated window with view

139

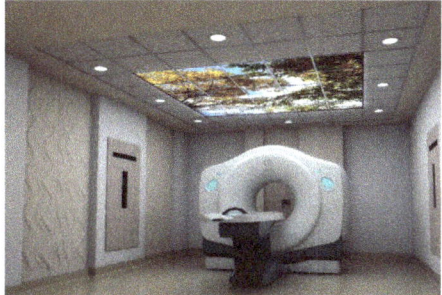

Figure 12. Textured beige wall; ceiling décor of trees and sky

Figure 13. Cove lighting and colored green wall; ceiling décor of trees and sky

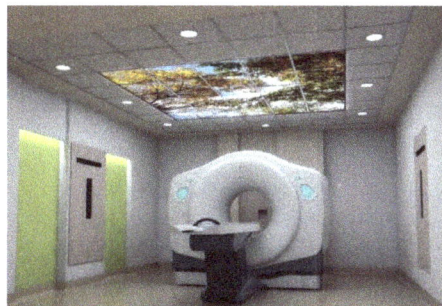

Figure 14. Textured green wall; ceiling décor of trees and sky

140

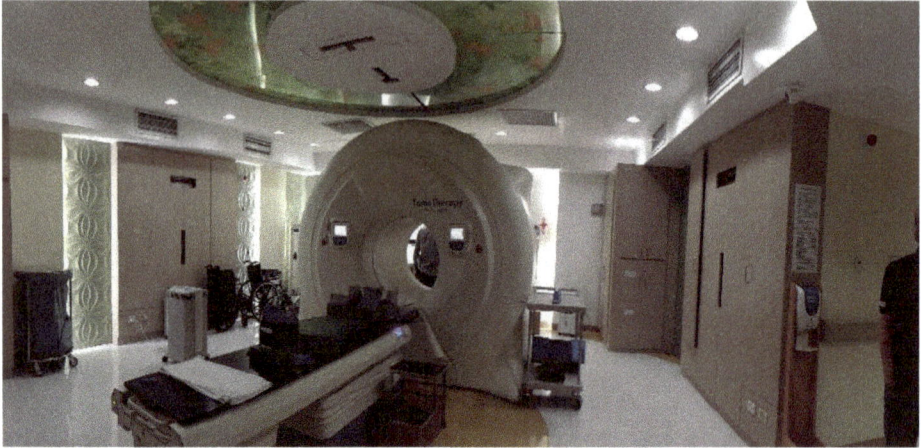

Figure 15. Overall ambience of a Tomotherapy Treatment Room

Figure 16. Maple leaves on green background as ceiling treatment, integrated with the laser beam enclosure

USNRC Technical Training Center. *Dose Standards and Methods for Protection Against Radiation and Contamination*

Veterans Health Administration Office of Facilities Management, Department of Veterans Affairs. *VA Design Guide Radiation Therapy Service*, April 2008.

Website: Cancer Treatment Centers of America

Website: National Cancer Institute

Wikipedia, the Free Encyclopedia. *Various information on cancer and radiation therapy.*

The Very Nature of Medicine has been Transformed and Hospital Design must Reflect that Change

Rodney Hill

rhill@arch.tamu.edu
Presidential Professor, Texas A&M University, World Future Society

Emerging technologies will shape and change hospital design due to a shortage of health-care personnel and expanding global population.

DESCRIPTION

Wearable monitoring technology exists today and is a rapidly expanding field with 500 million smart phones and 43,000 monitoring apps. Sensors are tiny, cheap, energy efficient and, most importantly, connected. High tech healthcare personnel can monitor all of their patients every day, hour and minute and when readings indicate a health problem, the patient can be notified to report to the hospital or physician's facility. This is important as it can indicate a disease before it becomes critical.

Contact lenses are being developed that monitor health by constantly being in contact with bodily fluids. An implant the size of a grain of rice can monitor your bodily functions and send data back to your healthcare provider.

How will space be reprogrammed to accommodate accelerating technology?

Architects must examine the space requirements for Robots, AI and healthcare technology personnel to monitor 7-11 billion patients between now and 2100.

METHOD & ANALYSIS

Articles from medical and technical journals, Internet blogs as well as research treatments in field trials, which show the accelerating, change of medicine and physical facilities.

Robots are increasingly proving beneficial helping healthcare providers with their duties.

Surgical robots are performing minimum invasive surgery.

Telemedicine can enable a physician to converse with patients globally.

Robots can also be directed by GPS to go to patients' rooms to deliver medicine and exercise patients.

Robotic limbs have been developed to function like natural body parts.

Hospitals will have to be reconfigured to combine high tech computer scientists, robots and physicians for the creation of the bionic man.

Will hospitals be more like high tech computer centers with cloud storage, and requiring many times more energy and technology than the present hospitals?

142

Doximity is a crowdsourcing App for physicians and has 400,000 members, about half of the country's active physicians.

A physician can post a problem or image and ask if anyone knows a solution or recommendation.
Washington Post, Dec. 9, 2014

With innovative digital technologies, cloud computing and machine learning, the medicalized smartphone is going to upend every aspect of health care.
Wallstreet Journal, Jan. 10, 2015

Colorimetrix, a new app developed by University of Cambridge researchers, turns a smartphone into a portable medical diagnostic device.

The app could make monitoring conditions such as HIV, tuberculosis, malaria, diabetes, kidney disease, and urinary tract infections clearer and easier for both patients and doctors, and could eventually be used to slow or limit the spread of pandemics in the developing world, the researchers say.
KurzweilAI, March 24, 2014

Google and Novartis announced that they're teaming up to develop contact lenses that monitor glucose levels and automatically adjust their focus. But these could be just the start of a clever new product category.

From cancer detection and drug delivery to reality augmentation and night vision, our eyes offer unique opportunities for both health monitoring and enhancement.
MIT Technology Review, July 29, 2014

In this session we will explore the facilities that require a separate clean building to eliminate the spread of pathogens into the integration of biological and medical combinations.

RESULTS & OUTCOMES

Gene therapy and stem cell research is changing the face of medicine.

Genetically modified humans can be constructed today and will be ubiquitous in the future. By 2020, your DNA can be sequenced for under $10. Medicine will be customized to the individual.

Almost every organ in the body can be printed using the patient's own cells.

What type of clean rooms and technology do you need to accommodate and combine surgical rooms, 3D printers, cognitive implants, brain-computer interface, exoskeleton fitting and spinal cord regeneration?

The new development of a MRI machine to the size of a briefcase and the scanner the size of an iPhone that sees vivid, moving, 3-D images of what is inside the body could reprioritize rooms and space in the hospital.

DISCUSSION & CONCLUSION

Should we call this facility something other than a hospital since the word hospital triggers so many images of past conformations?

Should we call this facility something other than a hospital since the word hospital triggers so many images of past conformations?

Strategic Design of Hospitals by Life-Cycles

Thomas Schinko
Heinrich Limacher

thomas.schinko@vasconi.fr
Vasconi Architectes

143

"The new construction of a building is the particular case of its conversion." (F. Haller).
The design of a hospital is a very complex task as the influences on the design are numerous. Hospitals have to deal with a great variety of services: highly technical examination areas, operation theatres, wards, logistics and sophisticated technical systems.
In many hospitals today, especially the new mono-bloc and mono-space structures, these services are mixed all together in the same building complex. Designs of processes are usually driven by short term considerations and neglect the fact that a hospital is facing permanent conversions, which risk to affect their functionality.
This way the lifetime of the whole complex is determined by the services with the shortest expected operating life causing major impact on the whole system: The reconversion works of these facilities impact the whole hospital, causing expensive temporary relocation of non-concerned services and sometimes demolishing and reconstruction.
The Life cycle hospital approach integrates already in an early design stage the lifecycle of different services by taking into account their specific lifetime. The design has to anticipate how to refurbish, extend or replace parts of the building without impacting the whole process. This design approach creates a new typology of hospitals and helps clients to schedule in advance refurbishments and minimize loss of investments.
The Lifecycle Hospital is a modular hospital design approach, looking to implement structures that offer a maximum of flexibility. The technical infrastructures are designed with the same modular approach and can this way facilitate maintenance by offering enough flexibility to adapt services to new technical constraints. By adopting a radical "object-based-design" approach these hospitals will rely on prefabricated module elements that only will be assembled on site. This will create the possibility to achieve better coordinated and maintainable building components with a high-end, industrial quality standard.
The object based design seeks to reduce the whole building's systems to a set of identical building components that enhance standardization.
The Lifecycle Hospital looks to anticipate future developments and new trends in healthcare to provide a prefect tool that can easily adapt to a changing demands by integrating latest technologies and providing space for dynamic examination- and therapy areas.
The Lifecycle Hospital design approach is illustrated on recent hospital projects of the office.

144

INTRODUCTION

Europe - especially France - has a long history of hospital design with a great variety of approaches. Starting from the medieval "Hotel-Dieu" right in the city centre next to the cathedral, a place that was dealing with a population that did not fit in the regulated system of the social community of the city (beggars, sick people, old people etc.) to the "hospices" outside of the boundary of the city, to protect the city from rising number of diseases. But over the centuries even these "hospices" were integrated in the expanding cities and within centuries these hospitals grew to cities within the city, offering a great variety of different buildings that tried to tie up with the growing demand of healthcare within our societies.

The historical plans of the "hospices civils" of Strasbourg illustrate in an exemplary way this juxtaposition of several typologies of buildings that create a living organism, that perfectly integrates into the city, but still confirmed its specific isolated condition. The hospices of Strasbourg were founded in 637 and became a civic hospital under the direction of the city hall in 1263.

The Hospices civils are still in use and collect a heritage of buildings representing all ages starting from the 13th century till today.

The heterogeneous juxtaposition of different buildings without a higher ranking organization illustrates that there has been no long term vision to develop a consistent and efficient operational masterplan layout.

The reasons are well known, as there are specific factors that were driving hospital design in the past:

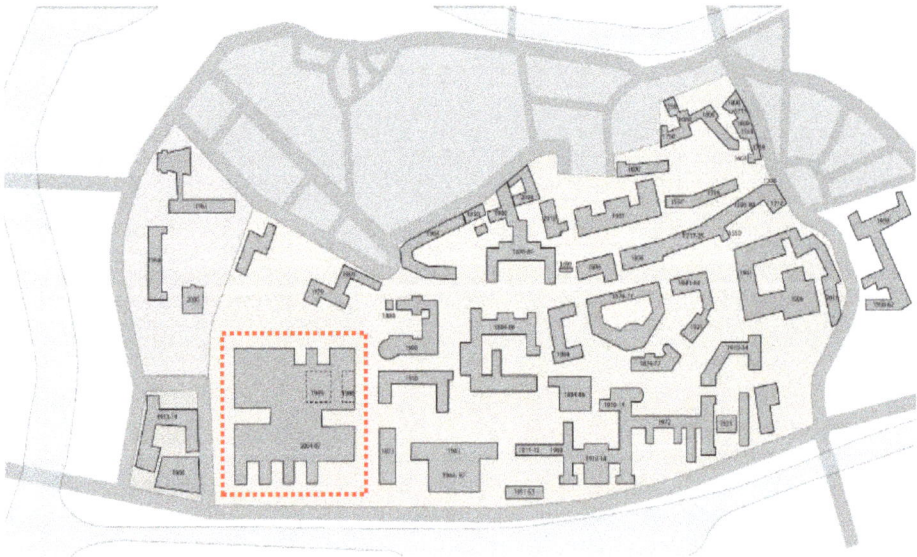

Figure 1. The medical campus of the civic hospital in Strasbourg showing the different stages of his development starting with the initial dark grey site of the "hospices" of the 13th century and the following extensions till todays new civic hospital in light grey on the lower left part of the site

- A financial split between investment and running costs, so there was never a strong incentive to consider the efficiency and recurrent costs of buildings.
- The primary target to keep capital projects within budget and time - this easily jeopardized the long term functionality and efficiency of facilities.
- The functional lifespan of a health building is usually shorter than its technical lifespan. In practice this has often meant holding on dysfunctional health buildings for far too long.
- Health assets – square meters – have been "free" for health care providers in the past. Once a capital project had been approved, the expense was covered by the government budget or from insurance funds and the providers ran little or no risks.
- The assumption that a hospital is a unique item of property that is suitable for few other functions and therefore cannot be released from the perimeter of hospital premises.

In 2003, the French government launched an ambitious plan to leave the old way of catching up with backlog maintenance and developed a forward-looking approach that considers the real cost of capital assets in the future. The investment plan 'Hôpital 2007" focused on a change of governance within the hospital facilities, providing more autonomy to the hospitals for their development and a benchmarking tarification per act ("t2a") rising awareness for a more efficient organization of the hospitals.
The trend was to concentrate care provision in large healthcare facilities and compounds. This has been driven partly by professional factors: different medical disciplines are encouraged to work together in a multidisciplinary context to enhance the quality of care (organized in so called "pôles d'activités").

As our office was working for the new civic hospital within the compound of such a historical "medical campus", we thought to bring this ancestral development to an end by gathering most of the services in a striking modern and efficient modular building.

145

But delivering the building in 2009 we already were confronted to major shift in the French healthcare system towards an increasing number of ambulatory care that needed additional operation theatres able to handle outdoor patience for day clinic interventions.
Once again the hospital reveals to be a place of eternal change and the new hospital will be just another facility in the medical campus and already next year a new building with 18 operation theatres will add a new asset designed for new activities.
Hospitals and hospital design is in a permanent change and it is difficult to predict the evolution of the future hospitals. In close collaboration with Heinrich Limacher and based on his long expertise in running and designing hospitals we developed an internal research about how we can design better hospital buildings able to adapt to future changes. As life is change, we call this new methodology: The Life cycle hospital ©.

THE HOSPITAL A VERY SPECIFIC BUILDING

What makes hospital design so unpredictable and what creates the dynamic changes in hospital design?
A simple answer is, that there is no other

146

building typology that has such a degree of complexity and integrates in one single envelope so many different functions as a hospital.

There are complex examination and treatment areas, where every space is different and has to implement different constraints. On the other hand a hospital is a hospitality facility that has to integrate all kind of logistical services like wards for patients with a complex kitchen and canteen for the stuff, a big laundry, a sterilization unit, a pharmacy and other logistical facilities.

A hospital has to satisfy as well all demands of a complex administration building, offering flexible and confidential office space, meeting rooms and public facilities like auditoriums and teaching facilities.

Then a hospital has to deal with a lot of very complex technical installations for the building services itself, as well as for the medical treatment (integration of medical gases, nuclear radiation, automatic vehicle systems etc. ...). Very challenging supply and disposal facilities represent another complex program to integrate, in order to avoid to mix clean and dirty logistical flows within the building. All these elements represent a very complex and sometimes contradictory program with very different operational demands.

THE MAIN CHALLENGES IN HOSPITAL DESIGN

Every hospital is a unique project and has to integrate very unique features, as hospitals are closely linked to the local demands of the community, the treated pathologies and activities.

The growing specialization in medicine asks for highest standards with regards to spatial and specific technical design.

Figure 2. The New civic Hospital delivered in 2010 should integrate in one modular building all services and was meant to be able to integrate future extensions – unfortunately an ambulatory care unit could not be integrated due to technical and administrative reasons – a new building will be added end of this year

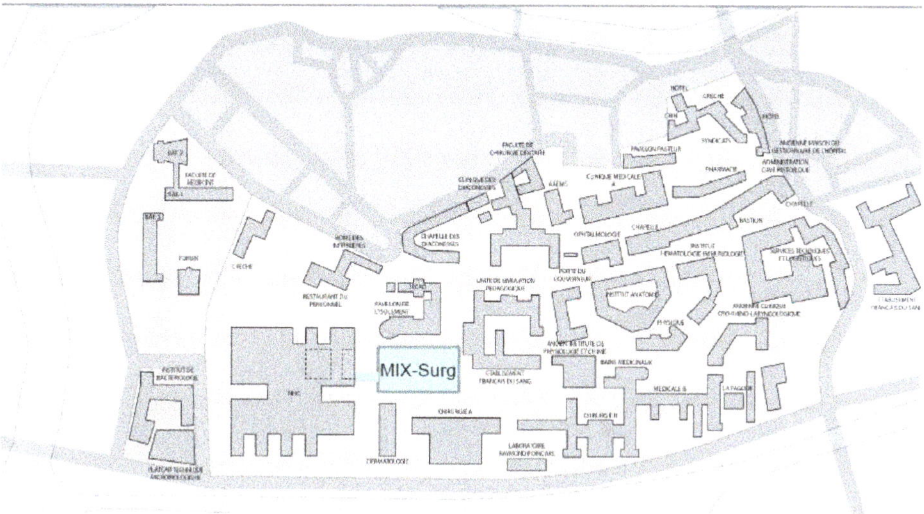

Figure 3. The medical campus will be extended this year by the new building of the "Institut de Chriurgie Guidée par l'image" on the campus of the IHU Strasbourg

Every service has a different layout and there is not a lot of repetitive elements.

The technological progress is another challenge for the architects, who have to integrate the latest technologies that rarely are clearly defined whenever architects start to work on the projects, adding a lot of unknown parameters in the design process.

This usually requires a permanent redesign or adaptation of the project to keep up with the technological progress. The technological progress is not only limited to the treatment, but includes new demands and desires of the patients, offering multimedia terminals, internet based information systems and enhanced patient centred care.

But the most difficult part of the project might be the intensive collaborative use of spaces. Hospital spaces have to satisfy the needs of numerous groups of users with conflicting interests. This means that the design has to include all concerned users in the design process to guarantee acceptable and practical solutions. A patient room is not like a hotel room designed to correspond only to the specific demands of the patients, but has to integrate the needs for treatment, as well as hygienic, operational and technical demands.

The design process is this very complex and needs a close collaboration of very different design partners. Every design partner has a completely different idea of how the hospital should work and the architects have to moderate and lead the design process without forgetting the view of the users.

A specific challenge is to find the right balance between the conflicting interests of the different groups of users, especially as rarely the stuff involved in the design process will be the stuff running the facility. Hospitals have an important turn over and the medical stuff is moving quickly between services and even different hospitals.

Figure 4. As experts flourish in the development of hospital-projects, it is difficult to find a common vision of the ideal hospital

148

COMMON DEFICIENCIES IN CURRENT HOSPITAL BUILDINGS

When we are looking closely in current hospital buildings we find the following problems:

- The offer and the layout of spaces are not satisfactory. Processes are usually complex and cumbersome.
- The technical building systems and the outer shell of the buildings have reached the end of their service life span (SLP) and whenever renovation of the services is decided, new regulations have to be integrated into the design.
- The room sizes and their standards are insufficient and old and because of reduced hospitalization due to permanent progress in the medical treatment, the number of beds are too high.
- Lack of ambulatory care and outpatient clinics.
- Different floor levels and heights make it difficult to connect or move services between buildings.

FINANCIAL TRAP: UPFRONT INVESTMENTS

Architects have a long run experience to develop flexible buildings and therefore tried to design hospitals that anticipate future changes in the services.

There are various approaches where some of the most advanced approaches are Moshe Zahry's masterplan for the Sheba Medical Centre in Ramat Gan or the "monospace hospital" as developed by Brunet and Saunier in France.

But all of these approaches seeking for flexible structures need upfront investments for later conversions. But even if we try our best to integrate future changes in the layout and organization of hospitals, we have to admit that:

- Technology and treatments develop so fast, that it is difficult to really know what will be needed in the hospital in the next years and therefore the infrastructure created to accommodate the extensions or implement new services are no longer up-to-date.

- Still, any changes within these flexible structures will need temporary structures and buildings to allow to maintain services in function. The heavy conversions within a flexible structures will still impact the hospital as a whole and deteriorate the exploitation of all other services.

Therefore the flexible and extendible structures are more a theoretical approach than a real solution for hospitals that want to be able to keep up with the future evolution of healthcare services. The investments needed to implement this flexibility are lacking in the immediate practice and have no significance in the near future.
It is undoubtedly a big advantage to have a flexible modular hospital design,

Figure 5. Integrate Moshe Zahry's hospital. Extensions laboratories: even extended still old structures within the laboratories avoid efficient and modern practice. The idea to strategically position changing rooms to be converted to future extensions

149

Figure 6. The Monospace hospital "Centre Hospitalier de Marne-la-vallée" represents the most radical model for a flexible hospital design. The continuous, homogeneous organisational structure of endless combinatory possibilities is secured by a three dimensional frame of 7.2m x 7.2m x 4.2 m, i.e. the slightest change in grid sizes will jeopardize the whole modular concept

but "monospace hospitals" have no significant advantage compared to other hospitals, as still future works impact heavily the whole hospital facilities.

These upfront investments are unnecessary and hospitals can be built far less expensive.

STRUCTURAL DIFFICULTIES IN CURRENT HOSPITAL BUILDINGS

Besides the complexity of integrating different functional services, hospitals have to deal with facilities with very different lifecycles.

While the average lifecycle of the building itself is around 40 years, the different facilities within the hospital have very different lifecycles:

- Highly equipped areas like operation theatres, radiology and imagery etc. have average lifecycles of 15 - 20 years
- Outpatient clinics and medical units 25 – 30 years
- Supply and disposal areas 30 - 40 years
- Administration 30 - 40 years.

The scheme below illustrates how a typical hospital integrates areas with different lifecycle within the same envelope, which means that finally the lifecycle of

150

the building as a whole is determined by the unit with the shortest service life period (SLP).

As hospitals are planned mainly due to functional demands all services are nested and interconnected in a way that whenever a service has to be restructured the hospital as a whole has to suffer the heavy intervention, causing a loss of activity and this way loss of revenues.

This nesting of facilities, the vertical and horizontal mix of facilities with different lifecycles, can even determine the whole lifespan of a hospital and still functioning services have to be sacrificed prematurely for the deficiencies of other services. On a long term this configuration of hospitals is very cost intensive!

CONCLUSIONS

Adaptability is a crucial point in a lifecycle perspective, in order to maintain the functionality of the hospital and thereby contribute to a positive value over the life-cycle. The period between each refurbishment is called the service

life period (SLP).

This is the period when the use of the building is more or less static. If the service life period is the same as the whole lifetime of the building, there is no need for adaptability, but if the service life period is particularly short, then the need for adaptability is particularly important. The use in hospital buildings is particularly dynamic with high demands for adaptability.

If the SLP is short, investment in adaptability will be worthwhile, whereas if the service life period is long, investment in long-lasting solutions will be advantageous.

Adaptability has three major dimensions:

- Flexibility: possibility of changing layout – the space distribution.
- Generality : the possibility of changing functions.
- Elasticity: the possibility of changing volume.

Different level of adaptability can be distinguished:

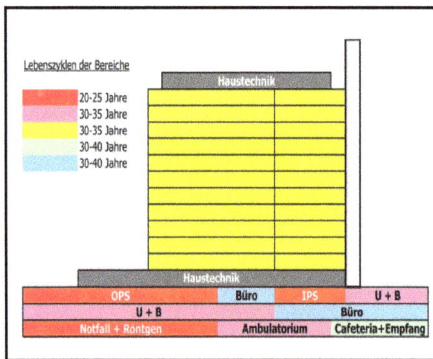

Figure 7. A typical hospital design with nested functions organized following operational constraints, but without consideration for the different SLP

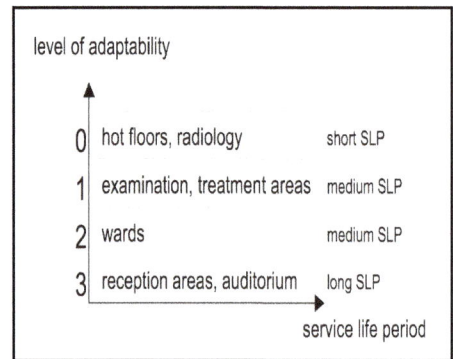

Figure 8. Scheme illustrating the different levels of adaptability in relation to the Service Life Period (SLP)

In order to create future-proof facilities, that can be easily adapted to future needs and demands of patients and treatment, we suggest to create a new approach, called the Life cycle Hospital.

This approach seeks to:
- Harmonize the life span of hospital buildings with their useful life.
- To anticipate within the design process renovation, conversion and extension measures for future generations.
- To take into account effective process orientation of the layout.

All this means that we have to develop new hospital structures able to adjust to the increasing demand for more flexibility without impacting the existing facilities. A solution can be the modular construction that combines units with equivalent life cycle in separate buildings. The hospital layout should of course be based on a modular structure and should respect the functionality and cost-effectiveness of internal processes. The layout of the masterplan should provide back-up areas for replacement and extension of buildings, quite like agriculture provides fallow land.

We will call this new hospital design approach the Life-Cycle Hospital.

SOMEWHERE IN SWITZERLAND: AN EXAMPLE OF REFURBISHMENT OF AN EXISTING HOSPITAL INTO A LIFE CYCLE HOSPITAL

We see here a showcase for a grown structure of modern hospital in Switzerland. The new extensions of the hospital are arranged right in the centre of the existing hospital site, maximizing this way the impact of the construction site on the surrounding existing hospital fa-

cilities. The consequences of conversions and renovations within ongoing operations:
- Great emissions of dust and noise, impacting the whole hospital site.
- Need of expensive temporary buildings to house services that are directly impacted by the works.
- All this represents a great strain to the constitution of patients and staff and causes loss of activity and occupancy of the existing services.

From a construction and economical point of view looking at the exploitation of the facilities, this is a very cost intensive way to adapt hospitals to future needs.

But how can the masterplan of the hospital be transferred in stages into a life-cycle hospital?

The following two elements are mandatory to succeed the transition:
1. Transition of the existing building organization in a new layout in several stages.
2. By assuring a good connection between existing and new buildings, recent investments will be saved.

This approach of renewal of the hospital site in stages will be far easier to finance and loss of already done investments will be considerably reduced.

The scheme below shows the strategic masterplan for the new hospital layout. A large gallery will interconnect the new with the existing buildings.

The new extensions of the hospital including the emergency unit and the ambulatory care for outpatients will be built in the remote eastern area of the site. New wards will be situated right in

151

TESIS Inter-University Research Centre "Systems and Technologies for Social and Healthcare Facilities"
University of Florence, Italy

TESIS

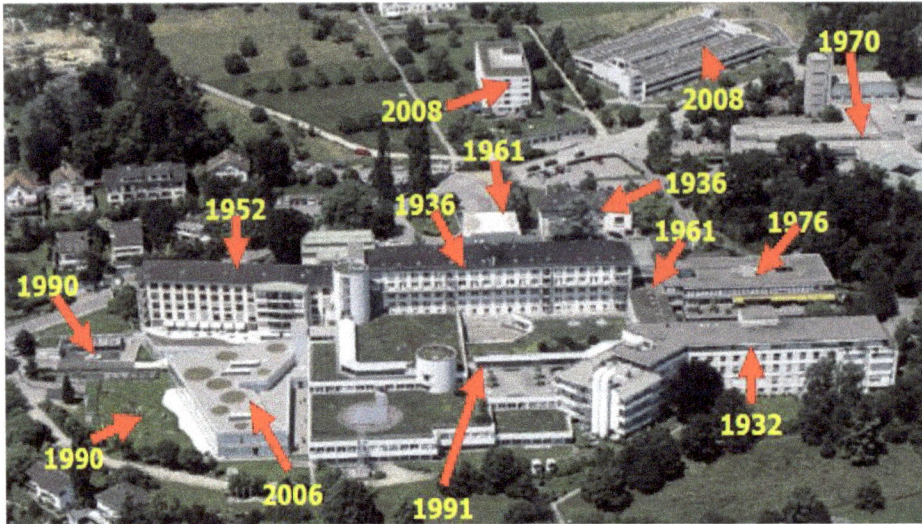

Figure 9. Example of refurbishment of an existing hospital into a Life Cycle Hospital in Switzerland

152

front. This way the hospital will be slowly transformed into a life cycle hospital and any change on one of the services won't affect the work of the other services of the hospital.

THE "LIFE-CYCLE HOSPITAL" APPROACH

A series of competitions in Morocco end of last year gave us the opportunity to look how the life cycle hospital approach can be applied in the design of new university hospitals of more than 500 wards, integrating a complete hospital with operation theatres, emergency units, radiology and imagery, wards and all logistical services.

The "Centre Hospitalier Universitaire" in Agadir (University Hospital in Agadir).

The building is divided in two volumes linked together by a large covered gal-

lery. Linking bridges are interconnecting the two volumes. A huge underground level integrates on the southern side the delivery and logistical areas (kitchens, sterilization unit, general warehouses and workshops, laundry etc.) and the parking for the visitors.

On the ground-level the northern lower building integrates all facilities that have a high level of heavy technical equip-

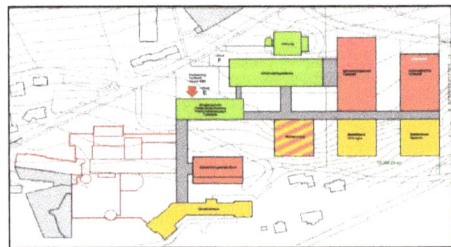

Figure 10. Scheme illustrating a stepwise transformation of an existing hospital masterplan in a life cycle masterplan. Investments of the past still will be integrated in the new scheme and actively support the new scheme. This way investments of the past will not be lost, while future extensions and changes can be anticipated

Figure 11. The life cycle approach allows to focus the architectural design on elements that have a longer lifespan and this way look for more durable design and materials, while the factory part of the building can provide a playground for new modular and adaptable structure systems and envelope materials. The life cycle approach is as well a way to better focus investments in the greater context of the huge hospital programs

153

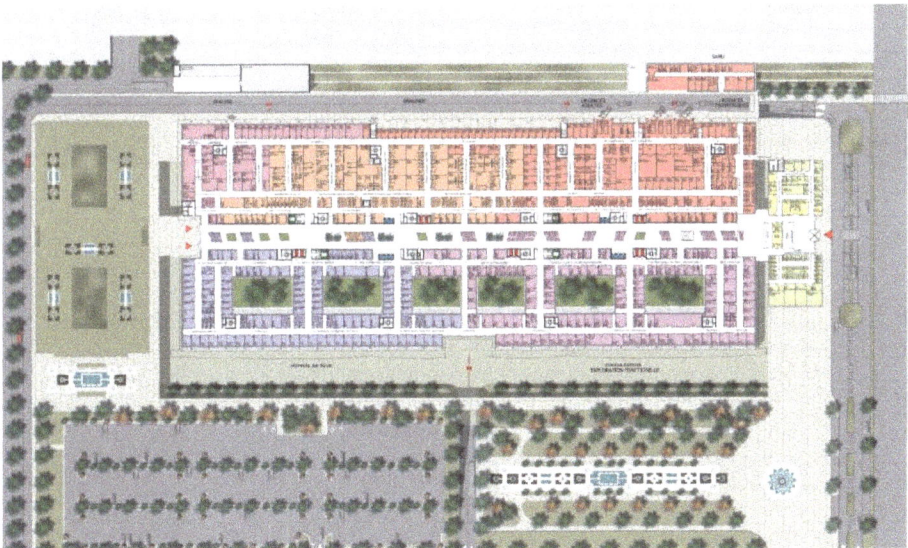

Figure 12. The life cycle hospital is not functionally different from other hospitals. It is therefore not less functional or less aesthetical as other hospital designs. It is just more performant in the near future and allows to better focus investments in the building and masterplan design.

ment like the radiology, imagery and the emergency unit right next to the front entrance.

The front desk is situated on the eastern side facing the medical university. He is inside a tensile structure, offering an inviting light flooded and stress relieved welcome experience in an atmosphere of lightness.

The day clinic and the outpatient's consultation are situated under the southern building that houses mainly the wards, gathering this way the longer life cycle facilities of the hospital. The northern lower building gathers on the first floor the operation theatres and combines all lower life cycles activities of the hospital. This way any refurbishment in the heavy technical parts of the hospital won't affect the hospital as a whole, but will remain limited to a small part of the hospital and causes minor impact on the functioning services of the hospital.

Art and Science of Health and Welfare Facilities and Town of the Sustainable Society

Masato Utsunomiya

mutsunomiya@k-ito.co.jp
K-ITO Architects & Engineers Inc., Tokyo, Japan

When viewing architectural issues from health and welfare facilities and considering how to lead and share in a sustainable society, we can present two design methods: the first, learning from medical "art and science": we rethink our design challenges in terms of "art and science"; the second, we consider clinical pathway-based design in the health and welfare space: this system suggests a way by which we can cooperate with medical and office staff as well as area residents.

Keywords: *art and science, clinical pathway-based design, sustainability, logistics, smart healthcare city*

BACKGROUND
Sustainability and Health

Attempts are being made to seek answers for the design of sustainable buildings through the reduction of environmental load and the improvement of environmental quality. The wisdom of life and health garnered from remaining indigenous traditional housing with high environmental performance is of value.

When we study environmental quality in contemporary architecture, we must consider not only environmental technology, but also the wisdom of housing and health.

As for living in sustainable buildings, it is important that there be a good structure for both human health and global environment preservation.

It is valuable for us to live with the feeling of light, air current, temperature, humidity and energy as well as to visualize them. It is important that this broadly nurtures a sense of values that are good for both humanity and the global environment.

Making a "strong intention toward health" is an important theme of the sustainable society.

Other than sustainable architecture, it is clear that methods of healthful living are not only brought about through sports clubs, but by better local communities as well.

In ancient times, tea was a medicinal herb, but it is spreading through the world as a source of rich communication now.

Moreover, we can also enjoy a rich commonality among traditional performing arts around the world.

We are consistent in valuing the residential and communal health culture that is rooted in each culture and climate. In essence, humankind's desire for health must be global. Surely, there is value in a sustainable society where collaborating on healthy living is important.

PROGRAM
Health and welfare architecture as a medical vessel for "Art & Science"

The future of healthcare design for everyone is basic and new.

A sustainable hospital building is a vessel for the recovery of health. It prompts people to recognize a healthy global environment in harmony with nature through cooperation based on shared values and participation in the planning. A life spent healthily through better communication and beneficial physical exercise was, is, and will continue to be most important.

We value "health" and life that cultivates a rich culture in which citizens cooperate on a daily basis. Achieving environ-

mental sustainability and housing is an important point of view.

To accomplish this, we should learn from "Art and Science" which continues to be a theme of medical care, more specifically: the art of medicine and the art of healing. Practicing the "Art and science of health and welfare facility architecture and towns in the sustainable period" is very effective.

When working harmoniously with the planning of a hospital, we are conscious of the ethics of architecture meeting medical ethics and nursing ethics.

The ethics of future hospital architecture may be created as a synthesis of these.

I cannot help but desire that hospital buildings that are vessels of health and welfare will be vessels of "art and science" as well.

As for "art" and "science," obviously the intention of the search is different: each one is developed and, then, a synthesis occurs.

For example: Japan is facing "an ultra-low birthrate and an aging society" ahead of the rest of the world; therefore, we will review the role of health and welfare facilities in every area; and are, then, going to begin strengthening and

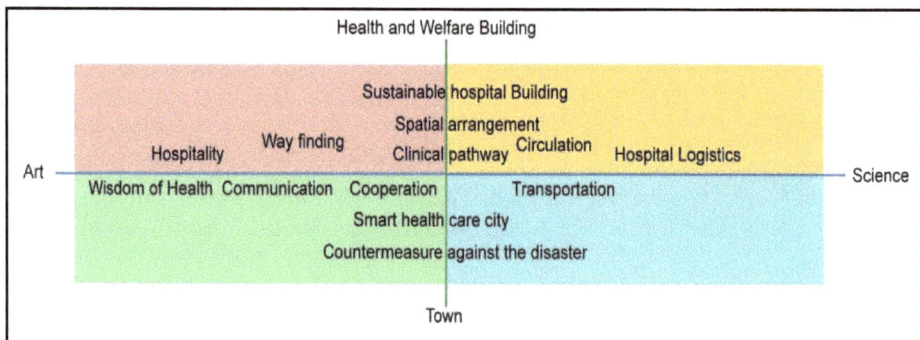

Figure 1. Terms located on "Art and Science" grid and "Health and Welfare Building–Town" grid

Figure 2. Nihon University Hospital (2014)

creating community, health, welfare and family cooperation.

The "Art and Science" of all the citizens of the whole area are necessary for this. A "clinical pathway-based design by regional alliances" will be created, and the role of each health and welfare facility clarified. It is important to design both town and architectural space that leads to continuous improvement and restoration of patients' health as well as to design a safe working environment for medical teams and staff.

Clinical- pathway partnership-based design

Partnership makes for wonderful and gratifying "art". A clinical pathway that is a partnership between the medical team and patient is expected to demonstrate an effect on the healing and recovery of health. It is prepared for both medical team and patient. The health recovery process created by a medical team makes full use of wisdom and is based on science.

On the clinical pathway of the medical team, the following information is diagrammed: When? Who? What kind of symptoms? What medical practice has been done? How will health be restored? The degree of freedom and time in a patient's daily activities is also recorded.

As for the clinical pathway of the patient, the preparation for the treatment and the degree of freedom in daily activities (meals, the range of walking, shower and bathroom use and discharge, etc.) are diagrammed and handed to the patient.

In the medical treatment "the person, action and time" are checked.

With the clinical pathway as protocol, hospital building design that harmonizes medical practice and architectural space is possible.

Specifically, in case of architectural de-

Figure 3. Niigata City General Hospital (2007)

Figure 4. Tochigi Prefecture Medical Association Hot Springs Shiobara Hospital (2007)

sign, the following can be checked and used to complement the medical treatment: What equipment is to be used? How can measurements for safe use in the area be ensured? What environment is it?

More importantly, through cooperation it becomes possible to establish medical risk management results and considerations in the building space.

Clinical pathway-based time and space is a medical tool whereby a medical team can practice a safe-care process. As for the patient, along with the recovery of health, it is a tool for living that leads to a continuous improvement in the range of activities and the degree of freedom.

These two spaces will merge, harmonize and separate in the hospital architectural space. One effective method: replace this spatial characteristic with a hospital architecture design challenge utilizing a clinical pathway to develop a protocol of hospital architecture section design.

Clinical pathway-based design adds the element of time flow to the creation of the health and welfare facility environment; therefore, the perception of a static environment would be perceived as a dynamic one.

And, this design will spread through the town with "Integrated Community Care". It begins with the basics, such as making the height of the handrails uniform in hospitals, welfare facilities and senior citizen's residences, thereby making them easier to use.

Art space

Some of the points regarded as "architecture for good health" from the standpoint of health and welfare architecture are the following:

1 Sick building syndrome is avoided.
2 Healthy materials are used.
3 Architecture and the environment ac-

tively encourage health maintenance.
4 Architecture whereby health and environment can be considered by the fact of being in the architectural space.
5 Architecture that can evoke one's own self-healing power.
"1, 2" are Environmental Assessment System points.
"3" corresponds to hospital and sports facilities rehabilitation areas and must depend on a type of science.
"4"appeals to human sensitivity and is a familiar space people prefer to go.
"5" may be a vessel of "healthcare design for the future" that we aim for together. It is worthwhile to continue the quest to make full use of "art and science". If our living environment is filled with art, we will be much healthier now and in the future.
It relates to a type of spirituality and also connects with the following definition of health prepared by the WHO:

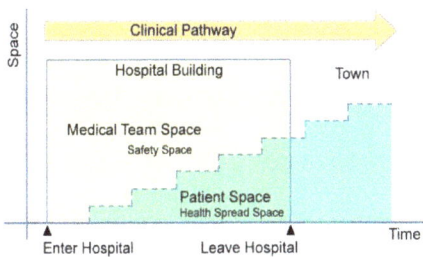

Figure 5. Time and space of clinical pathway-based design

Medical Team	Person, Action, Time
Patient	Preparations, Life discretion degree
Design Team	Where? What equipment? How safety space prepared?
Logistics	Material

Figure 6. Cooperation of clinical pathway-based design

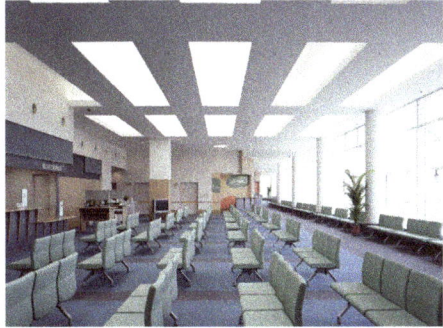

Figure 7. Ogachi Central Hospital (2005)

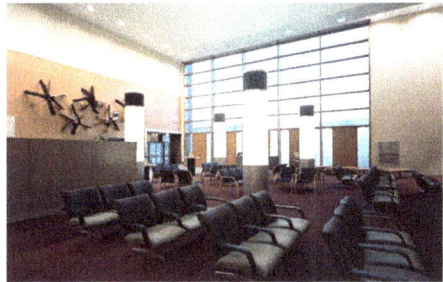

Figure 8. Ina Central Hospital (2005)

"Health is a dynamic state of complete physical, mental, spiritual and social well-being and not merely the absence of disease or infirmity."(Source: WHO ASSOCIATION OF JAPAN website).
Concerning the health definition of this Charter, a new proposal to add "dynamic" and "spiritual" was made in 1998; however, it was not adopted.
A spatial creation that evokes healing properties and the feeling of health is art. The space that evokes self-healing power and spreads health will become a goal for the future.

The richness of the communication of "art and science"

Consider that health can be built up through rich communication. A place for conversing expands the harmony

Figure 9. Shikoku Cancer Center (2006)

160

of familiar greetings over generations; and "living in the heart and omotenashi (hospitality)" is an art that all citizens can cherish in life.

Spreading hospitality throughout the town is the aim.

Both sustainable hospital buildings and hospital logistics use science. Sustainable hospital buildings make full use of techniques and wisdom that are good for the global environment and the health of all its citizens. Hospital logistics produces added value by linking commodity information to medical information.

Smart Healthcare Cities will create "Art and Science" by health and lifestyle information widely shared interactively through ICT utilizing smartphones and mobile devices; moreover, there will be mechanisms by which all citizens can quickly participate during an emergency or disaster.

We all need sustainability around the world. In addition to disaster-related medical care cooperation worldwide, it creates a new healthy symbiotic environment and achieves a sustainable society; In Japan, even with our ultra-low birthrate and aging society, our aim is to spend a healthy life together.

In cooperation with citizens from various fields, we spread Wa (harmony) and set a goal to make "buildings and environments that are good for health".

PROGRAM SPECIFICATIONS
Hospitality: Omotenashi

"Hospitality" is the etymology of the word "hospital." In the past when science was lacking, person-to-person contact through heart and mind.

It must have been expressed as caring for the patient as a person and through a sense of medical duty. And, the practice of hospitable living among the citizens of the town – between people and objects, people and society, people and nature – formed a co-creation between host and guest. This hospitality then spread to society beyond the two-party relationship between the host and guest. Speaking of hospitality in Japan, there is the "Cult of Tea" as seen in "Zen and Japanese culture". Ancient people began to drink tea from leaves as a medicinal herb. If we learn from this, it will become important that culture that values "health" information based on a rich and strong ethic, that can be created in a hospital in a sustainable society, be spread to enrich both town and people.

When delicious tea reaches the citizenry, various types of cooperation materialize, and hospitality spreads.

Sustainable hospital buildings

As for sustainable hospital buildings, selection can be best determined by the building scale, climate, diseases characteristic to the area and, then, cultural background. This method is not only possible for new buildings, but for renovations as well.

There is a demand for improving a building's environmental performance as well as for sustainable buildings that are good for both the earth and its inhabitants.

And we do need the concept of sustainable hospital buildings. That concept is to support the commitment to a sustainable society as well as to make further preparations.

161

Figure 10. China and Japan Friendship Hospital (Beijing 1984)

Figure 11. Children's Hospital (Islamabad 1985, 2006)

162

Figure 12. Samsung Medical Center (Seoul 1984)

Here, the sustainable hospital makes a commitment to act on global environmental issues. It will be positioned as a healthcare facility for the sustainability of society.

Medical practice sustainability is that of managing a healthy social environment; and the importance of this increases every day. Namely, if sustainable architecture deals with the support of societal life, sustainable hospitals have the large mission of leading healthcare in a better direction.

The goal is not only to reduce the global environment load as much as possible, but also to improve the environment of facilities both inside and outside, including disaster countermeasures.

Spatial Arrangement and Circulation

It is assumed that in the acute care hospital, hospital space is created by zoning, grouping and spacing as well as sequencing rooms; therefore, there is one line of thought that a certain spatial arrangement could be presented as a prototype while also reflecting the cultures of the world. Attempts based on this way of thinking are continuing.

However, an appropriate scale for a hospital building plan is decided by the necessity of circulation for persons and materials, and it must be devised using our common sense. In other words, the complex system of hospital architecture planning includes the following: the distance that staff is able to rush to immediately; a limit on the distance of patient movement; a limit on the nursing line of flow and the nurses' walking distance; the time required by the SPD (Supply Processing & Distribution) plan; and the addition of a time limit to the three-dimensional space.

Furthermore, the challenge of "concentration and dispersion" of important space in a hospital is increased.

Here may truly be where our professional ability as architects lies.

Figure 13. Kawaguchi City Hospital (1993)

Figure 14. Saitama Medical University International Medical Center (2007)

There are times when the science of spatial arrangement cannot be resolved through use of a computer. "The art of the architect that reflects medical methodology" is sometimes required.

However, "the challenge of spatial arrangement and circulation" often unavoidably spreads across the building itself.nMoreover, it is necessary for a hospital to be extended and connected to a ward and joined in a complex with a welfare facility.

By connecting through an aerial covered passageway crossing over the street, hospital architecture often merges into the cityscape. It is clear that medical welfare is simply not concluded only within a building alone. Health and welfare architecture cannot help but contribute to culture in a sustainable society at the same time as following up on life in the city. As for medical care and welfare, the range of choice has broadened even more. It is possible to conclude that the results of collaboration and complex buildings bring great change to these towns.

The possibility that communication can extend through "art and science" is sufficient.

Hospital logistics

By practicing "hospital logistics" in addition to "clinical pathway-based design," cooperation between the medical care information on patient treatments and

Figure 15. Oume Municipal Hospital, Rooftop Garden (2004)

163

164

Figure 16. Kobe General Hospital (1981)

Figure 17. Saitama Medical University International Medical Center (2007)

measures as well as information on the materials that are needed can be realized. An environment that unifies "the person, action and material" can be created. Hospital logistics can achieve necessary "materials" for "art" by means of "science." Then, from the point of time management, the set-up can be organized while being transported. In this way, added value is applied, and the logistics advances.

Accurate material information based on the medical information is prepared, and the material selection is carried out

and delivered. Here, information technology, including the traceability of medical activities, is in conjunction with the equipment use situation; it becomes more secure and has a higher degree of reliability.

Logistics produces cost cutting and added high value; it has traceability through information technology logistics, and there is the aspect of continually reviewing optimal transportation planning as well.

By this, intellectual productivity in the hospital is improved.

At the same time, rather than in-hospital SPD continuing with logistics outside of the hospital with manufacturing, transport, storage, conveyance, consumption to disposal and recycling being regarded as a total cycle, large hospital logistics can be formed.

Furthermore, joint use and networking among numerous hospitals will spread.

Hospital logistics at the time of natural disasters can be developed into a system to shift quickly beyond the regional medical sphere.

At the same time in this global environment era, a platform for a global viewpoint is needed to construct logistics to support urgent medical care when obstruction is caused by natural disasters.

Cooperation: from hospital architecture to the town (scale and space)

At the beginning of hospital function restructuring in Japan, the "regional medical care support hospital" was newly established, adding to the existing "general hospital" and "advanced treatment hospital". Further, a system was created for selecting and reporting the follow-

Healthcare	Medical Information	Clinical Pathway	
	Person, Action, Material		Time
Hospital Logistics	Material Information	Traceability	

Clinical Pathway-Based Design

Zoning, Grouping, Spacing

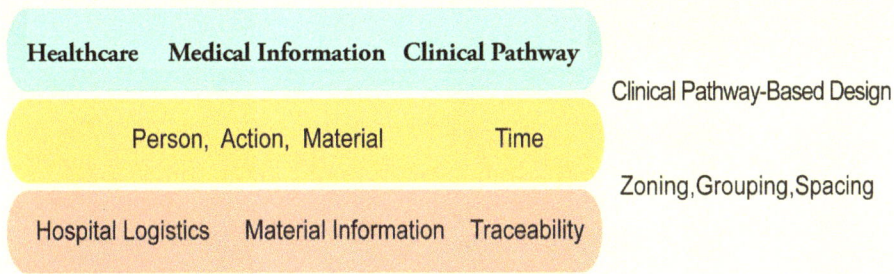

Figure 18. Clinical Pathway- based Design and Hospital Logistics

165

Figure 19. Yokohama City University Hospital (1991)

ing functions of general hospital beds and long-term care beds in each hospital ward: highly acute phase, acute phase, recovery phase, and chronic phase functions.

Healthcare cooperation between hospitals leads to a connection of the town's networks of space and time and circulation. This cooperation and time improves the environment of the town.

Health promotion, which originates from a medical facility, develops into town planning.

Hospital architecture is a point on a line within the city that ties together coop-eration and the role of the network. The result: the life of the people is fully covered in due time.

The network coordination pattern is selected by the distance and time at the time of use. Hospital transportation planning is also required at the same time. The health recovery process: the patient will be moved from an acute phase to recovery, then to long-term care toward rehabilitation.

Time begins to slowly flow. It will eventually become the same as the workings of everyday life.

"A strong intention toward health" is

Figure 20. Saitama Medical Center Jichi Medical University (1989, 2008)

166

Figure 21. Chiba-Nishi General Hospital (2013)

spread from the hospital network to the town. There is respect for environmental values that are good for health in variety of ways.

Wayfinding (signage as art)

Even if a hospital were able to be shown in a clear hierarchy in "spatial arrangement and circulation", even if it were a faithful repetition of a prototype, even if it could be reasonably explained to a user by the architect who designed it, it might still be difficult for a user to follow the route.

In particular, it's known that confusion often occurs when a user is moving alone through the sequence of outpatient, waiting space, consulting room, inspection room, diagnosis room and corridor areas.

In this time, a hospitable guide (con-

General hospitals	Special functioning hospitals	Regional Medical care support hospitals	Psychiatric hospitals	Tuberculosis hospitals

General beds	Long-term care beds	Infectious disease beds	Psychiatric beds	Tuberculosis beds

Highly acute phase,Acute phase,Recovery phase,Chronic phase

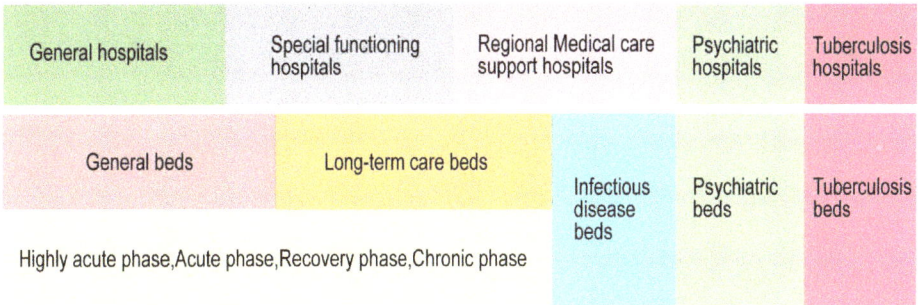

Figure 22. Bed classification revision (Source; Ministry of Health, Labor and Welfare; Report 2013-2014)

Figure 23. Tsuchiya Children's Hospital (2012)

Figure 24. Shinmatsudo Chuo General Hospital (2013)

168

Figure 25. Artemis Women's Hospital (2014)

cierge) plays an active part, and local volunteer participate, too. It becomes the culture of the hospital.

Nevertheless, basically, as long as way-showing, indicating the route, is performed or whether a user who reads the signage can use wayfinding with accuracy or not is literally affected by "signage art". Rather than an arrow or a logo design, we can better find our way by using a picture hung on the wall or by art that covers a large wall surface. A patient can gain confidence from a "healing design environment" in which he or she does not lose his or her way.

The art hanging on a wall, either through architectural planning or interior design, makes a place more recognizable than signage alone. Art greatly assists in learning the route. Therefore, "signage as art" is useful, and the need for art in an architectural space will increase for healthcare design in the future.

Urban hospital architecture is character-istic in cityscapes throughout the world. It is often the case that we can recognize a hospital even when visiting a city for the first time from common exterior characteristics. As sustainable architecture that creates "art and science" in a town, it is necessary that the hospital continues to enlighten a healthy environment going toward the future.

Hospital architecture, as a sustainable hospital building in a town, predicts the future and utilizes the present. "Art and science" are necessary to prepare for the future. Better guidance will create a healthy environment.

Smart healthcare city information cooperation

The smart healthcare city is science that's thinking about an information-oriented society from a health standpoint.

The smart healthcare city has information gathering and takes advantage of

Figure 26. Tokyo Kita Medical Center (2003)

Figure 27. Keiyu Hospital (1995)

Figure 28. Chiyoda Hospital (2012)

the state-of-the-art technology of medical care, nursing care, emergency, health and welfare; it incorporates network healthcare as a city function participated in by inhabitants and the local government. It is a city that richly grows and where life can be healthy, safe and secure. From the location-based information of smart phones and wearable devices, a system that watches over children and the elderly can be done.

Information management of an individual's healthy lifestyle can be extended from location-based information to include health information and medical care and pharmaceutical information.

It will be possible to coordinate health medical information through a regional medical information database center.

A regional medical information database can include the following: an emergency medical support system, a regional cooperation corresponding medical information sharing system (chart + inspection + imaging + medicine), a perinatal, maternal and child health information sharing system as well as a regional comprehensive care system.

It is possible for healthcare services to be performed by adding wearable devices and information collecting terminals.

Smartphone application development can perform personal information management of household information appliances and act as an automatic sphygmomanometer, a physical activity meter, body composition meter and sleep meter.

We are advancing from the provision of healthcare and medical-record management methods of the past to a future society in which an individual manages and shows his or her own health information.

169

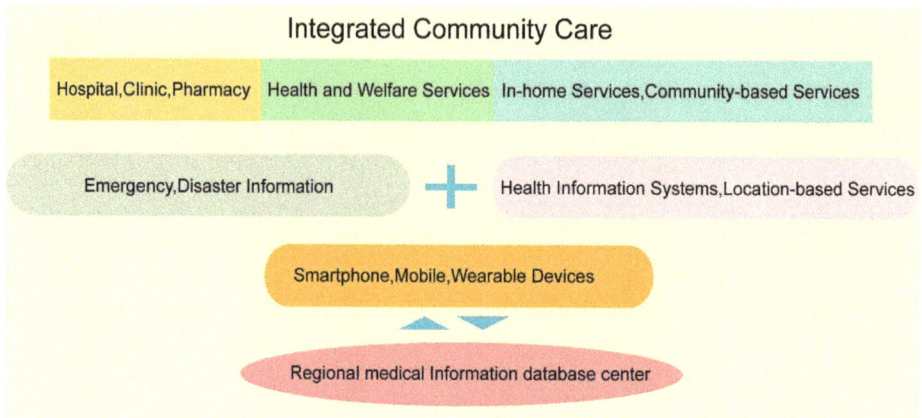

Figure 29. Integrated Community Care

Art and science as countermeasures against disaster

The scale of damage due to typhoons, heavy rain and drought from global warming and the signs of climate change are spreading in all parts of the world.
The Great East Japan Earthquake and the massive tsunami of legend occurred once again; and, we came to recognize the depth of the weight of disaster in history and lore.

We were struck with a sense of awe by the forces of nature.

We were living among the "art": the records that were expressed in the traditions and literature of the towns, the stone monument built by an ancestor that showed the tsunami arrival position, but we might have put too much confidence in the "science" of the embankment.

Even in daily life, there is a demand that we recognize the need to properly balance "art and science".

Correlated wisdom about the health of a town (affectionate communication)

There are people who have a friendly bond of activity based on attending to and greeting those who happen to live nearby; it must be one of the wisdoms of healthy life that traditional communities valued a strong relationship with each other.

Local communities make up our world: this begins at an agriculture harvest festival and a fishing festival for a large catch. It makes a traditional event or an entertainment and brings about the "art" that enriches life; they, then, spread out and call to each other, thereby making the world. The workings of the town, this "artful" life from ancient times together with the accumulation of the wisdom of "health," are very valuable.

In a sustainable society, these must become important as a basic responsibility for the culture of social life, together with the interchange of art and sports that goes beyond regional and national borders. There is an abundant future if we really notice once again that we are

global citizens in a sustainable society.
Regional comprehensive care is being promoted in Japan and the harmony of medical and nursing care spreads throughout the region with healthcare for the elderly.

The future is coming and the community, itself, is involved with sustainable society healthcare. It is possible to create "Art" together with a new "Science". There is a way

Toward Healthcare Design for the Future

The environment of the sustainable society will become a global network and healthcare will be well run and better made. It is important, at the same time, to develop in cooperation to resolve such issues as the following: sustaining better cooperation, moving toward global healthcare, presenting future challenges and sharing wisdom.

To value "health" and cooperate in the daily life of the town to create a life that fosters a rich culture: This is what is most precious.

What perspective is important when considering "healthcare design for the future" to achieve sustainability of buildings and the environment? That which makes full use of modern technology and knowledge effectively; and also learns from the wisdom of the "spirit of traditional housing as well as living in a natural climate.

And, we make sustainable hospital buildings in cooperation with logistics and environmental information bi-directionally. A Smart Healthcare City can be realized and expanded; in this way, we can reliably live in "the ultra-low birthrate and aging society" of the near future. Furthermore, we must achieve healthcare maintenance goals at times of natural disaster, not only through cooperation between locations nearby, but also remote ones using high-speed information sharing.

171

Figure 30. Ina Central Hospital (2005)

In collaboration with people in various fields, we spread Wa (harmony) and set goals to make "buildings and environments that are good for health".

REFERENCE

WHO ASSOCIATION OF JAPAN WEBSITE

Ministry of Health, *Labor and Welfare, Japan,* Annual Report 2013-2014

Murakami, S. et al. (2014). CASBEE. IBEC

Nagai, R. et al. (2014). *Smart Healthcare City*, Jichi Medical School

AIJ. (2011). *Going, looking, measuring, th inking for Architectural Design*, Kajima Institute Publishing

Kuse, H. et al. (2009). *Hospital logistics*, 22nd Century Medical and Research Center, Graduate School of Medicine the University of Tokyo. Hakutousho-bou

Nagasawa, Y. et al. (2007). *Architecture as a Geographic Environment: New Directions in Facility Planning Research,* University of Tokyo Press

Utsunomiya, M. (2010). *A Contemplation of Sustainable Hospital Building and Hospital Logistics*, IFHE Tokyo

Note: *Architectural photographs: K-ITO Architects & Engineers Inc., Tokyo, Japan*

172

New Frontier for Health Industry. Biomedical Research Innovation and Industrial Centers as an Alternative Model for Human Development in Frontier Markets.
The Case of Ustawi Biomedical Research Innovation and Industrial Centers of Africa

Macharia Waruingi

macharia.waruingi@ubrica.com
Professional Fellow, Center for Health Systems & Design College of Architecture, Texas A&M University, College Station, Texas;
Executive Member, Medical Advisor, Africa to International Union of Architects

After 10 years of exploration and research work, the U.S. to Africa wealth initiative (USTAWI) proposed the Ustawi Biomedical Research Innovation and Industrial Centers of Africa (UBRICA) as an alternative model for human development in frontier markets. UBRICA is a phenomenon where more and more Africans in the Diaspora, and in Africa are waking up to a deeper level of awareness that Africa's development is the work of Africans themselves, and not the work of international development agencies. UBRICA is the phenomenon where Africans are venturing deeper and deeper into this space of awareness as a point of departure for a creative process for bringing human development in Africa into reality. The bulk of members of UBRICA are Kenyan Americans, who propose the same standard of development in Kenya that they have come to enjoy when living and working in United States. UBRICA helps to construct a language that allows Africans to communicate at this deeper level of awareness that many Africans experience, but usually do not talk about, as is not a part of the mainstream development discourse. The works of indigenous organizations owned by Africans rarely find their way to the mainstream international media. By contrast, little action by the international development institutions, receives global media coverage, even though, indigenous organizations have, by far, much greater impact on human development in the countries where they operate.
UBRICA creates possibility for constructing a new language to explain such indigenous originated transnational organizations that create alternative forms of human development that have diaspora nationals of African countries and Africans in Africa leading change, and taking charge of the development of their own nations.
UBRICA is also a method that is helping Africans to be more effective operating at this

deeper space. The traditional method of national development in Africa, has involved African leaders taking trips to Western nations to borrow money to meet the annual budget for their respective nations. National leaders of African countries have been trained to believe that development comes from outside their nations. They have trained the people in their nations about this external source of development. This approach to development has had Africans become dependent on Western aid. In doing so, Africans overlook themselves as a source of development as they look outside of their countries for aid. In the new awareness, Africans have woken up to understand that development comes from within. UBRICA provides a method that helps to overcome the dependency on foreign aid.

174

Keywords: *Human development, research, science, innovation, industrial centers, architecture, master plan*

Ustawi is a U.S. based organization that is focused on knowledge emergence for human development.

Ustawi's work in knowledge emergence spans five phases of knowledge conversion continuum comprising knowledge exploration, research, publication, translation and application (Waruingi, 2010, 2012). Correspondingly, Ustawi has five major divisions, Ustawi Explorer, Ustawi Research Institute, Ustawi Publishing, Ustawi Translates, and Ustawi Applied.

The work of Explorer is discovery of knowledge through needs assessments, feasibility studies, and informal data gathering. The work of the Research Institute is formal research in diverse fields of human development.

The work of Publishing is production of peer and non-peer reviewed publications. Translates is involved in intellectual property management. Applied is involved in application of knowledge discovered through research.

Ustawi's work is mainly focused in frontier and emerging markets, generally speaking, and specifically in African countries. The sharp focus on Africa translates Ustawi to an acronym standing for United States to Africa Wealth Initiative (USTAWI). In this conception, Ustawi recognizes and is sensitive to contributing to America's economic growth as a fundamental business strategy for promoting wealth and human development in Africa. Since its inception in 2004, Ustawi has worked to discover knowledge about health and human development in Africa. After 10 years of exploration and research work, Ustawi Applied proposes the Ustawi Biomedical Research Innovation and Industrial Centers of Africa (UBRICA).

UBRICA plans to build many centers in Africa, with a first major project in Kenya known as UBRICA ONE. The project is on 4,000-acre ranch located in the Great Rift Valley of Kenya. The idea is to develop a well master-planned biomedical industrial park with hospitals, research facilities, residential areas, recreational areas and an industrial zone.

UBRICA ONE is designed as a sustainable human development enterprise that meets the needs of individuals, the society, the environment, and supports the Kenyan economy. The design work involves collaborating industry-university interdisciplinary research teams to help resolve a fundamental question about a theory that could explain strategic, operational and tactical structures of UBRICA ONE.

BACKGROUND OF THE PROBLEM

People living in Africa do not have access to good quality medical care. Where good quality care is available, it is out of reach of the majority. Much worse, African countries are not at the forefront of biomedical research, development, innovation, and commercialization of biomedical knowledge into commercial products and services.

For example, none of the countries in the sub-Saharan Africa (SSA) manufactures its own brand medicines or medical devices. Instead, the SSA countries rely on rarefied manufacture of generic medicines by a fragmented group of entrepreneurs, who are not grounded on a unified platform of knowledge production for scientific discovery of medicines and medical devices.

Indeed, the enterprise for translation of science into products for everyday domestic use and clinical care does not exist in Africa. For complete products, African countries rely on importation of all medical, scientific and technological goods and services.

Evidence indicates that no nation ever developed by reliance on importation of knowledge products from outside its boundaries.

Any nation that relies on importation of knowledge products becomes a slave to the exporting nation. There is ample evidence in history to show that a nation can only begin to comprehend its own development, first by comprehending its own knowledge through investment in cutting edge research for discovery of knowledge in all fields and translation of the discovered knowledge into commercial products and services that

175

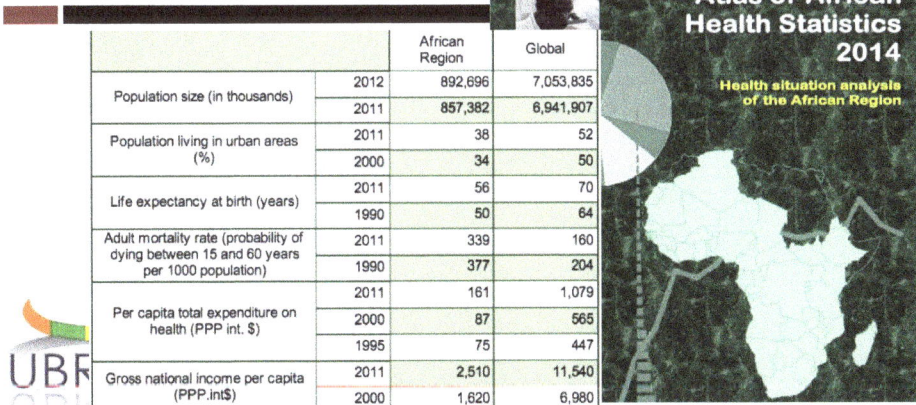

Africa Health Care Landscape

		African Region	Global
Population size (in thousands)	2012	892,696	7,053,835
	2011	857,382	6,941,907
Population living in urban areas (%)	2011	38	52
	2000	34	50
Life expectancy at birth (years)	2011	56	70
	1990	50	64
Adult mortality rate (probability of dying between 15 and 60 years per 1000 population)	2011	339	160
	1990	377	204
Per capita total expenditure on health (PPP int. $)	2011	161	1,079
	2000	87	565
	1995	75	447
Gross national income per capita (PPP.int$)	2011	2,510	11,540
	2000	1,620	6,980

Atlas of African Health Statistics 2014

Health situation analysis of the African Region

Figure 1. Africa Health Care Landscape

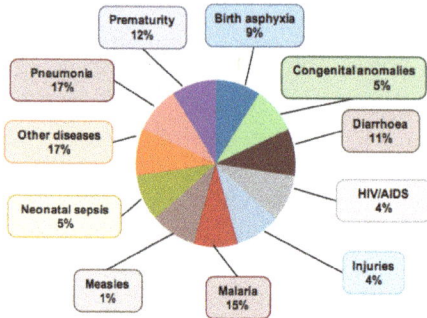

Figure 2. Africa: distribution of Causes of Death among Children

help solve problems of everyday life. Africa's development can only materialize if African countries aligned their vision with intent to build world-class capability for local knowledge production in biomedicine, science, technology, and engineering. Such world-class capability for knowledge production takes place in a center for excellence that integrates advanced scientific research, advanced scientific education and advanced scientific translation and commercialization of knowledge products. The absence of such a place means that the vision of many African countries to develop is not achievable.

In view of this problem, UBRICA intends to construct UBRICA ONE as a special place in Kenya for concentration and sharing of resources that will provide possibility for understanding disease and poverty in the country. UBRICA is envisioned as an organization that will create possibility of breakthrough research. The mission is to promote advanced research capability in Africa, in order to understand, prevent and treat diseases. Benefits of implementation of UBRICA ONE in Kenya cut across all

groups of stakeholders of health and human development.

Such stakeholders groups include the public, the government, health care providers (hospitals, physicians, nurses), the payers of care, the universities, and the industry.

The UBRICA ONE will create in Kenya a center for excellence capable of coordinated activities in key areas of human development that will include:
- translational research in human biology, human physiology, and human medicine;
- nano-science, biotechnology, molecular biology and human genetics;
- clinical medicine;
- organizations of systems for delivery of care;
- information systems for health.

UBRICA ONE is an all-inclusive development that is designed for innovative patterns of responsibility, ownership and management to attract best in class partners drawing from public and private institutions. UBRICA needs to work with interdisciplinary teams of leading American universities to comprehend itself and to bring to bear UBRICA ONE.

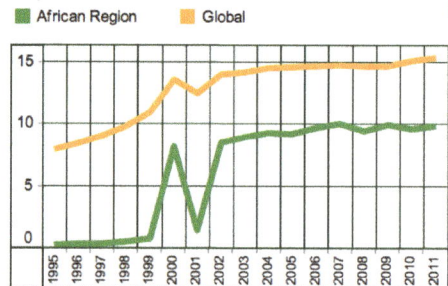

Figure 3. Africa: Trend Average Government Spending on Health

176

Nursing and midwifery personnel density (10,000 population)		Physician density (per 10,000 population)	
29.0			
		13.9	
	9.1		
			2.5
Global	African Region	Global	African Region

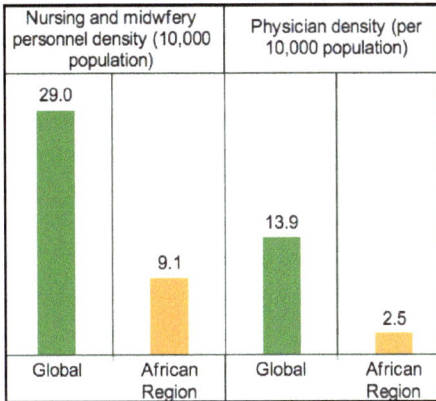

Figure 4. Africa: HealthCare Workforce

In an acceptance speech in 1994, the former President of the Czech republic Vaclav Havel lamented, "there are good reasons for suggesting that the modem age has ended". In that speech, Havel spoke of evidence in our times that "we are going through a transitional period, when it seems that something is on the way out and something else is painfully being born." He expressed a sentiment something "crumbling, decaying and exhausting itself, while something else, still indistinct, were arising from the rubble".

In essence, UBRICA embodies Havel's sentiment of "a transitional period, when it seems that something is on the way out and something else is painfully being born". In terms of international development, particularly, development in the so-called developing countries, the traditional development model is on its way out.

The World Bank, and its member institutions have become less and less effective, in the new millennium, and have less and less influence on national development decisions in developing countries. Local organizations owned and managed by people indigenous to these developing countries are "painfully being born" and investing in development of the local economies. Equity Bank in Kenya rose slowly from the rubble of World Bank's Structural Adjustment Program (SAP) of the 1980s, and was catalyzed by massive failure of Poverty Reduction Strategic Papers (PRSPs) of the 1990s, created to eradicate poverty. The widespread poverty that followed the SAPs and the PRSPs, evoked a deep awakening of the mind of some people in Central Kenya, who proposed an alternative way of financing development, that is built on pooling of resources of the individuals in the village to purchase property and buildings, in what was then called Equity Building Society (EBS). From these humble beginnings, Equity Bank grew to one of the largest banks in Africa providing financial resources to millions of people in the East African region, who were disenfranchised by the Western model of development, proposed through the World Bank.

More recently, Fountain Enterprises Program (FEP) has arisen from the rubble of failed development proposed by Kenyan state. FEP united Kenyans in the Kenya with Kenyans in diaspora to pool resources and invests through the power of many concepts. To date, FEP has enrolled hundreds of thousands of Kenyans world-wide, who have become shareholders of 14 companies involved in banking, media, real estate, schools, hotels, and health services.

Havel's observation that it "is as if something were crumbling, decaying, and exhausting itself, while something else, still indistinct, were arising from the rubble",

177

UBRICA THE PHENOMENON

☐ Economic development is by far the greatest cause of improvement in health.

☐ Ubrica is the phenomenon where more and more Africans are waking up to the realization that the work of developing Africa, is that of the Africans themselves.

Figure 5. UBRICA the phenomenon

Figure 6. Development. A metamorphic process

speaks to the crumbling decay of the international development organization, and the rise of indigenous grassroots development organizations that evoke the force of many so called poor people, to pool resources on one common platform for their own economic development. Grassroots organizations such as Equity Bank and FEP are grounded on the needs of the local people who are members of the organizations.

UBRICA steps in to epitomize this alternative to the human development establishment. As an organization owned by Africans in the Diaspora, UBRICA differs from, and is complementary to

Equity Bank and FEP, organizations owned by Africans in Africa. Members of UBRICA, having lived and worked in the Western countries, inject a fresh perspective to local development in developing countries, as they bring lessons learned from the two environments: their home country and their host country in the Diaspora. This transnational essence of members of UBRICA creates something new that is rising from the rubble of the crumbling human development enterprise. In this manner, UBRICA is a phenomenon where more and more Africans in the Diaspora, and in Africa are waking up to a deeper level of awareness that Africa's development is the work of Africans themselves, and not the work of international development agencies. UBRICA is the phenomenon where Africans are venturing deeper and deeper into this space of awareness as a point of departure, or a source of a creative process for bringing something new into reality.

It is in this phenomenon that UBRICA is able to propose sophisticated projects

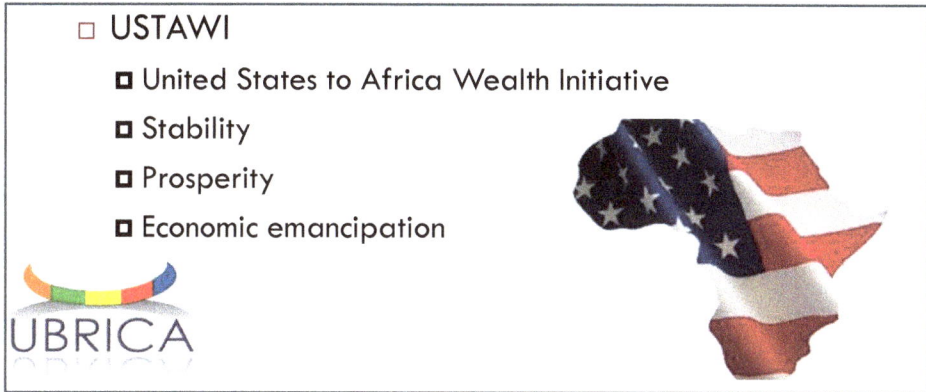

Figure 7. UBRICA the language

179

in Kenya such as UBRICA ONE, to be designed as a prominent high-tech research and development center of the standard to be found in United States of America. The bulk of members of UBRICA are Kenyan Americans, who propose the same standard of development in Kenya that they have come to enjoy when living and working in United States.

UBRICA helps to construct a language that allows Africans to communicate at this deeper level of awareness that many Africans experience, but usually do not talk about, as is not a part of the mainstream development discourse. The works of FEP and Equity Bank rarely find their way to the mainstream media. By contrast, little action by the World Bank, receives global media coverage, even though, FEP and Equity Bank have, by far, much greater impact on human development in the countries where they operate. UBRICA creates possibility for crafting a new language to explain such indigenous transnational organizations that create alternative forms of human development that have diaspora nationals of African countries

and Africans in Africa taking charge of the development of their own nations.

UBRICA is also a method that is helping Africans to be more effective operating at this deeper space. The traditional method of national development in Africa, has involved African leaders taking trips to Europe, Japan, United States and Canada to borrow money to meet the annual budget for their respective nations.
National leaders of African countries have learned that development comes from outside the nation. They have taught the people in their nations about this external source of development.
This approach to development has had Africans become dependent on Western aid. In doing so, Africans overlook themselves as a source of development as they look outside of their countries for aid. In the new awareness, Africans have woken up to understand that development comes from within.
The question is how?
UBRICA provides a method of pooling resources, and representing those resources by using shares of common stock, such that every African is aware

180

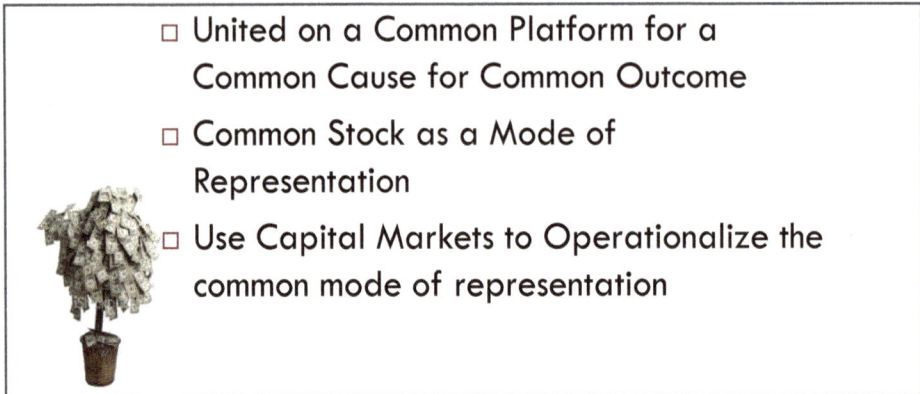

□ United on a Common Platform for a Common Cause for Common Outcome

□ Common Stock as a Mode of Representation

□ Use Capital Markets to Operationalize the common mode of representation

Figure 8. UBRICA the method

of how he or she is represented in the program.

UBRICA ONE

UBRICA ONE will be a master-planned biomedical park, built on an all-inclusive development that will have multiple land uses. Components of UBRICA ONE will include an academic medical district with five world class hospitals, a research district with biomedical research institutions, an industrial district with a full-scale diversified biomedical industries, and a residential district containing mixed-use real estate, residential and commercial real estate including world class shopping complexes, restaurants, and schools.

All UBRICA projects will be master-planned. Master planning minimizes the long-term cost of a project. UBRICA understands that producing a master plan does not have to be an expensive feat. Indeed, master planning saves much cost in the long-term from smart campus development. Master plans are beneficial to all stakeholders.

KEY FEATURES OF UBRICA ONE

The UBRICA ONE medical campus will comprise world-class academic medical facilities; an ultra modern research facility for innovative research in science, technology, medicine, biology, and health services; residential houses; and an industrial park for innovations leading to pharmaceuticals and medical devices manufacturing. Upon completion, UBRICA ONE's Academic Medical District will have several hospitals. In addition, to the hospitals, the medical campus will have a series of clinics, and research centers. All the hospitals and clinics will be concentrated in a defined area, with appropriate residential facilities and social amenities.

Clinical diagnostics will take place within the hospital and in the biomedical research facilities. The university general hospital will specialize mainly in infectious diseases, intensive care, endocrine diseases, kidney diseases, organ transplant, women's health, digestive diseases, orthopedics, neurosciences, emergency medicine and rehabilitation.

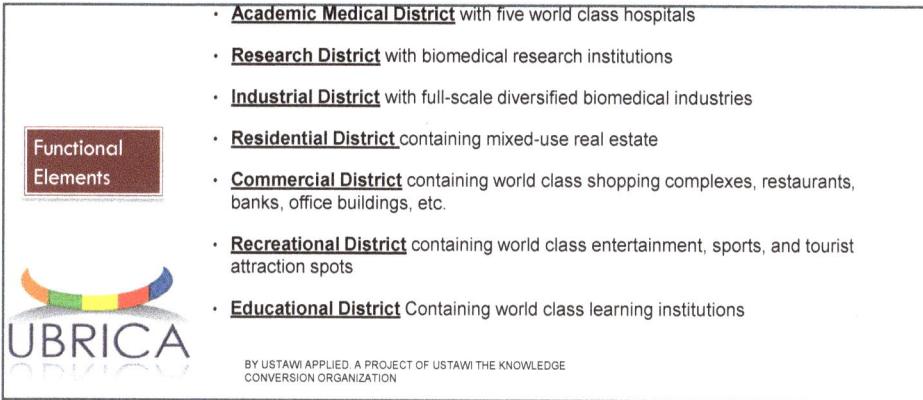

Figure 9. *UBRICA ONE Core*

The children's hospital will specialize in all childhood diseases, and will feature family medicine service, emergency service, in-patient and intensive care, and rehabilitation. The heart hospital will have latest technologies for cardiovascular care, and will be entirely dedicated to cardiac surgery and vascular medicine. Services will include clinical care, cardiac catheterization, angioplasty, open-heart surgery, cardiovascular imaging, vascular operations, minimally invasive robotic procedures, and a full range of tests and laboratory services for diagnosis of cardiovascular diseases.

The medical campus will feature a school of medicine, a school of allied health professions, and a school of biomedical sciences. Teaching facilities will include conference rooms located within the medical buildings. The school will provide first two years integrated basic sciences in histology, pathology, pathophysiology, pharmacology, and anatomy. In all cases, learning will be facilitated (as opposed to didactics), with structured objectives, resource guides and materials based on computerized self-study. Medi-

cal students will have first contact with patients in their first year of study.

Transparent spaces, awash with natural light, in the teaching and research facilities will serve as areas of advanced training and conference activities. These areas will be equipped with advanced communication systems built on a robust information platform. Technological devices will render training much easier with facilitated distant and even transnational learning. The transparent spaces will be areas to encourage spontaneous exchanges of ideas between and among multiple disciplines, supported by real-time web-conferencing technologies.

These spaces will be well designed to respond to the physiology and well being of the high-tech staff. The key drivers of the health care at UBRICA ONE will include robotics, intelligent patient, infection control, drug development, private finance, surgical techniques, alternatives, therapeutic environments, intelligent pills, DNA, RNA, stem cells, photo-acoustics, elderly, chronic diseases, affordability, home diagnosis, pandemic risk, artificial organs, public

181

TESIS Inter-University Research Centre "Systems and Technologies for Social and Healthcare Facilities"
University of Florence, Italy

182

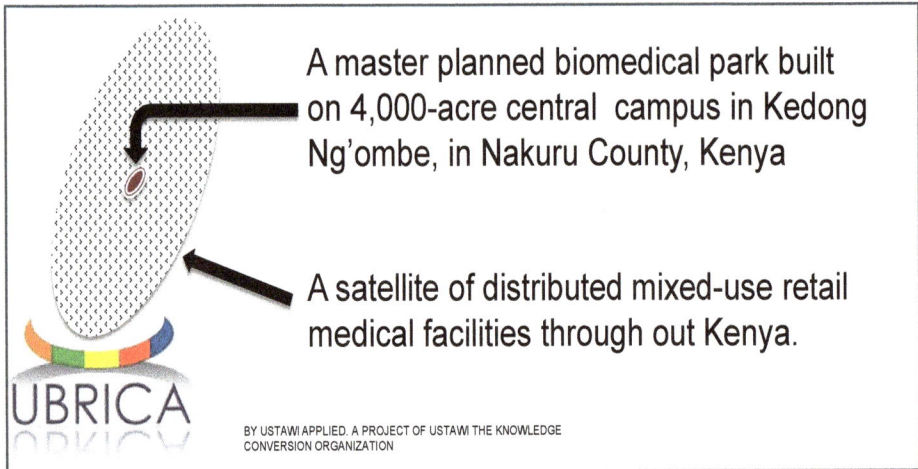

A master planned biomedical park built on 4,000-acre central campus in Kedong Ng'ombe, in Nakuru County, Kenya

A satellite of distributed mixed-use retail medical facilities through out Kenya.

UBRICA

BY USTAWI APPLIED. A PROJECT OF USTAWI THE KNOWLEDGE CONVERSION ORGANIZATION

Figure 10. UBRICA ONE

health, government legislation, information and communication technologies, and advanced imaging. Ubrica hospitals will be geared towards long-term sustainability, embedded in the communities.

The mode of production will be team based, continuous and integrated care delivery with patient as partner. Self-care will be encouraged and facilitated in Ubrica facilities. UBRICA will support caregivers as partners.

The UBRICA ONE Innovative Research District will comprise state-of-the-art laboratory buildings with research laboratories, centralized core facilities, and state-of-the-art equipment; facilities for preclinical in-vivo studies; a corporate incubator designed to facilitate the creation of new startups and accelerate the time-to-market of new products and treatment techniques. Research buildings will be conceived to interpret the most advanced principles of multidisciplinary research, in complete compliance with green design, and economic

sustainability.

Each building will accommodate at least 2,000 researchers, in different disciplines. The goal will be to concentrate all researchers in close proximity, and creating functional connections between hospitals and research building. This will help to maximize integration of research and innovation into clinical care of patients and teaching of students of medicine, nursing, health professions and basic sciences. The guiding principle of building design will be to create spaces that will facilitate spatial interdependence that would stimulate spontaneous interactions across the four functions of research, education, patient care, and innovation.

The research facilities will comprise a biomedical research unit, a tissue repository, a biostatistics unit and a clinical trials unit. Research activities will be conducted at the hospital and in the research centers at the school of medicine.

The focus will be to transfer research results into clinical practice, supporting

183

Figure 11. Residential district: illustrative example of low-density master planned living

Figure 12. Residential district: illustrative example of low-density master planned living

184

many research centers and laboratories in the UBRICA ONE to conduct various kinds of research ranging from basic research, to translational research, to clinical trials. UBRICA ONE will create a highly dynamic environment that will encourage collaboration among physicians, basic scientists and clinical researchers. The clinical research center will provide support for clinical trials and capabilities in project management, sample logistics and preparation, data compilation, genomics, histopathology and proteomics.

The buildings will have cozy large open areas that will serve as common areas for interdisciplinary and inter-professional meetings. These common areas will be carefully designed, with comfortable and soothing features, permeated with natural light for maximum visual relaxation, and other amenities such as cafeteria, and retail conveniences.

Clinical research centers will include a molecular biology and human genetics research center, a microbiology and immunology research center, an investigational medicine research center, a medical pharmaceutics research center, an oncology and onco-biology research center, a radiology research center, a health services research center and health systems and design research center. Biotechnology is one of the world's fastest growing industries.
UBRICA ONE will help advance the biotechnology industry in Kenya and beyond through its biomedical industrial park.

UBRICA ONE scientists will enjoy advanced and wellequipped laboratory facilities and the possibility to perform highly competitive research projects that will be evaluated only for their merit and translational potential. Thus, UBRICA ONE will help Kenya to retain some of its best medical and scientific talents, and attract some of the world's top researchers to Kenya. UBRICA ONE research programs will lead to new discoveries and inventions, new intellectual property, and to eventual yield of marketable products and start-up enterprises. The science developed will ultimately help to prevent or cure disease, or assist with our ability to improve the quality and longevity of life.

UBRICA intends to create a research culture that comprehends the local community. In order to understand the local community UBRICA ONE researchers will transact with local people radically. To facilitate radical trans-activeness, lower levels of UBRICA ONE research buildings will be open to the community. Members of the public can use the spaces for interacting with UBRICA research scientists in open lectures, seminars, workshops, and symposia. Spaces open to the community will demystify, encourage respect, and passion for research. The ground floors will contain retail operations including, clothing stores and restaurants.

The Industry Liaison Office in UBRICA ONE will co-ordinate industrial collaborations. The goal will be to facilitate the transfer of new discoveries and invention into utility products and services through transfer of these technologies to companies already on the market or to new enterprises. Technology transfer will occur by facilitating industrial commercialization of research outcomes from the research centers.

The role of the Industry Liaison Office will be to protect, manage, and promote intellectual property; to provide support for the industry, the faculty and staff, with high quality service guidance on matters relating to intellectual property and commercialization; to promote technology transfer and commercialization of university innovations; and to promote collaboration between academic research and industry.

The UBRICA ONE's master planned Industrial District, will be an epicenter of technological innovation, with a full range of R&D companies.
The research district will work closely to support the industrial district. The industrial district will be home to multinational corporations, university spin-offs and start-up businesses in pioneering industries, including biotechnology, information technology, and clean technologies. A diversified group of businesses such as financing organizations, venture capital firms, legal services, accounting firms, banking organizations, and other service providers will be co-located in the industrial district to provide services needed by people working in the cutting edge industries.

The growth of the UBRICA ONE's Industrial District will translate to growth of Kenya.

This growth will transform Kenya into an industrial nation. As such, UBRICA ONE will be one of the best places to live in Africa, with an above average per-capita income and high concentration of people with very advanced education.

The UBRICA ONE Residential Area will emphasize a density gradient development ranging from very low density to very high-density housing. UBRICA ONE will feature a light rail to transport people to the medical and industrial district. The Metro Center will be a mixed-use development in the residential district with a high-density development with retail and residential space near the railway line and luxury hotels.

UBRICA ONE represents a significant investment in biotechnology in Africa. The center will offer a unique opportunity to develop novel treatment and prevention strategies for diseases now afflicting humans. UBRICA ONE will significantly foster economic well-being, creating jobs and business opportunities on the local, national, and international level, while also helping Kenya to form and retain some of its best medical and scientific talents, besides attracting some of the world's top scientists to the region.

The development of medical products and devices in the Industrial District will provide a basis for future growth of Africa's biotechnology industry (including companies directly spun-off from UBRICA ONE's discoveries and inventions, as well as the center's intellectual property, which will be licensed to other companies, both nationally and internationally).
This will represent an opportunity to develop the venture capital industry in Kenya, by earning a reputation as a region with the available resources and capabilities to attract new businesses.

185

REFERENCES

Havel, V. (1994). Acceptance speech. Retrieved from http://constitutioncenter.org/libertymedal/recipient_1994_speech.html

Waruingi, M. (2010). Emergencing: Discovering the tacit dimension of global health. Minnetonka, MN: Global Health Care Systems.

Waruingi, M. (2012). Ustawi Research Institute's process of knowledge conversion by open innovation, in "The Journal of Global Health Care Systems", 2(1), 1-4.

Is "Architectural Planning" Evidence-based Design?

Kazuhiko Okamoto

Dr@okamoto-kazuhiko.com
Associate Professor, Tokyo University

187

Evidence-based Design (EBD) is the influential design approach in the present world. Japanese architects learn and apply EBD in hospital design field like most developed countries, however we often fall upon the same question; Is "Architectural Planning" Evidence-Based Design?

"Architectural Planning" was established in Japan based on the accumulation of academic researches conducted by Professor Yasumi Yoshitake at the University of Tokyo as well as Professor Uzo Nishiyama at Kyoto University around World War II in order to arrange modern public buildings like housings, schools, hospitals and so forth in damaged cities as soon as possible.

The concept of "Architectural Planning" developed parallel to the economic growth to fulfill the population growth which requires housings and public facilities, spread through university education system to help students efficiently understand and design, and published database of exemplary works in all kinds of building types since 1942. "Architectural Planning" was diversified in the bubble economy in 1980's which accepts superficial architecture like "deconstruction architecture" without any evidence.

The Great Hanshin-Awaji Earthquake stimulated the demand of "Architectural Planning" again to deploy temporary housings and rebuild city as well as community and "Architectural Planning" still works nowadays in the era of earthquake, tsunami and nuclear disaster.

Japan Institute of Architecture accepts 600 to 800 presentation papers in "Architectural Planning" field at annual conference. As mentioned above, variety of presentations are collected in which medical facility research occupies at a certain ratio. In this research, we are finding research trend and EBD shares by analyzing all research papers submit in the last 10 years.

Keywords: *Architectural Planning, Evidence-based Design, Hospital*

BACKGROUND AND AIM

Evidence-based Design (EBD) is one of the most influential design approach in the present world. Japanese architects learn and apply EBD in hospital design field like most developed countries, however we often fall upon the same question; Is "Architectural Planning" Evidence-Based Design?

Prior to the introduction of EBD in Japan, we have designed hospitals based on "Architectural Planning" (建築計画, AP) which is still popular academic field in Japan, Korea and a part of China. This paper aims to look back the history of AP and find how AP research includes EBD.

HISTORY OF AP

AP is a design theory especially focusing on the design process based on the analysis of human behavior, cognition etc. Originally, AP and structure, were big two majors in architectural university education system after western education theory was imported after Meiji evolution in 1868. Since then, AP required chairs(s) and lecture(s) at every university, however at that time, AP contains everything but structure.

In 1889, architect Kikutaro Shimoda (1866-1931) who worked for Daniel Burnham in the US published "Theory of Architectural Planning" after returning to Japan saying: Architecture should

188

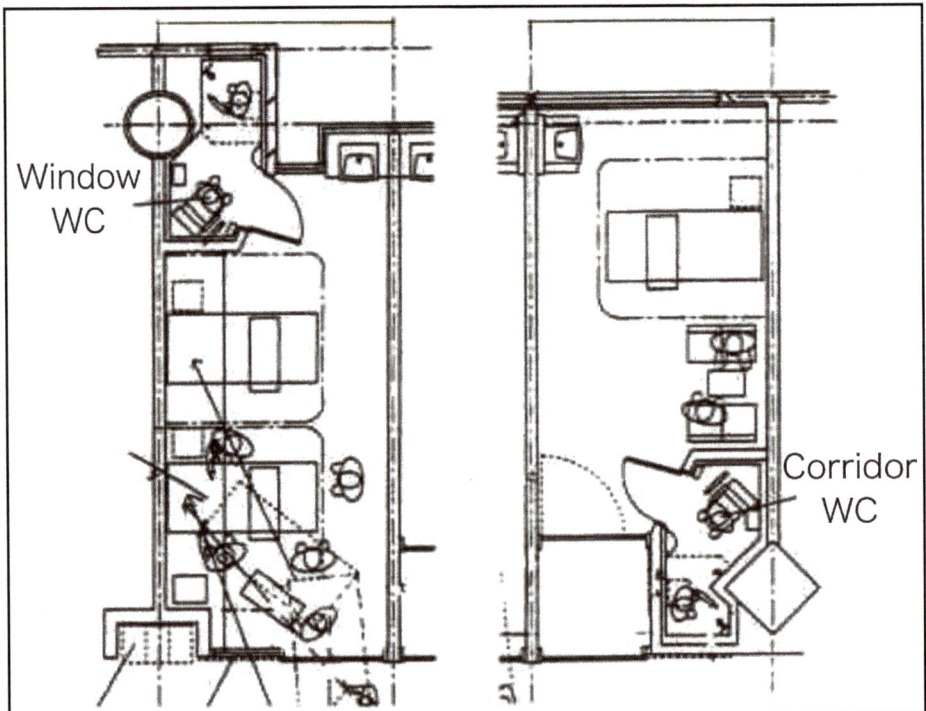

Figure 1. (see the text)

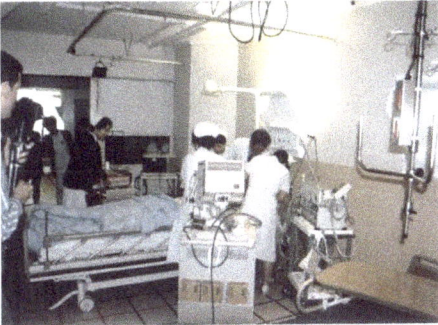

Figure 2. (see the text)

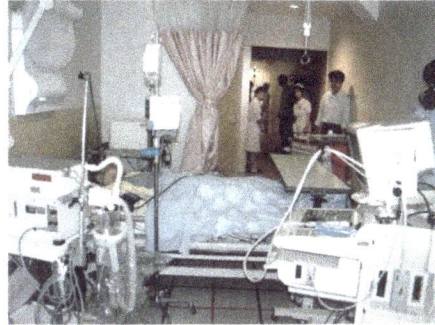

be 50% practical, 30% rhetorical and 20% aesthetic. This book is the first appearance of AP and showed its characteristics in a simple sentence.

Modern AP was established based on the accumulation of academic researches conducted by Professor Yasumi Yoshitake (1916-2003) at the University of Tokyo as well as Professor Uzo Nishiyama (1911-1994) at Kyoto University around World War II in order to arrange modern public buildings like apartment housings, schools, hospitals and so forth in damaged cities as soon as possible.

Nishiyama visited many houses to interview and sketch these interiors in detail in order to highlight ongoing problems to be solved by design. Yoshitake also collected numerical data from public facilities like schools, libraries as well as hospitals to find evidence contributing to efficient design. Foreign students from Asian countries studied AP in Japan and spread the concept in their home countries as they became professors.

The concept of AP developed parallel to the economic growth around 1970 to fulfill the population growth which requires more housings and public facilities, spread through university education system to help students efficiently understand and design, and published database of exemplary works in all kinds of building types to help practitioners. AP was diversified in the bubble economy in 1980s which accepts superficial architecture like "deconstruction architecture" with less evidence however, new concepts as window-side WC were realized through making mockup and simulating staff work (Figure1, Figure 2).

The Great Hanshin-Awaji Earthquake in 1995 stimulated the demand of AP again to deploy shelters and temporary housings, rebuild city as well as community and is still expected to grow nowadays in the era of earthquake, tsunami and nuclear disaster (figure 3)

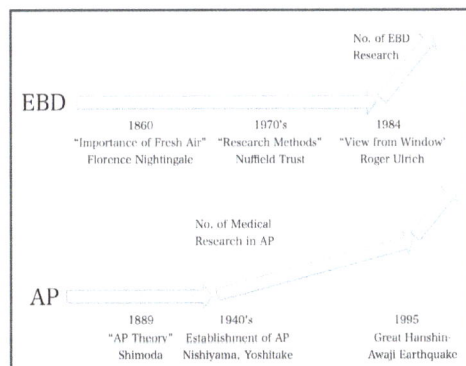

Figure 3. (see the text)

TESIS Inter-University Research Centre "Systems and Technologies for Social and Healthcare Facilities"
University of Florence, Italy

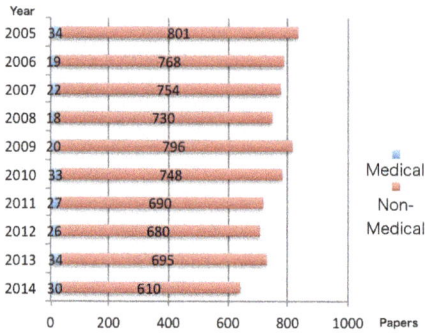

Figure 4. (see the text)

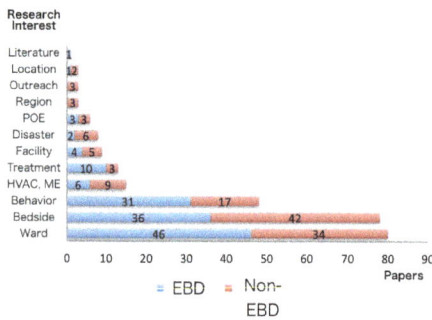

Figure 5. (see the text)

METHOD

Japan Institute of Architecture accepts 600 to 800 presentation papers in AP field at annual conference. As mentioned above, variety of presentations are collected in which medical facility research occupies at a certain ratio. In this research, we are finding medical research trend and its EBD shares by analyzing all research papers submit in the last 10 years. In addition, we organized what AP helped practitioners so far and discover the future task.

RESULTS

While total number of AP papers slightly decreased, medical research constantly increased every year. 52% of the medical research is related with EBD out of 267 medical papers submit in 10 years. When we classify the contents of papers, we can see that the major interest is patient's environment (figure 5).

One of the biggest works of AP is annual "Hospital Architecture Data Sheet" published by Japan Institute of Healthcare Architecture (JIHa). Every volume contains about 100 hospital floor plans completed in the year and what is intriguing on AP is that not only researchers but also practitioners voluntarily submit the data to be shared. Moreover, "Volume of Welfare and Medical Facilities, Handbook of Environmental Design" issued by Architectural Institute Japan (AIJ) includes detailed floor plans of important hospitals arranged in chronological order with explanations. This volume has been completely translated in Chinese.

FUTURE TASK

The concept of AP is popular in East Asia as explained above, however, English translation and delivery to EBD-advanced countries are necessary. Through comparing each other, we can truly understand the design of hospital by digesting its cultural background and research accumulation.

Make a Step Forward from 20th to 21st Century on Built-Environment of Healthcare Architecture

Yasushi Nagasawa

donpayasusin@gmail.com
Dr. Eng. (PhD), Executive Directors Board Member, Kogakuin University
Professor Emeritus, the University of Tokyo and Kogakuin University

When it comes to prospect future healthcare environment (HE), it will be a good way to consider historical view of development of HE.

In Ancient Greek, Asklepieon at Pergamon was one of the typical HE for patients and their families. Medieval Hospitals were the places to die because of primitive level of medical technology. The situation is symbolized in the words, famous surgeon, Ambroise Pare (1517-1590) said, "God will save her life, after I carried out surgery and dressing". Building shape looked like Monastery, e.g. St. Gall's monastic hospital in 9th AD. Until 19th AD, HE were in buildings converted from other public buildings, like palaces, prisons and mansions, e.g. Bethlehem (Bedlam) Hospital in London 17th AD. In 19th AD, Florence Nightingale (FN) defined hospital building function for the first time in history. In Notes on Hospitals (1853), she described, "It may seem a strange principle to enunciate as the very first requirement in a hospital that It should do the sick no harm".

FN improved nursing and care environment in wards, providing better nursing observation as well as fresh air, natural light and appropriate room temperature. As the result, hospitals were recognized as the places to be cured. Building shape was "Pavilion Type", i.e. each independent pavilion is connected by a corridor in order to prevent cross infection in a hospital, which was called, "Nightingale Hospital", e.g. Herbert Hospital (1864) in Woolwich, UK. This hospital prototype was prevailing all over the world.

From 19th to early 20th AD, extraordinary development of modern Western medicine was observed. For example, the symbol of physicians was changed from urine bottle to stethoscope, which French MD, Rene Laennec invented as excellent diagnosis hearing aid in 1816. Discovery of bacteria, e.g. by German pathologist Robert Koch (1843-1910),

192

revealed the cause of infection and sickness resulting in an establishment of pathological laboratories in hospitals. In the field of surgery, sterilizing technology was established e.g. by Dr. Joseph Lister (1827-1912) carried out his surgical procedure after sterilizing bandage by phenol in 1865. In addition Dr. William T.G. Morton (1819-1868) succeeded in a surgery under general anesthesia in 1846 at Massachusetts General Hospital (MGH). After German physicist Wilhelm Rontgen (1845-1923) discovered X-Ray in 1895, internal organ images were easily obtained. However, Tuberculosis (TB) therapy was not totally succeeded before the discovery of antibacterial drugs e.g. Penicillium in 1928 by Alexander Fleming (1881-1955). As the result of the fact, many sanatoria were built all over the world. Treatment was based on staying in the environment with fresh air, quiet rest and good nutrition. Building shape was still based on Pavilion Type.

In late 20th AD, centralized functional units in hospital organization were established which resulted in seeking for efficient hospital management, Architectural form looks like big factory buildings, what is called "Mega Hospital", symbolized in Archen University Hospital in Germany. Design target of 20th AD hospitals was to provide places for patients unable to die easily.

In conclusion, 21st century Hospitals will direct both to small scale mobile ICU orientating interventional tools as much as possible and to healing environment orientating natural, psycho-socio and artistic tools leaving from 20th AD concentrated mega hospitals.

There are quite a number of topics in recent Japanese hospital design trend against the background of the super aged society based on traditional national health insurance as well as recently developed care insurance schemes. The first topic is horizontal hospital shape, 2nd one is backyard of staff station and 3rd one is single bed nursing unit, and three actual hospital design were introduced respectively to the three topics.

Healthy Communities and Healthy Cities

Session introduction
Sandra Carlini
Arch., Research Fellow University of Florence

For some time there has been ever more widespread awareness of the fact that the health of people and of communities cannot be sacrificed for the modernization of living environments but that, in fact, modernization, from a sustainability perspective, must lead to the creation of healthy lifestyles for everyone and places where we can live better and longer.

The "Healthy Communities and Healthy Cities" session therefore addressed significant issues such as the development of strategic programming tools for the creation of modern cities of health in new contexts such as those represented, for example, by some African towns where there is a particular need to increase the quality of life and of care for the whole population, respecting the local history, culture and landscape.

The interest expands from more strictly healthcare contexts to the whole built environment for people's health, with proposed new interesting visions and readings for urban centres. The challenge, in an ever more globalized world, in many cases concerns emerging countries such as China and Brazil. Significantly, the reality of some large cities such as Rio de Janeiro or Singapore is highlighted.

The Brazilian metropolis, in particular, shows the intention to profit from the great opportunities offered by Rio 2016 in an attempt to combine, in terms of the strategic plan for the massive transformations underway, urban design with the promotion of health, also associated with prevention programmes in view of the Olympic games and a general review of the transport systems.

For Singapore, a city with one of the highest life expectancies, some decades ago the government made a decision to create, from a holistic perspective, an urban context within which the health of its citizens can be promoted thanks to the possibility of leading active lifestyles, preventing diseases and maintaining a good quality of life for the elderly population.

Once again the elderly are the centre of attention when referring to experiences such as Wanshou Park in Beijing, an initiative designed to encourage and favour their social reintegration in the community, increasing their physical health and mental well-being.

The session then addressed the serious problem of the increase in obesity. While the problem has existed for quite some time in the United States and is analysed in relation to the built environment of small cities.

From the perspective of promoting, for example, the "utilitarian" walk as a positive physical activity for health (in addition to being effective in combating pollution), the problem, with increased dependency on vehicle mobility, is clear in the significant rise also in contexts such as China where awareness of the importance of physical activity for health is also revealed in a study on the impact of the accessibility of sports facilities for the population.

Health Oriented Design in Singapore

Ruby Lai

ruby.lai@cpgcorp.com.sg
Senior Consultant - CPG Consultants Pte Ltd, Singapore

This paper will present the case for health-oriented design in Singapore. This requires a holistic view of all developments within the country, involving the coordination between various ministries and agencies. The aim is to promote health and reduce chronic illness, and thus reduce the number of sick people requiring treatment and support.

INTRODUCTION

Hospitals are places designed to cure sickness and diseases, and to take care of patients. However, are there places specially designed to promote health? Can design really promote health?

In Singapore, Health-Oriented Design has been a primary driver in the development of the nation. This has been consolidated in the Healthy Living Master Plan which was published in 2014 after a 2 year study on how healthy living can be made Available, Accessible and Affordable.

Singaporeans now enjoy a long life span – the World Health Organisation (WHO) in 2011 ranked Singapore as 4th in the world for life expectancy with average life span of 82.14 years. However, it is not enough to just live long – we would be miserable if the last decade of our lives are spent in ill health and pain. In a survey done by the Ministry of Health, it was found that 26% of the population aged 18 to 69 did not have sufficient physical activity. Simple changes to lifestyle such as exercising regularly, eating healthily, adopting smoke-free lifestyles, and undergoing regular health screenings can help prevent the onset of diseases and ensure a more enjoyable healthy life into our old age. The Healthy Living Master Plan was developed to help encourage more people to engage in healthy activities.

The Healthy Living Master Plan identified 3 goals:

a) To develop a conducive environment, created through the integration and connectivity of physical environments for seamless access to healthier options.

b) To encourage the development of a socially inclusive healthy community, through pervasive programmes, messaging, role models and advocates.

c) To provide affordable healthier options that are within the reach of all, through using financial micro-incentives as nudges to create both supply and de-

196

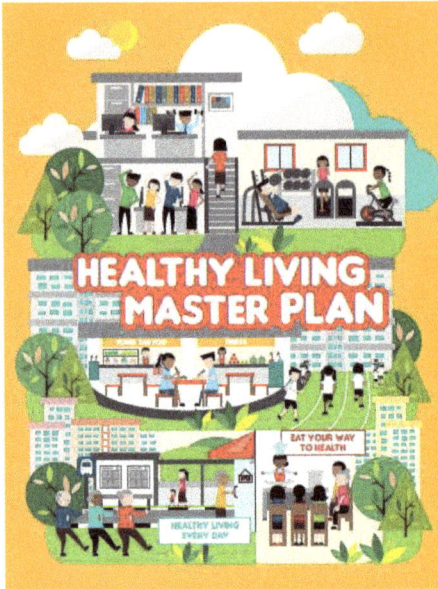

Figure 1. Healthy Living Master Plan

Several government agencies have also developed various programmes in line with the Healthy Living Master Plan such as the National Well Programme, Sport Singapore Vision 2030 and updating of the Urban Redevelopment Authority (URA) and Land Transport Authority (LTA) master plans to develop more parks and cycle paths.

The main objective is to promote healthy living so we can enjoy a better quality of life to be able to pursue our goals and dreams, and be able to spend more time with our loved ones.

mand for healthy living.

The Healthy Living Master Plan helps to ensure all public agencies are involved in an integrated manner to develop a clean and healthy environment in general, and in particular to design facilities that help promote healthy living, which will help to reduce chronic illnesses. People will be encouraged to live independently at home instead of moving into institutions such as nursing homes.

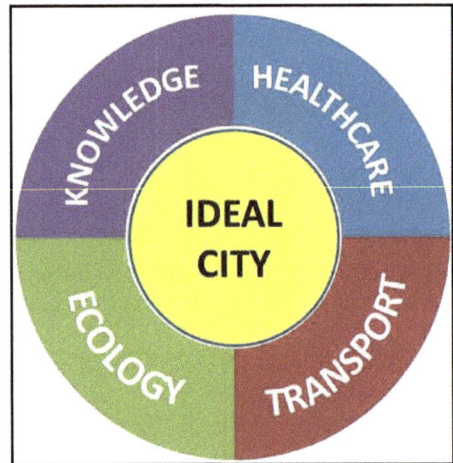

Figure 2. Creating a healthy environment

Figure 3. Singapore River in 1960s

Figure 4. Singapore River today

Figure 5. Reservoirs turned into recreation areas

Figure 6. The Marina Barrage – a favourite place for kite flying

HEALTHY ENVIRONMENT

Different cities concentrate on different aspects in their long term plans for their development. There are those that are Transport Oriented, Health Oriented, Knowledge Oriented or Ecology Oriented.

Health Oriented Design of a nation focuses on the health and well-being of the people in its developments.

Creating a healthy environment requires an integrated approach to develop healthy landscapes, clean water, and a health-oriented community.

Water

Our late former Prime Minister, Mr Lee Kuan Yew, was the driving force in creating a healthy Singapore. In the early 1960s, the rivers of Singapore were filthy with years of neglect.

He determined to have clean flowing water within 10 years, and this was achieved.

198

Today the rivers of Singapore are clean and beautiful, and attract many activities. They are used for recreation, a barrage has been built to control floods, and the water is treated to become drinkable water.

Housing

Housing was another problem to be tackled. Up to the 1980s, there were still squatters and derelict housing. The Housing and Development Board (HDB) set about developing new towns, and today Singapore's public housing is clean, beautiful and provided with excellent facilities. Over 80% of Singaporeans are proud owners and live in these public housing flats.

Food

Our Environment Ministry was also busy ensuring that new markets and food centres were developed to provide clean and hygienic food. The Agri-food and Veterinary Authority set stringent standards on the quality of food, animals and plants.

Parks

The 1970s also saw a transformation in Singapore's landscape. The city started planting trees, and Singapore has since been transformed into a Garden City. Beautiful new parks have been developed throughout the island to provide spaces for people to exercise, with trees

Figure 7. Present-day public housing

Figure 8.   Foodstalls in 1970s

Figure 9.   Present-day foodstalls

providing shelter from the sweltering heat. Nearly 46.5% of the island city is covered in greenery.

HEALTHCARE INFRASTRUCTURE

Singapore's approach to the provision of healthcare is a combination of strong government intervention through both provision and payment, and aggressive use of market mechanisms.

The five principles from the Singapore Government White Paper on Affordable Healthcare, October 1993 are:

a) To nurture a healthy nation by promoting good health.

b) To promote personal responsibility for one's health and avoid over-reliance on state welfare and medical insurance.

c) To provide good and affordable basic medical services to all Singaporeans.

d) To rely on competition and market forces to improve service and raise efficiency.

e) To intervene directly in the healthcare sector when necessary where the market fails to keep healthcare costs down.

Much attention has been paid to improving the healthcare infrastructure through the years. In the last decade, the Ministry of Health has concentrated on the development of a variety of healthcare infrastructure for acute care, intermediate care and long term care, as well as promoting primary care delivery by the private sector.

In the 1960s, the healthcare scenario in Singapore faced many challenges such as:

a) Dilapidated living conditions.

b) Unemployment.

c) Traffic congestion in the city.

199

Figure 10. Creating a garden city

Figure 11. Trees providing shade for roads

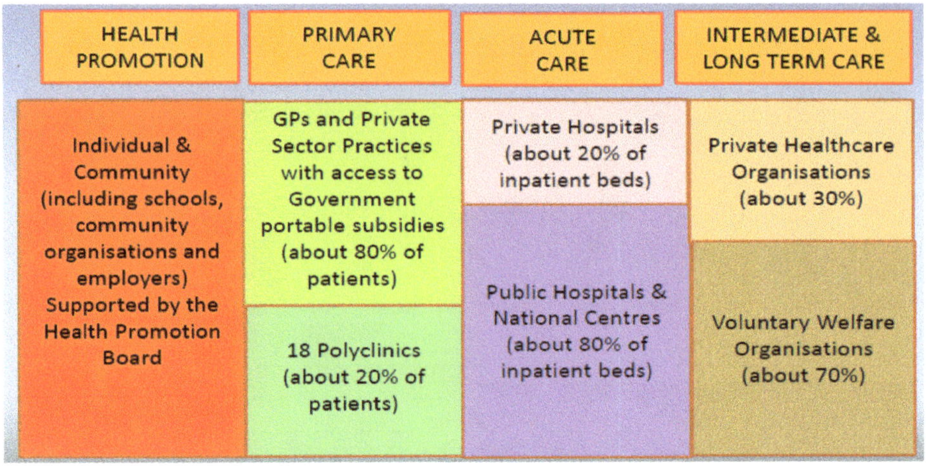

HEALTH PROMOTION	PRIMARY CARE	ACUTE CARE	INTERMEDIATE & LONG TERM CARE
Individual & Community (including schools, community organisations and employers) Supported by the Health Promotion Board	GPs and Private Sector Practices with access to Government portable subsidies (about 80% of patients)	Private Hospitals (about 20% of inpatient beds)	Private Healthcare Organisations (about 30%)
	18 Polyclinics (about 20% of patients)	Public Hospitals & National Centres (about 80% of inpatient beds)	Voluntary Welfare Organisations (about 70%)

Figure 12. Improving healthcare infrastructure

d) Inadequate infrastructure
e) Unregulated healthcare system.
f) Poor health standards.
g) Most of the island was farmland.

HEALTHCARE CONCEPT PLANS

In 1981, based on a projected population of 3.4 million by 1992, a Healthcare Concept Plan was developed to de-centralise and modernise the existing hospitals. 6 new hospitals were built in the following decade, located near the housing estates.
In 1991, the Concept Plan was revised to enable more efficient usage of services by regional clustering. 6 clusters were identified, each served by a general (acute) hospital, supported by polyclinics for outpatients and community hospitals and nursing homes for sub-acute and long term care.
The Concept Plan has been fine tuned in the recent years, to address the revised projection of 6 million population in 2020. Several new hospitals have been constructed.
Some examples of the clusters are Out-ram Medical Campus, National University Health Services and Health City Novena.

ACUTE GENERAL HOSPITALS & COMMUNITY HOSPITALS

Many new hospitals are being constructed (figures 16, 17, 18, 19, 20)

Intermediate Buildings

Apart from the acute general hospitals and community hospitals above, a new genre of healthcare facilities is being developed: the Integrated Building. These are designed to provide an environment that aims to empower patients to live as normally as possible in a hospital setting, to regain maximum independence before heading home. These are built next to the acute hospital, and the patients are provided a wide range of services to enable a smooth transition from acute to sub-acute care, and on to outpatient or home care services.
The wards are designed in a cluster concept, with home-like settings such as liv-

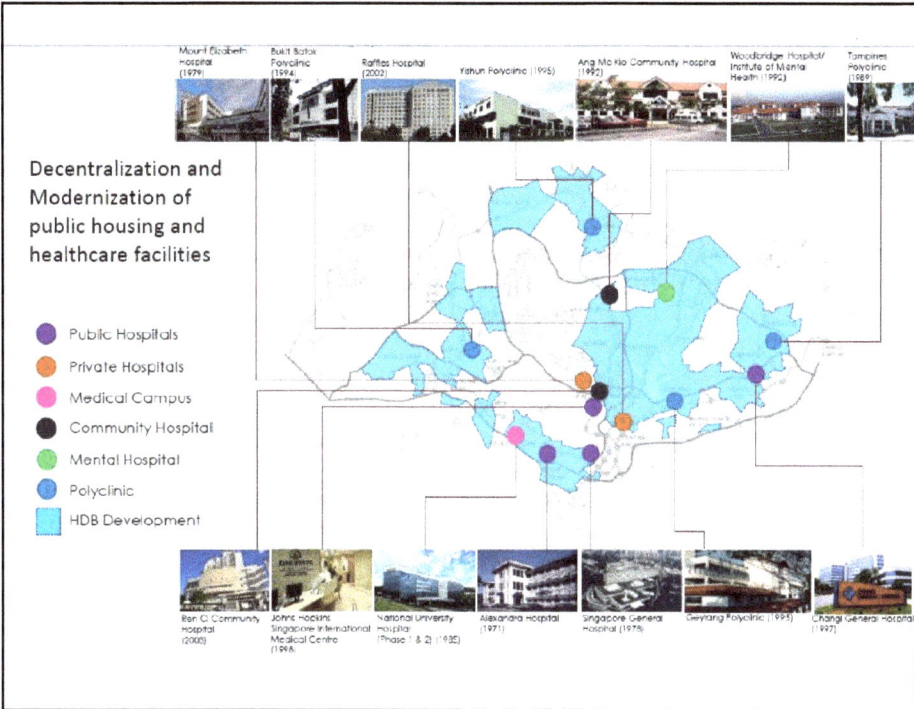

Figure 13. Concept Plan 1981

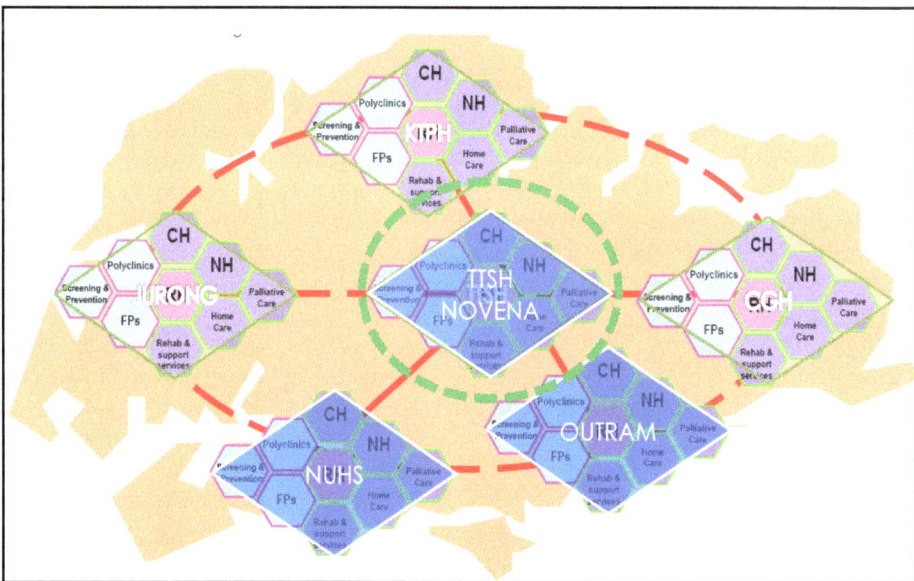

Figure 14. Concept Plan 1991

202

Figure 15. Khoo Teck Puat Hospital (2012)

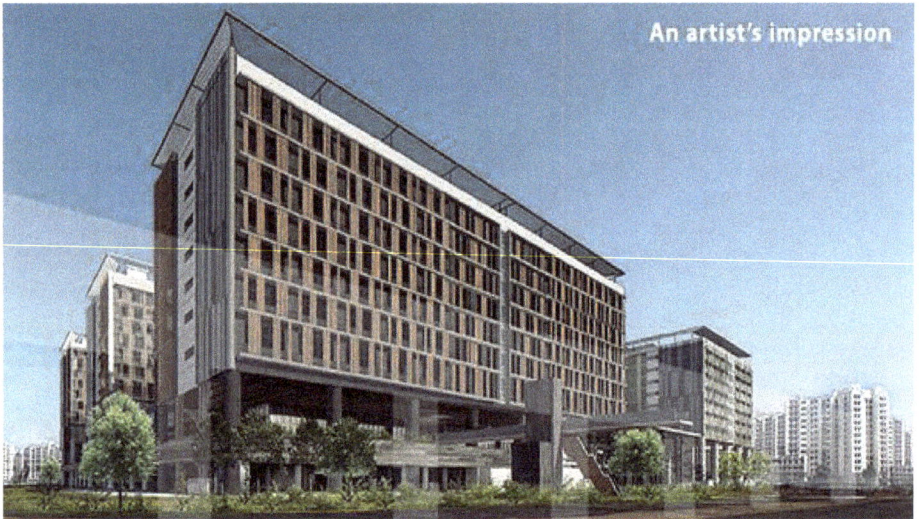

Figure 16. Seng Kang General Hospital (2018)

Figure 17. Ng Teng Fong General Hospital (2015)

Figure 18. Yishun Community Hospital

Figure 19. National Centre for Infectious Diseases (2018)

Figure 20. Jurong Community Hospital (2015)

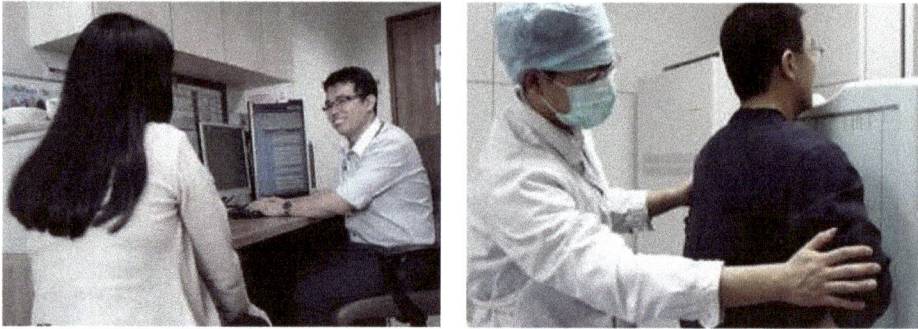

Figure 21. Subsidised healthcare and co-payment through Medi-save and introduction of CHAS

204

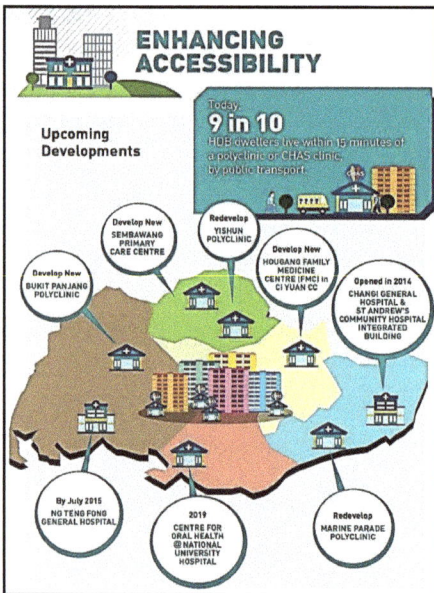

Figure 22. Improving accessibility for primary care (Source: Ministry of Health, Singapore)

Primary Healthcare

Improving primary healthcare is also important to keep the people healthy and reduce dependence on hospitals. In Singapore, over 80% of the primary healthcare service is provided by the private general practitioners (GPs). Subsidised primary care is provided in public polyclinics.

To improve accessibility to subsidised primary care, the government has started a scheme allowing the lower and middle-income households to receive subsidised medical and dental care from a group of participating GPs and dental clinics near their homes. The patient is also able to use his Medisave for healthcare expenses for chronic conditions.

New polyclinics are also being built, and existing ones enlarged and upgraded, to provide new facilities for eldercare and community services. The aim is that 90% of the people living in public housing will be within 15 minutes of a polyclinic or CHAS clinic by public transport.

A multi-pronged approach is proposed to transform primary care and enhance chronic disease management in the community. Apart from enabling infra-

ing room and family area, and patients are encouraged to live as independently as possible, and to interact with other patients. Two such Intermediate Buildings are being built – the one next to Changi General Hospital has recently been completed, and another one next to Tan Tock Seng Hospital will be completed in 2020.

structure and reviewing financing, this includes a shift towards team-based care, which brings together GPs, nurses, allied health professionals and other healthcare providers in an integrated services delivery model. This will enhance primary care providing easier access and more holistic care for patients thereby facilitating better management of chronic ailments.

The Ministry of Health is working with private GPs in providing better care to their patients in various forms including:

• Community Health Centres (CHCs) which aim to provide off-site ancillary support services (such as health education, Diabetic Retinal Photography and Diabetic Foot Screening) to GPs.

• Family Medicine Clinics (FMCs) bringing together doctors, nurses, allied health professionals and other related services in an integrated service delivery model to enable resource sharing, economies of scale and team-based care.

• Medical Centres (MCs) to provide ambulatory procedures (such as day surgery for cataract removal) in the community. Specialists will also work with GPs to co-manage patients with more complex but stable conditions as part of shared care programmes, to enable the right-siting

205

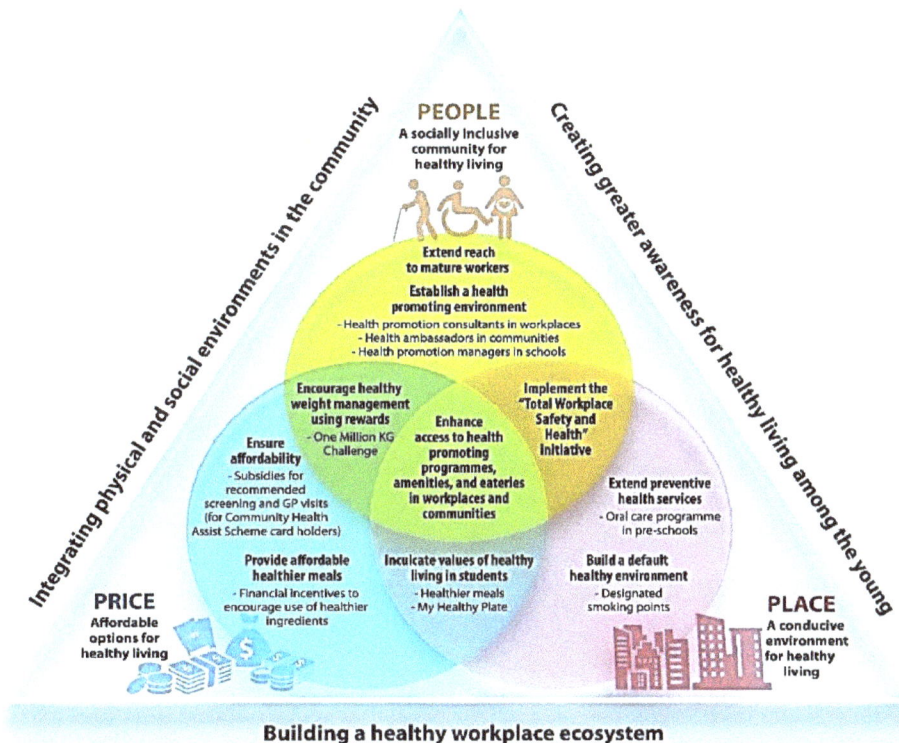

Figure 23. Promoting healthy lifestyle

TESIS Inter-University Research Centre "Systems and Technologies for Social and Healthcare Facilities"
University of Florence, Italy

of stable patients from acute hospitals' Specialist Outpatient Clinics (SOCs).

PROMOTING HEALTHY LIFESTYLE

Exercise plays an important role in a healthy lifestyle. To encourage people to exercise more, the various agencies have worked together to:

i. Develop places and environment conducive for healthy living.

ii. Develop facilities and programmes to encourage people to exercise.

iii. Ensure the options are accessible and affordable for the general public.

Where possible, facilities and programmes will be provided free, or at heavily subsidised rates.

Neighbourhood Facilities

Every housing estate has well developed parks and recreation facilities to encourage the people to go outdoors.

Figure 24. Exercise areas within the neighbourhood

Figure 25. Safe bicycle paths

Exercise areas for young and old and safe bicycle paths are provided to encourage people to keep active.

Community Centres, Senior Care Centres, etc., actively promote activities for the elderly to keep them active and healthy. In the new estates, more elaborate public parks are developed.

Island-wide Facilities

One of the major developments is the construction of a cycling network that links all the parks throughout the island. Apart from neighbourhood parks, national parks are also provided throughout the island.

The main park in Singapore is the Botanic Gardens which has been named "Asia's Best Urban Jungle" by Time Magazine, with its vast range of foliage and educational signs. The National Orchid Garden, the Ginger Garden and the Evolution Garden are part of the Botanic Gardens. There is also a Band Stand where people gather on weekends to enjoy an afternoon of jazz.

Other more specialised facilities are developed to attract the general public to go outdoors and enjoy the scenery and facilities.

One of the most popular recreation facilities is the Marina City Park with the Gardens by the Bay. Marina City Park is a public park built on 26.2 hectares of reclaimed land. It has been developed to be the premier park for the new downtown of Singapore, dubbed the "City of the 21st Century" and "City in a Garden".

The 101 hectare Gardens by the Bay is located within the Marina City Park. The park houses two air-conditioned conservatory complexes – the Flower

Figure 26. New public housing estate at Punggol with Water Park and boardwalk

Dome and the Cloud Forest which are favourite places for locals and tourists.
Many other popular recreational facilities lure people to get outdoors with family and friends.

Sports Facilities

Sports is actively encouraged, and many new facilities have been constructed and existing facilities upgraded. Mass sports encourage greater participation for the young and old.

In 2014, the new Singapore Sports Hub was completed. The 35 hectare facility comprises a 55,000 capacity stadium with a retractable roof (the largest free spanning structure in the world) and comfort cooling for the spectators, a 6,000-capacity Aquatics Centre, a 3,000-capacity Sports Arena which is scalable, modular and flexible in layout, a Water Sports Centre and other community spaces such as a skate park, hard courts, beach volleyball, playground, rock climbing, etc., and commercial

Figure 27. Cycling network linking all parks in the island

Figure 28. Marina City Park, with Gardens by the Bay

Figure 29. Waterpark at Sentosa

Figure 30. Singapore Zoo

spaces.

Other sports facilities within the island have also been upgraded to encourage the population to take part in different forms of sports.

SENIOR HOUSING OPTIONS

Singapore's population is ageing fast, and by 2030 about 20% of our population will be above the age of 65. The elderly will have special health requirements, and housing for the elderly is thus a concern. Where one should live when one ages depends on several factors:

a) Physical and medical needs

As you age you generally would need some help with physical needs including activities of daily living. In Singapore, our family ties are strong, and we try to take turns caring for our elderly parents. We are also fortunate that the cost of domestic help is relatively low, and many can afford the expense of engaging a maid to take care of our parents. However, of course there are elderly people without children, or their children are too busy at work and can't spend time at home.

Some elderly may need medical or nursing care. Alternatives thus have to be made available.

b) Home maintenance

Figure 31. Singapore Sports Hub

210

Figure 32. Water Sports Centre

All homes need some form of maintenance. If the elderly were to live alone at home, he or she may not be able to manage the tasks of housekeeping, etc. Unless there are people who can help carry out the tasks, or they can afford the cost of engaging people to do the work, the elderly may not be able to continue living at home as they age.

c) Social and emotional needs
A major problem for the elderly is the lack of social interaction. As they age, their social network decrease (friends die; or they don't venture out of their homes, thus they loose contact with

friends, etc). They may be less mobile – being wheelchair bound, or being unable to walk far – and find it too bothersome or difficult to travel around. They thus may become isolated or housebound, and become depressed.

d) Financial needs
Finances are often a major concern for the elderly. Medical costs are getting higher, especially when you age. In addition, you may need funds to renovate your house to make it more accessible.
The above factors have to be taken into consideration when making decisions of where to stay as one ages.

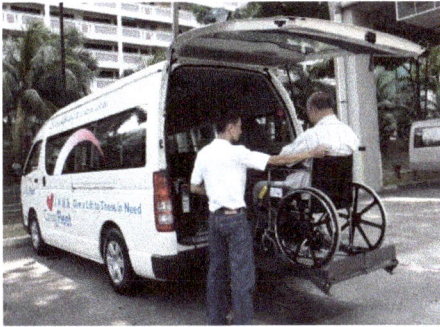

Figure 33. Transport service

Ageing in place

The elderly are generally happier to continue living at home in familiar surroundings, being taken care of by their family members. The government's goal is to help them to do so. To assist the elderly to continue living in the community, the government has come up with various schemes:

a) Bonus schemes in providing additional funding for children to buy public housing near their parents.

b) Providing some 2-generation flats for the elderly to live with their children.

c) Building apartments with special features for the elderly.

d) Providing subsidies to carry out alterations in public housing apartments to make the apartment elder-friendly.

e) Redesigning and upgrading public parks and community areas to make them elder-friendly.

f) Encouraging the development of various types of facilities and developments that are elder-friendly.

Improvements to Public Housing

The Housing Development Board (HDB) has made tremendous efforts to improve public housing to make it elder friendly. Formerly, lifts for public housing apartment blocks used to serve only alternate floors. In the last decade, the HDB has had an extensive Lift Improvement Programme, adding lift landings, and in some cases, additional lifts, to ensure all residents are served by lifts. In addition, HDB introduced Enhancement for Active Seniors (EASE) programme in 2012 where improvements are made to existing apartments to enhance safety and comfort of seniors living in HDB flats.

211

These improvements include changing floor tiles to slip-resistant floor tiles for the toilets, providing grab bars to the bathrooms, adding ramps, etc. These improvements are provided at highly subsidised rates.

There are also some estates where some apartments are specially designed for the elderly and are provided with fully accessible toilets and bathrooms, emergency call bells and healthcare facilities nearby.

The Ministry of Health (MOH) has also introduced many schemes to help the elderly including subsidised health checks, home nursing, transport service and the provision of senior care centres. There is also support available, such as the Seniors' Mobility and Enabling Fund that provide subsidies for devices and consumables needed by frail seniors, and some voluntary organisations provide ambulances and other forms of transport for the elderly.

SPECIALLY DESIGNED COMPLEXES

Kampong Admiralty

Kampong Admiralty is a specially designed building in the form of a "ver-

212

Figure 34. The Hillford – Singapore's first retirement village, to be completed in 2017

tical village". It is planned with apartments with elder-friendly features, and has healthcare and eldercare facilities within the complex.

To encourage a 3-generation lifestyle, there are also childcare facilities provided. Shops, foodcourt, supermarket and other conveniences are planned on the lower floors, and children play areas and exercise areas for adults and elderly are provided on the roof decks.

Lush landscaped areas encourage the people to spend time outdoors, and there is even a communal garden to keep the residents active.

The Hillford

In land-scarce Singapore, property prices have been too high for the development of retirement villages.

In 2014, the Urban Redevelopment Authority (the planning arm of the government) released a land parcel for development into apartments of 30-year lease, with features for the elderly.

This will be the first private development suitable to be a retirement village, and will be run by a voluntary welfare organisation.

NURSING HOMES

Ageing at home, however, may not be possible, or even the best solution for everyone. There may not be anyone at home, and the elderly could become very lonely and isolated. Or the elderly may not be physically mobile, and may need more professional help.

There is, thus, still the need for nursing homes. Currently there are about 69 nursing homes, providing about 10,000 beds. MOH is planning to increase the number of nursing beds by 17,150 by 2020. Up to date, nursing homes have been run by voluntary welfare organisations, with the government bearing a large percentage of the development cost.

Recently, MOH has announced that it is considering running 3 to 4 of its own nursing homes to allow the ministry better understanding of the issues faced by operators, and come up with solutions and innovations in eldercare. It is also looking into releasing land for new facilities and giving a hand to operators to help them scale up more quickly.

Ang Mo Kio Nursing Home

The Ang Mo Kio Nursing Home will be a new generation nursing home funded by the government, and will be one of the nursing homes run by MOH. It will have 455 beds. Instead of the traditional 8-bed institutions, the nursing home will be based on a cluster design, with landscaped courtyards.

NTUC Nursing Homes

The National Trades Union Congress (NTUC) recently announced that its first nursing home will open in Jurong West next year, and that it will be investing in another five homes in the next 3 to 5 years. The larger role of the government in preparing for the silver future is to be welcomed. Together with NTUC, the Ministry can help create baseline standards, for example, in ensuring the

213

Figure 35. The proposed Ang Mo Kio Nursing Home

Figure 36. Home-like design with cluster concept and landscaped courtyards

Figure 37. New NTUC nursing home at Jurong Westig.

TESIS Inter-University Research Centre "Systems and Technologies for Social and Healthcare Facilities"
University of Florence, Italy

correct staff-patient ratio to deliver adequate care and guard against abuses arising when staff are over-stretched.

SUMMARY

Health-oriented design looks at development of the city in a holistic manner. Firstly, the fundamental basic needs must be met – clean water and food, adequate and safe housing, and a safe and relatively comfortable environment.

Singapore spent the first 30 years since Independence in 1965 working on achieving the fundamentals.

In the last 20 years, as economy prospered, the country was able to build new facilities, improving its hospitals, housing and recreational buildings. More attention was paid to health and sports promotion, and to encourage active healthy living.

In the last few years, more attention has been paid to caring for the aged. Public housing has had additional facilities added to homes to help the aged, and new types of private developments are being built to address the special needs for the elderly.

The government has invested in many developments and programmes to promote healthcare and to try to make it available, accessible and affordable. Many recreational facilities have been built – these are freely accessible or heavily subsidised to encourage usage.

Singapore celebrates its 50th Anniversary since independence this year. It is hoped that in future as the people age, the environment will become even more elder-friendly. As the Minister of Health said in his Committee of Supply speech, the aim is to build Singapore to be a place where everyone can look forward to their happy golden years, leading active, healthy and fulfilling lives.

REFERENCES

Ministry of Health & Health Promotion Board, 2014. *The Healthy Living Master Plan*, Singapore

Department of Statistics, Singapore. *Complete Life Tables 2008 - 2013 for Singapore Resident Population*

Singapore Government. *White Paper on Affordable Healthcare*, October 1993

Lim, J. and Tan, C. (2011). *Strategic Orientations in Singapore Healthcare*, Singapore

Lim, MK. (1998). *Health Care Systems in Transition II*. Singapore, Part I. An overview of health care systems in Singapore. J Public Health Med, 20, pp. 16-22

Gan, KY. (2014). *Committee of Supply speech by Minister for Health* – better health for all (Part 1 or 2), Singapore.

Ibrahim, MF. (2013). *Committee of Supply Speech By Parliamentary Secretary for Health*, - Healthy Together, Anytime, Anywhere - Making the Connections, 12 March 2013

Robinson, Lawrence, Saisan, Joanna, White, Monica (2015). *Senior Housing Options* – Making the Best Senior Living Choices

The Straits Times. (2014). *Nursing Homes as Test Bed for Aged Care*, Singapore.

Evidence-Based Approaches to Medical City Master Planning in a Frontier Market: a Case Project in Akwa Ibom, Nigeria

Chanam Lee

clee@arch.tamu.edu
Texas A&M University

This presentation is to explore how existing theories and empirical evidence can be used to guide the development of a medical city master plan in a frontier market, using a project case in Akwa Ibom, Nigeria.

DESCRIPTION

While the Niger Delta region is known for it rich natural and ecological resources, its residents have suffered from inadequate access to healthcare. The region's infant mortality rate is among the highest in the world. According to World Bank, life expectancy of Nigerians as of 2012 was only about 52 years, compared to 79 for Americans and 75 for Chinese. Large-scale interventions like the implementation of a comprehensive medical city can respond to the urgent need to improve health and heath care among this vulnerable segment of the population.

METHODS

A qualitative approach was used to collect inductive data from several sources to cover all critical elements needed for developing a comprehensive medical city in a frontier market. Data originated from: (1) case studies of ten most relevant examples, (2) literature reviews and research on nine most relevant substantive topics, (3) in-depth interviews with the clients and stakeholders of health and human developments in Nigeria and the US, and (4) field observations to gather all necessary physical and socio-cultural data from the project site. The evidence-based design/planning approach offered a valuable framework to guide the master-planning decision-making process.

RESULTS

The data gathered were synthesized and analyzed to extract most salient elements of medical city master planning, which were then categorized into 'people,' 'economy,' and 'environment.' This led to the development of three overarching guiding principles for the master planning: (1) healthy living for all, (2) economic and cultural developments, and (3) sustainable and low-impact development. In addition, eleven master plan objectives including active living, safety/security, food systems planning,

216

economic development and education, etc., and 60 performance measures were derived from the data gathered.

The ten-month master planning process involving multidisciplinary team and advisor members resulted in a comprehensive plan that will serve as the basis for implementing the medical city within the next three years. The final Thompson & Grace Medical City master plan was developed to create a sustainable and self-contained mixed use community anchored by a world-class teaching hospital on a 100-acre green field property. It provides a full range of healthcare services, including curative and preventive cares, and traditional and alternative cares, to residents, employers and visitor. It proposed optimal spatial arrangements of diverse land uses including an urban center, hotel, conference center, diverse residential communities, artisan village, entertainment center, elementary school, and industrial park. The City's land uses are supported by multi-modal transportation systems and extensive green infrastructure, while responding to the local history, culture and landscape. It was prepared to serve a model for future healthcare development in Africa and other frontier markets.

CONCLUSION

This project offers theoretical and practical insights into the design, planning, and implementation processes for developing healthcare projects and communities in a frontier market.

Walkable Communities and Obesity: the Relationship between Community Environments and Utilitarian Walking among US Adults with Overweight and Obesity

Chanam Lee

clee@arch.tamu.edu
Texas A&M University

Walking is a low-impact, low-cost form of physical activity with potential to offer considerable health benefits, especially to those who have overweight or obesity. Walking for utilitarian purposes holds additional benefits as a transportation mode as it can help lower pollution and congestion. We examined the relationship between the built environment and utilitarian walking among US adults with overweight and obesity compared to adults with normal weight.

METHODS AND ANALYSIS

We interviewed adult residents from nine small towns in three US regions: Washington State, Texas, and the Northeast. Through telephone surveys (n=2,152) we obtained data on demographics, race and ethnicity, health and socioeconomic status, walking barriers and facilitators, behavioral factors, and neighborhood perceptions.

The outcome variable was utilitarian walking at least once a week in the neighborhood, and the main independent variables were the environmental variables that included both objective measures (Geographic Information System, GIS) and subjective measures (survey).

The GIS measures were taken within a 1-km street-network buffer around each survey respondent's home, or as the shortest street route distance from home to each target destination.

Mixed-effect logistic regression models were used to predict the odds of walking for groups of adults with normal weight, overweight, and obesity separately.

RESULTS

Over 15% (335 out of 2,152 respondents) had obesity (BMI of 30+); 36.7% had overweight (25-29.9); and 34.2% had normal (18.5-24.9) weight.

Controlling personal covariates, only one environmental variable was correlated with walking in all three BMI groups: perceived presence of a trail/path/track (+). Significant subjective measures were perceived presence of parks (+ in groups with normal weight and overweight), grocery stores/supermarkets (+ in overweight group), coffee places (+ in obesity group), and schools (+ in obesity group). From the GIS variables, the ratio of re-

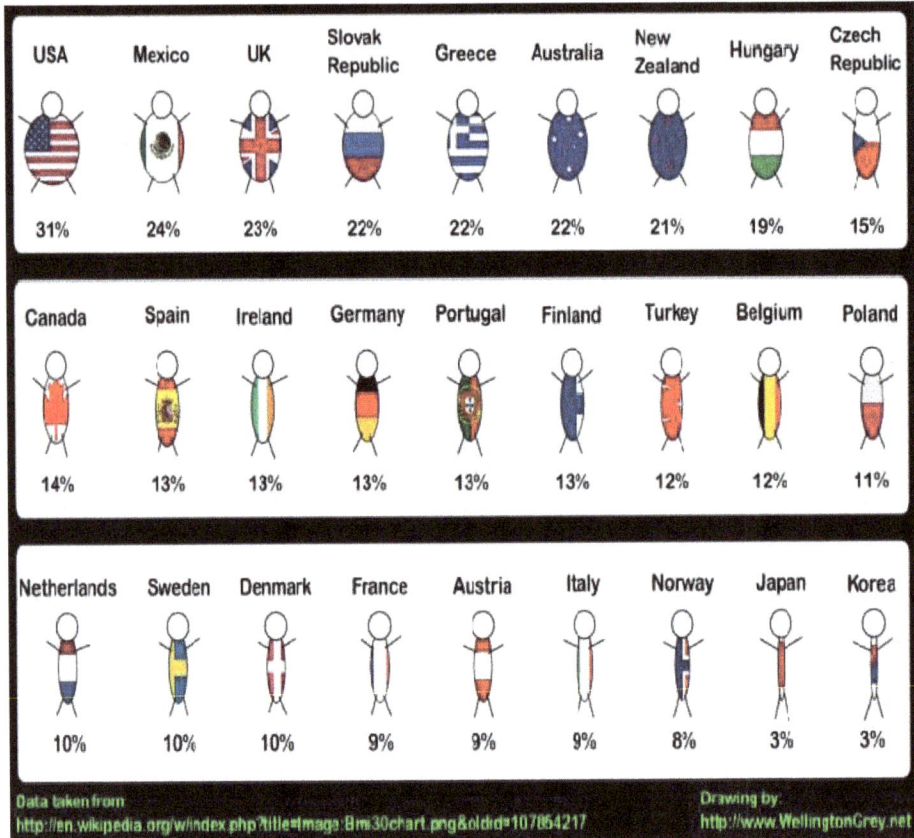

Figure 1. Obesity: the percentage of the population older than 15 with a body-mass index greater than 30

Table 2. Actual Causes of Death in the United States in 1990 and 2000

Actual Cause	No. (%) in 1990*	No. (%) in 2000
Tobacco	400 000 (19)	435 000 (18.1)
Poor diet and physical inactivity	300 000 (14)	400 000 (16.6)
Alcohol consumption	100 000 (5)	85 000 (3.5)
Microbial agents	90 000 (4)	75 000 (3.1)
Toxic agents	60 000 (3)	55 000 (2.3)
Motor vehicle	25 000 (1)	43 000 (1.8)
Firearms	35 000 (2)	29 000 (1.2)
Sexual behavior	30 000 (1)	20 000 (0.8)
Illicit drug use	20 000 (<1)	17 000 (0.7)
Total	1 060 000 (50)	1 159 000 (48.2)

*Data are from McGinnis and Foege.[1] The percentages are for all deaths.

Figure 2. Actual Causes of Death in the United States, 2000, Ali H. Mokdad, PhD; James S. Marks, MD, MPH; Donna F. Stroup, PhD, MSc; Julie L. Gerberding, MD, MPH, JAMA. 2004

Obesity Trends* Among U.S. Adults
BRFSS, 1990
(*BMI ≥30, or ∼ 30 lbs. overweight for 5' 4" person)

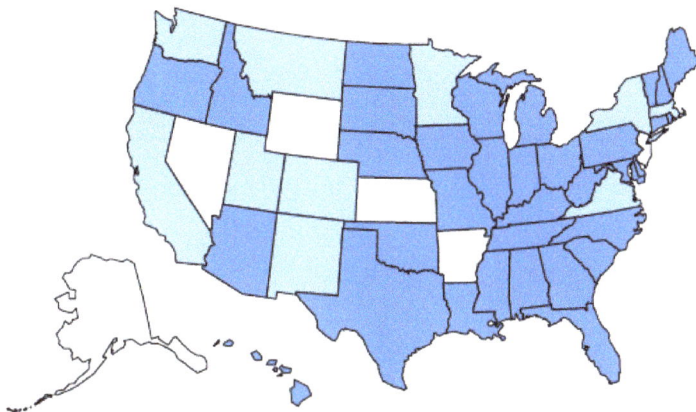

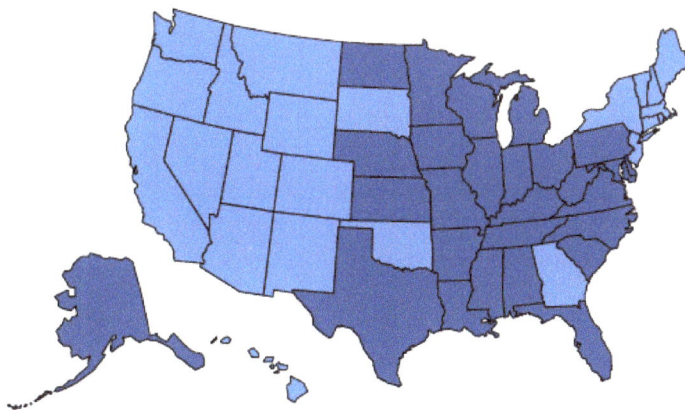

No Data   <10%   10%–14%

Obesity Trends* Among U.S. Adults
BRFSS, 1995
(*BMI ≥30, or ∼ 30 lbs. overweight for 5' 4" person)

No Data   <10%   10%–14%   15%–19%

TESIS Inter-University Research Centre "Systems and Technologies for Social and Healthcare Facilities"
University of Florence, Italy

TESIS

220

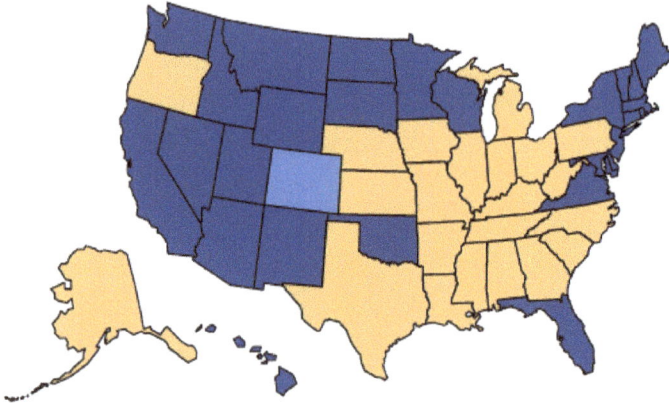

Obesity Trends* Among U.S. Adults
BRFSS, 2000
(*BMI ≥30, or ~ 30 lbs. overweight for 5' 4" person)

No Data   <10%   10%–14%   15%–19%   20%–24%

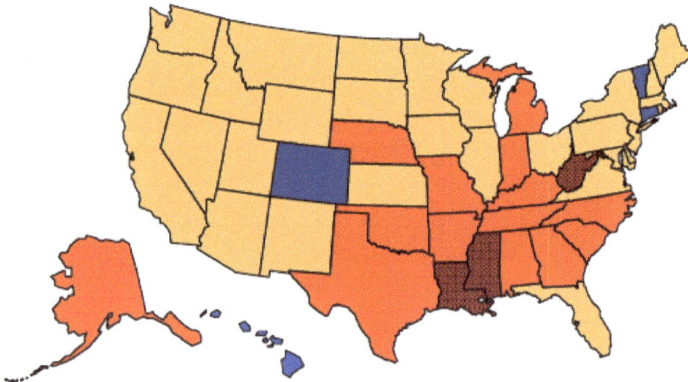

Obesity Trends* Among U.S. Adults
BRFSS, 2005
(*BMI ≥30, or ~ 30 lbs. overweight for 5' 4" person)

No Data   <10%   10%–14%   15%–19%   20%–24%   25%–29%   ≥30%

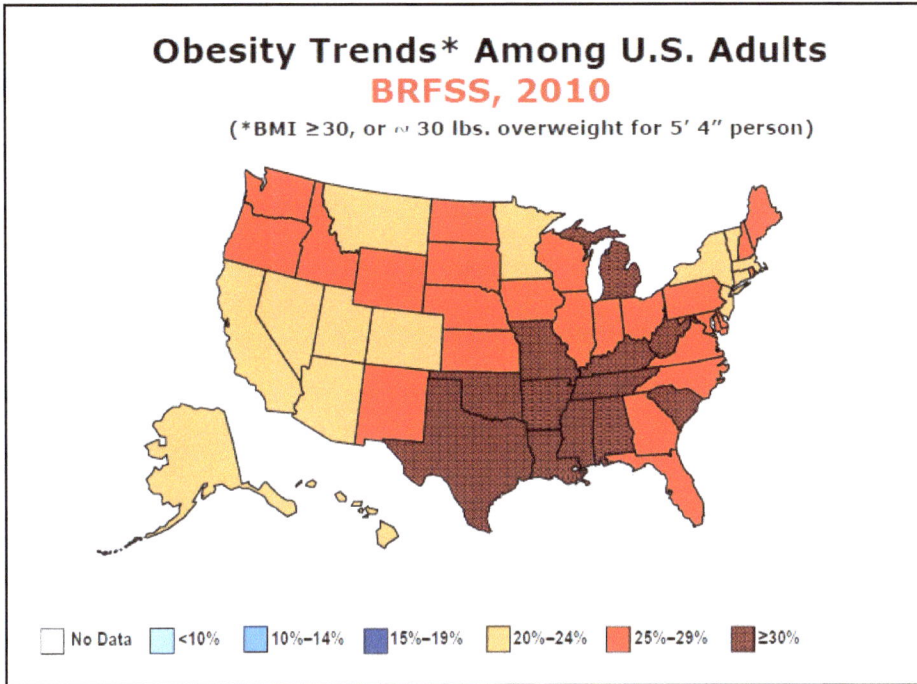

Figure 3. Obesity Trends Among U.S. Adults (Source: Behavioral Risk Factor Surveillance System, CDC)

source production/extraction land use area within the buffer was negatively correlated with walking among groups with overweight and obesity.

The numbers of parks (+), banks (+), and pizza places (-) were significant only in the overweight, while the number of drugstores (+) was significant in the obesity group only. For the normal weight group, only two GIS variables were significant, both of which were related to transportation infrastructure: number of crosswalks (+) and sidewalk length (+).

DISCUSSIONS AND CONCLUSIONS

This study identified variations in the characteristics of the built environment in small US towns and their relationships to weight status.

Infrastructure-related variables were more relevant to promoting walking among normal weight adults, while recreational facilities such as parks, trails, and schools (local schools in our town often have walking tracks available for public use) and certain service destinations such as drug stores and banks were more relevant for adults with overweight or obesity.

Future research on the relationship between the built environment and walking could explore how people of different weight, health, and income status may perceive or react to a range of environmental features differently as the barriers or facilitators of walking; and how communities in different settings (urban, suburban, rural) may require different environmental strategies to promote residents' walking.

TESIS Inter-University Research Centre "Systems and Technologies for Social and Healthcare Facilities"
University of Florence, Italy

222

Figure 4. Urban Sprawl and Auto-Centered Infrastructure

Figure 5. Lack of Adequate Pedestrian Infrastructure

Figure 6. Automobile Dependency

Longevity Park

Donald A. Grant

grantd@silktreegroup.com
Australian Institute of Landscape Architects

223

An exploding aging population in China (WHO figures show that by 2050 China will have more than 330 million Chinese aged 65 or older, with 100 million of them aged over 80), has prompted the Chinese government to try different ways in which to "manage" this aging population trend and the consequences of it. This management includes not only programs and funding for aged care facilities but funding for the redevelopment of parks and gardens to promote an healthy and active lifestyle. Wanshou Park in Beijing is a shining demonstration of one of these initiatives. The park has been redesigned to reintegrate the elderly into the community, encouraging them to age "actively" by fostering participation in physical and social activities and using the park and its surrounding facilities to offer additional services such as health and mental wellbeing.

INTRODUCTION

World Health Organisation figures show that by 2050 China will have more than 330 million Chinese aged 65 or older, with 100 million people aged over 80. The Chinese government needs to "manage" this ageing population trend and the consequences of it by introducing different initiatives.

Wanshou Park in Beijing is a shining demonstration of one of these initiatives. The park has been redesigned to reintegrate the elderly into the community, encouraging them to age "actively" by fostering participation in physical and social activities and using the park and its surrounding facilities to offer additional services such as health and mental wellbeing.

If the Wanshou Park redevelopment is successful, it could become a model for other parks and a driver for urban development with a focus on rehabilitation and aged care facilities.

CONTEXT/BACKGROUND

Typically the health, mobility, physical and mental abilities of elderly people deteriorate with increased age. This deterioration can be minor or major depending on the individual.

The individual then needs to be assisted (to varying degrees) by support from family members, medical or health care professionals. This support system made up of workers, families and friends, can

TESIS Inter-University Research Centre "Systems and Technologies for Social and Healthcare Facilities"
University of Florence, Italy

TESIS

be given a numeric value called a PSR. The PSR (potential support ratio) of a society indicates the dependency burden on a societies support system. This value is determined by the ratio of the number of persons aged 15-64 years per one older person aged 65 years or old.

The impact of the above mentioned rise in the global elderly demographic is visible in the global PSR, which has fallen and will continue to fall. In the 50 years between 1950 and 2000, the PSR fell from 12 to 9 people.

In the next 50 years the global PSR is projected to be 4 persons for each person 65 years or older. China's PSR currently stands at 8 and will fall faster than the global trend. It is projected that by 2050 China's PSR could be as low as 3. PSR's are important indicators for our society because they signal major implications for our social security systems, health care infrastructure and family support systems. The lower the PSR the greater pressure on the support mechanism.

There are two ways in which this PSR pressure can be addressed. The first is by strengthening the existing support systems, which can be done in a variety of ways. We can create more health care positions that cater for the aged or provide financial support for families to be able to provide for health and aged care, again this requires an increase in the numbers of health care professionals. We can also build more aged care facilities and other facilities whereby the aged can find it easier to take care of themselves, again increasing manpower. These steps are by no means extensive and a full array of other steps and measures could be introduced by families, societies and governments.

These steps can all be seen as being reactive solutions to the ageing issue and can be seen as one way of handling the situation. A second way to address this pressure would be to create a proactive scenario whereby the burden on the system is lessened, before it actually happens. One of these proactive steps will be expanded on later in this paper.

ACTIVE AGING

1999 was declared by the WHO (World Health Organisation) the International Year of Older Persons. During this year the WHO reinforced the benefits of

Figure 1. Active aging?

active ageing for older persons and the need for social integration and a healthy lifestyle throughout someone's life.

The main emphasis of the WHO initiative is to highlight the fact that ageing not only has to be active but it had to be something that happens with the involvement of the family, society as a whole and it has to happen in a supportive environment.

The active ageing process also needs to be able to maintain autonomy and independence for the elderly. This is a key goal in the policy framework for active ageing, the role that the rest of society has to play is also important.

The concept of active ageing is the maximisation of opportunities for health and wellbeing, involvement, comfort and freedom in order to enhance the quality of life as people age.

Active ageing allows people to realize their prospects for social, physical and mental well-being throughout the rest of their life and to participate in society, while providing them with adequate protection, security and care when they require it.

The concept of active ageing is aimed at providing the best possible future for the elderly throughout their twilight years but it also has a secondary effect in that it lessens the burden on the support system. The healthier and more active the individual the less support required. Increasing the quality of life of older people and compressing the period of time in which they can find themselves living in a state of dependence and morbidity lessens the support required on those that care for them both in terms of its intensiveness and its duration.

The term "active" is not limited to one's physical ability to participate in sports or the labour force, it means involvement in society as a whole, being involved in economic, cultural, spiritual and civic affairs. Older people who retire, have disabilities or have chronic illnesses can and should remain active contributors to society, by keeping the elderly active and healthy it extends their quality of life and their continuing involvement in society.

People of different age groups, ethnicities and social classes have different spiritual, physical, and psychological needs, these make up who we are as individuals and how we behave.

All of our needs and behaviours need context, that is, a set of circumstances or facts that surround that particular requirement. For example spiritual behaviour may mean that people need a church or a mosque.

They may need private space or public space. They may need particular times of the day to be with their spirituality. Peoples' physical requirements also need specific context, that is sports fields, walking areas, exercise equipment, swimming pools or just areas where people can be with their families to interact with. Both peoples requirements/behaviour and the context in which they occur go hand in hand.

While it is important to state that specific individual requirements or behavioural patterns need context the reverse is also true. Specific context can lead to specific behaviour. In his book *The Tipping Point* (2000) Malcolm Galdwell states that "the power of context is crucial to all varieties of human behaviour. We are, he argues, exquisitely sensitive to changes in context".

Context can drive behaviour; slums tend

225

226

to breed crime more than affluent areas, loving caring relationships usually breed loving caring people, good educators usually develop intelligent thinking people. This being the case we must strive to develop a context whereby the elderly can be active. We must provide the framework and the support mechanisms that underly this, physically, socially and politically. Nursing homes provide some of that context but they tend to lack the ability to provide the support for the requirements of active ageing.

If we consider an active social, economic, cultural, spiritual and civic and put these into the context of a nursing home, does the behaviour match the context? Are the facilities provided by a nursing home or aged care facility providing adequate context for aged people to be active? In its base form the word active means to participate or to engage in, can people participate and engage in all of the above activities confined to a building. A single building or group of buildings provides some context or place for these active events but it is limited in its ability to be dynamic, it is limited in ability to link in with the environment, it is limited in its ability to provide a multitude of different spaces for different uses for individuals and groups at the same time.

Architecture and buildings have important roles to play in aged care but to limit the support mechanisms for active ageing to bricks, mortar, glass steel and concrete is to limit the ability of people to be active.

Buildings are primarily static objects. Just like society as a whole needs to be able to move through varieties of spaces, to observe and experience varieties of stimuli, to interact with people and places and to actively engage with the environment, people and places, the elderly need to do this as well, if not more so, as their needs and support requirements become greater with age.

Global development trends for better communities espouse the need for an integrated approach to new communities and cities. We need buildings to nestle into open spaces, we need efficient and effective transport routes, we need green networks connecting major hubs, we need a good mixture of residential, commercial and recreation land use to be easily accessible and available, this is good planning practice.

Why then shouldn't these essential planning goals be dropped down to the micro level and be used when planning for aged care communities and development for the elderly. Aged care facilities whether they are individual buildings (which goes against the grain of community interaction) or larger scale developments need to have greater focus on integrated design.

Currently the design process for these types of facilities are limited to healthcare professionals and architects. This means that the focus is on the building envelope and the facilities within. This diametrically opposes the notion of "activeness". Open space networks or parks need to be incorporated into the design as well as upgrading of access and egress routes. Shops and transport options need to be close at hand.

People need these to be "active". In a lot of societies (mainly western societies) the elderly are seen as burden and put somewhere where someone else can manage the "problem". This scenario means that the major players in the ageing industry are governments, health providers and developers. Governments tend to push difficult problems aside for others to solve (at a cost) and the providers and developers are only involved in projects that make money. The driving force behind health care for the elderly is economic not social.

WANSHOU PARK

For humans to survive we must cohabitate and provide for all levels of society, for all age groups. If the majority of the population are going to be elderly then services, programmes, infrastructure all need to cater for the elderly. But it is not just good enough to have relative programmes and infrastructure, it is not good enough to be reactive we need to be proactive in our approach.

We need to provide the infrastructure for active ageing. This can be done more readily in open space, parks and gardens that it can be in buildings. People are dynamic entities that have moods, change their minds, prefer different activities, different interactions. Buildings are limited in their ability, tend to be static in their form and one dimensional in their

uses. They provide the infrastructure for many requirements of an ageing population, such as health care facilities and spaces for aged care requirements.

They also provide shelter and protection from the elements but they lack the dynamism that is required for active ageing. Open space and parks on the other hand have this dynamism. The ability of a park to be able to provide different settings at different times of the year give a park an ability to appeal to the widest range of active person.

In 2012-13 Silk Tree International was invited to design a refurbishment for Wanshou Park, Beijing that specifically focused on the use of the park by the elderly to promote active ageing. Wanshou Park (Wanshou is the Chinese symbol for longevity) sits in an older area of downtown Beijing and the district surrounding it has one of the oldest demographic profiles in the country.

Silk Tree initially used the "active ageing guidelines" outlined by WHO as the base point for our design. A survey was carried out with the existing elderly users

227

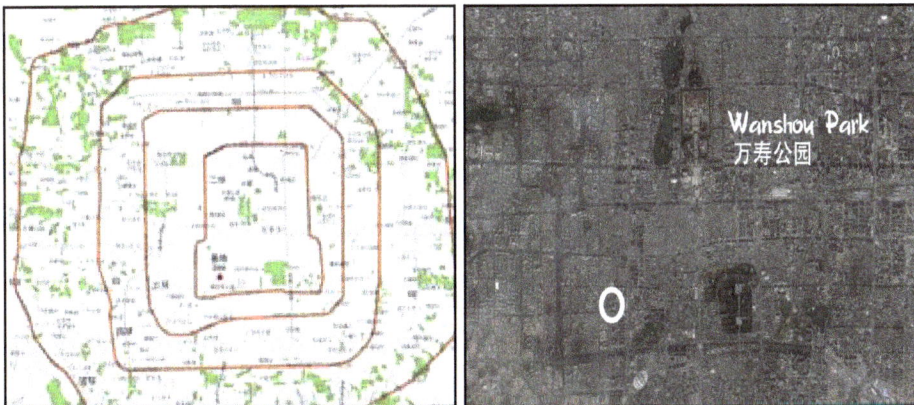

Figure 2. Wanshou Park, Beijing showing its proximity to the centre of the old city

of the park as well as a physical survey of the park and its immediate surrounds. Once this initial phase of survey and inventory was carried out interviews were carried out with expert in feng shui as well as interviewing an expert in *xiao*.

Xiao in Chinese means filial piety, which in layman terms is being good to your parents and taking care of them. *Xiao* is also about conducting ones self in a way that brings a good name to your family and ancestors and to carry out all of your duties in a courteous, respectful and righteous way. *Xiao* is considered a key virtue in China and respect for ones family is one of the major ethical values that is common to the majority of Chinese. To understand *xiao* in the context of Chinese culture and the way in which the park was to be redesigned was important because we had to understand how interaction occurred not only between the elderly but also between the younger and older generations.

The Chinese character for *Xiao* is 孝
This character is combination of two other Chinese characters, the first is 老 (lao) which is the symbol for old and 字 (zi) which is the symbol for son. Combined they form the character for *Xiao* 孝 which represents an elder being carried by a son, filial piety.

When we first started looking at the park design we also wanted some background on design issues that made parks multigenerational.

The need to include different generations is important, as inclusion in a greater society rather than seclusion and isolation is important, even more so in a society such as China. In 1986 an industrial design professor named James J. Pirkl at Syracuse University coined the term "transgenerational design". This term described the way that products and environments can cater for a wide range of people who will use them. From young to old from physically abled to physically challenged. We wanted our park to be truly transgenerational.

Wanshou park design has been driven by seven major design drivers:Rehabilitation, Exercise, Connections, Leisure, Amenities, Initiatives and Music.
RECLAIM is the philosophy of our design. We want the elderly to reclaim their lives and not be sedentary and dependant on others.
We want to reclaim the park for the people who want to use it, the most. We want to reclaim the way societal needs are addressed and most of all we want to reclaim the rights of people to be able to live and age the way they want to.

Rehabilitation

The rehabilitation area of the park focuses on both physical rehabilitation and psychological/mental rehabilitation. The physical rehabilitation area is centred around 3 small core gardens, these gardens are based on the three major principles of rehabilitating people who require it; strength, balance and resistance.
The three gardens are joined together so that people can move from one to the other easily and also see how friends and/or family are progressing. Psychological/mental rehabilitation is also considered in several other ways.
Firstly we have designed and built sev-

Figure 3.   New siheyuan entrance

Figure 4.   The family/xiao sculptures

Figure 5. Horizontal maze

eral elements that represent old Beijing. As the city has developed, the traditional old 4-sided housing compounds (*sihey-uan*) have been knocked down to make way for newer residential areas and/or commercial facilities. These siheyuan are representative of the architecture of Northern China, where people used to live as a family unit.

We have rebuilt a siheyuan as the main gate on the eastern side of the park, so that when people enter the park they have to walk through the old style courtyard. We wanted people to remember and reflect on their youth, thus stimulating memory and recall.

Towards the southern entrance of the park we have created a horizontal maze, this is stimulate memory and to help people with longer term disabilities such as Dementia and Alzheimer's. Traditionally a maze would have been a nightmare for people with these conditions, but we have created a maze that is totally at ground level so that no-one is unseen and if people get disoriented they can just walk out. It is thought that this maze could be used as therapy and it would be best to be done with helpers. A horticultural therapy area is set up in the south west of the park. This includes raised garden beds for people who have issues with movement. The beds are to be planted with mainly vegetables and herbs, as well as plants used traditionally in Chinese herbal medicine.

The Horticultural area also has a glasshouse to contain floral display all year round. As Beijing experiences extremely cold winters indoor facilities are essential. Both the glasshouse and the horticultural area accessible year round.

Exercise

Exercise opportunities takes place all over the park. These opportunites take the form of exercise equipment (adult playground), formalised play areas such as croquet courts and badminton courts and more informal exercise areas such as a walking track which circumnavigates

230

the park.

Large grass areas and large hard paved areas are provided for activities such as Tai chi, kite flying etc. Depending on the levels of fitness ad mobility there are opportunities to exercise through the park. In the more focused and consolidated exercise areas we have placed children playgrounds close by. The sounds and sights of the younger generations help the elderly to feel "at home".

Connections

The majority of modern built facilities, including parks and gardens are usually designed in isolation, they shouldn't be. The way in which people travel to, move in and around facilities is of the utmost importance.

The way in which a facility sits in a broader context is also very important. The redesign of Wanshou park looks at both of these aspects in relationship to the elderly and all of the people who want to use the park. The park is approximately 500 metres away from the subway, so connection to the Beijing metro is close at hand.

We have recommended to the local government that the footpath between the station and the two park entrances be relaid to cater for people with diminished mobility. The park also has eight bus routes that pass the park, we have relocated two of the major bus stops to the two entrances to the park on the East and South.

Within a 2 kilometre radius of the park lies a number of facilities that can enhance the use of the park from an elderly persons perspective. Inside this radius there are two public libraries, many local restaurants, two schools (one primary and one secondary), a mosque, church and a hospital. All of these are important to the life and wellbeing of the elderly some for physical reasons (hos-

231

Figure 6. Glasshouse

TESIS Inter-University Research Centre "Systems and Technologies for Social and Healthcare Facilities"
University of Florence, Italy

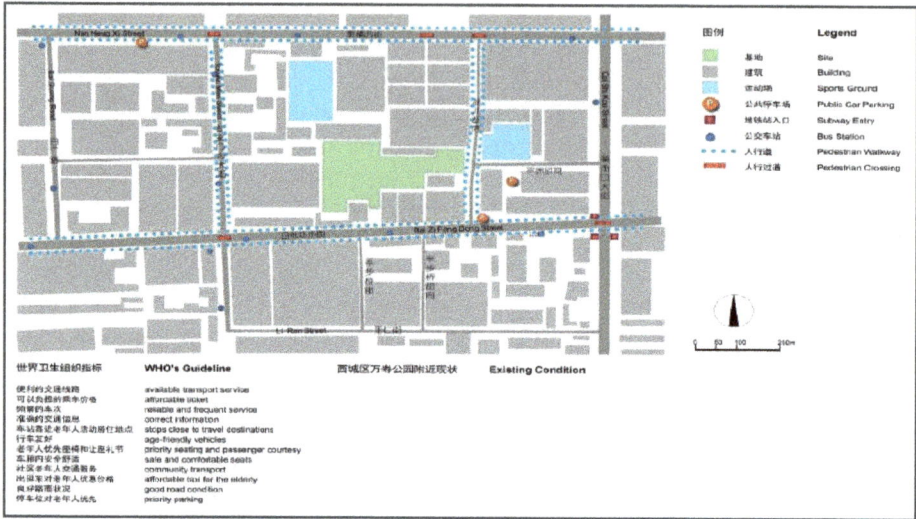

Figure 7. Surrounding facilities

pital, restaurant), some for spiritual reasons (mosque, church), some for mental wellbeing reasons (library) and some for family reasons (schools).

It is envisaged that in the future all of the physical connections to these facilities will be upgraded and that a shuttle service loop goes past all of these facilities on a regular timetable.

Leisure Activities

Leisure activities for the park occur both indoors and outdoors. Leisure activities for the Chinese are very similar to that of western elderly in some ways but different in others.

Similarities include such outdoor activities as chess, backgammon, checkers, sitting and chatting and indoor activities such as cross stitch, knitting, weaving and watching tv. The differences are minor with differences in board games and crafts. The park caters for all of these activities, both indoors and outdoors, night and day with the facilities all lo-

cated within the park.

Amenities

Amenities and facilities provided for in the park include as much as possible to make the park as comfortable as possible for the users. Specific benches and seats have heating which can be turned on during winter. The park also has a collection of air conditioned fans that can be provided throughout the park during the hotter months. Seating throughout the park is located every 20 metres providing ample opportunities for rest. Panic buttons on well marked bollards are located at strategic locations to enable park staff to assist anybody who is under duress. Shade in the form of trees, shelters, pavilions and arbours are located throughout.

In the centre of the park is a large famous temple that is to be upgraded to provide both amenity and spiritual activity. A "bird" area is to be enlarged for the elderly to listen, look and enjoy the old men and their pet birds who come to the park on a regular basis. The park is well lit enabling night time activities. Drinking fountains and hot water taps are located to enable cold and hot drinks year round.

One of the smaller buildings in the park is to be provided with a new digital screen, which will be located to convey messages about health and well being for the elderly, including cooking and hygiene tips, weather forecasts and local news. Mobile phone chargers have also been placed both indoors and outdoors for the convenience of the users.

Initiatives

To involve the community and the greater society more we have tabled some initiatives that can be incorporated into the park. It is forecast that within the next 10-15 years most medical practitioners will have had to have some training or exposure to the care of the elderly.

We have proposed to two hospitals in the area to have a medical station permanently manned at the park so that, doctors, nurses, interns and other health care professionals can provide a free medical service to the park. It is intended that the service be limited to blood pressure testing, eye sight testing, reflex testing, initial consultations, discussions, workshops etc. We see this as being a double win situation, where:

i. The people who attend the park get medical professionals to discuss their issues and maybe give them initial consultations.

ii. It gives medical staff, in particular interns, the opportunity to get accustomed to and familiar with issues of the elderly, in a calmer environment than that of a hospital.

The local schools have been approached to provide school monitors for the park during school hours. These children would basically walk around the park, keeping an eye on the elderly and offering a helping hand where needed. Again we see this as a double win situation, where:

i. The elderly people who attend the park have a helping hand and keen eye on them at all times helping if situations become more than they can handle.

ii. It gives the children a sense of purpose, of community pride and responsibility. It give the children a very real sense of the meaning of xiao.

We have also approached supermarkets and food suppliers to look at ways in which market days for the sale of fruit and vegetables and other items can occur in the park on a regular basis. This could occur purely as a vendor of goods, or provide some incentives to people to eat healthy and buy organic products. There could be a greater community involvement in this as well. Again a win-win.

i. The elderly have the opportunity to buy fresh produce without the hassle of having to travel or shop. This produce could even be cooked on site as part of cooking demonstrations.

ii. Secondly it gives suppliers and food chains an opportunity to meet their CSR requirements and be a marketing tool for them in the greater scheme of things.

Music

Music is a large part of most cultures and the Chinese are no different. One of the great sights in any Chinese city

233

Figure 8. Leisure activities

Figure 9. Music

234

is to see the elderly (and sometimes the not so elderly) dancing with their friends and partners in the local parks.

This occurs most evenings, all year round, in large and small plaza spaces all around China. On weekends and at night the sounds of the elderly playing traditional musical instruments fills the air around parks and gardens. Both of these activities require hardscape areas and seating so that groups of people can play sing and/or dance. These areas we have placed very close to the rehabilitation area so that people will be inspired to get well and be mobile.

CONCLUSIONS

The great ramifications of population ageing present enormous opportunities as well as enormous challenges for our society, it is our responsibility to make the most of these opportunities.

George Bernard Shaw said "We don't stop playing because we grow old; we grow old because we stop playing." Roget invented the thesaurus at the age of 73, Colonel Sanders was 65 when he launched KFC, Ronald Reagan was 74 when he started his second term as President of the United States, Warren Buffett is 77, William Gladstone was 82 when

he became Prime Minister of the United Kingdom. Oscar Swahn from Sweden won three olympic medals at the 1908 Olympics, he won two olympic medals at the 1912 Olympics and one olympic medal at the 1920 Olympics. In 1920 Oscar Swahn was 72 years of age. This list is by no means extensive but it goes to show that people after the age of retirement (60-65) can achieve greatness. This greatness was and is achieved by being both active in mind and body, and having the opportunity to use this active mind and body. Hopefully as a society that is ageing realises that to be active throughout ones life and to have facilities and abilities to age actively will be one of the most important things we do. Hopefully Wanshou becomes the start of a whole new direction in age care.

Learning with Events Legacies: Health Promotion and Urban Changes with the Rio2016 mobility projects

Jorge Azevedo de Castro

georgecastro55@gmail.com
Architect, Prof. Dsc EAU UFF & Oswaldo Cruz Foundation, Sanitation and Ambiental Health Dept.
Researcher

The article develops health promotion and healthy community concepts and to relate the concept of urban health with the Olympic Legacy definition, that is the argument most commonly used for public policy Rio 2016 scenario, a planning and implementation sequence from 2009 choice of Rio de Janeiro as the host city to nowdays, a period where urban policy is structured from the mega projects transformation on the port area and the Barra da Tijuca, revealing the possible relationship between urban planning and promotion of urban health, a concept that makes room for predictive and preventive programs in the study area impacts and risks to public health on mega events, also supported by recommendations on urban design and transport infrastructure projects oriented to urban health, which reaches the guidelines of mobility policies, translated on large ongoing investments in strategic works in the mass transport system, concluding by observing their absence in municipal health plans.

Keywords: *legacy, events, health promotion, urban planning*

INTRODUCTION

The last decade the Brazilian urban transportation public politic generates the motorized individual mode growing with the low prices to fuel and cars, and easier financial credits to buy and sell automobile industry products, and now the great cities mobility is a great problem to urban managers and to the everyday modal transportation users.

Specially Rio de Janeiro is a urban transformation scene, cause we have the Rio 2016 and the Sea Port area projects implementation, with great urban design changes.

We try to cross public health data and transportation index data analysis to understand where and when the mortality index and other health indicators are modifying their values appointing the high individualization on transport system.

The urban reality changes under individual car market explosion, the medium rent grow income and government lack of proposals to invest on public transport systems.

There were no urban planning answers to these national economy factors, and now 80% or more of the Brazilian pop-

TESIS Inter-University Research Centre "Systems and Technologies for Social and Healthcare Facilities"
University of Florence, Italy

TESIS

Figure 1. Rio de Janeiro: The City, The Bay and Tourism Points

ulation lives at the twelve great metropolitan areas with infrastructural questions. There were no previsions to health promotion and now the healthy ways to move are impossible to practice to the majority of urban users.

Brazilian federal government public policies are under discussion with climate change impacts on the great cities and on the transport model and oil pollution, with no public health issue presence.

A model to identify ways to cross health and transport public politics indicators may underline the health promotion impacts on the healthy cities management.

DEFINING OLYMPIC LEGACIES

Legacy has come to prominence in Olympic discourse in recent years because this term offers managing capacity with tensions between Olympic dreams (or promises) and municipal-financial realities.

Olympic "legacy" offers bridges between two potentially divergent narratives setting the practical accountancy of host city planning, against the "creative" accounting that underpins Olympic dreams and promises. Every Olympic host city dreams of accomplishing at least three things: first, to provide the best conditions for the competing athletes; second, is to stage a top standard Olympics with distinctive features that

Figure 2. A view from Niterói City

237

create memorable impressions of the host city and its culture, and that will reverberate throughout the world – called "immaterial legacies"; and third, to leave something to the host community and country that will benefit their inhabitants for many years to come – called "material legacies".

Among the legacies, the most recognizable impacts include those related to urban planning, architecture, city marketing, sports infrastructure, economy and tourism. However, in the Olympic Charter, the International Olympic Committee plan clearly defines from the earliest stages the objectives to leave a public health legacy.

PUBLIC POLICIES

The National Sports Policy, National Sports Council Resolution no. 05, guides the National System of Sports and Leisure work, and is synthesized in the Sport Development Plan (2007-2010), with guidelines (Filgueira, 2008) to democratize access to sport and leisure; promote human development and social inclusion through sport and leisure; promote sport and leisure scientific technological knowledge production and dissemination; to foment sports and leisure domestic industry and its supply chain; improve the sports and leisure infrastructure in the country; at last, strengthen high performance sport and articulate intersectoral policies implementation that enable the development of citizenship, the promotion of health and quality of life.

Quality of life, according to WHO, is the Healthy City beginning (see the Ottawa Charter), where health is conceived as something more than the absence of diseases. Other authors define this perspective aligning the ten principles of building a healthy place in the definitions to put people first; recognize the economic value; empower champions for health; energize shared spaces; make healthy choices easy; ensure equitable access; promote access to healthy food; make it active.

According to the Rio de Janeiro Municipality Strategic Plan, health promotion responsibility in health services must be shared among individuals, community groups, health professionals, institutions providing health services and governments. They must work together building a health care system to achieving a high level of health.

THE MEGA EVENTS URBAN POLICY

The town planning changes milestone to do a new urbanism so was the launch of Rio-City program, an early 1990s initiative which handled the urban debate, with the public selection of projects and execution of works in various neighborhoods.

Then came the experiment conducted by Oriol Bohigas before the preparations for the 1992 Olympics in Barcelona, where specific interventions in public spaces were carried out, with the unit neighborhood as reference.

The Olympic infrastructure activities take advantage with sports equipments and infrastructured places at City four areas (Sugar Loaf, Barra da Tijuca, Maracanã and Deodoro), internally homogeneous, but distinct from each other by the location and distance from the city center, by socioeconomic status (high and middle-income) and urban construction typology, resulting from occupation and development circumstances. Taking diversity in account, the four areas can be taken as representative of the municipal territory. In 2007 Pan American Games, much of the new spaces and half of the event activities were allocated in Barra da Tijuca.

This region improves urban occupation in accordance with the Lúcio Costa Plan, 1969. Its connection with the rest of the city has been improved in the 1970s, thanks to municipal government

Figure 3. A study of Urban Waterfront revitalization: Light Rail Train (LRT system)

238

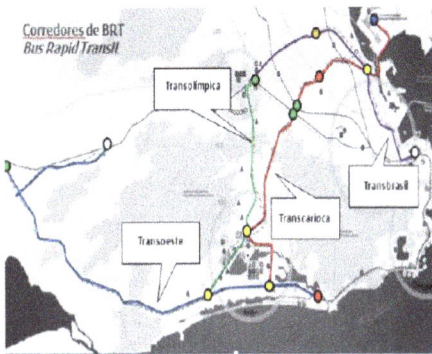

Figure 4. BRT System Axes

road works. Barra da Tijuca has been treated as expansion area, being of great interest the real estate market, especially for middle and high income groups. In the last two decades public resources in infrastructure were intensified, followed by private investment, stimulated by specific changes in planning legislation that made the region attractive for new developments. In 2007 Pan American Games proposal, sports facilities concentration and activities was strengthened by the restructuring of the urban mobility system. Such interventions completed a ring road around the municipality and the implementation of three axes intercepting this ring and converging to Palmeiras Highway Clover, nodal point of the Barra da Tijuca.

This road system also provided waterways and rail links between the International Airport and Santos Dumont Airport (in the central area of the City). Assigning centrality to Barra da Tijuca prevailed in the two proposals that succeeded the PAN 2007.

For the 2012 Olympics were considered necessary 31 facilities, most, including the main ones in the region (RIO 2003). The proposed mobility system general structure was similar to the Pan 2007,

239

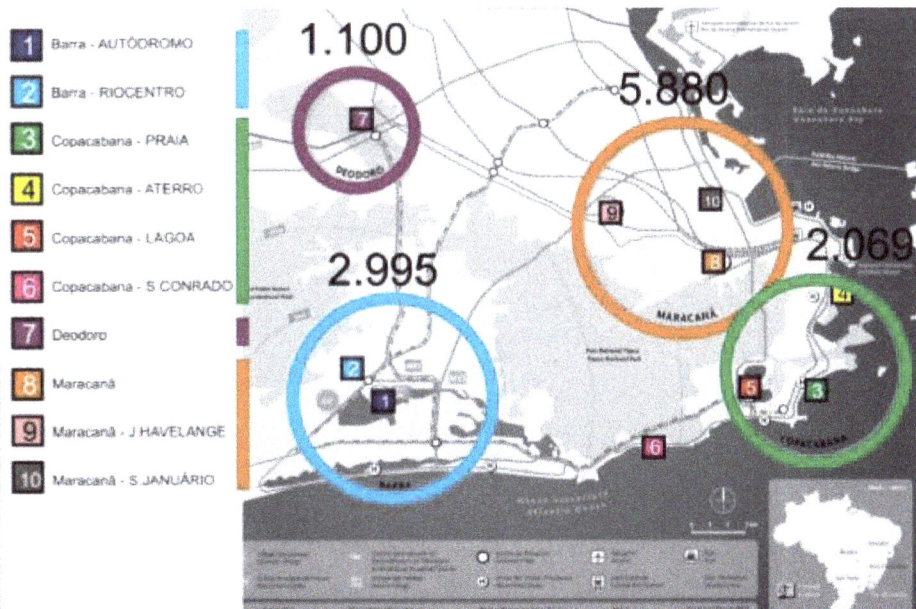

Figure 5. Rio 2016 Main Location: 1 – Barra da Tijuca-Olimpic Park

TESIS Inter-University Research Centre "Systems and Technologies for Social and Healthcare Facilities"
University of Florence, Italy

PROJECT/INTERVENTION	RESPONSABILITY/MANAGEMENT
THE CITY METROPOLITAN ROAD ARC	RIO DE JANEIRO STATE GOVERNMENT
BUS RAPID TRANSIT (BRT)'S ROADS AND AVENUES: TRANSOESTE, TRANSOLÍMPICA, TRANSCARIOCA E TRANS BRASIL	RIO DE JANEIRO MUNICIPAL GOVERNMENT
METRO LINE NUMBER 4 FROM IPANEMA STATION TO BARRA DA TIJUCA STATION	RIO DE JANEIRO STATE GOVERNMENT
METRO LINE NUMBER 3 FROM RIO TO NITERÓI & ITABORAÍ (EAST SIDE RIO METROPOLITAN AREA MUNICIPALITIES)	RIO DE JANEIRO MUNICIPAL GOVERNMENT
LIGHT RAPID TRANSPORT (LRT) AT RIO DE JANEIRO CITY CENTER	RIO DE JANEIRO MUNICIPAL GOVERNMENT
PETROBRAS ITABORAÍ PETROCHEMICAL PLANT	FEDERAL GOVENMENT
RIO DE JANEIRO WONDERFUL PORT (PORTO MARAVILHA) REURBANIZATION	RIO DE JANEIRO MUNICIPAL GOVERNMENT
SLUM'S URBANIZATION PROGRAM, AND HABITATIONAL PRODUCTION	RIO DE JANEIRO STATE GOVERNMENT
BARRA DA TIJUCA OLYMPIC CITY/PARK	RIO DE JANEIRO MUNICIPAL GOVERNMENT

Figure 6. Rio de Janeiro main interventions projects on course

however public transportation news included the expansion of Metro lines to the Barra da Tijuca, the regional system like Light Rail Vehicle (LRV) implementation, besides the waterway linking the City Center.

For the Olympic Games in 2016, most of the activities were held in the same region, called Olympic and Paralympic Games Rio 2016 "heart". The transport system disposal for the event structure, resembled the previous proposals: one ring intercepted by axes that converge in Barra da Tijuca. There were also modal changes in the Bus Rapid Transit (BRT) system, and it is now implemented in two stretches of the expected ringt.

The subway between the South Zone and central region was added to these projects, as we can see in the section Mobility Issues and the Context.

Barra da Tijuca centrality is highlighted in events documents presentation (RIO, [between 2001 and 2002]; RIO, 2003). Concentric circles form a graphic scale that measures the distance of each Olympic area to the core of the Games. The circles highlight one of the challenges for the event, the displacement of athletes teams, which should be solved by structuring the road system.

Phisycal support creation, that is, facilities and infrastructure that connects the different spaces where an event happens, perpetuates what is accepted as ephemeral. The emergence of legacy idea when attributed to these urban interventions. The term "legacy" suggests, however, a challenge: "city project", an expression that indicates the intentions of the city to take place along with the preparations for the event beginning.

Figure 7. New Transolimpic Road Map

Analyzed in urbanistic terms, not just operational terms, Barra da Tijuca activities centralization, a urbanistically qualified economical dynamic region, helps to keep the daily flow pendulum motion of the metropolitan periphery transportation to the center. The emphasis in Barra da Tijuca contributes to imbalance conservation investment that feeds the metropolitan flows. It also contributes to distances maintenance, that is, the unequal conditions for access to the city, experienced by surrounding areas residents.

HEALTH RISKS AND IMPACTS

A solid indicator of urban health is in the transport system impacts until event dates - a present factor is population treats with everyday mobility difficulties changes in one hand, and with Olympic Legacies Plan in the other hand.
The research proposes some comparative studies development based on urban design, transport systems and health indicators approach and health equipment, to examine urban interventions impacts of large projects in the host city, and Public Health in all policies, with health promotion included in planning and project activities, also monitoring results after the events.

Hosting the Olympics is a long and expensive commitment to the city of this mega event, the impacts can be divided into four different periods:
1. the preparation of the competition to win the right to host the Games;
2. the seven-year period of preparation for hosting the Games;
3. a short period (about 15 days) when the Olympic Games are succeeded by the Paralympic Games;
4. a long time after the Games.
Brazilian Law n. 10671 of 15 May 200347, provides the Statute of the Fan defense during sporting events, provides

TESIS Inter-University Research Centre "Systems and Technologies for Social and Healthcare Facilities"
University of Florence, Italy

TESIS

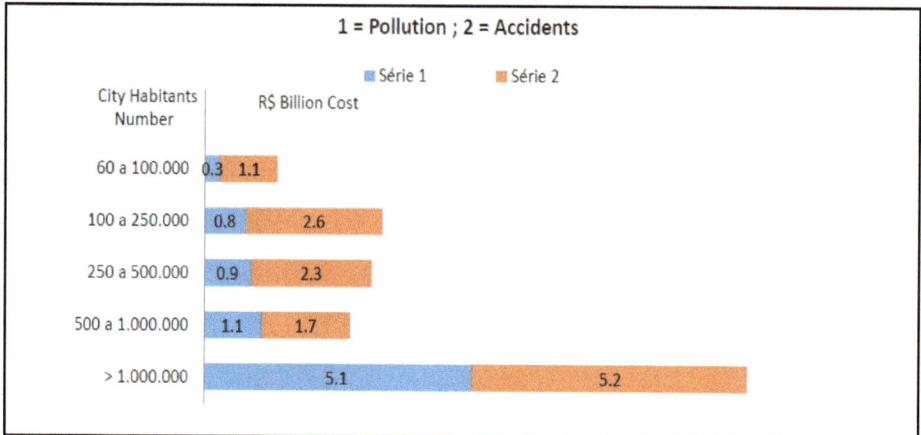

Figure 8. Brazilian Cities Ministry: Transports Systems Externalities within cities with more than 60.000 habitants

duty organizer to provide a doctor and two nurses for every ten thousand fans, and provide an ambulance for every ten thousand fans, short of the recommendation suggested by Hartman et al the organizers are jointly liable when there is damage to the fan, caused by security flaws in stadiums. The Brazilian standard, is right supporter hygiene and quality of the physical facilities and food products sold at the event, with the last verified by the health surveillance.

The WHO proposes strategies for the health sector to build its disaster response capacity. One of the key initiatives is the considered assessment of risk and danger, with emphasis on retrospective data from previous situations that are not limited to disasters, but that address accidents in events.

The lessons learned during the Olympics show a number of relevant aspects, including the need for planning and disaster management. Some issues considered important were those related to leadership, operations and unified command and international cooperation in public health for large events and emergency situations.

Respect to health itself, the advisory composition groups was suggested, with health experts on issues related to disease prevention, health promotion, analysis and risk management, health security, surveillance and alert, laboratory, medical services, infection control, water and food security, disaster and emergency response. Some areas were considered strategic, such as:

1. Hospital capacity preparation, health care and medical emergencies in accidents with multiple victims.
2. Diseases surveillance and response to outbreaks, including surveillance and response to communicable diseases.
3. Syndromic surveillance system, Public Health preparedness and response accidents involving explosives, biological, chemical and radiological and nuclear agents.
4. Environmental health and food safety, including topics on environmental health surveillance, water quality, laboratory support.
5. Monitoring and control of mosqui-

toes and vectors.

Preparing response plans to accidents with multiple victims, the steps of needs assessment and risks can elucidate potential hazards of specific geographic areas, facilitating preparation with the institutions concerned, anticipating problems, aiding the prioritization process of policies to be adopted and avoiding no necessaries preparations.

With respect to issues related to disasters, some authors suggested defining the psychosocial processes demanded to support the victims, their families and professionals involved in the first response steps. They suggested also set mutually supportive plan and international assistance for cases beyond the capabilities of local response.

Lund et al. consider relevant experience gained by cities that hosted mass events, even when surprised by the disaster occurrence. The availability of information aimed at contributing to the prevention of risks related to the concentration of large numbers of people. The higher the experience in the planning, preparation and provision of services related to health in mass events, most health professionals tend to strengthen their practice in providing medical care.

The Federal Government Ministry of Cities, points out urban transport model externalities in the above table, presenting all Brazilian metropolitan araes. In Rio de Janeiro case, the mobility issue was decisive in the victory to host 2016 Olympics games, with local authorities promises to the IOC (International Olympic Committee) a profound restructuring public transportation local delivery. This "transportation revolution" focused on public transportation systems, aims to remedy the current mobility conditions, that is nowdays a collective public service currently offered which constitutes expensive, poor and inadequate for existing demand. In Brazil, this speech touchs a very sensitive item to the public since these are problems that affect the daily well-being of the people involved.

There are plans for construction of Bus Rapid Transit systems (BRT), the stretch of Line 1 of the Metro, the implementation of Bus Rapid Sistem (BRS) and the construction of a Light Rail Vehicle (LRV) in the port area, among other interventions. Some of them are already operating.

Over 26 kilometers long, connects the shaft TransOlímpica Deodoro to Recreio, crossing the Sierra Old Mill, the Road Catonho, through a tunnel being drilled in the Massif of Pedra Branca. The Transolímpica will carry 70,000 people daily.

With R $ 1.6 billion total investment, the Transolímpica 26 km axis extension will link with two other BRT corridors. The project also provides for the duplication of important roads, as well opening new avenues for the Pedra Branca Massif with the construction of a tunnel with four emboques. With the Transcarioca axis inauguration, passengers who make the journey between Barra da Tijuca and the International Airport Tom Jobim, reduced by 60% the time spent in this shift. To optimize the time, they were built along its route three loons, 10 viaducts (including duplicates) and nine bridges. Also track duplication works were performed in addition to the urbanization of areas covered by BRT.

With 52 km long, the Transoeste have on your route works as the Grota Funda Tunnel, along with a deployment of oth-

243

er 522 thousand square meters and the installation of 3,650 new points of light. By 2016, the Transoeste will reach the Garden Ocean, in Barra da Tijuca, integrating with the future station of Metro Line 4. At the end of the works, will be 58 km and 63 stations.

Those who live in suburbs have the so-called feeder routes, taking passengers to the nearest BRT station. Other public transport projects are underway in several communities and in the central area of Rio De Janeiro.

The expected path investment and territorial distribution carried out so far in the mega-events context seems to play the same space organizational logic. With the information publicized until now, there are no elements that allow us to say that huge investments in mobility produce a better distribution of people and jobs in the metropolitan territory. On the contrary, in the Rio de Janeiro metropolis, the major investments in transport for the 2014 World Cup and the 2016 Olympics are mostly concentrated territorially. An example is the implementation of BRT systems. First, there is a strong concentration in Rio de Janeiro city, noting that Rio de Janeiro metropolitan area (RJMA) has 20 municipalities. Second, there is an unequal shares distribution within the Rio de Janeiro municipality, with a massive concentration in the South Zone and Barra da Tijuca.

According to Census 2010, approximately 2.9 million people travel daily to work inside the RJMA. Of these, more than 849,000 - or 22.1% - moving from one municipality to another. Moreover, in the context of the interventions in

the mobility system for the 2014 World Cup and 2016 Olympic Games has not been submitted, so far, no integrated plan that considers Rio de Janeiro as "metropolitan city", and the last Master Plan Urban Transport in the metropolitan area is 2003 made and is not being used to plan the current interventions. Thus, as noted by Abreu (2010) the opportunity to overcome the challenge of planning and finance infrastructure in the metropolitan scale, may be lost, due to the territorial concentration of interventions and insistence on road model, reproducing concentrator policies and practices, which tendence to accentuate the intra-metropolitan disparities.

We consider that it is necessary to advance in research on the impact of mobility projects on cities restructuring, which in turn focus on urban dynamics. In the context of mega-events, it is considered that this research should be directed primarily at exploration of three hypotheses about these interventions and their ability to restructure the urban space. In this regard, first, to analyze the impact of mega-events in the field of mobility should evaluate the real possibility of playing the rodoviarista model, which historically guided the urban mobility policies in Brazil since the 1950s. Therefore, it is considered that the provision of means of movement in the context of mega-events favors the reproduction and the affirmation of this model does not address the other modes of transport, such as walking.

DISCUSSION: PUBLIC POLICIES

This data analysis check-up two important conclusions: first, that both the cost

Projects	Description	Value(1)
Metrolines	Line 1 Modernization	438
	Line 2 Modernization	384
Trains	Line 4 Construction (Ipanema – Barra da Tijuca)	7000
	Stations renovations, railway sign systems, lines extending	2400
	New trains acquisition	
BRT	Transbrasil	1300
	Transcarioca	1500
	Transoeste	1001
	Transolímpica	1600
VLT	Light Train Rails	1500
Total		17123

Figure 9. Public transport projects

of displacement as their externalities per capita, grow with the size of cities, mainly for individual transport, ranging far less in the case of public transport . This contribution to the UIA health care architectural conference may underline the health promotion impacts on the healthy cities management. The public health perspective may be applied to urban design projects effectiveness.

CONCLUSIONS

Tangible or intangible legacies: planning and control structures are suitable targets on schedule, and the technical and managerial capacity of project control is conditioned by the events.

A few months of the Olympic Games of Rio de Janeiro-2016, institutions of researchers from Brazil, Australia and the United Kingdom met to discuss the possible legacy of the event to public health. According to the researchers, the Olym-

pic legacy refers to forms of compensation to the host country in areas such as sustainability, infrastructure, employment, tourism, accessibility and promotion of health, given the huge investments in the organization of these mega-events. Highlights the lack of studies on the impacts of the Olympics for the public health context and suggests that among the possible legacy, is the increase in physical and sporting activity levels among the population.

Olympic legacy plan depends on city planning goals. In this sense the realization of major events serve as a catalyst of urban strategic plans, which otherwise would take more time for your more successful conclusion. Cities spent more time in the planning demands of medium to long term coordinated with the short-term demands.

The transfer of knowledge is one of the strategic principles of management development plans and implementation of projects of previous locations for the next location. To organize this knowledge you need to research the host cities before and after the Olympic Games in aspects such as design principles, effectiveness of investments, resulting for the resident population and the visitor population, effectiveness of the indicators used in the application for city - based, etc. The absence of master plans did not prevent the continuation of short-plans and medium local time, when it was possible to transfer experience between host cities of past events with evaluation of the generation of context and use of facilities.

REFERENCES

Abreu, M. A (2010). *Evolução Urbana no Rio de Janeiro, Rio de Janeiro, Prefeitura do Rio de Janeiro*, Ed. Instituto Pereira Passos

Bonduki, Nabil (2002). *Origens da Habitação Social no Brasil, São Paulo* Ed.Estação Liberdade

Brunet, F. (1995). *Na Economic Analysis of the Barcelona 92 Olympic Games*; Auditor General's Report to Parliament 2002, vol. 2, "Cost of the Olympic and Paralympic Games" Sidney: NSW Government 2002 Relatório da Comissão de Avaliação do COI da XXX Olimpíada 2012

Caiaffa, Waleska (2008). Ferreira, Fabiane Ribeiro; Ferreira, Aline Dayrell; Oliveira, Claúdia Di Lorenzo; Camargo, Vitor Passos; Proietti, Fernando Augusto, Urban health: "*the city is a strange lady, smiling today, devouring you tomorrow*" Belo Horizonte, Revista Ciência & Saúde Coletiva, 13(6):1545-1536, 2008

Castro, Camilla Figueiredo de; Simões, Dayane; Menezes Carla; Delamarque, Elizabete Vianna; Pepe, Vera Lucia Edais, *Health risk, Disasters*, Ed. UERJ, 2008

Hartman, Stefan; Zandberg, Tjeerd, *The future of mega sport events: examining the "Dutch Approach" to legacy planning*

Lamartine DaCosta & Miragaya, Ana, Olympic Studies Group, UGF: Sede à Franquia Olímpica: Um Estudo Exploratório com Base no Pan 2007, Universidade Gama Filho – RJ

Lund et al., Revista Ciência & Saúde Coletiva, 19(9):3717-3730, 2014

WHO, *Carta da Primeira Conferência Internacional Sobre Promoção Da Saúde - Ottawa, novembro de 1986 WHO 2004 2009 2003*

Eitler, Thomas W.; McMahon, Edward T.; Thoerig, *Theodore in Building Healthy Places Initiative*, Urban Land Institute, 2014

Rio de Janeiro Strategic Plan Municipality Policies of Health Area

Leon, 2008, National Plan of Mass Destruction Event Management

Lúcio Costa Plan, 1969

246

Active Living by Design: State of Knowledge and Practice and Implications for China

Xuemei Zhu

xzhu@arch.tamu.edu
Ph.D., Associate Professor
Department of Architecture, Texas A&M University

This study first reviewed the state of knowledge and practice in active living by design, and then explored the implications of these findings for design and planning in China.

INTRODUCTION

Obesity is becoming a leading public health problem in many countries. Physical activity (PA) helps combat the obesity epidemic and bring other health benefits. Traditional PA promotion focused on individual factors but have not been very successful. Recently, there has been a paradigm shift toward a socio-ecological approach addressing multi-level (i.e., personal, social, and physical environmental) factors.

The focus has shifted from exercise to active living —a way of life that integrates PA into daily routines. The built environment has been increasingly recognized as an important venue for PA premonition.

RESULTS

State of Knowledge

There is now a substantial body of evidence on the relationship between built environments and PA, mostly from developed countries. "Walkable communities" with compact and mixed land uses and well-connected streets encourage PA, especially active transportation (walking and biking).

Other factors such as rich pedestrian/bicyclist infrastructure, safety from traffic and crime, and good visual quality and maintenance, may provide additional support. Gaps of knowledge exist in terms of the causal relationships between environmental changes and PA improvement, and relevant policy approaches and economic impacts.

State of Practice

The growing literature has informed the recent upsurge of multi-level environmental and policy interventions in some countries to promote PA through collaborative efforts by design/planning and health organizations.

They focus on diverse environmental factors such as safe streets, compact communities, local parks, and neighborhood schools; as well as multiple domains of

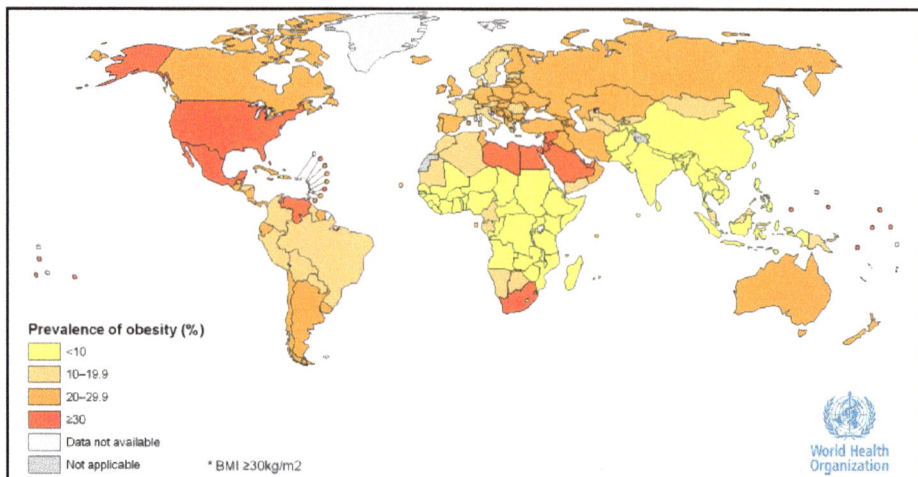

Figure 1. Prevalence of Obesity, Age 20+, Age Standardized, Both Sexes, 2008 (World Health Organization)

248

PA, including occupation, recreation, transportation, and household activities.

IMPLICATIONS FOR CHINA

In China, the prevalence of overweight and obesity increased from 14.6% in 1992 to 21.8% in 2002.

The rise of automobile dependence and reduction of walking and biking likely played a significant role in this change.

There is a urgent need for more active living research in China. Empirical findings from other countries provide useful references, yet need to be interpreted with extra caution, because environments in China are dramatically different. Meanwhile, methodologies from previous research provide excellent tools for Chinese studies.

CONCLUSIONS

There is a substantial body of cross-sectional knowledge on the relationship between built environment and active living in some developed countries.

In China, the rising rate of obesity calls for more active living research, which can benefit from methodologies developed in other countries yet needs to be context-sensitive in conceptual understanding of the problem.

Such studies will also enrich the knowledge base about environment-PA relationships by testing them in different contexts and populations.

Figure 2. Can bad design make us fat?

Impacts of Sports Fields Accessibility on Physical Activity Levels in Harbin, China

Shanshan Zhang
Weiwen Cui
Xiaopeng Bai

249

cww66@sina.cn
zhangshanshan@hit.edu.c
Harbin Institute of Technology, China

The purpose of this study is to examine whether the access to sports fields is related to physical activity levels in Harbin, China.

Sports fields provide opportunities for everyone to do physical activity. The increasing of physical activity can have a significant impact on promoting healthy living. However, the available for sports fields has so far not been a focus of sports facilities research. We performed a survey to assess the effects that different distance to the nearest sports fields have on physical activity levels with adjustment for potential confounders.

A cross-sectional study was conducted in a representative sample of 300 residents living in three adjacent residence communities in Harbin, China. Distances from each participant's home to the nearest sports fields within 500m from home were calculated from geographic coordinates. We assessed levels of physical activity ("active," "moderate," and "inactive") in relation to distinct distance to the nearest sports fields ("nearest", "medium", and "farthest") regarding to Chinese government guidelines. Regression models were used to determine the associations between sports field accessibility and physical activity level.

There were significant correlations between sports fields accessibility and the levels of physical activity (p<0.05). The average increased physical activity was greater for those whose distance to a sports field decreased. Therefore, physical activity was positively associated with the sports field accessibility.

The findings from this study suggest that changes in accessibility of sports fields may affect physical activity levels but it is not the major impact factor. To reach the recommended levels of physical activity in China, it is necessary to propose the development and implementation of national guidelines for health-enhancing physical activity. As a result of the success of this initiative, other districts in China can begin to replicate it.

Abbreviations: PAL, physical activity levels; OR, odds ratio; CI confidence interval: Adj, adjusted

Keywords: *Sports fields; Physical exercise levels; cross-sectional study*

INTRODUCTION

Regular physical activity has been shown to have significant health benefits and contributes to prevent noncommunicable diseases (NCDs) such as decreasing heart disease, colon cancer, high blood pressure, feelings of anxiety/depression and weight, especially when maintaining and building muscles, healthy bones and joints (U.S. Department of Health and Human Services, 1996).

However, globally, 1 in 4 adults is not active enough and more than 80% of the world's adolescent population is insufficiently physically active (WHO). Due to the prevalence of sedentary lifestyle as well as an increasing trend relying on motorized transport, leisure-time physical activity based on community open sports facilities may be an integral part to enhance physical activity levels.

Typically, research on the prevention of disease has targeted changing behaviors over which individuals theoretically have control. Because such approaches alone have not made sufficient inroads in promoting physical activity, there have been recent calls for interventions such as built and social environmental approaches in order to encourage a more active healthy lifestyle (Humpel, Owen, Leslie, 2002; McCormack, Shiell, 2011).

The intervention of environmental features has been demonstrated in numerous studies examining, e.g., availability of green areas (Toftager, Ekholm, Schipperijn, et al., 2011) and parks (Prince, Kristjansson, Russell, et al., 2012). However, studies about assessed availability of sports fields and physical activity have been less consistent reporting both null (Troped, Saunders, Pate, Reininger, Addy. 2003) and weak (Karusisi, Thomas, Meline, Chaix, 2013).

In China, sports fields are common community features established regarding to the community population size in many disciplines (Code for Planning and Design on Urban Residential Areas), yet we know little about sports fields proximity that are most related to physical activity.

This paper highlights how sports fields accessibility might influence public health through a conceptual framework relating sports fields to physical activity and, ultimately, the health of users. Finally, field research is encouraged in

Figure 1. How to Enhance Physical Activities

order to examine sports environmental attributes and physical activity levels.

METHOD

Study Sample

From property lists provided by municipal officials, total 300 residents (100 residents per neighborhood) were randomly selected for participation in the study. We took significant steps to ensure that multi-residents properties from diverse sociocultural, educational and economic background were appropriately represented in the sampling frame.

Data from 300 participants were included: randomly selected respondent from each unique resident that provided valid physical activity data. Participants ranged in age from 16 to 88 years; their mean age was 54.8 years (SD = 15.6). Most participants were female and these and other characteristics of the study sample are summarized in Table 1.

Sports Fields

The locations of built sports fields were obtained by site investigation. The database included co-ordinate based information on the outdoor sports fields (including running tracks, soccer fields, parks, school yards, and ice skating rinks), and indoor sports fields (including public and private sports halls e.g. for tennis, badminton, and soccer as well as gyms, dance studios, school gymnasiums, pools, and indoor ice rinks).

Sports Fields Accessibility

The most important factors influencing perceived accessibility to sports fields were physical and locational features such as proximity to the fields, a pleasant walking experience, and a sufficient number of fields in the neighborhood. Data were collected in 3 neighborhoods, designated by a random selected medium-sized community in Harbin, China.

The community was approximately 1 square mile in size and each neighborhood was 0.1 square mile in size, with 10000-15000 size of population.

Therefore, we focused on the proximity to the sports fields with the control of the number of fields in the neighborhood. The distance from neighborhoods to the nearest sports fields was ranked as "nearest"(within 3 minutes walking distance), "medium" (3-5 minutes walking distance), and "farthest"(5-10 minutes walking distance).

Physical activity levels

The Global Physical Activity Questionnaire, which is widely used in population health surveillance systems, was used to collect information on physical activity by face-to-face interview. A reliability and validity study carried out in 9 countries indicated that this questionnaire was a suitable and acceptable instrument for monitoring physical activity (Bull, Maslin, Armstrong, 2009).

Frequency and daily duration of different types of physical activities in 1 typical week were recorded, and the total amount of weekly physical activity was accordingly calculated. On the basis of both frequency and total amount of weekly physical activity, PAL was categorized into the following: "active,"

251

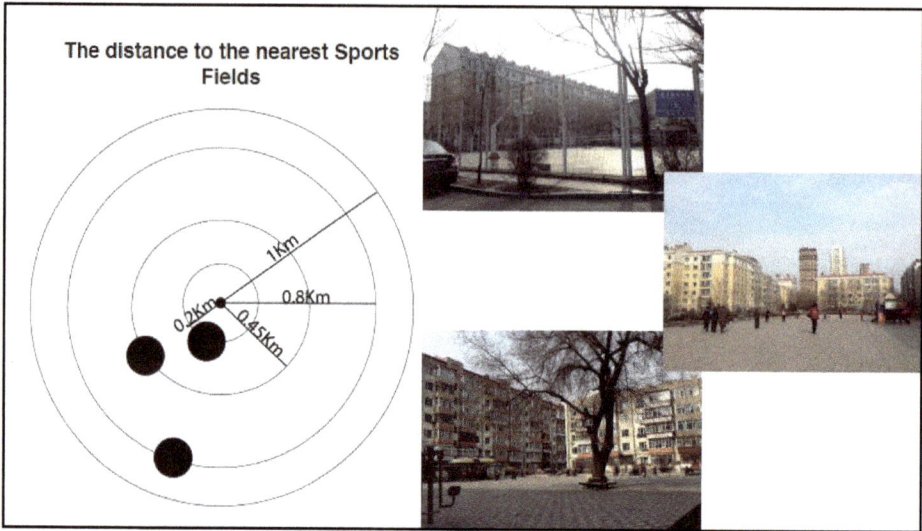

Figure 2. The distance to the nearest Sports Fields

equating approximately 1 or more hours of at least moderate-intensity physical activity per day; "moderate," equivalent to half an hour of at least moderate-intensity physical activity on most days; and "inactive," not fit any of the criteria of previously mentioned categories (Global Physical Activity Questionnaire - Analysis Guide).

Statistical analyses

In this cross-sectional study, data were collected through questionnaires, interviews, and observation methods. Linear regression models were used by SPSS 21.0.0.0 to examine differences between different neighborhoods physical activity with respect to their distance from participants' homes and their 95% confidence intervals. The models were adjusted for sex, age at baseline, level of education and body mass index as well as baseline and follow-up neighborhood socioeconomic disadvantage.

RESULTS

Of the 300 respondents, the majority were older, female. The percentage of participants for the five age groups was as follows: 18- years =3.3%, 18-29 years =10.0%, 30-40 years =14.0%, 41-65 years =38.7%, 65+ years =34.0% which can be concluded from Table1.

Regression models were established to analyze the impact of individuals' socio-characteristics (gender, age, level of education) and sports fields accessibility on physical activity levels (Table 2-1, 2-2, 2-3). The differences in levels of physical activity were significant related to age ($F=17.604$, $p=.00<0.05$) and distance to the nearest sports fields ($F=17.604$, $p=.006<0.05$). However, gender ($p=.159>.05$) and levels of education ($p=.107>.05$) had no significant association with PAL.

The results of Table 3-1 and Table 3-2 indicate that middle-aged Chinese individuals who do not spend much time for the upbringing of children and the care of relatives per week and live close to a sport field are more likely to participate in sport in general.

The model also shows that the highest physical activity levels were related to nearest distance to the sports fields. Likewise, an increase in availability of sports fields near home was associated with an increase in activity in our study.

DISCUSSION

We studied physical activity in general and our findings provide additional longitudinal evidence that decreased availability of sports fields may be associated with a more pronounced decrease in physical activity. Although decreases in physical activity related to changes in availability of sports fields were moderate, this may increase individuals' risk of chronic diseases.

Some prior studies of availability of sports facilities and physical activity in different countries have been conducted. In studies from the US, higher density of recreational facilities has been related to participation in the corresponding activities (Diez Roux, Evenson, McGinn, et al., 2007).

However, no associations were observed between count or presence of recreational facilities near home and recreational activity (Hoehner, Brennan Ramirez, Elliott, Handy, Brownson, 2005). In China, the Neighborhood Destinations Accessibility Index was fairly strongly associated with transport-related and leisure-time physical activity as well as walking, but the exposure included a range of community services such as transport, recreation, social and cultural as well as food retail destinations (Witten, Blakely, Bagheri, et al., 2012).

One of the longitudinal studies examining changes in the environment was a natural experiment from Australia in

253

Statistical Analyses			Participants	
			n	%
Total			300	100
Gender				
		Men	130	43.3
		Women	170	56.7
Age. y				
		< 18	10	3.3
		18-29	30	10.0
		30-40	42	14.0
		41-65	116	38.7
		> 65	102	34.0
Level of education				
		High	188	62.7
		Intermediate	52	17.3
		Low	60	20.0
Distance to the nearest sports fields				
		Set A (nearest)	100	33.3
		Set B (medium)	100	33.3
		Set C (farthest)	100	33.3

- Participants ranged in age from 16 to 88 years;
- Their mean age was 54.8 years (SD = 15.6).

Table 1. Sample Socio demographic Characteristics: Harbin (2015)

TESIS Inter-University Research Centre "Systems and Technologies for Social and Healthcare Facilities"
University of Florence, Italy

TESIS

Table 2-1   Model Summary

Model	R	R Square	Adjusted R Square	Std.Error of the Estimate
1	.306(a)	.093	.081	.854

a. Predictors: (Constant). distance to the nearest sports fields. age. gender. level of education

Table 2-2   ANOVA(b)

Model		Sum of Squares	df	Mean Square	F	Sig.
1	Regression	22.203	4	5.551	17.604	.000(b)
	Residual	215.344	295	.730		
	Total	237.547	299			

a. Predictors: (Constant). distance to the nearest sports fields, age, gender, level of education

b. Dependent Variable: physical activity levels

Table 2-1 e 2-2

Table 2-3   Coefficients

Model	Unstandardized Coefficients		Standardized Coefficients	t	Sig.	correlations			95%C.I.for EXP(B)	
	B	Std. Error	Beta			Zero-order	Partial	Part	Lower	Upper
(Constant)	2.991	.281		10.660	.000				2.438	3.543
age	-.186	.046	-.226	-4.006	.000	-.244	-.227	-.222	-.277	-.095
gender	-.143	.101	-.079	-1.411	.159	-.038	-.082	-.078	-.341	.056
education	.054	.033	.091	1.616	.107	.074	.094	.090	-.012	.119
distance	-.170	.061	-.156	-2.767	.006	-.184	-.159	-.153	-.290	-.049

a. Dependent Variable: physical activity levels

- The differences in levels of physical activity were significant related to age ($F=17.604$, $p=.00 < 0.05$) and distance to the nearest sports fields($F=17.604$, $p=.006 < 0.05$)
- gender ($p=.159 > .05$)and levels of education ($p=.107 > .05$) had no significant association with PAL

Table 2-3

which the effects of moving to "a livable development" (designed to increase local walking and cycling by community design, movement network, public parklands, and lot layouts) on walking behavior were examined (Christian, Knuiman, Bull, et al., 2013).

In the other longitudinal study, however, an increase in the recreational facility density within a one mile buffer of one's home was associated with less decrease in recreational physical activity during a 3-year follow-up (Ranchod, Diez Roux, Evenson, Sanchez, Moore, 2014).

Some studies suggested that the uses of sports fields differ widely from different ages through psychological elements. Other studies have suggested that peo-

254

Statistical Analyses

Table 3-1   crosstabs between PAL and distance to the nearest sports fields

		distance to the nearest sports fields			Total(%)
		nearest(%)	medium(%)	farthest(%)	
Physical Activity	active	47.2	31.9	20.8	100
	moderate	32.1	39.3	28.6	100
	inactive	14.0	32.0	54.0	100

- highest physical activity levels were related to nearest distance to the sports fields

- an increase in availability of sports fields near home was associated with an increase in activity

Table 3-1

Statistical Analyses

Table 3-2   crosstabs between PAL and age

		age . y					Total(%)
		<18(%)	18-29(%)	30-40(%)	41-65(%)	>65(%)	
Physical Activity	active	2.8	2.8	6.9	43.1	44.4	100
	moderate	0.0	21.4	28.6	35.7	14.3	100
	inactive	6.0	14.0	16.0	34.0	30.0	100

- middle-aged Chinese individuals who do not spend much time for the upbringing of children and the care of relatives per week and live close to a sport field are more likely to participate in sport in general

Table 3-2

ple place value on the existence of sports fields even when they do not use them. Ulrich and Addoms (Ulrich, Addoms, 1981), for example, found that college students derive substantial psychological benefits, including "feelings of open space," "change of scenery," and "place to escape campus," from their experiences in or nearness to the park. These psychological benefits ranked higher in importance than the recreational and social aspects associated with parks. Several reviews of exercise and depression research indicate that exercise reduces depression symptoms among people diagnosed with depression by three fourths to one standard deviation and among people without depression by about one half standard deviation (Craft, Landers, 1998; Lawlor, Hopker, 2001; Morgan, 1994). Therefore, combining the beneficial effects of physical activity on depression with the restorative effects of nature would indicate an important role for sports fields in improving psychological health.

This study has several limitations. First, although the model assessment indicated a good fit of both models, the R2 values for the individual level (micro level) were relatively low. This is a common problem as low R2 values have also been reported in previous studies on sport participation (Hallmann, Wicker, Breuer, Schüttoff, 2011; Wicker, Breuer, Pawlowski, 2009).

Nevertheless, the low share of explained variance indicates that further variables can be relevant to explain sport participation. Second, it is problematic to calculate the actual distance with geographic coordinates. Two variables (X and Y coordinates) are used to describe the exact location, a straight line would have to be calculated between the two locations (individual's home and sports fields), and the result has to be translated into an actual distance.

This calculation would have to be done for all individuals in combination with all sports fields. Consequently, every sport field would result in one infrastructure variable leading to a total number of 23 infrastructure variables in the selected community.

This total number is high to be included into a statistical model. Therefore, some type of aggregate measure of sport fields has to be used. Third, only the air distance could be calculated which does not necessarily have to be associated with the actual distance to the sports fields. In order to fully understand residents' use of sports fields, future research could focus on relating accessibility to sports fields usage.

Furthermore, obtaining information on items such as sports fields maintenance, amenities, and programming (club activities, etc.) would be an important extension to the research presented here, since sports fields users at different ages will likely have varying preferences and needs. This would require purposive data collection, since currently no inventories exist for these data items in the region. Field surveys could focus on the characteristics and patterns of active mobility of residents accessing sports fields. Furthermore, accessibility was calculated based on sports fields.

To summarize, a key contribution of this study lies in the potential for analysis and policy makers to use this methodology to improve accessibility to sports fields, by addressing transportation components of accessibility. Further, the results of the analysis could be used as an input in ulterior investigations of the impact of accessibility in other outcomes, such as for instance health of adults.

CONCLUSION

This study provided evidence on the impact of sports fields accessibility on physical activity levels using cross-section study. Regression models were estimated to analyze whether the distance from individual's home to the nearest sports fields had a significant influence on physical activity. The application of data and analyses could be considered an improvement to previous research. Nevertheless, there are still some challenges regarding a more holistic modeling of sports fields accessibility.

REFERENCES

Bull, F. C., Maslin, T. S., Armstrong, T. (2009). *Global physical activity questionnaire (GPAQ): nine country reliability and validity study*, in "J Phys Act Health", 6, pp. 790–804

Christian, H., Knuiman, M., Bull, F., et al. (2013). *A new urban planning code's impact on walking: the residential environments project*, in "Am. J. Public Health", 103 (7), pp. 1219–1228

Code for Planning and Design on Urban Residential Areas GB 50180-93. China Craft, L. L., Landers, D. M. (1998). *The effect of exercise on clinical depression and depression resulting from mental illness: a meta-analysis*, in "J Sport Exerc Psychol", 20, pp. 339–357

Diez Roux, A. V., Evenson, K. R., McGinn, A. P., et al. (2007). *Availability of recreational resources and physical activity in adults*, in "Am. J. Public Health", 97 (3), pp. 493–499

Global Physical Activity Questionnaire (GPAQ) Analysis Guide http://www.who.int/chp/steps/resources/GPAQ_Analysis_Guide.pdf

Hallmann, K., Wicker, P., Breuer, C., Schüttoff, U. (2011). *Interdependency of sport supply and sport demand in German metropolitan and medium-sized municipalities*, Findings from multi-level analyses, in "European Journal for Sport and Society", 8 (1/2), pp. 65–84

Hoehner, C. M., Brennan Ramirez, L. K., Elliott, M. B., Handy, S. L., Brownson, R. C. (2005). *Perceived and objective environmental measures and physical activity among urban adults*, in "Am. J. Prev. Med.", 28 (2 Suppl. 2), pp. 105–116

Humpel, N., Owen, N., Leslie E. (2002). *Environmental factors associated with adults' participation in physical activity: a review*, in "Am. J. Prev. Med.", 22 (3), pp. 188–1994

Karusisi, N., Thomas, F., Meline, J., Chaix, B. (2013). *Spatial accessibility to specific sport facilities and corresponding sport practice: the RECORD Study*, in "Int. J. Behav. Nutr. Phys. Act.", 10 (1), p. 48

Lawlor, D. A. Hopker, S. W. (2001). *The effectiveness of exercise as an intervention in the management of depression: systematic review and meta-regression analysis of randomized controlled trials*, in "BMJ", 322, pp. 1–8

McCormack, G. R., Shiell A. (2011). *In search of causality: a systematic review of the relationship between the built environment and physical activity among adults*, in "Int. J. Behav. Nutr. Phys. Act.", 8, p. 125

Morgan, W. P. (1994). *Physical activity, fitness, and depression*, in C. Bouchard, R.J. Shephard, T. Stephens (Eds.),

257

"Physical activity, fitness, and health", Human Kinetics, Champaign IL, pp. 851–867

Prince, S. A., Kristjansson, E.A., Russell, K., et al. (2012). *Relationships between neighborhoods, physical activity, and obesity: a multilevel analysis of a large Canadian city*, in "Obesity (Silver Spring)", 20 (10), pp. 2093–2100

Ranchod, Y. K., Diez Roux, A. V., Evenson, K. R., Sanchez, B. N., Moore, K. (2014). *Longitudinal associations between neighborhood recreational facilities and change in recreational physical activity* in the multi-ethnic study of atherosclerosis, 2000–2007, in "Am. J. Epidemiol.", 179, pp. 335–343

Toftager, M., Ekholm, O., Schipperijn, J., et al. (2011). *Distance to green space and physical activity: a Danish national representative survey*, in "J. Phys. Act. Health", 8 (6), pp. 741–749

Troped, P. J., Saunders, R.P., Pate, R. R., Reininger, B., Addy, C. L. (2003). *Correlates of recreational and transportation physical activity among adults* in a New England community, in "Prev. Med.", 37 (4), pp. 304–310

Ulrich, R. S., Addoms, D. L. (1981). *Psychological and recreational benefits of a residential park* J Leisure Res, 13, pp. 43–65

U.S. Department of Health and Human Services. *A report from the Surgeon General: physical activity and health Centers for Disease Control and Prevention,* National Center for Chronic Disease Prevention and Health Promotion, President's Council on Physical Fitness and Sports, Atlanta GA (1996)

WHO. http://www.who.int/topics/physical_activity/en/

Wicker, P., Breuer, C., Pawlowski, T. (2009). *Promoting sport for all to age-specific target groups: The impact of sport infrastructure,* in "European Sport Management Quarterly", 9 (2), pp. 103–118

Witten, K., Blakely, T., Bagheri, N., et al. (2012). *Neighborhood built environment and transport and leisure physical activity: findings using objective exposure and outcome measures* in New Zealand, Environ, in "Health Perspect.", 120 (7), pp. 971–977

DESIGN FOR CHILDREN, SENIORS, AND OTHER VULNERABLE POPULATIONS

Session introduction

Valentina Santi
PhD. Arch., Research Fellow University of Florence

Research in the field of healthcare facility design finds fulfilment in analysing the needs of a vulnerable population.
People who have a biological or social frailty defined as problematic and that would require them to turn to a hospital for treatment fall into this category. They may be foetuses, newborns, children, pregnant women, elderly people, people with reduced or compromised mobility capacity, mentally disabled people, and disadvantaged people from an economic and cultural point of view.

Research concerning paediatric hospital services in recent years has raised the attention to solutions aimed at improving the physical and psychological well-being of children based on different diseases. Studies concerning spatial perception in children who suffer from hypersensitivity caused by autism, for example, highlight the need to work on reducing acoustic impact and offering intuitive spatial orientation solutions.

As regards the design of residential spaces for the elderly, the need to create solutions with direct access to nature, by taking walks and engaging in outdoor activities, has been confirmed.
Another aspect that research into spaces for the elderly highlights is the need for a strong connection with the external world, so that elderly people who are still active do not live in social isolation. The need for communication continuity between interior and exterior spaces also came to light, so that even the lives of elderly people who are confined to bed can benefit from contact with nature, the continuous passing of day into night and the cycle of the seasons.

A different but still important vulnerability condition is identified as people who are the victims of natural disasters and the conflicts of war.
From the perspective of the growing humanization of care, the well-considered planning of the reception area in hospitals must seek to remove the cultural and linguistic barriers that certain users may experience and ensure that access to the health service also becomes an opportunity to assess the fragility of the individual, where this has not yet been done, and to start the process of preventing it from worsening.

Refurbishment of the "Spedali Civili" Hospital Complex of Brescia

Romano Del Nord

romano.delnord@unifi.it
Professor, University of TESIS Inter-University Research Centre, Director of CSPE professional Office, Italy

The article outlines the Refurbishment of the Civil Hospitals of Brescia project currently in progress and is broken down into two main sections: the construction of a new outpatient facility and the redevelopment of an existing pavilion to house functions relating to paediatric activities.

The project to build a new outpatient clinic aims to improve the outpatient management processes, with particular regard to patient-directed discharge , as well as improve the distribution and management of personnel and the spaces set up for outpatient activities in order to facilitate the use of the areas available for care activities and opportunities for communication between the various specialists.

The redevelopment project for the existing pavilion instead is aimed at ensuring greater flexibility and adaptability for the increasingly pressing healthcare and technology requirements, starting with a careful analysis of present-day and future needs.

Both projects pursue the maximum humanization of the environment objectives in line with the consolidated philosophy of the value attributed to comfort and psychological well-being in the treatment process. To this end the size of the reception areas, spaces for training and therapeutic education, and for the rehabilitation and recreational activities of paediatric patients, is particularly important.

PROJECT AREAS AND BUILDINGS

As indicated in the Work Programme for the Refurbishment of the Civil Hospitals of Brescia project, the planned execution of the design activities includes a series of works for the overall refurbishment of the Hospital which concern in particular:
- the construction of a new outpatient facility;
- the redevelopment of an existing pa-vilion to be used for functions related to paediatric activities (Pavilion B).

Despite the numerous adaptation works carried out over time, the Hospital was in need of a refurbishment that would allow the new general objectives of the healthcare programme to be implemented through practical integration between the hospital and the region in harmony with the current national and regional policies which impose a reduction of beds and multi-disciplinary outpatient care with low clinical complexity and high care complexity.

As regards the more design-related issues, on the other hand, the works had to ensure the maximum humanization of the environment, according to the now consolidated philosophy of the value attributed to comfort and psychological well-being in the treatment process. To this end the project studied the correct sizing of the reception areas, the spaces for training and therapeutic education, and the rehabilitation and recreational activities of paediatric patients.

With this intention logic the new outpatient hub will act as a centre of outpatient activities with medium to low clinical diagnostic complexity and distinct and separate areas for paediatric services and adults. The aim is to distance the"daily" patient flows within the departments of the Civil Hospitals complex in order to make the services more accessible in the territory and integrate them thereby making it easier for citizens to access and use them, reducing the risk of infection.

The redevelopment of Pavilion B mainly concerns the North Wing (used for in-patients) and the South Wing. The building, started in 1938 and completed in 1951, required a significant improvement of the functionality and usability of the spaces in order to achieve the requirements of the current legislation on accreditation.

ORIGINS AND EVOLUTION

The history of the present-day Civil Hospitals complex dates back to the 15th century and is closely interwoven with that of the city of Brescia.

The Civil Hospitals in fact derive from the "Hospitale unum magnum et universale" built in 1427 to bring together in one building the many institutions that were involved in assisting the sick and destitute; institutions whose symbolic references were found in the crest still used as the corporate logo. The crest

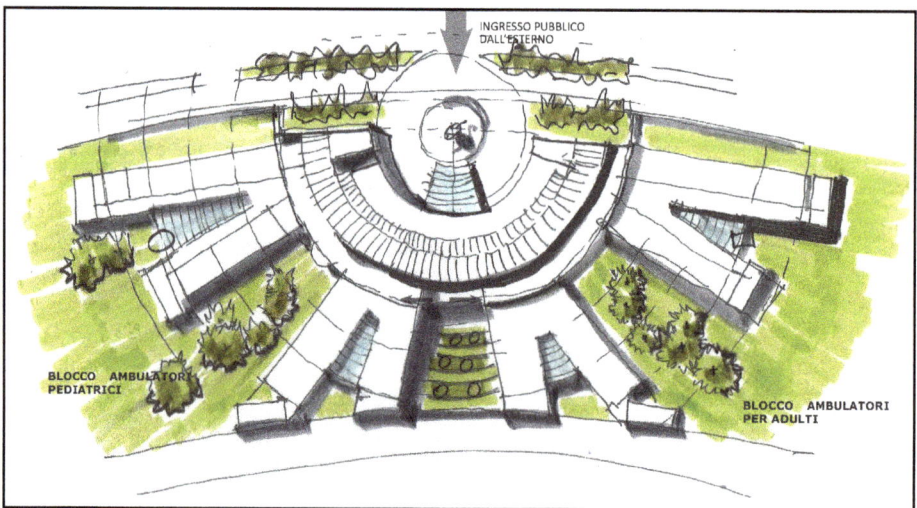

Figure 1. Concept of the new outpatient facility

of the Civil Hospital of Brescia, the sixteenth-century heir to various forms produced in the fifteenth century, is composite, bearing within it symbols pertaining to some of its predecessors.

The dove at the top concerns one of the major players of the Hospital foundation, the Consortium of the Holy Spirit. It refers to the ancient symbol of the Holy Spirit, merged with the biblical dove, the bearer of peace, characterized by the olive branch carried in its beak. The dove rests its feet on a book thought to be the Gospel of St. Luke, considered the designation of the first Hospital, the "Ospedale di S. Spirito e di S. Luca della Misericordia" (Hospital of the Holy Spirit and St. Luke of Mercy).

The name "Spedali Civili" (Civil Hospitals) of Brescia was confirmed at the end of the 1800s; the hospital building was located in the city centre at the time. At the start of the 1900s, however, the insufficient spaces with respect to the citizens' requirements brought about the construction of a new functional and modern hospital, started in 1938. The design was innovative in that – for the first time – it reconciled the characteristics of the old hospital divided into pavilions with the more recent single-block structures.

The new hospital was only opened on 10 December 1950 due to the signifi-

263

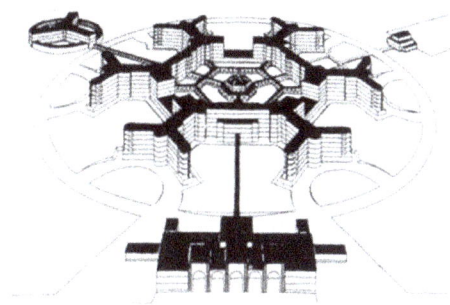

Figure 2. Civil Hospital of Brescia: original plan

Figure 3. Civil Hospital of Brescia: original configuration

264

cant slowdowns experienced during the second world war.

In 1953 the old hospital was finally decommissioned and all the departments were relocated to the new site. In the following decades several works were carried out with the intention of expanding and adapting the hospital building to the citizens' requirements: the construction of the Satellite Polyclinic, started in 1966 and completed in 1972; the construction of the Pavilion for Infectious Diseases in 1976; the refurbishment of the wing in front of the chapel.

ARCHITECTURE & PROJECT FUNCTIONALITY

The project for the new Outpatient facility involved the creation of a new building on the eastern border of the hospital area (previously a green area and car park) with a semi-toroidal plan (partially opening up towards Via Antonio Schivardi with the rooms in blocks arranged in a radial pattern) with a three-storey volume and a direct entrance from the outside (created by a new opening in the present-day enclosure wall).

Inside the building there are around 150

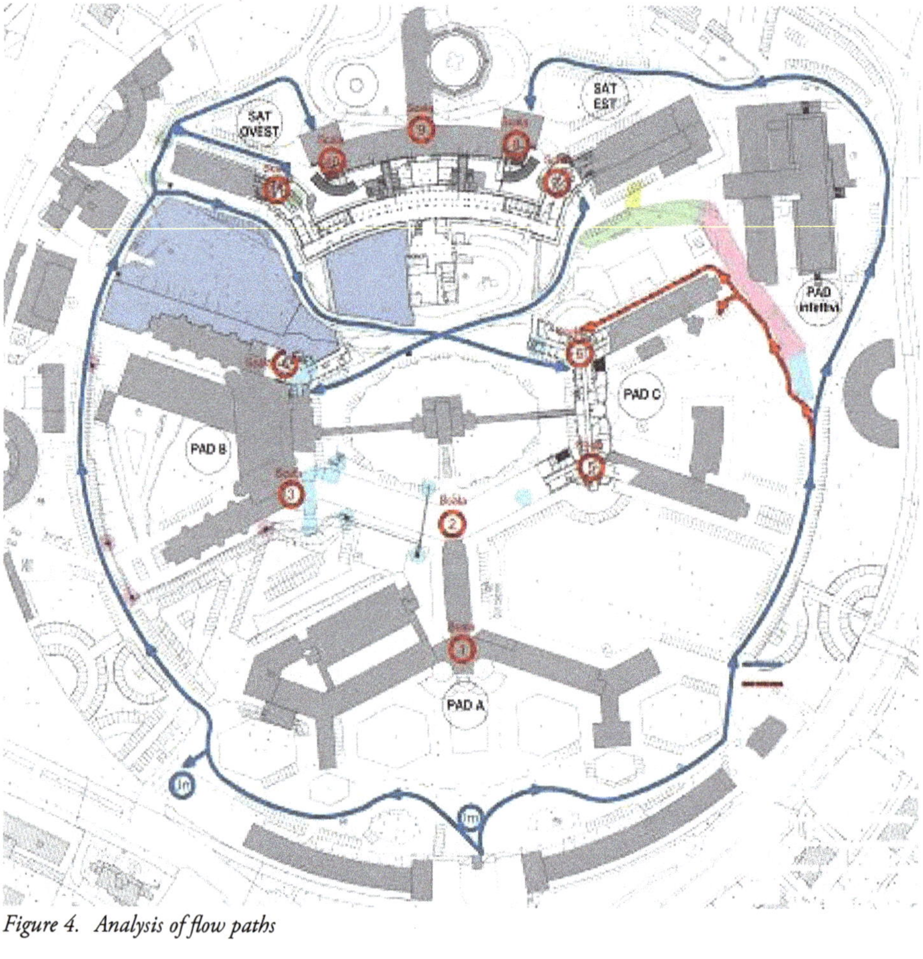

Figure 4. Analysis of flow paths

examination rooms, an auditorium with a capacity of approximately 300 seats and a reception and admissions point.

The architecture style is repeated over three floors: a central corridor in the radiating blocks onto which all the rooms face, staircases at the end of each block and two at the ends of the semicircular entrance area.

The first design schemes, assessed with the Healthcare Management Office of the Civil Hospitals complex, were focused on the need to separate the outpatient blocks (paediatric-adult), creating an atrium for public access along with separate admissions areas and waiting rooms. The two square-shaped outpatient blocks were designed with a large internal courtyard with a path leading to the various floors winding around it.

The ground floor gives access, in addition to the public areas, to the auditorium in the basement, with a capacity of 300 seats, which can be adapted to the internal organization of the spaces.

Subsequently, following further meetings with the Healthcare Management Office, a semicircular plan was agreed on for the new project which integrates with the pre-existing structures (occupational medicine).

The solution chosen thus provides a separate access for the two outpatient blocks. The entrance square provides direct access to the paediatric area and the adult area through two separate revolving doors. Moreover, the square also provides direct access to the auditorium in the basement.

The paediatric area on the ground floor has a waiting room with 50 seats, situated in front of admissions, and it is integrated with a recreational area for children who can use it while they wait.

Figure 5. Hospital humanization lies also in the choice of colors

After the admissions procedure patients are directed towards the relevant department where specific secondary waiting rooms are provided within the outpatient areas. In this case too, each secondary waiting room has a play area for children. Similarly, access to the adult area leads to a specific waiting room.

The shape of the outpatient blocks, arranged in a radial pattern, and the layout of the examination rooms along the façades, allows natural light to penetrate each examination room. The secondary waiting areas instead receive natural light from the ends of each block.

GENERAL DESIGN CRITERIA

Flexibility

Flexibility concerns not only the possibility to alter and adapt the architectural components and installed plants, but also and especially the system of interactions between diagnosis, monitoring, care and intervention; it therefore involves the architectural components and above all the installed plants themselves

265

Figure 6. Elevations and Section

in terms of their interface. To ensure distribution and plant flexibility, and therefore the possibility to rearrange the spaces each time the introduction of new activities or care methods makes it necessary, all the typological and technological aspects that allow the modifications requested to be made were developed during the design phase.

This objective was possible by envisaging, among other things: the ability to alter the spatial distribution, obtained by using division systems based on dry technologies integrated with the plant networks.

To divide up the areas partitions were planned, made of plasterboard panels or other advanced composite materials on metal frames, a solution that allows:

- dry processing on the already finished floor;
- possible relocation due to changed functional requirements;
- the internal passage of the plants, benefiting from the simplicity and cleanliness of the works (absence of chases in the walls) and hygiene (smooth surfaces without parts of the plant protruding visibly and collecting dust and dirt);
- excellent acoustic insulation performances that can be scaled according to use;
- pre-determined fire resistance and reaction performances;
- flexibility in the technological subsystems, with the possibility of changing the distribution and power outputs.

This means adopting a modular and section-based plant system.

The plant solutions meet the environmental comfort requirements necessary for each functional area, allowing the following to be obtained:

- great flexibility to allow future distribution and functional adaptations;
- linearity and logic in the plant so-

Figure 7. Render of the project

lutions to optimize the management and maintenance;
- flexibility in the set up of the equipment and furniture, positioning the fixed furniture in areas that are not subject to change, such as the external closures or internal divisions not subject to repositioning.
The main sectors affected by flexibility are: diagnostics, examination rooms.
These functional areas house a series of equipment and technological set-ups that evolve quickly and may require adaptations in the short/medium term.
This involves the application of morphological and plant-based flexibility and the evaluation of alternative locations within the same area.

THE ROAD SYSTEM AS RESULTING FROM THE PROJECT AND PARKING AREAS

The project included an integrated road system that guarantees a direct connection with the main urban infrastructures. In particular an entrance square was planned, slighted raised and connected, via a canopy, to the nearby subway station. The road system design also planned for a bike sharing point.

As for patients arriving by car, the project allowed them to arrive as far as the square in front of the entrance so patients can be accompanied as close to the entrance as possible (drop-off). Vehicle access to the hospital area was planned for disabled people (south entrance) so they could get to the controlled access area situated behind the outpatient facility. This is also where the entrance reserved for healthcare personnel is found.

Public and reception areas

Particular importance was given to the public spaces and reception area. The criteria followed for the waiting areas included a series of integrated waiting spaces (waiting and secondary waiting

Figure 8. Render of the project

areas), relating to paediatrics, with recreational and play areas for children. Access to the outdoor green areas is planned on the ground floor from the waiting areas.

HUMANIZATION AND ENVIRONMENTAL COMFORT

The New Outpatient facility focuses on humanization and the functional livability of the entrance, resting and orientation space. The project aims to create spaces available to the public.

Humanization and wayfinding, connecting corridors

The corridors, in terms of forms, colours and decoration, are designed to avoid institutional monotony.
This objective, which does not detract from the functionality but rather is synergic to it, is achieved through various construction solutions such as:
- avoiding a repetitive layout that would create orientation problems for users: the distribution spaces are designed differently in terms of the colour of the floors and walls, natural and artificial lighting system, and signage;
- distinguishing the circulation spaces with small rest and information areas;
- installing all safety features for users: protective strips on the walls, non-slip floors, shatter-proof glass for the interior window fixtures, etc;
- using different colours to promote recognizability and orientation;
- spotlights and lighting that highlights the entrances to the bedrooms.

Natural lighting

The utmost attention was paid so that there would never be dark areas but above all so that the perception of the outside is enhanced, avoiding that sense of "closure" and introversion typical of hospital environments. Visual relationships between the inside/outside maintain their relationship with day/night and seasonal rhythms. As we know, light is the main environmental stimulus that tells our body what time of day it is. The lighting design in accordance with circadian needs concerns both patients and healthcare staff and affects their physical and emotional well-being.

The lighting design concerns areas that support orientation and wayfinding, circadian rhythms, affective processes, operability and visual functionality. Humanization means also introducing natural lighting into areas that are normally neglected.

Colour study

The role of colour and decoration as a resource mainly consists of:
- supporting the sensory well-being of the occupants of the various healthcare environments creating perceptibly comfortable environments;
- supporting the affective processes helping to create an emotionally positive environment;
- supporting the operability of the personnel not interfering with visual tasks that require colour recognition;
- supporting cognitive-fruition processes helping to understand the function, use and structure of the environments.

General philosophy for preventing infections

The design philosophy for new hospitals provides for a global approach to prevent the spread of infections.

This approach is expressed in both the distributional organization of the spaces and the separation of routes, and in the provision and quality of the finishes and equipment, the most appropriate and

269

Figure 9. Render of the project

advanced plant technologies, up to the widespread application of the simplest and most effective prevention measures, such as frequent hand washing; in order to facilitate this multiple hand-washing facilities with disinfectant were introduced along the main routes, available to staff, patients and visitors alike.

Applying the Seniors' Outdoor Survey (SOS) in Practice: an Observational Tool for Assessing Outdoor Environments at Residential Care Facilities for Aging

Eric Bardenhagen

Bardenhagen@tamu.edu
Texas A&M University, Department of Landscape Architecture & Urban Planning, Center for Health Systems & Design, Assistant Professor, College Station, TX, USA

271

As many world populations age, increasing numbers of older people are making their homes in residential care facilities in countries around the world. Where facilities allow residents to age in place, they become the settings in which seniors experience major changes in their physical, cognitive, and functional abilities. As a result, supportive outdoor spaces associated with these facilities play an increasingly important role, to take advantage of multiple health benefits that can be derived from contact with nature and the outdoors. While research has mainly focused on the indoor environment, new models of design for aging encourage the incorporation of usable outdoor environments, to supplement the quality of livability found in existing care facilities.

In 2014, the Seniors' Outdoor Survey (SOS) assessment tool was developed to evaluate how well outdoor spaces in long-term care settings support the preferences and outdoor usage of aging residents. The instrument contains 60 ratable items organized in five domains drawn from the literature. Content validity of the SOS was initially based on relevant literature and preliminary studies in diverse long-term care settings, with item validity examined using content analysis of resident survey responses (N = 1,128) in a large multiregional study. Further validity was supported through subject matter experts (N=53) and the tool was then rigorously tested for both inter-rater and test-retest reliability with highly satisfactory results. This innovative tool will allow multiple stakeholders to share a common platform to evaluate the spatial continuum that connects the natural and built environments, in a wide range of long-term care settings. Having a reliable and easily understandable tool to assess usable outdoor space will provide decision-making support for facility and programmatic changes, toward the goal of promoting positive change and improved health in the lives of older adults in long-term care facilities.

Keywords: environmental assessment instrument, outdoor usage, aging, access to nature, long-term care residents

INTRODUCTION

Importance of outdoor spaces for older adults

As many world populations age, increasing numbers of older people are making their homes in residential care facilities in countries around the world. Where facilities allow residents to age in place, they become the settings in which seniors experience major changes in their physical, cognitive, and functional abilities.

As a result, supportive outdoor spaces associated with these facilities play an increasingly important role, to take advantage of multiple health benefits that can be derived from contact with nature and the outdoors.

Research has clearly shown that access to nature and the outdoors can provide numerous observable health-related benefits for older adults. Time spent outdoors is linked to lower blood pressure, improved mood, improved sleep patterns, greater vitamin D absorption and reduced fall risks (Cohen-Mansfield & Werner, 2001; Detweiler, et al., 2012; Joseph, 2006, Okubo et al., 2015, Ulrich, 1999; Wang & MacMillan, 2013). Time spent outdoors also carries behavioral benefits such as increased physical activity, which subsequently can lead to greater physical and psychological benefits (Berto, 2007, Jacobs et al., 2008).

Specifically, in the case of long term care facilities, outdoor spaces are often provided for residents and include features such as seating and walkways, shade structures, plantings and gardens and

Figure 1. Health Benefits of Therapeutic Landscapes (photo courtesy of Access to Nature)

water features that satisfy many of the needs and preferences of older adults.

Increasingly, studies have shown that overall, outdoor usage is strongly linked to the characteristics of the physical environment even despite challenges of weather, individual health conditions, and staff abilities/attitudes to facilitate outdoor usage.

Thus, as disabilities increase throughout the aging process, it becomes increasingly important that supportive outdoor spaces be provided as a means of positively influencing behaviors (Cutler, 2000; Lawton, Weisman, Sloane, & Calkins, 1997; Sugiyama & Ward

272

Thompson, 2007). Low-cost, non-invasive and non-pharmacological interventions such as healing gardens and green spaces hold promise as strategies for senior housing facilities that are seeking to improve resident quality of life (CDC, 2003, 2013; Cooper Marcus & Sachs, 2014; Lee, 2007; Mowen et al., 2007; Takano, Nakamura, & Watanabe, 2002; Wang & MacMillan, 2013).

Finally, beyond the physical and psychosocial benefits that access to outdoor spaces can provide, financial analysis has supported the hypothesis that improvements to outdoor spaces can also lead to higher levels of resident or patient satisfaction. This, in turn, results in both greater overall occupancy that is often

brought about by word-of-mouth referrals (Rodiek, Boggess, Lee, Booth, & Morris, 2013).

Low levels of outdoor space use

Although research has shown clear linkages between time spent outdoors and therapeutic benefits to seniors, outdoor spaces in many long term care facilities are very often reported to being underutilized (Rappe & Kivelä, 2005; Grant & Wineman, 2007; Kearney & Winterbottom, 2006). Low levels of use can be linked to uncomfortable weather conditions and restrictive facility policies, but often this can also be attributed to the physical design and layout of a fa-

273

Figure 2. Design & Usage of outdoor spaces among seniors

cility such as how interior and exterior spaces support easily traversable connections. This can also be attributed to specific features such as chairs, walkways and shade structures that are provided for residents (Brawley, 2006; Cooper Marcus & Sachs, 2014; Regnier, 2002; Rodiek, 2009; Rodiek & Lee, 2009; Rodiek, Lee, & Nejati, 2014; Zeisel et al., 2003). With many residents spending nearly all of their time within a care facility, this lack of outdoor space usage concerns researchers and facility administrators alike.

Lack of instruments

A great challenge for facility administrators and executive decision makers seek to improve their residents' quality of life, a great challenge arises in how to utilize this knowledge of both the benefits of access to nature and the general underutilization of outdoor spaces and prioritize scarce financial resources as they seek improvements in their outdoor spaces.

While researchers have provided many assessment tools to evaluate physical environment features at long-term care facilities most assessment tools that focus on senior environments have few, if any, items related to assessing the quality of outdoor space (AHRQ, 2007; Cutler, 2000).

This lack of evidence-based tools for evaluating outdoor spaces in senior living environments makes it difficult to clearly and systematically assess the features of an outdoor space that tend to encourage or discourage use by residents.

THE SENIORS' OUTDOOR SURVEY TOOL (SOS TOOL)

Development and format of the SOS Tool

To fill this gap, the Seniors' Outdoor Survey (SOS Tool) was recently developed. This evaluation tool was designed to specifically assess the quality of an outdoor space in its ability to support the physical and psychosocial needs of older adults in long term care settings (Rodiek, Nejati, Bardenhagen, Lee & Senes, 2014). The SOS Tool identifies the key outdoor features that support older adults and is envisioned as a practitioner-focused tool that can be used in the field at single facilities or across networks of facilities.

Figure 3. Access to Nature

Figure 4. Outdoor Comfort & Safety

The tool can also be utilized prior to any construction when planning for resident usage of outdoor space is more manageable. The tool includes 60 discrete items to be rated on a 7-point likert scale. To facilitate usage, the 60 items were subdivided into five domains that were derived from literature reviews of key resources that support outdoor usage by frail older adults. These domains include:

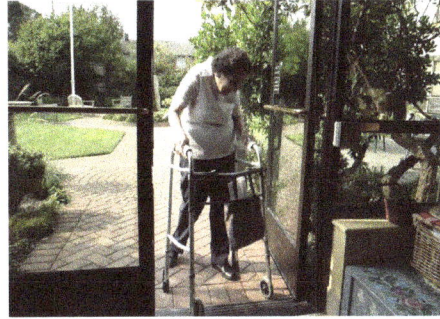
Figure 6. Indoor-Outdoor Connection

1. Access to Nature – greenery, views, water, other aesthetic features (14 items)
2. Outdoor Comfort & Safety –seating, climate control, & comfort issues (15 items)
3. Walking & Outdoor Activities –safe & accessible walks, destinations (14 items)
4. Indoor-Outdoor Connection –doorways, physical/visual outdoor access (11 items)
5. Connection to the World – providing contact with nearby surroundings (6 items).

Scoring of the tool is currently completed by simply calculating the total of rated values within each of the domains and for the overall instrument. The relative relationships between the scores of

Figure 7. Connection to the World

each domain within the tool can then be compared to assist in prioritization and decisions related to improvements to outdoor spaces. A full listing of SOS Tool items can be viewed below.

Utilizing Gibson's theory of affordances The SOS Tool is designed to be completed by an individual while moving within an outdoor space. Further, it specifically emphasizes the usability of the features of the outdoor space rather than a simple inventory of whether or not a feature is present. Raters administering the tool are encouraged to put themselves in the mindset of a frail older adult that may be hindered by limited physical abilites such as sight or mobility, or may experience the outdoor space while seated in a wheelchair.

This approach that focuses on the us-

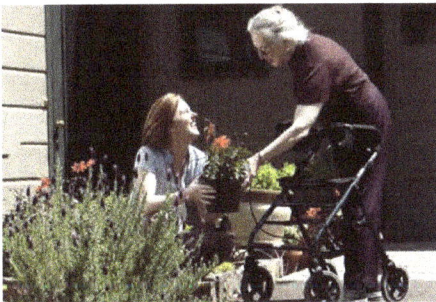
Figure 5. Walking & Outdoor Activities

276

SENIORS' OUTDOOR SURVEY (SOS)

©2014, Susan Rodiek, Center for Health Systems & Design, Texas A&M University, College Station, TX

Access to
Nature

Your Name: _____ Your Role/Position: _____

Facility: _____ Name of the outdoor space you are evaluating: _____

Date: _____ Day: _____ Time: _____

PLEASE READ before using this tool:

<u>STEP 1</u>: **Choose an outdoor area** – First, decide on the boundaries of the outdoor space to be evaluated. (Features that are viewable should be included when appropriate, even if beyond the space itself.)

<u>STEP 2</u>: **Walk and sit in the area** - Imagine **YOU** are a senior resident with sensory and functional disabilities, using a walker or wheelchair. Walk around slowly, test the furniture, look at the area from different positions – including wheelchair height.) **ASK:** "How well does this space support the needs of frail older adults?"

<u>STEP 3</u>: **Evaluate the area** – Rate each item from 1 to 7 (1 = worst, 7 = best), based on the climate, context, and functional level of residents, considering what you could *reasonably expect* in this type of setting. If there are several features in an item, rate overall how well they support outdoor usage.

OVERALL, how well does this outdoor area provide a real sense of escape and relief from being indoors? (a feeling of fresh air, views, sky, sunshine, lush plantings, other senses)   **Very well** _____ **Fairly well** _____ **Not well** _____

1. ACCESS TO NATURE   *Subtotal ____ Divide by 14 = ____ Score for this category*

Abundant greenery - Does this area include or view a substantial quantity of healthy green plants ___; with a diverse mix of trees, vines, flowers and shrubs ___? (instead of all hard paving, or just a few types of plant)

Flowers and color - In season, would residents see an abundance of color, as flowers or bright foliage ___?

Reachable plants - Can residents in wheelchairs see, touch, or smell attractive plants at hand or eye level ___?

Viewscapes - Does seating have pleasant views ___, and are hard boundaries partly screened by plants ___?

Water and motion - Can residents see, hear, or interact with water, such as fountains, ponds, birdbaths, etc. ___? Do any features have movement ___? (e.g., wind chimes, waving banners, spraying fountains, grasses moving in the breeze)

Wildlife/ pets - Does this area provide amenities for pets ___; or to attract wildlife, such as squirrels, birds, and butterflies ___; or does it have views of domestic or farm animals ___? (such as rabbits, chickens, grazing cows or horses)

Private and quiet - Is the area overall fairly quiet, and free from obnoxious noises ___; with privacy from nearby resident rooms ___; and at least one or more private outdoor places to sit ___?

2. OUTDOOR COMFORT AND SAFETY   *Subtotal ____ Divide by 15 = ____ Score for this category*

Available seating - Is there plenty of seating available ___; with at least a few different types of seating ___?

Sitting choices – Are there places to sit in sun or shade ___; with some seating easily movable by residents ___?

Safe seating - Is the seating stable so it will not tip over ___; with backs and arms to help residents get up safely ___?

Sitting comfort - Are chairs and benches comfortably shaped ___; made of materials that do not get too hot or cold ___; with at least some seat cushions ___?

Sitting amenities - Are there tables near some of the seating, to place a cup of coffee or food ___; and are there any rocking chairs, swings or gliders available ___?

Restroom/ drinking water - Is there a nearby restroom, with access to a drinking fountain or water cooler___?

Maintenance/ air quality/ climate control - Is the outdoor area well-maintained ___; are any smoking areas well-separated from other areas ___; and is there any microclimate control ___? (e.g., outdoor fans, heaters, etc.)

Figure 8. The SOS Tool as used in assessments of senior living facilities

ability of elements within a space rather than their presence alone is based on Gibson's (1979) theory of affordances. From his work, an affordance can be described as the functional potential that a feature in an environment provides to specific further as it captures the meanings and values for these items in terms of how they support usage. As an example, while a series of benches in an outdoor space may be present, they may not be placed in such a way that allows easy or comfortable use by older adults.

They may be located too far from building entries, set along uneven walks or not able to take advantage of any shade protection. Older adults (and indeed all humans) make decisions regarding the value and supportiveness of elements such as this example both consciously and unconsciously very quickly as they move through a space which, in turn, influences behavior patterns (Chemero, 2003). By focusing the items of the SOS Tool on the usability and support of features, critically important interrelationships between multiple features can be captured as raters seek to assess an overall space.

Psychometric testing

Psychometric testing of the SOS Tool was conducted for both the validity and the reliability of the tool to shed light on how well an outdoor space and its environmental features support usage by older adults. Validity support for the tool was initially drawn from both literature reviews and preliminary studies that included:
1. Resident preferences from written surveys with 1,128 residents. Respondents identified relevant outdoor space features through open-ended questions that focused on usage and/or satisfaction.
2. Outcome-based findings were utilized from a comparison of reported resident usage to the SOS Tool ratings in corresponding spaces and found significant positive associations with many tested environmental features (Rodiek, 2009).
3. Expert opinions were sought grom 53 subject matter experts based on their publications within fields of research related to outdoor space use by older adults. Participating experts provided feedback on each item within the SOS Tool as to whether it had a high, medium or low potential to record support for usage by older adults. This information was used for refinements to the wording and inclusion of tool items.

Combining these diverse sources of validity of items to be used in the SOS Tool tool allowed for a more balanced instrument to be created that could more completely reflect the needs of older adults.
The reliabilty of the SOS Tool was also tested by using trained researchers in 22 outdoor spaces located at 12 senior living and care facilities which ranged from assisted living to skilled nursing. Results from these outdoor spaces showed high levels of inter-rater reliability (.83 to .98 for the five domains, and .91 for the overall instrument).
These same 22 outdoor spaces were then re-evaluated after seven weeks and test-retest reliability found similar results (.81 to .98 for the domains, and with a mean of .92 for the overall instrument) (Rodiek, Nejati, Bardenhagen, Lee and Senes, 2014).

277

Using a combination of both a triangulation of source validity inputs upon which the tool is founded and clear reliability testing results, the SOS Tool can be seen as a reliable way to accurately and consistently assess the quality and supportiveness of outdoor spaces across diverse senior living contexts.

ADMINISTERING THE SOS TOOL
Field raters

278

Outdoor spaces can be assessed using the SOS Tool by any number of raters which can include facility personnel and administrators as well as designers and facility space planners. Though a single rater can successfully evaluate a space, using multiple raters from differing roles or backgrounds allows for comparisons of results. Raters are not required to have any prior special training or expertise. Instructions within the SOS Tool guide them to view the space and its environmental features 1) from within the context of the facility, residents and community, 2) from the perspective of how features 'afford' usage by older adults, and 3) by moving through the space and actively engaging with or trying each feature as they conduct the assessment. Typically spaces can be evaluated within one hour after an initial orientation or review of the tool domains and items and an understanding of the space(s) to be assessed.

Figure 9. A Trained rater using the SOS Tool at one of 22 outdoor spaces assessed in Bryan/College Station, Texas, USA (photo courtesy of Access to Nature)

In some cases, a provider may have multiple facilities and desire to conduct assessments across outdoor spaces within a care system. In these situations, it is recommended that either some members of assessment teams be consistent across all facilities or, a dedicated team of raters be used to assess all spaces to improve consistency of administration and comparability of results.

Resulting scores from tool administration

Current scoring of the SOS Tool in the field simply relies on comparison of 1-7 ratings for each item or comparison of average scores for each of the five domains which can be calculated by adding the total of all items in a domain and dividing by the number of items in that domain. Based on feedback from industry representatives and testing of the tool in the field, a differential weighting and scoring framework is currently being developed to increase the tool's usability. While all of the 60 items in the tool are supported by at least one validity source, many items naturally can have a greater impact on older adults' preferences for outdoor spaces or in how well that environmental feature supports health outcomes.

As examples the "presence of automatic doors" to allow access to outdoor spaces and "amenities for pets" are both supported in prefence surveys, however, the presence of automatic doors has a greater overall impact on access, and thus health outcomes.

The weighting protocol being developed will assign weights based on the levels of support from validity sources. Using differential weightings, rated scores for items multiplied by weightings will better illustrate differences among items assessed in outdoor spaces. Then, to achieve an even more intuitive score, a consistent multiplier and addend to bring the score range within a commonly understood 60-100 grading scale. This 100-base scoring system will provide a more intuitive way to understand the implications of possible improvements to outdoor spaces and allow for clearer comparisons across facilities.

279

CONCLUSIONS

The use and enjoyment of outdoor spaces such as courtyards, front porches, gardens and terraces supports many physical and psychosocial needs of older adults in long term care settings. The resulting increases in quality of life and satisfaction with long term care facilities that can be associated with these amenities are of great interest to care provider organizations.

The SOS Tool fills a gap in the decision making process of these care providers by offering a way to systematically evaluate the quality of outdoor spaces with a valid and reliable tool. Through a better understanding of the successes and shortfalls of outdoor spaces in senior living facilities, these care givers, facility planners and researchers can be better equipped to provide supportive environments and access to nature for older adults.

ACKNOWLEDGMENTS

The author appreciates the assistance of Dr. Susan Rodiek, Dr. Adeleh Nejati and Dr. Chanam Lee at Texas A&M University, for their roles in the SOS Tool development. Early development of this work was supported in part by the National Institutes of Health (R44 AG024786).

The content is solely the responsibility of the author and does not necessarily represent the official views of the National Institute on Aging or the National Institutes of Health. The College of Architecture, Texas A&M University supported participation in the UIA/PHG in Dalian, China through an international travel grant to.

REFERENCES

AHRQ - Agency for Healthcare Research and Quality. (2007). *Environmental scan of instruments to inform consumer choice in assisted living facilities.* Retrieved from http://www.ahrq. gov/legacy/research/ltcscan/ltcappa.pdf

Berto, R. (2007). *Assessing the restorative value of the environment: A study on the elderly in comparison with young adults and adolescents,* in "International Journal of Psychology", 42, 331-341

Brawley, E. C. (2006). *Design innovations for aging and Alzheimer's: Creating caring environments.* Hoboken, NJ: Wiley

(CDC) Centers for Disease Control and Prevention (2013). *The state of aging and health in America 2013,* in "Atlanta, GA: Centers for Disease Control and Prevention, US Department of Health and Human Services"

(CDC) Centers for Disease Control and Prevention (2003). *Trends in aging--United States and worldwide,* in "MMWR. Morbidity and Mortality Weekly Report", 52(6), 101. www.cdc.gov/mmwr/preview/mmwrhtml/mm5206a2.htm

Chemero, A. (2003). *An outline of a theory of affordances,* in "Ecological Psychology", 15(2), 181 195. doi: 10.1207/S15326969ECO1502_5

Cohen-Mansfield, J. & Werner, P. (1998). *Visits to an outdoor garden: Impact on behavior and mood of nursing home residents who pace,* in B. Vellas, J. Fitten, & G. Frisoni (Eds.), "Research and practice in Alzheimer's disease" (pp. 419-436). Paris, France: Serdi

Cooper Marcus, C. & Sachs, N. A. (2014). *Therapeutic landscapes: An evidence-based approach to designing healing gardens and restorative outdoor spaces.* Hoboken, NJ: Wiley

Cutler, L. J. (2000). *Assessment of physical environments of older adults,* in R. L. Kane & R. A. Kane (Eds.), "Assessing older persons: Measures, meaning, and practical applications" (pp. 360– 379). New York: Oxford University Press

Detweiler, M. B., Sharma, T., Detweiler, J. G., Murphy, P. F., Lane, S., Carman, J., Kim, K. Y. (2012). *What is the evidence to support the use of therapeutic gardens for the elderly?* in "Psychiatry Investigation", 9(2), 100-110

Gibson, J. J. (1979). *The ecological approach to visual perception.* Boston: Houghton Mifflin

Grant, C. F., & Wineman, J. D. (2007). *The Garden-Use Model: An environmental tool for increasing the use of outdoor space by residents with dementia in long-term care facilities,* in "Journal of Housing for the Elderly", 21(1-2), 89-115

Jacobs, J. M., Cohen, A., Hammerman-Rozenberg, R., Azoulay, D., Maaravi, Y., & Stessman, J. (2008). *Going outdoors daily predicts long-term functional and health benefits among ambulatory older people,* in "Journal of Aging and Health", 20(3), 259-272

Joseph, A. (2006). *Health promotion by design in long-term care settings.* Concord, CA: Center for Health Design.

Kearney, A. R., & Winterbottom, D. (2006). *Nearby nature and long-term care facility residents: Benefits and design recommendations,* in "Journal of Housing for the Elderly", 19(3-4), 7-28

Lawton, M. P., Weisman, G. D., Sloane, P., & Calkins, M. (1997). *Assessing environments for older people with chronic illness,* in "Journal of Mental Health and Aging", 3(1), 83-100

Lee, C. (2007). *Environment and active living: The roles of health risk and economic factors,* in "American Journal of Health Promotion", 21(4s), 293-304.

Mowen, A., Orsega-Smith, E., Payne, L., Ainsworth, B., & Godbey, G. (2007). *The role of park proximity and social support in shaping park visitation, physical activity, and perceived health among older adults,* in "Journal of Physical Activity & Health", 4(2), 167

Okubo, Y., Osuka, Y., Jung, S., Rafael, F., Tsujimoto, T., Aiba, T., Tanaka, K. (2015), *Walking can be more effective than balance training in fall prevention among community-dwelling older adults,* in "Geriatrics & Gerontology International". doi: 10.1111/ggi.12444

Rappe, E., & Kivelä, S. L. (2005). *Effects of garden visits on long-term care residents as related to depression,* in "HortTechnology", 15(2), 298-303

Regnier, V. (2002). *Design for assisted living: Guidelines for housing the physically and mentally frail.* New York: John Wiley and Sons

Rodiek, S. (Director). (2009). *Access to nature for older aAdults* [set of three 30-minute DVDs]. (Available from the Center for Health Systems & Design, Texas A&M University, Langford Architecture Center, College Station, TX 77843, and www.accesstonature.org)

Rodiek, S. & Lee, C. (2009). *External space: Increasing outdoor usage in residential facilities for older adults,* in "World Health Design", 2(4), 49-55

Rodiek, S., Lee, C., & Nejati, A. (2014). *You can't get there from here: Reaching the outdoors in senior housing,* in "Journal of Housing for the Elderly", 28(1), 63-84. doi:10.1080/02763893.2013.858093

Rodiek, S., Boggess, M. M., Lee, C., Booth, G. J., & Morris, A. (2013). *Can better outdoor environments lead to cost*

281

benefits in assisted living facilities through increased word-of-mouth referrals?, in "Health Environments Research & Design Journal", 6(2), 12-26.

Rodiek, S., Nejati, A., Bardenhagen, E., Lee, C., & Senes, G. (2014). *The Seniors' Outdoor Survey: An observational tool for assessing outdoor environments at long-term care settings,* in "The Gerontologist". doi: 10.1093/geront/gnu050

Sugiyama, T. & Ward Thompson, C. (2007). *Outdoor environments, activity and the well-being of older people: Conceptualising environmental support,* in "Environment and Planning", 39, 1943-1960

Takano, T., Nakamura, K., & Watanabe, M. (2002). *Urban residential environments and senior citizens' longevity in megacity areas: The importance of walkable green spaces,* in "Journal of Epidemiology and Community Health", 56, 913–918

Ulrich, R. S. (1999) *Effects of gardens on health outcomes: Theory and research.* In C. Cooper Marcus & M. Barnes (Eds.), "Healing gardens: Therapeutic benefits and design recommendations" (pp. 27-86). New York: John Wiley & Sons.

Wang, D. & MacMillan, T. (2013). *The benefits of gardening for older adults: A systematic review of the literature,* in "Activities, Adaptation & Aging", 37, 153-181. doi:10.1080/01924788.2013.784942

Zeisel, J., Silverstein, N. M., Hyde, J., Levkoff, S., Lawton, M. P., & Holmes, W. (2003). *Environmental correlates to behavioral health outcomes in Alzheimer's special care units,* in "The Gerontologist", 43, 697–711

Creating Spaces for Children with Special Needs Specific for Those with Autism

Shireen Kanakri

smkanakri@bsu.edu
PhD, Assistant Professor, Ball State University, USA

Autism has been generally ignored by the interior design community and excluded from building codes and guidelines, even those developed specifically for special needs individuals. In reference to this exclusion, Baron, of the International Code Council stated, "I know of no building or accessibility code that incorporates requirements specifically to address children with autism. However, accessibility in general is addressed in the codes developed by the International Code Council" (Baron-Cohen, 2003; UN Global Program on Disability, 1993).

Therefore, one of the primary aims of this research is to correct this exclusion by developing a preliminary framework of interior design guidelines for autism. Deasy and Laswell discuss the architect's use of common patterns of cognition to guide and manipulate user behavior in a space (Deasy & Laswell, 1990). If one looks at the meaning, or the cognitive value given to an experience, it becomes clear the way in which a user typically interprets his interior environment.

Acoustics is one of the most important issues in interior design. No specific references are made in the mandates regarding individuals with developmental disorders or autism, but the term "consideration" is used in reference to "other communication disorders" (UN Global Program on Disability, 1993). Individuals with developmental and psycho-social disorders, of which autism is one, have been overlooked (UN Global Program on Disability, 1993).

To reach this goal of developing a framework for architectural guidelines for autism, an extensive literature review was conducted.

Research results indicate that environment is important to the treatment of autism because it influences behavior. This research gives practical solutions that architects and designers can use to modify the environment for children with autism. These modifications will help these children develop their skills, cope with auditory problems and improve their behaviors.

LITERATURE REVIEW

Classroom and Home Design

An important part of school design is the classroom environment, and one of the most important features in any educational environment is quietness in the classroom. To reach this goal schools typically teach the students to be well-behaved so that the classroom environment will be healthy for academic and behavioral learning.

Lehman and Gratiot (1983) reported that reductions in classroom noise (via acoustical modification) had a significant effect on increasing concentration, attention, and participatory behavior in typical children. Interestingly, noise levels were reduced from typically reported noise levels of 35–45dB (A) to the suggested guideline of 30dB(A) (Lehman and Gratiot,1983).

Literature shows that most families who have a child with autism will realize quickly that the best is to simply home-school there child. There are so many reasons why parents prefer do this, one of these reasons is minimizing distractions and control noise level will be easier in the home environment (Crandell et al, 1995; Sapienza, Crandell & Curtis, 1999).

Many children with autism are affected of distractions in the environment and noise impacts them strongly (Caldwell, 2006). In a typical school classrooms there are many environmental distractions and a large classroom is has a high level of noise. Children with autism do not tolerate with this environment well, and have difficult achieving their maximum ability. However, if the child with autism is homeschooled the parents will be able to control the noise level and make the environment quiet; they will minimize distractions, and help their child succeed at their abilities and improve their skills (Nabelek & Nabelek, 1985).

There are no statistics showing the number of families who homeschool their children with autism. Obviously, these learning environments are important for children and more research is needed on these environments.

Impact of Noise on Communication

Communication is the use of nonverbal (eye gaze, facial expression, body posture, gestures) and verbal (speech or spoken language) behavior to share ideas, exchange information, and regulate interactions (Autism Speaks, 2013).

Speech produced in one place in a room should be clear and intelligible everywhere in the room (Nabelek & Nabelek, 1985). Depending on this simple statement, as researchers, designers and educators we should create classrooms with minimal acoustics barriers; a well-designed learning classroom should have low noise level and minimal reflections.

Our effort should focus on providing an appropriate education in excessively noisy and reverberant rooms, a good acoustics room design with no acoustics barriers will cover the needs of the teachers and the students in their learning environment as a user's of the classrooms. To this end, the American National Standards Institute (ANSI) has approved a standard for maximum levels of classroom noise and reverberation

(ANSI S12.60-2002. Acoustical Performance Criteria, Design Requirements, and Guidelines for Schools; Nelson, Soli & Seltz, 2000).

Adults have sentence thresholds of about -4dB signal- to-noise ratio, or SNR, and understand familiar sentences perfectly at 0dB SNR. Young children, children with hearing loss, children learning a second language, and children listening in reverberant rooms require a higher signal-to-noise ratio in order to understand the spoken message (Nabelek & Nabelek, 1985). From this evidence, we can see that it makes sense that children with autism who are over-stimulated will be affected by high noise levels. This research study was done in schools focused on teaching children with autism, and the results of the data show the strong side effects of the high sound levels. At the same time we can imagine that if the noise level is decreased, behaviors will be observed and student performance increased.

Other evidence of the effect of the high dB level of noise was studied by Mohr et al. (1979). The results of the Mohr study suggested that a high dB level will lead to serious problems in the human behavior.

One neurobiology research study has shown that children with learning problems experience difficulty understanding speech sounds in noisy environments. Cunningham, Nicol, Zecker, Bradlow, and Kraus (2001) measured brain responses to speech sounds that are often confused ('da" and "ga"). The children with documented learning problems were no different from typical children in their discrimination "da" and "ga"

in quiet settings. They were, however, poorer than other children in their discrimination of the sounds in noisy settings. These results support the general impression that background noise causes excessive difficulty for children who have learning disabilities and attention deficit disorder (Nelson, Soli & Seltz, 2002). As (Nelson, Soli and Seltz, 2000, p.55) mentioned "schools are places of learning where speaking and listening are the primary communication modes. Until recently neither school planners nor were the general public aware of the significant negative effect of noise and excessive reverberation on learning process."

The positive effects of low noise levels are shown in the literature. Young children are ineffective listeners for speech in noisy environments until they reach the adolescence (Johnson, 2000). Also, young children do not effectively listen and understand speech in reverberant conditions in the classroom or any other environments (Johnson, 2000). A deep understanding of the ANSI S12.60 standards criteria indicates that communication will occur at a clear signal-to-noise ratio (SNR). One of these required standards is reducing the background noise to 35dB(A) in an unoccupied classroom.

THEORETICAL CONTRIBUTIONS

As discussed above, a clear understanding of how noise affects the behavior of children with autism is lacking in the extant literature. Different scholars hypothesize about the various mechanisms to deal with over-stimulation in children with autism (e.g. arousal, coping, stress),

285

but do not provide rigorous empirical evidence (Khare & Mullick, 2009). The results from the literature review show that increasing noise levels leads to a higher discomfort level, overstimulation and inappropriate behaviors. That is, both moderate and high noise levels lead to more negative behaviors as compared to low noise levels.

286

General Recommendations for Healthy Acoustical Environments

The impact of noise on children's health and development in schools is a major public health concern but is even more important for the health of children with autism. These children have sensory issues such as hypersensitivity to environmental features such as noise, textures, smells, lighting and taste. The increase in the number of children who are diagnosed with autism means that even more children are being negatively impacted by their environment.

The impact could be greatly reduced if noise problems were taken into consideration as early as possible when a school is being designed. According to Sergeant and Dewsbury (2004) sounds commonly identified as causing stress to the hypersensitive are those associated with heating systems, domestics appliances, and ventilation fans.

From this literature review, the HVAC equipment is one of the sources of noise in the classroom, but it is often the biggest source of noise. Schools commonly in this study choose HVAC systems that place equipment within one room shared with both classrooms, rather than opt for more expensive centralized systems. The

researcher recommends that the schools use the central HVAC because it is more efficient and easier to acoustically isolate than the other HVAC systems.

Discussing these conditions and simplifying the sensory environment is critical and important. A specific level of stimulation will keep people involved and focused. A neutral sensory environment can be designed so that elements and features can be added to accommodate the sensory sensitivity of children in their schools (Ahrentzen & Steele, 2009).

Solutions include arranging classroom and non-classroom spaces to minimize the effect of occupancy, equipment, and environment related noise that originates beyond the walls of the classroom and specifying construction that provides ceilings, floors, and partitions (including doors and other openings) with suitable STC ratings, ANSI/ASA S12.60-2002.

It may be necessary to avoid the open-plan classroom layout. The more structured the layout, the more acoustical barriers will be created. Also, this structured layout will seriously upgrade the speech intelligibility and will result in a low level of the background noise that fits with the maximum limit set by ANSI/ASA S12.60-2002.

The American National Standards Institute has not put any specific acoustical design standards for children with autism. From this research study we can see the need for paying attention to the effect of noise on the children with autism. Designers, parents and schools should increase their insistence on greater attention to this issue.

Practical Applications for Classroom Acoustical Modification

The following recommendations and methods have been proposed to modify the environments that have been designed to support children with high functioning level of autism. Some of these methods are:

Acoustical Ceiling

- First the ceiling should have a high AC rating, the AC ("articulation class") rating is a measure of its performance in limiting the sound reflection off the ceiling plane over an angle of approximately 45 to 60 degrees (American Society of Interior Designers, 2005).
- Second, the ceiling should have a high NRC rating. Classroom interiors should provide surfaces that can absorb or reflect sounds. The NRC and sound absorption coefficients over the frequency range of speech are the most important rating (American Society of Interior Designers, 2005).

It is important to avoid both the use of large air diffusers and flat lens lighting fixtures that can become significant reflectors of conversational noise. A better alternative to these are liner air bars for supply air and recessed 18-or 24-cell 2-by-4 parabolic lighting fixtures (American Society of Interior Designers, 2005).

Designers and acoustical consultants could use different techniques to create improved sound masking. The following are sound masking techniques;

Sound masking

- Careful placement of absorptive and

287

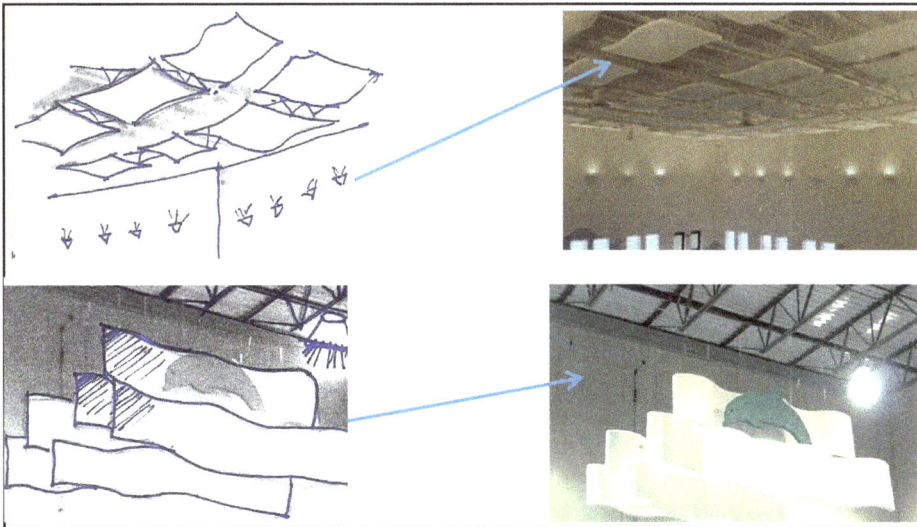

Figure 1. Ceiling Design with A high Absorbing Sound Materiel (Source: http://www.tandfebooks.com/doi/abs/10.4324/9780203879801)

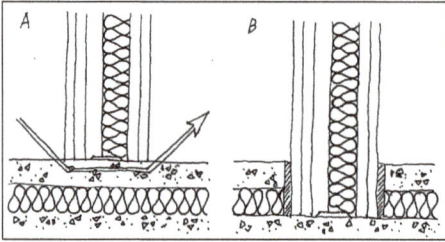

Figure 2. Flanking Transmissions Via Floating a) Incorrect Detail, b) Correct Detail (Source: http://www.tandfebooks.com/doi/abs/10.4324/9780203879801)

288

non-absorptive materials can direct the teacher's voice to students without inappropriate reflections (ANSI/ASA S12.60-2002).

- It is important that before the sound masking system can be used, the architectural system must have been designed "to provide the capability of achieving the desired level of noise".

- Employing a low-voltage electro-acoustic background sound system of proven quality that has qualified professionals to improve the acoustics of classrooms (Sykes, 2004).

- The materials that we use on the floors, walls and all the classroom features should absorb the sound energy, so the careful choice of the material as absorptive or non-absorptive can directly affect the voice of the teacher without inappropriate reflections (Sykes, 2004).

The recent change in industry standards regarding HVAC is an advantage to using central HVAC in classrooms environment. The dramatic differences in

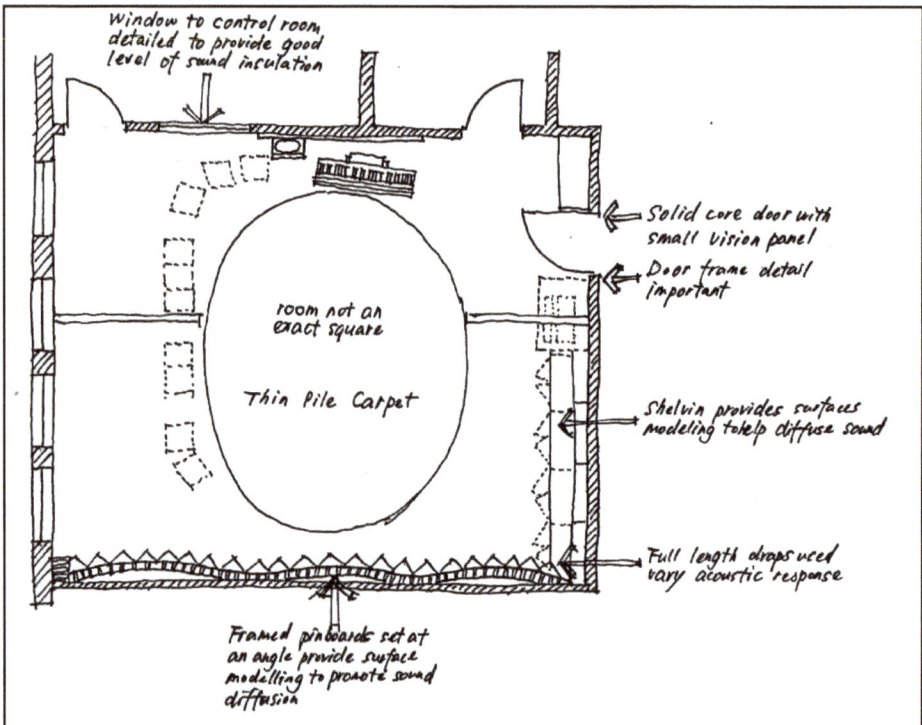

Figure 3. Flooring and Walls Material Recommended Reducing Noise

Figure 4. Wood Furniture Recommended to Reduce Noise (Source: http://www.tandfebooks.com/doi/abs/10.4324/9780203879801)

decrease the noise level values show central HVAC to have the advantage over the other HVAC that currently used in the classroom.

The flooring material specified in classrooms for children with autism should enhance the acoustical environmental quality. When considering using carpets or floor covering different features should be discussed as in the following:

Carpets

- Serves to absorb airborne sound, reduce surface-generated noise (often called "football noises") and help block sound transmission and reflection. It is recommended using carpet in the classroom areas. The new technology for manufacturing commercial carpet with integrated cushion allows for the greater use of cushion in the classroom environment, and it offers superior acoustical and ergonomic properties and benefits (Schmitz, Liu, Jaeger & Horne, 1997).

Floor Covering

- Floor covering, like ceiling tile and systems furniture, is NRC rated- the higher the NRC rating, the greater the ability

of the floor covering to absorb airborne noise. Sound Absorption in Corridors, Entrance Halls and Stairwells. The objective is to absorb sound in these areas so that it does not interrupt the teaching and the study activities inside the classrooms. The amount of additional sound absorption should be calculated.

We can use pin-boards and noticeboards with absorption coefficients suited to the area and the volume of the classroom. Just a note - the absorption coefficients vary from one space to another because it depends on the area and volume of the studied room (Schmitz, Liu, Jaeger & Horne, 1997).

289

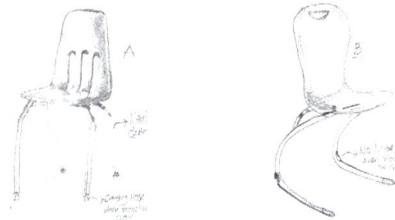

Figure 5. Chair A Not recommended but Chair B Recommended because it didn't Produce Noise

Figure 6. 3D Layout Recommended Reducing Noise

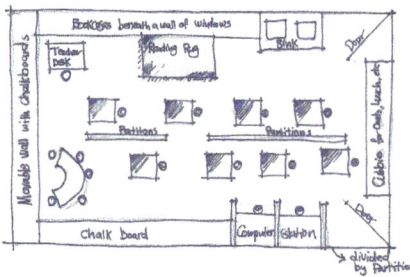

Figure 7. Layout Recommended Reducing Noise with Movable Partitions Allow Visual Access while Controlling Sound

290

Noise-canceling window sensor, is noise-cancelling tool that can convert a specific unpleasant background noise into a pleasant sound, such as calm music (Roach, 2013). The device sticks to the window because the glass surfaces will senses the noise vibrations. In this method the noise-cancelling window sensor generate a signals to cancel out the unpleasant background noises (Roach, 2013).

The differences in furniture material and shape affect the level of noise inside the classrooms. Providing wood furniture to reduce the noise is recommended.
The differences on the furniture layout affect the behaviors of children with autism and affect the level of noise inside the classrooms. Providing a maximum enclosure by orienting the furniture and use panels to divide the spaces and observe the noise is recommended.

FUTURE STUDIES

The researcher has studied the overall impact of loudness on the behavior of children with autism; future studies could elaborate on this research by studying the effects of every feature of noise, for example; sound frequency, pitch, musical tone, echo and reverberation, on the behavior of children with autism. The findings from this study could be further strengthened by doing environmental interventions to study the impact of different acoustical environments on the behavior and performance of children with autism. The economic implications of acoustical design could also be explored in future.

REFERENCES

Ahrentzen, S. & Steele, K. (2009). *Advancing Full Spectrum Housing: Designing for Adults with Autism*, in "Research Report", Arizona State University

American Society of Interior Designers, (2005). Available: http://greenhome-guide.com/residential/partner/267

ANSI S12.2-1995, American National Standard. *Criteria for Evaluating Room Noise*

Autism Speaks, (2013). Available: http://www.autismspeaks.org/School II house, (2011). Available: http://www.School IIhouse.org/

Baron-Cohen, S. (2003). *The Essential differences: Male and Female Brains and the truth about autism.* New York: Basic Books

Caldwell, P. (2006). *Finding You Finding Me.* Jessica Kingsely Publishers, London, UK

Crandell et al, (1995). *Classroom Acoustics for Children With Normal Hearing and With Hearing Impairment*, in Jara, Crandell "An Update on Counseling Instruction", 77-86

Cunningham, J., Nicol, T., Zecker, S., Bradlow, A., & Kraus, N. (2001). *Neurobiologic responses to speech in noise in children with learning problems: Deficits and strategies for improvement*, in "Clinical Neurophysiology", 112(5), 758-767

Deasy, C.M., and Laswell, T. (1990). Designing Places for People- *A Handbook on Human Behavior for Architects, Designers and Facility Managers*. Watson Guptill Publications, New York, USA

Johnson, C. M. (2000). *A survey of current research on online communities of practice*, in "The Internet and Higher Education", vol. 4, Issue 1, 1st Quarter 2001, Pages 45–60

Khare, Rachna, and Abir Mullick (2009). *Incorporating the Behavioral Dimension in Designing Inclusive Learning Environment for Autism*, in "ArchNet-IJAR: International Journal of Architectural Research", vol. 3, issue 3

Lehman. A. & Gratiot, A. (1983). Effects du bruit sur les enfants a l'ecole, in "Proceedings of the 4th Congress on Noise as aPublic Health Problem" (pp. 859–862). Milano: Centro

Mohr et al., (1979). *Clinical manifestations and pathogenesis*. Oxford University Press

Nabelek, A. K., & Nabelek, I. V. (1985). *Room acoustics and speech perception*, in "Handbook of Clinical Audiology", 4th ed., edited by J. Katz (Williams and Wilkins, Baltimore), pp. 624-637

Nelson, P. & Soli, S. (2000). *Classroom Acoustics II. Acoustical Barriers to Learning*. A publication of the Technical Committee on Speech Communication of the Acoustical Society of America

Roach, J. (2013, October 14). *Noise-canceling window sensor helps you enjoy the silence amid cacophony*. Retrieved May 20, 2015, from http://www.wirelesssensors.co.uk/noise-canceling-window-sensor-helps-you-enjoy-the-silence-amid-cacophony/

Sapienza, C., Crandell, C., & Curtis, B. (1999). *Effects of sound-field frequency modulation amplification on reducing teachers' sound pressure level in the classroom*, in "Journal of Voice", 13(3), 375-381

Schmitz F., Liu, S., Jaeger, S.M., & Horne, W.C. (1997). *Noise Reducing Screens for In-Flow Pressure Sensors*, U. S. Patent No. 5,684,756, Nov. 1997

Sergeant, L., G. Dewsbury, and S. Johnston. 2004. *Smart Thinking: Supporting People with Complex Behavioural Difficulties and Autistic Spectrum Disorder* in a Community Setting. Retrieved from: http://www.smartthinking.ukideas.com/ Designs%20for%20Autism.htm

Sykes, D. M. (2004). *Productivity: How Acoustics Affect Workers' Performance In Offices & Open Areas*. Retrieved February 1, 2009, from "Office Sound Masking Solutions", by Speech Privacy Systems: www.speechprivacysystems.com/files/Productivity.pdf

291

UN Global Program on Disability
(1993). *Mandates of the UN Global Program on Disability: Standard Rules on the Equalization of Opportunities for Persons with Disabilities.* Target Areas for Equal Participation: Accessibility, United Nations General Assembly resolution 48/96, annex, 20/12/1993

The Lady Cilento Children's Hospital.
Research, Consultation and a Focus on the Child in Design

Ian Mitchell

imitchell@conradgargett.com.au
LFRAIA Conrad Gargett

During the past 10 years Conrad Gargett has designed a number of hospitals of vary-ing types and in a diversity of locations; the most recently completed of these is the Lady Cilento Children's Hospital (LCCH), in Brisbane, Queensland, Australia, designed in collaboration with Lyons (Conrad Gargett Lyons).

The expectations surrounding the realization of the project were based in concern for the well-being of patients, their families and the staff; the much vaunted, patient centred care, here given tangible expression. This paper provides insight into the values underpinning the project and how they translated into a design process to achieve an outcome which is already receiving acclaim. While the thrust of the paper deals with this major hospital designed to deliver high level or leading edge pediatric care, the design was informed by our other projects and in turn has informed our subsequent work. Aspects of these are woven into the narrative and serve to illustrate the interdependence of some of the major themes of the conference. Our work in regional hospitals informed the requirement for dealing with aboriginal communities; consideration of ethnic culture informed in part our working in China recently and the response to change and advancing technology has developed from initial work here.

The outcome is a building, sustainable at all levels, environmentally, economically and socially. It includes energy efficiency measures and mechanical and passive; it provides a significant level of urban renewal and it connects with and is embraced by its community.

Keywords: *Values, research, consultation, healing, context*

BACKGROUND AND INTRODUCTION

During the past 10 years Conrad Gargett has designed a number of hospitals of varying types and in a diversity of locations; the most recently completed of these is the Lady Cilento Children's Hospital (LCCH), in Brisbane, Queensland, Australia, designed in collaboration with Lyons (Conrad Gargett Lyons).

294

Some statistics, the Lady Cilento Children's Hospital:
• is a Queensland Health facility, a public hospital;
• provides principally tertiary, quaternary services;
• forms the hub of a state wide tertiary network of paediatric services;
• has 359 inpatient beds;
• provides for 70,000 presentations per annum in its Emergency Department;
• includes a mental health unit;

• is 75000m2 in area;
• has a project value $A 1.5 billion;

...all in a single building on an inner-urban site in Brisbane Queensland.

The expectations surrounding the realisation of the project were based in concern for the well-being of patients, their families and the staff; the much vaunted, patient centred care, here given tangible expression.

This paper provides insight into the values underpinning the project and how they translated into a design process to achieve an outcome which is already receiving acclaim. While the thrust of the paper deals with this major hospital designed to deliver high level or leading edge paediatric care, the design was informed by our other projects and in turn has informed our subsequent work.

Figure 1. The completed hospital

Our work in regional hospitals informed the requirement for dealing with aboriginal communities; consideration of ethnic culture informed in part our work in China recently and the response to change and advancing technology has been reflected in a developing approach to hospital planning.

As many such health projects are, this was a product of a joint venture. Conrad Gargett and Lyons established a joint team to design the building, without the often adopted demarcation of architecture and health planning. The work was shared allowing the planning to inform the architecture and the architecture to challenge the planning, identifying and capitalising on the opportunities.

CONSULTATION AND BRIEFING

Briefing and planning for the hospital was supported by a process of applied research which expanded the conversation with stakeholders beyond their experience. This, together with a wide-ranging and sophisticated consultation process allowed the boundaries of health care design to be explored.

The new hospital is an amalgamation of two existing and highly regarded paediatric facilities, each with its own culture and traditions. The imperative was therefore that the design process was inclusive and collaborative, actively involving all key stakeholders in the formulation of the project brief and the in shaping of the evolving design.

Significant consultation was undertaken through a series of workshops, focus groups and planning forums covering aspects of a technical nature (e.g. environmentally sustainable design workshops, architectural peer reviews and buildability workshops), clinical aspects

295

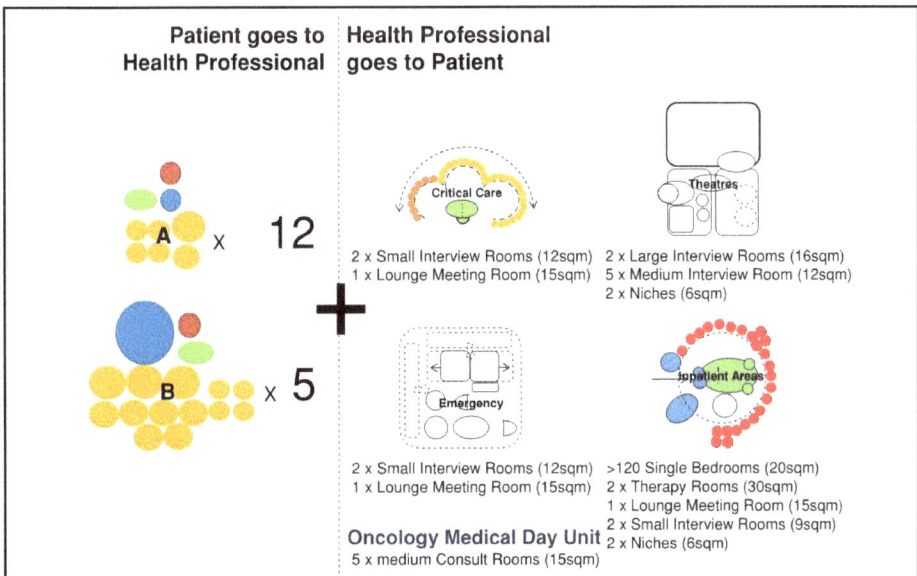

Figure 2. Alternative service delivery models were considered at all levels

(e.g. departmental planning teams and lean thinking workshops) and project management aspects (e.g. value management reviews).

The needs and views of the primary users were sought with the establishment of a Family Advisory Council comprising parents and carers of current and former patients and a Youth Advisory Forum comprising young people aged 12 to 18 years who were current or former patients of the State's paediatric cardiac program.

During this process no aspect of the patient journey or the modes of service delivery model was left unexamined. Extensive use was made of the available technology in the recording and communication of information and presentation of concepts. Real time recording and review of briefing meetings and virtual modelling of all of the spaces from a very early stage facilitated the delivery of design approaches.

The process evolved using an evidence base where design decisions were guided by sound design principles, designer knowledge, client input, but most importantly on scientifically sound research. Results from such research demonstrate a positive correlation between evidence-based design and improved quality of care. Evidence based design also seeks to systematically measure whether design interventions have generated the intended outcomes by comparing pre- and post-occupancy data. In the case of healthcare environments, positive measurable outcomes have included medical error reduction, improved nursing recruitment and re-

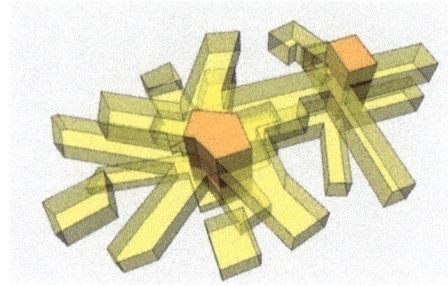

Figure 3. The trunks and branches

tention, patient and family satisfaction, and utilisation of specific areas such as healing gardens.

Practice based research was used by the design team across all areas of the design. The project team had the benefit of an in-house research assistant specialising in evidenced based design, working as part of the design and planning team.

Planning for future expansion such a constrained site required a number of strategies. Some "shell" space is provided within the current envelope; "soft" expansion space is provided where possible adjacent to clinical areas and strategies for decanting administrative spaces and the identification of an adjacent zone for expansion within the master plan were also implemented.

SITE AND CONTEXT

The site is located in inner-urban South Brisbane in an area undergoing urban renewal. A brown-field site adjacent to the existing private and public hospital facilities of the Mater Hospital and two private schools, the site was constrained in size and constricted by traffic. The LCCH represented the first stage of a master plan for the precinct which includes a Central Energy facility, producing chilled water and generating power for the precinct a major research facility (nearing completion), and ultimately family accommodation developed by a not-for-profit group which will support families who travel from the regions for long-stay treatment.

This inner urban context required considerations beyond the site, establishing the connection to adjacent parklands to provide public amenity and to stitch the building into the precinct.

DESIGN

The design harnesses the healing power of nature – light ventilation and connection to gardens and landscape all in a joyful and supportive environment. Intuitive wayfinding limits many everyday stresses and the vibrant arts program: visual and performance,

provides welcome diversion.

A concern for legibility and navigability was central to the concept. The hospital provides clear wayfinding and easy access to services and facilities for staff, patients, families and visitors.

Conventional wayfinding devices include signage, floor treatments, "links" and other graphic cues to make connections between departments, often through a mazelike "institutional" hospital corridors are prone to failure.

The hospital's design provides an intuitive navigable approach with an interior design strategy which is both generous in its scale and legible. A hierarchy of circulation systems and spaces- from urban scaled to people scaled – connect the various zones of the building together and importantly connect inside and outside, allowing people to orient themselves to outside views. Colour is used to provide a key to orientation.

297

Figure 4. Extensive use of colour throughout

298

Figure 5. The main atrium showing artwork and colour coding for wayfinding

The design concept is of a "living tree". Double height spaces (branches) radiate from two vertical atria (trunks) in the centre of the plan. These extend to the street to form framing portals and balconies and the branches also bring light and air into the building. Each branch is oriented toward a landmark to provide orientation for users within the building. Colour is used to provide a key to orientation. The colours used inside of the building were distilled from the colours of the Queensland landscape. They include the muted neutral colour tones of the outback together with the more vibrant colours of the State's exotic birds, rainforest butterflies and flora.

The hospital's colourful exterior incorporates the variegated greens and purples of the Bougainvillea plantings of the adjacent parklands. Its massing presents a sculpted building form incorporating green spaces and landscaped green roofs.

While the focus of the design is on patient well being, it is recognised that the hospital is also a significant workplace with issues of attracting and retaining staff, staff satisfaction and productivity. Many staff working in this building work in open planned offices for the first time and the design places considerable emphasis on the amenity of these spaces. Windows in operating theatres, landscape staff terraces and well designed and resourced education spaces are all outcomes of considerations for staff amenity.

A low rise solution, nestled into its context, the building responds to the Southeast Queensland sub-tropical climate with its emphasis on indoor-outdoor connection, its landscape and it sun shading. The sunshades are a prominent element of the envelope, excluding summer sun while maintaining views. This is a building of its place.

ART

The Arts Program at the Lady Cilento Children's Hospital was developed to provide exceptional cultural experiences for children, families and staff. The program includes an exciting contemporary art collection and, with assistance of several cultural organisations in Brisbane, a regular program of performances, activities and workshops.

The program includes works showcasing Aboriginal and Torres Strait Islander Artists. This ongoing investment ensures the LCCH generates the warm, safe and supporting environment needed to improve the health and well being of children and young people.

The inclusion of arts programs within hospital settings is changing the face of healthcare. Art is not just about absorbing visual or cultural information; it is an experience which engages all of the senses. The LCCH Arts Programs helps to create a sense of normality and interest within the clinical setting.

SUSTAINABILITY

A significant ambition for the project was that it should be environmentally responsive and responsible.
The building is sustainable at all levels, environmentally, economically and socially. It includes energy efficiency measures and mechanical and passive; it provides a significant level of urban renewal and it connects with and is embraced by its community.
While the building engages with issues of sustainability in ways which could be expected: natural ventilation to public areas, environmentally attuned mechanical and electrical systems including tri-generation, water harvesting and use particularly in irrigation, it goes beyond these in its relationship and impact on the community. The community engagement process
which traced through all stages of the design of LCCH provides mechanisms for ongoing community involvement with the hospital.
Over time this has the potential to renew, reinforce and otherwise benefits the local built, social, environmental and economic structures, providing a sustainable basis and a template for design for a healthy community.

LANDSCAPE

Pre-design strategies for the landscape comprised considerable consultation and extensive research of healing gardens. The landscape design philosophy

Figure 6. One of 11 rooftop gardens

focused on holistic healing, the health of both the body and mind. Research into healing gardens led to two key messages that underpin the design; the power of nature and the benefits of contextual design on health and wellbeing. These two driving principles reinforce the philosophies and contemporary research that discloses access to gardens and nature enhance people's ability to deal with stress and therefore potentially improve health outcomes.

The landscape design incorporates eleven rooftop gardens for recreation, rehabilitation and therapy, providing amenity and respite and redefining the notion of healing gardens. A new public forecourt is a gesture to the community and a means of integrating the building into it context and amplifying its connections to its surroundings.

The driving ideas in the landscape design recognise the power of nature and the benefits of the connection to landscape on health and wellbeing; that access to gardens and nature enhance people's ability to deal with stress and therefore potentially improve health outcomes. The design and plant selection reflect the local climate and subtropical character of Brisbane, aiding the through the association of an environment synonymous with 'home'.

The design sends a resounding message on the importance of established trees to make an impact and provide instant shade. Six 30-year-old fig trees were procured sourced locally for the project and

Figure 7. Lady Cilento Children's Hospital with a backdrop of the Brisbane CBD

later transported to the new public plaza at street level. The trees soften the built form and provide scale, amenity, rejuvenating and activating the streetscape. The fig trees define the now pedestrian friendly streetscape. They reflect planting in the surrounding parklands, reinforcing a strong contextual relationship.

URBAN DESIGN

An important objective for the project is to fit the new building in to its urban context. The scale of the proposed development as an urban intervention (the size of a city block) means that it will have a significant impact in creating an almost entirely new context for this part of South Brisbane.

The new building and its associated urban spaces create an important new children's precinct, improving the urban design and amenity for those parts of Stanley Street, Raymond Terrace and Graham Street which abroundings, to

Southbank, (and the city), and adds a significant new urban amenity to this part of Southbank.

Consideration of the building in its place was critical to the urban design approach. Sustainability is addressed in urban design with this focus on place making. The building is concerned with durability of function and materials, response to context, both in terms of planning and form and generosity to the community. All of these contribute to establishing an important and memorable place. The extent to which it is embraced by its community determines its longevity and its contribution to economic and social sustainability.

The building in the city

Traditionally Brisbane is navigated by hilltop landmarks, external to the CBD. Mater Hill is one of these hilltops and the building would inevitably be prominent on the city skyline. As one of our major health and public institutions it

301

Figure 8. Sunshine Coast University Hospital Master Plan

302

Figure 9. The local landscape informed the design of the Zhejiang Hospital

was important that this be considered.

The building in the precinct

The building is located in South Brisbane, surrounded by health, education and recreation precincts. The existing health precinct in particular dominates and while it was important to create a strong relationship with it the establish-

ment of an individual identity was also important. The development has transformed the environment with some simple generous gestures to its context; the colours, the major circulation and the landscape architecture connect the building.

The building on its site

With a large footprint the building occupies almost its entire site. The site constraints were realised as opportunities Resolution of precinct traffic issues created the opportunity to create a significant public space reinforcing the connection to Southbank Parkland and enhancing the relationships with the heritage listed former South Brisbane Town Hall (Somerville House).

IMFLUENCE

The design process developed and the outcomes of the Lady Cilento Children's Hospital have had a major impact on how we approach hospital design which is reflected in two subsequent projects, one locally in south-east Queensland and one in China.

Planning for the Sunshine Coast University Hospital, (SCUH) currently under construction north of Brisbane is based on a similar range of principles to the LCCH but in a vastly different context, addresses them in a different manner.

By contrast, the SCUH is a green-field development which in addition to its attendant goals for healthcare and research has been designed as a progenitor of a new town centre for Kawana on Queensland's Sunshine Coast.

Master planning and initial design for the Sunshine Coast Hospital were car-

Figure 10. Zhejiang Hospital main entrance

303

ried out simultaneously with the latter stages of design of the LCCH. The lessons learned and the insights gained were applied in that project and the underpinning approaches to community engagement and patient welfare were translated into a development on a green field site. In this case the role of the facility embraced a contribution to the development of an emerging community, in one of our urban growth corridors.

Particular to the needs of the Sunshine Coast was the requirement to expand the hospital over time while maintaining its operation. This resulted in a model with a chassis of structure and services which could be adapted and extended over time, essentially a 'shell and core' or open building approach.

The plan links into and reinforces community infrastructure and initiatives – the active transport network of pedestrian and cycleways and high quality open space - space for play, for patients,

staff and visitors to escape the clinical environment, providing respite and relaxation and importantly, for formal and informal therapies. Planning maximises views to and from the site amplifying the healing value of the natural environment.

The development establishes a framework that considers the connection and relationship to the Kawana community it is part of.

Our recent competition entry for the design of the Yuhang Division of the First Affiliated Hospital of College of Medicine, Zhejiang University, a 1200 bed tertiary hospital (expandable to 2500 beds) collocated with the Medical Research Centre of Zhejiang University on a green-field site in the Future Sci-Tech City in Hangzhou was informed by our work on both the Children's Hospital and the Sunshine Coast University Hospital projects.

304

The concern for patient and staff wellbeing and efficiency of operation informed a building design which responds to its setting.
- A high level of amenity in public areas.
- Clear circulation paths and wayfinding and separation of public and staff circulation.
- Narrow footprints which allow all habitable spaces access to light and view.
- Responding to the climate in Hangzhou offered the opportunity for mixedmode air-conditioning in appropriate areas.

While the client's brief was for a state-of-the-art hospital, the design responds to its location with the use of local materials, reference to the climate of Hangzhou and the rich scenographic nature and form of Chinese landscape.

CONCLUSION

The design of the Lady Cilento Children's Hospital promotes a positive, rich and stimulating architectural experience, incorporating landscape, maximizing daylight and views, and facilitating wayfinding. It also incorporates a vibrant art program embracing both visual art and performance. The focus is on legibility and connection with public spaces, connected to landscape at all levels.

From the outset there was an implicit understanding that this hospital would be a special place. An enlightened client team and engaged stakeholders allowed the design team to realise this objective. The building is a significant addition to the health facility landscape in Australia; delivering leading edge functionality. It does this in a joyful but nonetheless sophisticated environment which com-

municates with its primary clients at a visceral level.

The consultation processes, the research foundations and design intentions are what make Lady Cilento Children's Hospital an innovative and thoughtful project. The project is an excellent case study illustrating the health and environmental benefits that can be achieved through contemporary evidence-based design.

The Lady Cilento Children's Hospital has been influential in our subsequent but measuring and evaluating the level of success of the project is a further stage in its development. Our colleagues, Lyons and the University of Melbourne are currently undertaking a joint Australian Research Council funded project that will investigate ways in which environmental design contributes to patient well-being. Founded in existing research the project will seek to quantify and qualify the value of good design in the health sphere.

The Global University Program in Healthcare Architecture (GUPHA) is a subgroup of UIA-PHG. It dedicates to promote international exchange, collaboration and knowledge dissemination between educators involved in teaching and research, along with UIA member practitioners and representatives of academic institutions, governmental and non-governmental agencies with an interest in architectural education and academic research in the area of healthcare architecture. Since founded in 2000, GUPHA has grown to include 25 member institutions. The Chair of GUPHA is Professor David Allison (adavid@clemson.edu) from Clemson University, U.S.

Session 1
News Updates and Introduction of Architecture for Health Education Programs Worldwide
Hui Cai, University of Kansas, USA
Walkiria Erse, Institute for Hospital Researchers Architect Jarbas Karman, Brazil
Gelun, Beijing Architecture University, China
Prosperidad Luis, University of the Philippines, Philippines
Yasushi Nagasawa, Kogakuin University, Japan
Norwina Mohd Nawawi, Internatioanl Islamic University Malaysia
Romano Del Nord, TESIS, University of Florence, Italy
Kazuhiko Okamoto, Toyo University, Japan
Thomas Schinko, Vasconi Architects, France
Shanshan Zhang, Xiaoxia Bai, Xiaopeng Bai & Yi Qi, Harbin Institute of Technology, China
Ying Zhou, Southeast University, China
Shireen Kanakri, Ball State University
Zeyad Al-Swaidan, Ministry of Health, Saudi Arabia
Zhipeng Lu, Texas A&M University, USA

Session 2
Innovative Approaches for Architecture for Health Education

The Berkeley Prize
Benjamin Clavan (USA)

Teaching "Healthcare Architecture & Environment" at Harbin Institute of Technology in China
Zhang Shanshan, Bai Xiaoxia, Bai Xiaopeng & Yi Qi (China)

The Latest New Research & Design Projects at Texas A&M University
George J. Mann (USA)

The GUPHA workshop was comprised of two sessions:

In the first session entitled: "**News Updates and Introduction of Architecture for Health Education Programs Worldwide**" the representatives of the institutions involved in the GUPHA programme meeting presented the activities in progress, the most significant initiatives, some works developed during the workshops, the publications, research activities, etc. A brief excerpt of the only documents received is set out below.

The second session of the workshop entitled "**Innovative Approaches for Architecture for Health Education**" was divided into three topics: "The Berkeley Prize", "Teaching "Healthcare Architecture & Environment" at Harbin Institute of Technology in China" and "The Latest New Research & Design Projects at Texas A&M University".
On these three topics, the articles received from the authors Benjamin Clavan, Zhang Shanshan, Bai Xiaoxia, Bai Xiaopeng & Qi Yi, and George J. Mann are reproduced in full.

Hui Cai
University of Kansas, USA

The University of Kansas School of Architecture, Design & Planning.
The University of Kansas Schools of Medicine and Nursing.

Healing a Nation: Healing the Wounded
(Finalist 2012 Architecture for Humanity Competition)

Rana is a Libyan student who is committed to rebuilding her country after the events of 2011/2012. In this proposal she has redesigned the military compound of Gaddafi as a public memorial to the dispossessed and wounded of the revolution. Her own focus is a rehab and training facility for amputees.

Graduate Studio ARCH 808, Spring 2012
Rana Elmghirbi
Professor Kent Spreckelmeyer
Sponsors: Architecture for Humanity

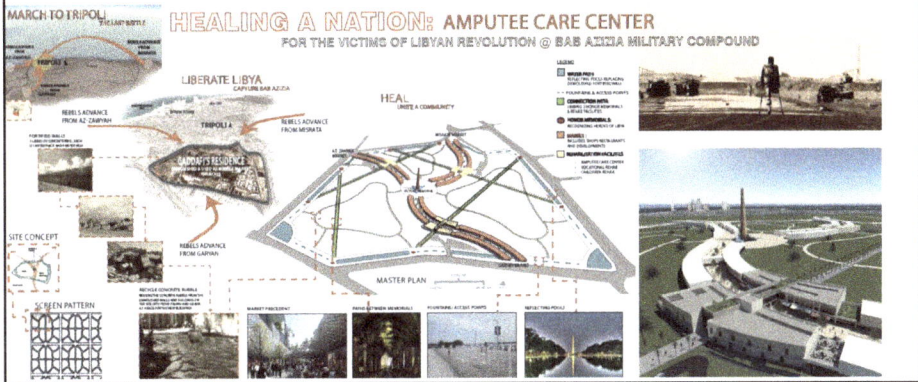

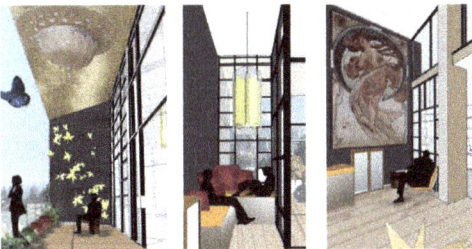

Nourish Newborns
(Winner of 2011 Steelcase Nurture Competition)

A student design competition that explored the social and physical issues of improving the environmental conditions in neonatal intensive units.

Graduate Seminar ARCH 731, Spring 2011
Professor Frank Zilm
Sponsor: Steelcase Corporation

Nurturing U
(Runner-Up of 2012 Steelcase Nurture Competition)

The project stems from a need to improve the check-in and waiting experience for patients in the Watkins Memorial Health Center, located on the Lawrence campus of the University of Kansas.

Graduate Seminar ARCH 731, Spring 2012
Professor Frank Zilm
Sponsor: Steelcase Corporation

WALKIRIA ERSE
Institute for Hospital Researchers Architect Jarbas Karman, Brazil

The Tripod: Architect + Hospital + Comprisement of Knowledge. A study to create a post graduation in Brazil.

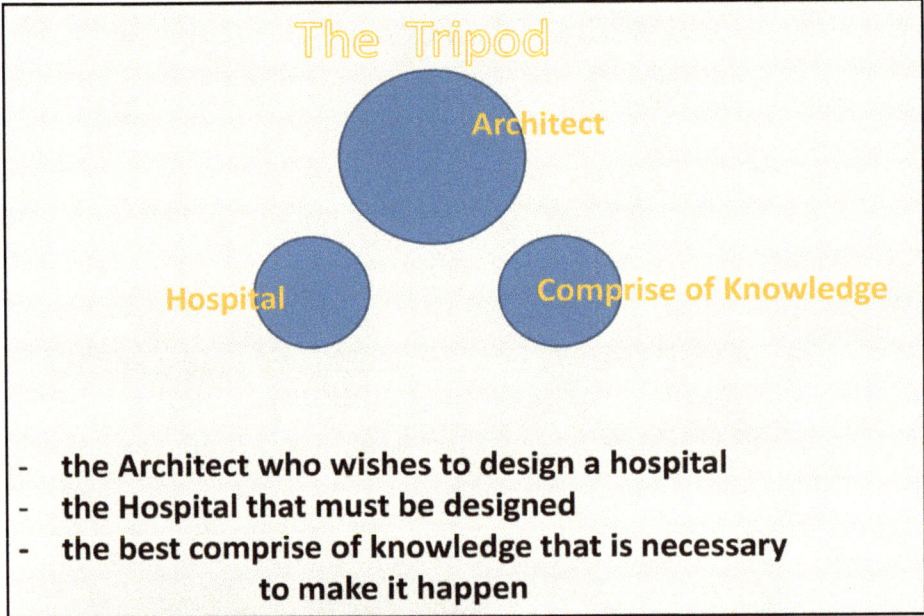

The Tripod

Architect

Hospital

Comprise of Knowledge

- the Architect who wishes to design a hospital
- the Hospital that must be designed
- the best comprise of knowledge that is necessary to make it happen

BRAZILIAN ARCHITECS

90,000 in Brazil

45,000 are in São Paulo

92% like their profession

64% speak english

25% post graduated

2% teach architecture

PROSPERIDAD LUIS
University of the Philippines
The Program in Master in Hospital Administration, College of Public Health University of the Philippines, Manila (Health) Campus.

Course Outcomes:

- Discuss the basic concerns, principles, and practice in planning, design, construction, equipping and maintaining a hospital, its equipment and facilities.

- Describe the roles of the administrator, architect, engineer, and other members of the planning team in over-all hospital planning.

- Formulate an architect's brief for the design and construction of a new hospital or the expansion, modification of an existing hospital.

- Discuss the concepts of "safe hospital" and "green hospital" and the importance of their integration in the planning and design of hospitals

Session	Topic	Session	Topic
1	Course Orientation; History of Hospitals	9	Design of the Service Zone; The Special Service Zone: *Dietary, Laundry, Engineering, Morgue*
2	Functional Concepts in Hospital Design and Organization; The Architect's Brief	10	Fire Safety in Hospitals
3	Methodology of Planning and Design	11	Safe Hospitals: Hospitals Safe from Disasters
4	Nature of Hospitals in the Philippines	12	Green Hospitals
5	Design of the Outer Zone: *Emergency, OPD, Admission*	13	Hospital Equipment Planning
6	Design of the Second Zone: *Imaging, Laboratory, Pharmacy*	14	Hospital Engineering and Maintenance
7	Design of the Inner Zone: *Wards*	15	Group Hospital Case Oral Presentations
8	Design of the Deep Zone: *OR, Delivery, Nursery, ICU*	16	Group Hospital Case Oral Presentation

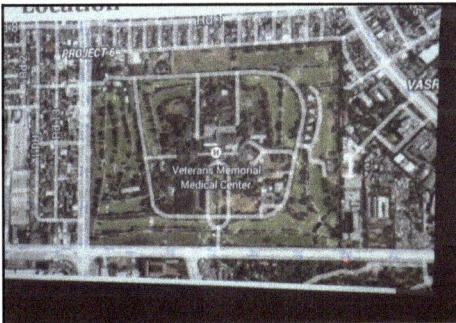

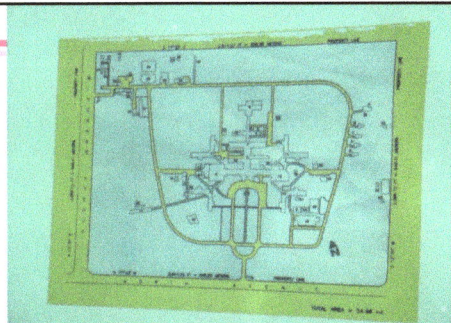

NORWINA MOHD NAWAWI
Internatioanl Islamic University Malaysia

Public Health-Healthcare Architecture initiatives, International Islamic University Malaysia.

(Assoc. Prof. Ar. Datin Norwina Mohd Nawawi Department of Architecture,Kulliyyah of Architecture and Environmental Design, IIUM, Kuala Lumpur, MALAYSIA).

310

IIUM VISION AND MISSION

Vision

Inspired by the world–view of Tawhid and the Islamic Philosophy of the unity of knowledge as well as its concept of holistic education, the IIUM aims at becoming a leading international centre of educational excellence which :

i) Revitalizes the intellectual dynamism of Islam and the Ummah

ii) Integrates Islamic Revealed Knowledge and Values all academic disciplines and educational activities

iii) Seeks to restore the leading and progressive role of the Muslim Ummah in all branches of knowledge; thereby

iv) Contributing to the improvement and upgrading of the qualities of human life and civilization

Mission

- Integration
- Islamization
- Internationalization
- Comprehensive Excellence

INTERIOR SPACE PLANNING OF MEDICAL SUITES
LABORATORY

Lab Office

Bleeding room

Blood Bank

INTERIOR SPACE PLANNING OF MEDICAL SUITES
OBSTETRIC AND PAEDIATRIC CLINIC

Afiq

Hilmi

3 students work

AAR 4202 Architectural Design 8
VERTICAL HOSPITAL

Workshop in Interior design exercises in proposed Office building block by industry to be transform to medical use

INTERIOR SPACE PLANNING OF MEDICAL SUITES

ADULT

PAEDIATRIC

Hazwan

ROMANO DEL NORD
University of Florence, Italy

TESIS, Systems and Technologies for Healthcare Facilities provides a scientific approach to the planning and design of architectural healthcare facilities.

311

The Center promotes the training of specialized competences in the field of planning, design and managing of health facilities by means of seminars, meetings, conferences.

IFHE 2014
Buenos Aires
13-16 Oct.
2014

Second Saudi Forum for Planning and Design for Hospitals
Riyadh
22-24 April 2014

get better! UIA/ PHG
Toronto
24-28 Sept.
2013

Hospital Planning and Building.
UIA/PHG Oslo
22-24 March
2012

30th Annual Congress of Turkish Pediatric Surgical Association and 16th Annual Congress of Turkish Pediatric Surgical Nurses Association
Ankara
17-20 Oct. 2012

Arquitetura de Sistemas de Saúde,
Universidade Católica de Brasília
Brasilia
31 Aug. 2012

LAST CONFERENCES

Congresso Brasileiro para desenvolvimento do edificio hospitalar
San Paolo
4 – 7 Sept. 2012

The 24th World Congress of Architecture
UIA /PHG
Tokyo
25 Sept-1 Oct . 2011

7th International World Congress & Exhibition
Academy for Design and Health
Boston
6-10 July 2011

The making of Affordable and Safe Healthcare Facilities for all
UIA /PHG Kuala Lumpur Malaysia
29 Nov. – 1 Dic. 2010

6th International World Congress & Exhibition
Academy for Design and Health
Singapore
24-28 June 2009

The Culture for the Future of Healthcare Architecture
UIA /PHG
Florence
28 June 2008

Research

Within the conceptual framework the Center's teaching and research activities have been structured in four different levels, related to actual phases of the building process:
- general planning and healthcare facilities;
- design of healthcare buildings;
- the tender process and construction of healthcare buildings;
- use and maintenance of healthcare buildings.

SCIENTIFIC ISSUES OF COMMON INTERNATIONAL INTEREST

The new strategic dimensions of teaching and research hospitals

Environmental stress prevention in children hospital design

The humanization of healthcare facilities environment

Systems, buildings and technologies supporting physical, psychic and sensorial handicaps

SHANSHAN ZHANG, XIAOXIA BAI, XIAOPENG BAI & YI QI
Harbin Institute of Technology, China
Program of "Healthcare Architecture & Environment" at Harbin Institute of Technology.

312

学生实践项目-2
Students Project Examples - 2

滨海新区公共卫生服务机构社区卫生
Community Health Service Center

学生实践项目-3
Students Project Examples - 3

平山医院
Pingshan Hospital

DESIGNING FOR HEALTH:
Teaching the Social Art of Architecture

Benjamin Clavan

Benjamic@earthlink.net; info@BerkeleyPrize.org
Ph.D., AIA Coordinator, Berkeley Undergraduate Prize for Architectural Design Excellence

It is clear that healthful architecture starts with a deep and empathetic understanding of the people who will use a building or place. The goal of such an understanding is rarely part of contemporary architectural school curricula. For 17 years, an online competition, the international Berkeley Undergraduate Prize for Architectural Design Excellence (the PRIZE), has worked to change this deficiency by directly challenging architecture students to go into their local communities for the purposes of thinking and writing about the meaning of an architecture that originates from this broader perspective. Nearly 1900 students from 62 countries have participated in the PRIZE's Essay and Travel Fellowship competitions.

In 2014, the PRIZE topic was, "The Architect and the Healthful Environment." There were four student Essay winners responding to the competition question: How do you Design a Healthful Environment? Simultaneously, the PRIZE launched its second Teaching Fellowship in the Social Art of Architecture, reflecting the year's competition topic. Three undergraduate studio faculty from around the world were selected to integrate the ideals of human-centered ideals and values into their current course syllabi with a focus on healthful architecture. Their work is ongoing.

Based on the history of the PRIZE; the results of 2014 Essay competition; and the collective analysis of the results of all of the Teaching Fellowships, the author investigates the problems and potentials of shifting the focus of architectural education to people-driven design. In doing so, the idea that new approaches need to be adopted in order to learn, teach and design healthful architecture is examined. A basis for the adoption of these approaches is proposed.

INTRODUCTION

Someone realized that the health of the city people has to be achieved with the health of the city. And thus with the resurrection of a canal in the city's heart, a happy healthy story began. This initiative is part of a utopia of connecting all the dying water channels of Dhaka reviving the hydro-logical balance of this liquid landscape. The name of the project is 'Hatirjheel' which means 'lake of elephants'. History claims that before Dhaka was soaked dry, the elephants of the royal family had bathed here which resulted in this nomenclature.

Public health has not been the primary concern of the Hatirjheel. Yet it is the enthusiasm of people that completes this partially complete design.
The implication of the basic idea – sun, water, flora and fauna attracts health conscious people here. Health is not confined in physical health only. The same slums dwellers who used to live by the fetid water have painted some of their houses in bright blue and pink. It shows a recovering mental health.

The spirited youth, the enthusiast photographers all gather here because of the mental uplift. Everyday all the people who pass by the lake in speedy vehicles or walk by it, feel their umbilical connection to the water.
The nostalgia of the river by their village calms them. Sound of rain on water brings monsoon in the city. The therapeutic design for the city heals the citizen too.

(From the 2014 PRIZE First Place Essay, "Livability vs. Lovability" by Tazrin Islam, Bangladesh University of Engineering and Technology, Dhaka).

Healthful architecture is about creating healthy, productive and emotionally-satisfying communities for the people who reside there.

Healthful architecture is about creating healthy, productive, and emotionally-satisfying personal environments.

And yes, healthful architecture is about creating the best possible healthcare facilities not only for the benefit of the patients, but for the vast array of people who constitute today's healthcare infrastructure. Healthful architecture is at heart about creating places where people flourish in whatever the context or situation.

Teaching and learning about people-centered architecture is critical for the making of such environments. Yet seldom is this social art of architecture used as a benchmark against which to evaluate the quality of buildings and places. Part of the problem is how to interest young architecture students and their faculty in exploring these issues for themselves, in the field, directly interacting with the users of the buildings they propose to design.

This paper explores what can and should be done to make the human-centered ideals of the social art of architecture the primary focus of architectural education in the coming years. It is no coincidence that this is also the starting point for the creation of healthful architecture.

It is important to stress that teaching and learning about the social art of architecture does not end with architecture students, but could and should be extended to healthcare policy makers, medical planners, program and project managers, and staff. The questions and analytical methods explored in this project can and should be applied universally in healthcare environments to boost not only the wellness of the patients, but to enhance the lives of all the people involved in the healthcare delivery system.

CONTEXT

There is now a half-century of groundbreaking studies of the sociology of architecture by such figures as MacKinnon, Blau, Larson, Gutman, Ghirado, Cuff, Crawford, Jenkins, etc. All of these researchers have attempted in one way or another to apply the lessons of the social sciences to the development of (an) architectural theory.
This energy has, so far, not resulted in any new lasting architectural pedagogy.

Part of the problem has been that, however committed to the goals of social justice and public health, architects and architecture schools do not know what to do with seemingly extraneous theoretical, experimental, and/or practical social and behavioral information bubbling up, or more succinctly lying fallow, around them.
Accepting the tenants of what is now called "evidence-based design" is one thing; qualifying that evidence and applying it to architectural design is another.

This actual how (not to mention the ever-present, why) of applying the findings and lessons of the social sciences to the teaching of architecture remains largely unanswered.
There are signs that it is beginning to

be addressed in a more systematic way[1]. Whatever the results of these efforts, the over-riding objective must be to discover ways to discharge the false dualism that has emerged in architecture between social concerns and creative design, and between people-driven design and object-driven design.

The international Berkeley Undergraduate Prize in Architectural Design Excellence (the PRIZE) strives to show architects-in-training and their teachers that the smallest act of building has global implications: that design can and does play a major role in the social, cultural, and psychological life of both the individual and society at large.

315

---

1. In March of this year, a major initiative in the United States by the fraternal professional organization, the American Institute of Architects (AIA), and the Association of Collegiate Schools of Architecture (ACSA) called the "AIA Design & Health Research Consortium," was introduced at an inaugural conference. The Consortium looks to utilize the resources of some of the top schools of architecture and public health in the country to advance, "revolutionary, university-led research in the area of design and health" (See, Schneidawind, J. 2015). There are 11 inaugural members of the Consortium, including 2013 BERKELEY PRIZE Teaching Fellow Eve Edelstein's current home, the NewSchool of Architecture and Design in San Diego, U.S.A. Edelstein has, in addition, organized and become Director of a major cross-disciplinary research and development laboratory, the Design + Health Research Collaboratory, for the purposes of investigating and providing real-time solutions for health and design issues as a handson offshoot of the AIA effort. The potential for these initiatives to influence educational programs in the United States and internationally is real and substantial.

As such, it directly impacts the health and well-being of each inhabitant and their community. It is not design or health, but both working to enhance the other.

LEARNING AND WRITING ABOUT HEALTHFUL ARCHITECTURE

"…healthful design is multidimensional but by no means unattainable. I discovered through a comparison of the Halifax Seaport Farmers' Market and Dalhousie University's Killam Memorial Library, that the key to environmental health include: cooperation between architects, clients, and user-groups; a holistic approach to design that considers environmental, physiological, and social environments; and the thoughtful renovation of previously designed buildings.
While a wider study would likely uncover far more nuance in the design of healthful environments, the present comparison is, for me, a starting point. I have become more aware of the considerations behind healthful design, and more perceptive of architectural responses to these considerations in my city. I have come to realize the influence that architecture - and architects - have on the health of built environments, and my own responsibility to design towards a more healthful city".

(From one of the two, 2014 BERKELEY PRIZE Third Place Essays, "Healthful Halifax: Designing Healthful Spaces, Learning by Example"; by Michael Philpott, Dalhousie University, Halifax, Canada.)

The format for the PRIZE competition, founded in 1998 by Raymond Lifchez, Professor of Architecture and City and Regional Planning at the University of California, Berkeley (Berkeley, U.S.A.), is straightforward. Each year we select a topic integral to the social art of architecture and pose a question, really a prompt, to which the students respond online at www.BerkeleyPrize.org.

From the first topic, "The Architect Meets the Nursing Home" to this year's, "The Architect Confronts Poverty," we have strived to encourage these young architects to go out into their communities and explore the world in which they live in light of the topic and question[2]. A substantial cash award is given for the best essays on the subject.

It is often a baffling task for the student, made all the more difficult by most schools of architectures' reluctance to see – and teach – social purpose as a subject that is at least as important and integral concern as the design of the building form and facade. For 2014, we asked the question:

HOW DO YOU DESIGN A HEALTHFUL ENVIRONMENT?

"In your city, find a building or a public place that helps create a healthful environment. Describe the features of the healthful environment that you admire and why. Tell us what you believe the architect did specifically to make the healthful environment work as it does.
Then, find a building or a public place that offers an unhealthful environment.

---

2. *See Appendices "A"-"C" for a description of how the PRIZE works, and the participants and results of the 2014 PRIZE Essay competition.*

316

317

Figure 1. From the 2014 PRIZE Second Place Winners, "Spaces to Grow in – A Comparative Study of Two Orphanages," by Nipun Prabhakar and Gupta Sukruti, School of Planning and Architecture, Bhopal, India

Describe the features of the unhealthful environment that you do not admire and why. As an architect, describe specifically what you would have done differently, including working with what governmental and civic resources to improve the situation. Tell us what you have learned by this comparative analysis".

The comparisons we received were far-ranging, from a Singapore Bachelor of Architecture Studies student at the Unitec Institute of Technology in Auckland, New Zealand who offered, "Healthful Environments: Architecture and The Human Experience"; to a Chinese-native, Bachelor of Architecture student at the University of Notre Dame School of Architecture, U.S.A. who studied, "Residential Design and Physical Health: A Comparison of Two Communities in Beijing, China"; to the two winning students from Bangladesh and Canada who have been quoted above. What all had in common was both their eagerness to address the issue, but also the realization that the subject and how they gathered information was hugely different from the normal classroom and studio experiences.

Some random comments by the reviewers substantiate this excitement:

- I feel enlightened from reading your essay. The comparison is extremely well visualized. You chose buildings you know then explored them more fully.
- This is a sensitive and probing essay addressing how distinctly opposed two

318

college spaces can be regarding basic human health and more subtle psychological wellbeing. I appreciate how you have engaged with people-more in discussion at the museum and as a seemingly more formal interview at the motel dorm. Just this distinction of discussion versus interview tells lots about the different dynamics of each space.

- This essay has some marvelously poetic concepts (health as the "fruit of a well-lived life"), and is a powerful and nicely unfolding revelation, full of vivid examples. The two urban spaces compared are the grand bazaar as the heart of the social city and the street as a conduit only for the car, and the proposal is to give the streets back to the people.

- The street as public space, and the act of moving through cities is a fascinating place to commence discussions around healthful cities.

- The way you captured how the (buildings) affect the health of the community is absolutely essential to architecture's role in the public space.

The idea is sound and the history is there: good architecture starts with an understanding of the people who will use a building or a place. If you do not understand how architecture can contribute or be detrimental to the mental and physical health of its users, no medical or health services building will answer the needs of its clients adequately. Somehow, these seemingly basic concepts must be integrated both into the traditional architectural curriculum and into mainstream thinking about health-care architecture.

TEACHING HEALTHFUL ARCHITECTURE

"I have made a decision to create a fairy tale for old people wanting them to experience - one more time - the gratuitous joy and innocence only a child could feel. A

Figure 2. Entry from student blog, 2014 PRIZE Teaching Fellow's class. Student: Milica Stojanovic, University of Belgrade

location for the fairy tale would be where all fairy tales take place - in a land far, far away, outside the framework of reality - above their (apartment) Block 28. Since at Televizorke two long buildings are the main characteristics of the block, they have to disappear, so the fairy tale could happen on their roofs which represent two extremes, two opposites that (reflect) each other and (together) make a balance".

The primary goal of the BERKELEY PRIZE Teaching Fellowship is to support innovative thinking by architecture faculty as they work to focus their students' attention on the social, behavioral, and physical characteristics of the users of the buildings and spaces they design.
This is simultaneously a curriculum-development project and a teaching-development project. One major element is to actually implement/teach a specifically designed syllabus.
The second Teaching Fellowship coincided with and was tied to the 2014 PRIZE topic of the "Architect and the Healthful Environment." The three selected Fellows were: Guari Bharat from India; Dr. Ružica Božović-Stamenović from Serbia and Singapore; and Dr. Joseph Wong from Hong Kong[3].
Elaine Ostroff, Hon. AIA, who developed and has worked to popularize the term "user/expert" (Ostroff, E. 1997), coordinated the work of the Fellows for the PRIZE.

319

_____
3. See Appendix "D" for the Fellows' full university affiliations.

Figure 3.   Observing and sketching people in public places. Student: Shivani MehtTable

320

The Fellows agree on a variety of core principles:

- Healthful architecture encompasses both physical and mental health;
- Healthful architecture is a reiterative process that must start and end with the input and acceptance of the user/ experts;
- The teaching of healthful architecture requires a sensitization of the student's mindset to fully understand the complexity of issues that must be addressed for a successful design.

Within this community of agreement is a great range of perspectives, all of which are informed by the special context in which the Fellows' courses were taught.

(Guari Bharat)
Bharat led her 2nd and 3rd year students in the design of a public library with both a strong emphasis on the requirements and demands of different user groups, and an equally strong requirement for the library to clearly demonstrate its contribution to the public health of the community.

More specifically, she focused on having her students develop a program and select a site by utilizing the input of users/experts as the basis for creating the physical design. Some of the key tasks in the studio were:

1. Observing and understanding people's behavior in public places in order to select the site, develop a program and develop design concepts.
Two specific observations and documentation tasks were assigned - first, the mapping of density of people and the

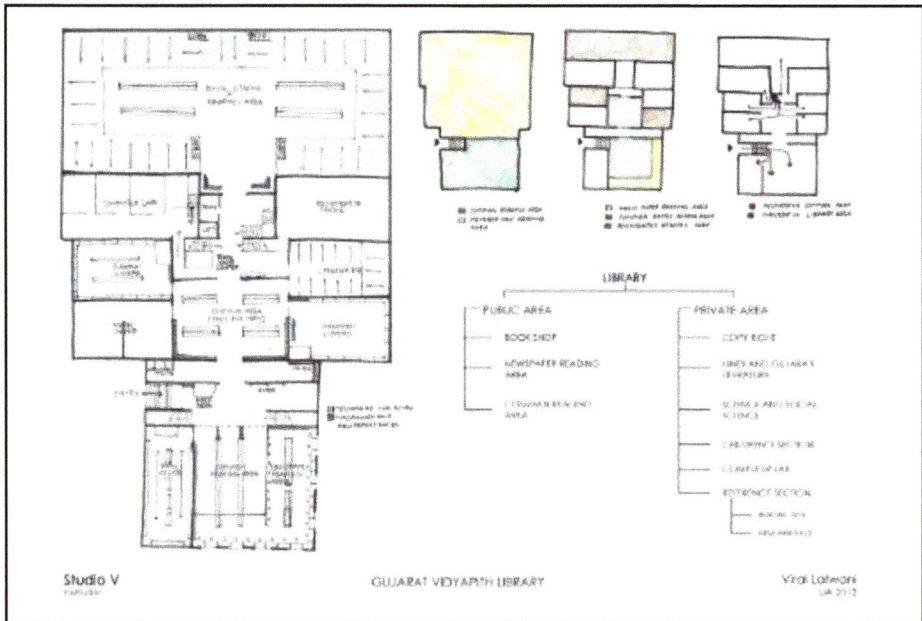

Figure 4. Study of existing library in Ahmedabad. Student: Viral Lalwani

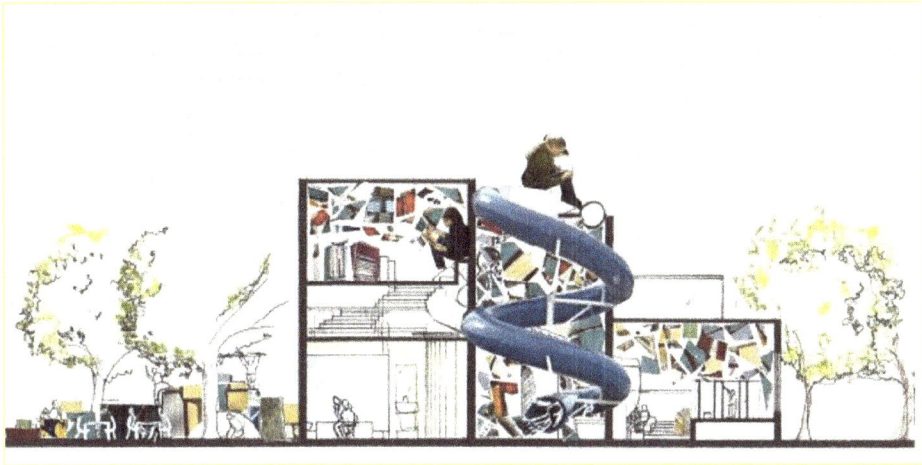

Figure 5.   Collage, imagining the library as a public place. Student: Surabhi Khanderia

physical elements that provided anchors for people in public places, and second, sizes of gathering and the surroundings that encouraged such behavior.

This became the basis for identifying sites that had the potential to develop into public places.

2. Identifying site, program and user/experts.

Students were continuously involved in discussions about where the library could be located such that it could become a potential public place. The involvement of students in the understanding and selection of sites was an important departure from previous studios where students are typically given a site, and encouraged students to think critically about the situating and making of public places.

3. Developing an architecture brief through in terms of users' requirements.

Unlike typical studios where students are given a specific design brief with an area statement that specifies sizes of spaces to

be designed, students in this studio were encouraged to develop a design brief by observing libraries where the sites was located. These exercises served two purposes. First, students were beginning to think of their designs in terms of the workings of a library rather than as forms or volumes, and second, students were considering dimensions in terms of users' requirements rather than in terms of abstract, pre-determined sizes.

4. Concepts, as if users mattered.

Unlike concept models that are typically made on the basis of massing or volumes that will make up the buildings, in this studio, students made concept models on the basis of different levels of access within the library.

This exercise of developing concepts in terms of relationships was one of the most important lessons of the studio given that it clearly shift the emphasis of design from visual forms to users and their relationships to each other and their environments.

322

5. Exploring sense of place by inhabiting one's own design.

A key challenge for the students attempting people-centric design was to integrate inputs from user/experts and observations of people and places into their own designs. One of the ways in which the studio attempted to deal with this challenge was to encourage students to 'inhabit' their own designs in order to evoke its sense of place. This was done in two ways. First, students were encouraged to orally describe their design in terms of how different users may move through the place. Second, in the later stages of design, students were required to make large scale drawings including people, furniture and activities as they imagined taking place within their proposed buildings. These two methods were intended to help the students think about their designs from inside out i.e. as places to be inhabited by people rather than as forms or elevations to be seen.

(Dr. Ružica Božović-Stamenović)

If architects are to be the major mediators of a new, integrative design process, then the question is how to teach them to become sensitive, relevant, reliable and accountable in the field of the social art of architecture. The change begins with changing the students' perspective on the issues, the users, and the needed dialogue between all those involved in the design process.

It also requires changing their own attitudes, views, and sensitivity to social issues in general. In other words, the need is to energize students at an early point in their education to give a priori attention to responses to the social and behavioral factors that will create healthful architecture.

In her Fellowship year, Božović-Stamenović explores specific methods and experiences, based on the work of two design studios located on opposite sides of the globe in Serbia and Singapore.

The juxtaposition of these two venues provides clues as to what is universal about teaching the social art of architecture and what, perhaps, is not. Her initial results of the two semester's comparison shows:

- Students' reaction to the same methodology indicates differences triggered by and based on cultural context, social expectations and common behavior.

- The similarity is evident on higher levels of perception and cognition where basic human needs are addressed and managed: safety, empathy, and social support.

- Student's ability to recognize and deal with users' needs and expectations is closely dependent on their

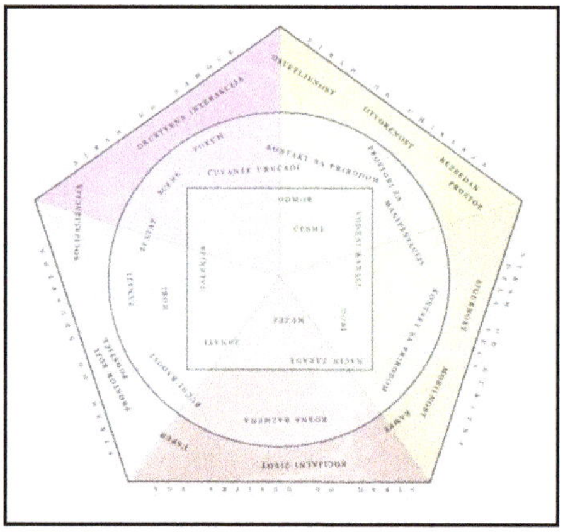

Figure 6. Diagram of influences on users (in Serbian) showing students' awareness of the complexity of issues. Student: Milos Mitrovic

own sensitivity and ability to exceed strictly professional codes of conduct and insert different modes of design thinking. The difference in this respect between the two groups of students was extremely high, reflecting different attitudes regarding power, empowerment, rules, and self-initiative in the two countries.

Božović-Stamenović posits that healthful architecture is an intersection point of social ("1"), technical ("2"), and design ("3") issues. The investigation of specific parts of this triad is important, however, the healthful effects of design rely on the harmonious coordination of the three parts throughout the entire design process. The mediators in this process should be the architects. Still, in practice it is very common to see a different sequence: "3,2,1" with architects' engagement being focused primarily on design issues and technical properties while turning attention to social aspects comes only much later (if it comes at all), in post- occupancy evaluation exercises.

Teaching exercises centered on raising awareness in students by putting them physically in the situation that mimics the everyday problems of people with disabilities and the elderly. This includes maneuvering through the city in a wheelchair; having to deal with uncomfortable positions for tasks such as writing with the non-primary hand; and darkness, simulating not seeing well for a task. The result is confusion, poor performance, loss of confidence: very similar to what the disabled and elderly people experience on a daily basis in their living environment.

(Dr. Joseph Wong)
Using his local Hong Kong context of ultra-high density residential skyscrapers, Professor Wong has led his 4th year design studio in the investigation of creating healthy vertical environments. This studio project focuses on a real govern-

323

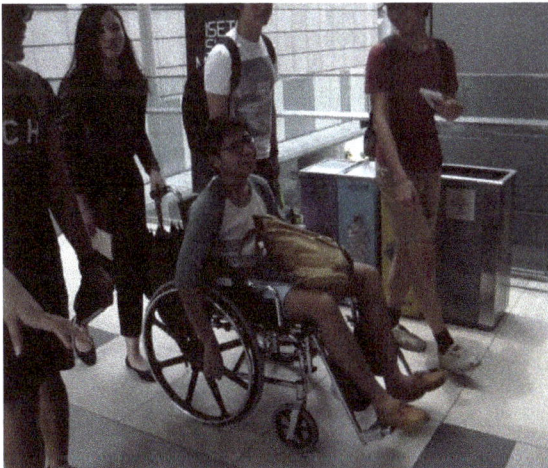

Figure 7. Introducing students to the lives of the "other"

324

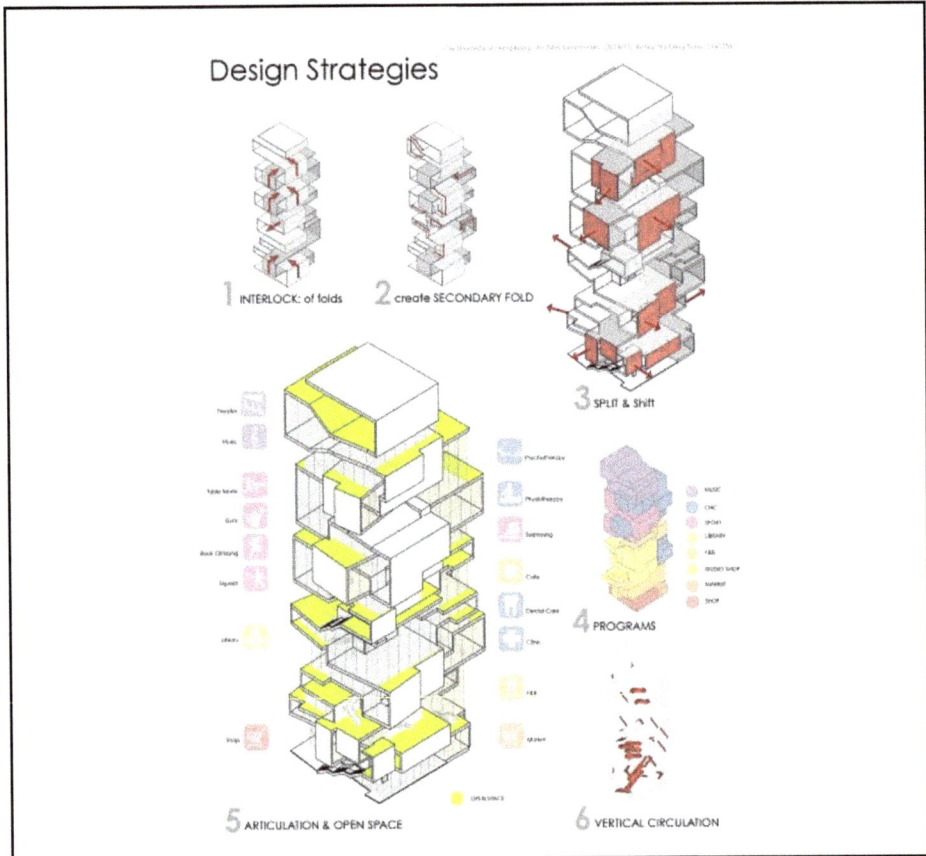

Figure 8. Massing Analysis for a "Healthful Vertical Village." Student: Kenny Ng

ment redevelopment project located at a busy city corner in Mongkok. Despite the rundown state of the built environment around Mongkok, it is home to a vibrant community of "mom-and-pop" shops, markets, Chinese medicine practitioners, local food stalls, etc, that have grown into an integral part of the lives of the mostly under-privileged families in the vicinity.

The studio project examines the possibilities of regenerating the community by rebuilding a better environment to house these local features and extend

this vibrant fabric to form a healthful vertical city.

Let us concentrate here on one specific initiative. With an aging population, one of the most affordable and readily available forms of exercise for the elderly is sitting right outside the doors of their very own apartment units – the staircase. However, most staircases in high-rise buildings are hardly used because they are fire escape staircases intended for use only in times of emergency. As a result, staircases are designed to be hidden away inside the central service core of the building with little or no sunlight and with the steepest gradient allowed to save space.

It is not the most suitable staircase for the elderly to use.

In this redevelopment of the old market building into a high-rise building consisting of a Community Health Centre, Elderly Centre and other community facilities, Wong's students were encouraged to explore the possibility of using programming to create local movement "networks" to encourage the users, especially the elderly, to make use of staircases instead of elevators for vertical circulation when they move up or down only a few floors.

"The individual health benefits of daily exercise are clear; in this instance, the mental health benefits of greater direct interaction with their neighbors might surpass the physical benefits."

Dr. Wong has also experimented with using graphic networking programs to systematize his students' nascent social and behavioral research. He asked students to chart a mind map of their conversations with their user/experts, including every concept mentioned and if they are mentioned in the same sentence or related concepts then to create a link between them. Using the social network analysis software, Gephi, these are then combined to form a larger map for each group of students, who are working on a (library) project for different user groups.

The result is a "more objective analysis of their user expert interview data rather than only choosing bits that they like." Like Božović-Stamenović's student graph(s), this shows the complexity of the issues, but takes that effort one step further by providing a cross-cultural platform and set of tools to examine these complexities.

A subtext in all of these excellent efforts and results by the Fellows was the role and efficacy of evidence-based design. Each of the Fellows approached collecting data in a completely different way. There was little time to prepare students how to ask questions to provide the best results and the responses were catalogued in widely differing fashions. Interviewing techniques and date collection in the social sciences is a much-studied topic and the proven findings are widely utilized. There was sense of "re-inventing

325

Figure 9. Renderings for a "Healthful Vertical Village." Student: Matthew Fong

the wheel" with the students' efforts. Whether students should be introduced to these techniques for their own use, or work and study with social science experts to execute the interviews and surveys is an open question. Perhaps, architecture students should join with social science students in joint research/learning efforts.

Overshadowing this methodological issue is the further question of how the architect's traditional creative and often intuitive approach to problem-solving should be integrated into an evidence-based architecture process. It is possible that architecture requires a new model for collecting "evidence."

A BASIS FOR CHANGE

"In much of mainstream architectural education, terms such as 'context' and 'user' are loosely defined and casually engaged with. Often, they translate into some preliminary documentation of the physical surroundings of sites by way of contextual analysis and profiling abstract and imagined users rather than engaging with real people. This leads to working with preconceptions about users and it is not surprising then that architectural education, and indeed the profession at large, has come under criticism as facing a crisis of relevance in recent times".
(Guari Bharat, 2014 BERKELEY PRIZE

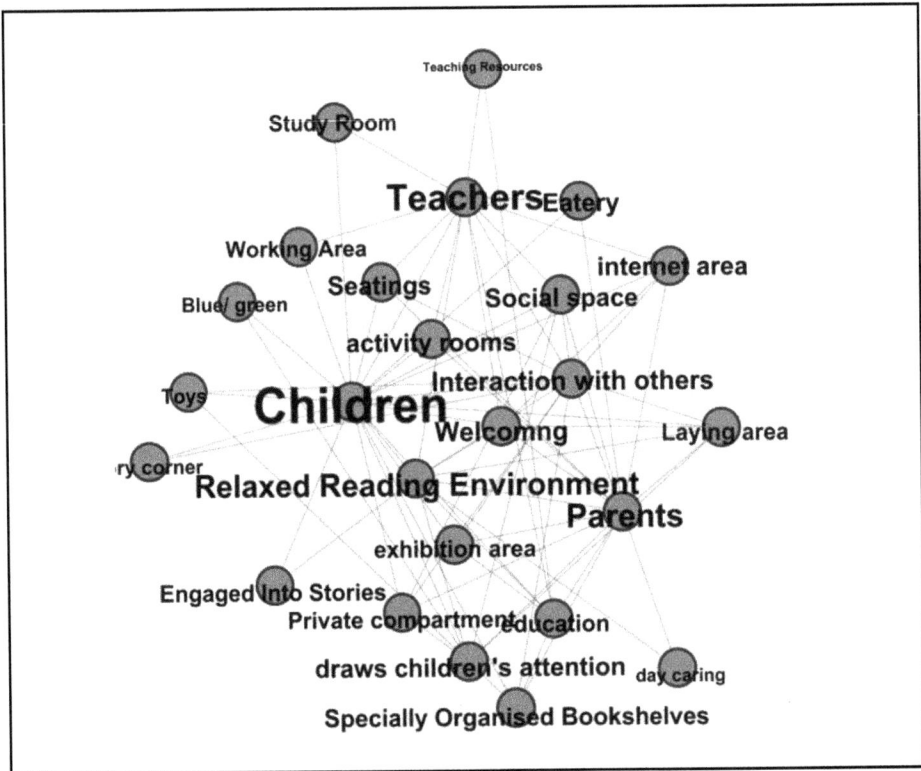

Figure 10. The graph of the combined students' mind map. Bolder/larger entries shows "closeness" among concepts

Teaching Fellow, Interim Report on Fellowship year.)

All three Fellows, their students, and the work of the Essayists have shown how, when faced with talking about architecture in non-traditional ways not only does the process of teaching change, but the interests and motivations of the students themselves change. The subject of "The Architect and the Healthful Environment" puts these issues in stark relief, but they point to the same conclusion: the attitudes of students about what is important in design and what is merely style can readily and rightly be changed by faculty who are equally motivated.

The experiences also point to the need to more systematically investigate a series of largescale changes that would be required to fully implement the teaching of the social art of architecture. I have previously reported on five that remain most apparent (Clavan, B. 2014). These are:

1. The emphasis must be on place, not studio.
2. User/experts must become an integral part of the learning environment.
3. Different standards must be adopted for course outcomes.
4. Social scientists must be (re-)integrated into the design process.
5. The idea of empathy must be consciously incorporated into the architectural studio and classroom.

If architecture is to ever truly reflect its importance as a social art, and if healthful architecture is to be accepted as a prerequisite for good design, a completely different approach to the teaching of architecture, the preparation of teachers of architecture, and the motivation of students is required. First and foremost, we must open the door to the question of value, of what works and what does not, of what is good and bad.

- Inside the academy, this new approach questions the accepted dogma of subjectivity and neutrality in traditional teaching, particularly as it applies to subjects of taste and perception in architecture.
- Outside the academy, this new approach requires a willingness to engage with the community in ways much different than traditionally accepted and much more difficult to organize and control. The result is a different and more sensitive relationship between the teacher and the student, and between the student and their peers, and yes, between teachers and their peers. These reinvigorated relationships will, without question, change the way architecture is taught and learned.

APPLYING THE LESSONS LEARNED

Adopting these goals to ongoing and planned healthcare projects will not be easy. The design and construction process in any country is complex, hierarchical, and above-all, steeped in the tradition of the local environment.

The new generation of architects, aware of the limitations of formal design and skilled in becoming mediators for people-centered architectural design is not yet in the field. Nor is the healthcare system itself prepared for such changes.

What is clear is that the lessons from teaching healthful architecture are widely applicable to the day-to-day operations in the healthcare environment. Learning in-depth about the people involved at all levels of the system is

327

the first priority: not technologies, not building systems, not therapies – simply, people.

Engaging users in a much more systematic and participatory way is a methodology that can be adopted almost immediately. At the very initial stages of a project, user/experts – those who have actually lived the situation - should be identified. These new participants in the design process should become a constant presence both in developing theoretical responses, interacting during the various stages of design, and even through construction. These same participants should be prepared now to amend the environment later, after occupancy, to reflect what will undoubtedly be a series of changing needs and desires. The result is a design based on consensus and flexibility, not simply rigid geometry imagined in the all-too-common isolation of an architect's office.

The patients top the list, but all of the individuals caring for them and the physical plant are of equal importance in he design process. The tasks that these people undertake are at the heart of a flourishing and well-designed healthcare environment. The physical component of their situation - the setting - should to the greatest extent possible reflect their preferences, their stated and implicit needs, and their thoughts and aspirations. This might seem all too obvious, but surprisingly even the most rigorous programming often overlooks what we know and what we do not know about human factors in design.

This commitment by those who design, build and manage ultimately requires a seminal change in the way we look at the production of architecture as a whole and the relationship between architects, their clients, and society at large. But that is a subject for another paper.

(APPENDIX "A")
HOW THE PRIZE WORKS

Each year, the BERKELEY PRIZE Committee poses a Question on the competition website. Students enrolled in any undergraduate architecture program throughout the world or those in collateral disciplines teamed with such students are invited to submit a 500-word essay proposal in English responding to the Question. From this pool of essays, approximately 25 are selected as particularly promising by the PRIZE Committee, a group of 63 international architects, architectural educators, social scientists, writers, and general thinkers. (See: http://www.berkeleyprize.org/endowment/berkeley-prize-committee/).

The 25 semifinalists are then asked to submit a 2,500-word Essay expanding on their proposals. The Committee then selects five to eight of the best Essays and sends these finalists on to a jury of international architects and academics to select the winners. The BERKELEY PRIZE Essay Competition is announced, papers submitted, and reader- and jury-reviewed all online. During the past seventeen years, 1870 students have submitted essays and proposals, representing dozens of schools of architecture from 62 countries.

Students are also given a further incentive to compete: each year the selected 25 or more semifinalists are given the opportunity to propose a study trip outside

328

of their home country that is linked to that year's topic. This trip, the BERKELEY PRIZE Travel Fellowship, is hopefully part of a social service event or conference. Twenty-five students have been awarded Travel Fellowships over the last eleven years. Their travelogues speak to the extent to which on-site, face-to-face investigations transform the landscape of architectural inquiry.

As the positive results of this effort multiplied, it became equally clear to the PRIZE Committee that architecture faculty were still not encouraging much, if any, shift in the ways of looking at the art and task of design. This was an issue of teaching. Starting in 2013, a Teaching Fellowship in the Social Art of Architecture was initiated as a first step to encourage and foster a new approach among faculty.

In recognition of these efforts, the BERKELEY PRIZE is the recipient of the 2008 American Institute of Architects Collaborative Achievement Honor Award; and the 2002 American Institute of Architects' Education Honor Award.

The BERKELEY PRIZE has also garnered international acclaim, not the least reason for which is its complete embracing of digital technology.

In partial recognition of this outreach, the 2003 BERKELEY PRIZE competition was named a special event of "World Heritage in the Digital Age," a virtual congress helping to commemorate the 30th anniversary of the UNESCO World Heritage Convention.

In 2014, a total of 237 students responded to the competition announcement. Of these, 141 undergraduate ar-

chitecture students from 28 countries were qualified to participate.

(APPENDIX "B")
LIST OF THE 2014 BERKELEY PRIZE JURY

Arza Churchman: Professor Emeritus, Technion Faculty of Architecture and Town Planning, Haifa, Israel; past President, International Association for People-Environment Studies; 2001 Career Achievement Award of the Environmental Design Research Association (EDRA).

Susan Goltsman: Children's Environmental Designer with degrees in Architecture, Landscape Architecture and Envrionmental Psychology; Founding Principal of Moore, Iacofano, Goltsman (MIG), Inc., Berkeley, California, U.S.A.; author of Play for All Guidelines and The Inclusive City.

Daniel Karlin, M.D.: Medical Resident, University of California, Los Angeles Combined Program in Internal Medicine and Pediatrics with an emphasis on underserved medicine and global health; Recipient of the Albert Schweitzer Community Service Fellowship, and the Fogarty International Clinical Research Scholarship; Member, BERKELEY PRIZE Committee.

Adriano Pupilli, RAIA: Sydney, Australia-based architect working at the junction of art, architecture, ethics and the environment; Collaborator in Healthhabitat, and on communityled development initiatives, including Fixing Houses for Better Health; First winner of the B. PRIZE Travel Fellowship (2004); Member, B. PRIZE Committee.

329

(APPENDIX "C")
LIST OF THE 2014 BERKELEY PRIZE ESSAY WINNERS

Tazrin Islam, Bangladesh University of Engineering and Technology, Dhaka, Bangladesh: "Livability vs. Lovability" (First Place);

Nipun Prabakar and Sukruti Gupta, School of Planning and Architecture, Bhopal, India: "Spaces to Grow: A Comparative Study of Two Orphanages" (Second Place);

Michael Philpott, Dalhousie University, Halifax, Canada: "Healthful Halifax: Designing Healthful Spaces, Learning by Example" (Third Place, tie); and

Aparna Ramesh, Visvesvaraya National Institute of Technology, Nagpur, India: "The Architecture of a Healthful Learning Environment" (Third Place, tie).

(APPENDIX "D")
LIST OF THE BERKELEY PRIZE TEACHING FELLOWS

Gauri Bharat, Assistant Professor of Architecture, CEPT University, Ahmedabad, India.

Ružica Božović-Stamenović, Ph.D., Associate Professor, Faculty of Architecture, University of Belgrade, Serbia (first semester); Visiting Senior Fellow, Department of Architecture, National University of Singapore (second semester). She is also a Faculty Fellow at the Center for Health Systems and Design, Texas A&M University.

Joseph Francis Wong, Ed.D., M. Arch., Assistant Professor, Department of Architecture and Civil Engineering, The City University of Hong Kong.

Allan Birabi, Ph.D., Senior Lecturer, Makerere University Department of Architecture and Physical Planning, Kampala, Uganda.

Eve Edelstein, Ph.D., Associate AIA, (Then) Associate Professor, University of Arizona College of Architecture, Planning and Landscape, Tucson, U.S.A.; (Now) Faculty, NewSchool of Architecture & Design, San Diego, U.S.A.

Ajay Khare, Ph.D., Founder-Director and Professor, School of Planning and Architecture, Bhopal, India with Rachna Khare, Ph.D., Professor of Architecture, SPA, Bhopal.

Alex MacLaren, RIBA, Design Tutor, Edinburgh School of Architecture and Landscape Architecture (ESALA), Edinburgh, United Kingdom

Josh Safdie, Associate AIA, Adjunct Faculty Member, Massachusetts College of Art and Design (MassArt), Boston, U.S.A.

Faiq Mari (Associate Fellow), Teaching and Research Assistant, Department of Architecture, Faculty of Engineering, Birzeit University, Palestine.

REFERENCES

Clavan, B. 2014. *Teaching the Social Art of Architecture: The Transformation of the Studio from Object-Centered to Human-Centered Design.* In Proceedings, 5th International Association for Universal

330

Design (IAUD) Conference, Fukushima and Tokyo, Japan, November 9-13.

Clavan, B. and Lifchez, R. 2006. *The Berkeley Prize: Those Who Make it Work.* In Places Journal, 18(2).

Dutton, T. A. 1996. *Cultural Studies and Critical Pedagogy: Cultural Pedagogy and Architecture,* In Dutton, T. A. and Mann, L.H. (eds.), Reconstructing Architecture: Critical Discourses and Social Patterns, University of Minnesota Press.

Hatch, C. R. (ed.) 1984. *The Scope of Social Architecture, Van Nostrand Reinhold,* New York.

Iacofano, D. and Clavan, B. 2013. *Either/Or? There is very little grey in creating healthful environments,* Berkeley Undergraduate Prize for Architectural Design Excellence, 2013 Essay Competition Introduction, <http://www.BerkeleyPrize. org>.

Lifchez, R. and Clavan, B. 2005. *Competing to Learn: The Berkeley Prize and the Social Art of Architecture,* In Places Journal, 17(1).

Ockman, J. (ed.) 2012. *Architecture School: Three centuries of educating architects in North America,* MIT Press, Cambridge, Massachusetts.

Ostroff, E. 1997. *Mining Our Natural Resources: The User as Expert.* In Innovation, the Quarterly Journal of the Industrial Designers Society of America, 16(1).

Schneidawind, J. 2015. *Share the Health.* "

In AIArchitect, Practicing Architecture, American Institute of Architects, <http:// www.aia.org/practicing/AIAB105810>, accessed March 20, 2015.

331

332

Teaching "Healthcare Architecture & Environment" at Harbin Institute of Technology in China

Zhang Shanshan, Bai Xiaoxia, Bai Xiaopeng, Yi Qi

zhangshanshan@hit.edu.cn
School of Architecture, Harbin Institute of Technology, China

The earliest research of healthcare facilities at HIT started from 1980s by Prof. Zhi Yi-chun and Prof. Xu Baichang. They were also the pioneers about ICU and sterile operating room in China. In 2006, Prof. Zhang Shanshan who was the dean in College of Architecture, formally established "Healthcare Architecture & Environment" program based on HIT's previous research and her engineering practice. This program focuses on the growing healthcare facilities demand in China and preparing students for such kind of complex functional design through both teaching and research. In order to link theory and practice, "Engineering Practice Education Center" for healthcare facilities between HIT (China) and HKS (USA) was established in 2014 which will provide an opportunity for students to learn from architects with practice experience and international perspectives. Our program sets different education objectives and teaching methods for different stages, including undergraduate students, master students and PhD students. For undergraduate students, the purpose is to encourage students' interest and introduce basic healthcare facilities knowledge through teaching. During this four-week class, professor from university and architect from design firms together teach all students who major in architecture at HIT. Each student needs to submit a four -"one" report as their homework, including reading one book, analyzing one healthcare facilities in developed countries, visiting one local hospital and studying one copy of design guidelines. For master students, we pay more attention to practice. Students at this program will take 2.5 years for further study such as typological studies, design strategies, the latest development trends. Each student needs to complete a master's thesis and take part in at least one healthcare project as training. For PhD level, students mainly undertake the specific research contents. During the past 8 years, our team accomplished two "National Natural Science Foundation of China" focusing on healthcare facilities. One is "City Planning and Architectural Design to deal with Public Health Emergencies", the other is "Construction and Evaluation for Prevention and Control of Infectious Diseases". PhD students in our team mostly choose related research topic, such as healthcare efficiency and safety. To sum it up, our team have already cultivated more than 20 masters on this specific direction, and right now 7 PhD candidates are working on it. Our researches keep pace with hot problems and development of healthcare facilities in China. We also pay close attention to international healthcare trends and education.

334

BACKGROUND OF HEALTHCARE ARCHITECTURE EDUCATION IN CHINA

Traditional Chinese architectural education is committed to the training of basic knowledge for being an architect, including architecture history, design theory and construction technology. Further research of stereotype architecture design and theory mostly begins from the graduate or above.

Education program for healthcare architecture started relatively later in China and even right now only few influential architectural colleges could offer courses, representative ones such as Chongqing University, Beijing University of Civil Engineering and Architecture, Harbin Institute of Technology(HIT) and so on.

In addition, there are teachers and students from other universities do healthcare architecture research based on their interest, showing the characteristics of individual and scattered.
It is not easy for them to inform a comprehensive research system, not even to reflect the effect on a wide range of teaching. Most architects have little or no education in this specific direction in China.

They do healthcare buildings design based on their experience at work, however, this kind of background and method may leave lots of problems. Healthcare architecture is always considered as one of the most complex type and has more demanding, therefore, architects should constantly strive for perfection and healthcare architectural education should also be further strengthened.

PROGRAM OF "HEALTHCARE ARCHITECTURE & ENVIRONMENT" AT HIT

Background and History

The earliest research of healthcare facilities at HIT started from 1980s by Prof. Zhi Yichun and Prof. Xu Baichang.

They were also the pioneers about ICU and sterile operating room in China. At the beginning, teaching was only for graduate students and presented a number of papers during the early healthcare architecture research in China. In 2006, Prof. Zhang Shanshan who was the dean in College of Architecture, formally established "Healthcare Architecture & Environment" program based on HIT's previous theoretical research foundation and her engineering practice.

This program relies on Public Architecture and Environment Institute, which focuses on the growing healthcare facilities demand in China and preparing students for such kind of complex functional design through both teaching and

Figure 1. Lectures of Healthcare Architecture

Figure 2. Discussion with architects using Patient-room models

Figure 3. Courses for Design Practice

research. Main concept of this program is to integrate teaching, research and practice of three-in-one throughout the healthcare architecture education.

Teaching and Research Plan

To complete learning of healthcare architecture design and research requires a lot of time and there is no need for everyone to get the same degree, so this program sets different education objectives and teaching methods for different stages, including undergraduate students, master students and PhD students.

Each level of teaching is composed of two parts, professional content and related methods.
- For undergraduate students, the pur-

pose is to expand their professional knowledge through introduction of basic healthcare facilities and encourage their research interest in this field. The task of teaching is to know "what is healthcare architecture" and the international forefront of development. Since most undergraduate students will work as a designer in their future, the key point is not to require them to remember too much about professional knowledge, but to help establish some design concept of healthcare architecture and learn how to deal with the similar complex design. If there is such an opportunity of designing healthcare architecture at future work, they should know research-based design, how to collect research information and use it during the design process. Courses for undergraduate students usually last for four weeks, including lectures (Fig.1), discussion with architects from design firms (Fig.2), and visiting local hospital. This class covers all students who major in architecture at HIT. After class, each student needs to submit a "four-one" report as their homework, including reading one book, analyzing one healthcare facilities in developed countries, visiting one local hospital and studying one copy of design guidelines. In summary, we promote basic healthcare architecture education through courses among all undergraduate students.

- For master students, we pay more attention to practice and fundamental research. The task of teaching is not only to know "what" is healthcare architecture", but also "why". Since master graduate education is a state between specialist and generalist, therefore, our purpose is to use healthcare architec-

335

336

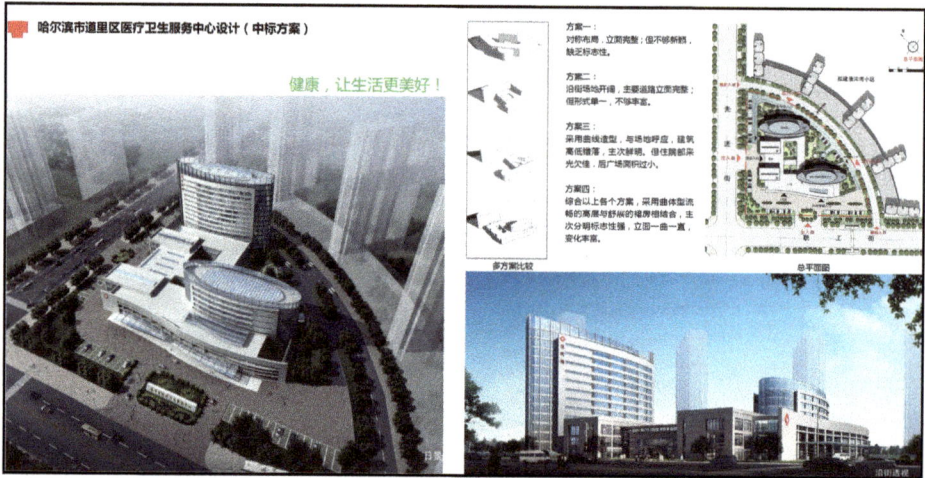

Figure 4. Student Project1: Center for Disease Control and Prevention of Harbin

ture design as training materials and to cultivate students' ability of transferring the design similarity to other types of buildings. This program covers 10 to 12 students each year. It will take 2.5 years for further study such as typological studies, design strategies, the latest development trends. Students are required to complete some reading, survey and design practice. Each student should at least take part in one healthcare project as training (Fig.3).

Figures 4-5-6 are some student projects through our teaching and they are all real projects, for example, Center for Disease Control and Prevention of Harbin (Fig.4), Community Health Service Center of Binhai (Fig.5), Pingshan Hospital (Fig.6) and so on. Actually, it is not easy for students to participate in real healthcare project practice, so teachers will try hard to create opportunities for them. If they do not get projects to design, they will use healthcare architecture design competition program instead. In addition, all students at HIT need

to get their degree through completing a master dissertation and students at this program usually choose related topic to healthcare facilities. For example, streamline design, different types of healthcare facilities, new technologies using in this direction and so on. Table 1 shows our recent master dissertations.

- For PhD level, students mainly undertake the specific research contents. The task of teaching is not only the present situation, but also leading them to explore "what should it be". The research scope is not limited in the hospital buildings ontology, also into a more macro and micro two-way level, including the national medical environment and micro hospital environment control technology. It usually takes 5 to 6 years for PhD students to study. Their training program includes healthcare architecture courses, exchange of learning abroad, design practice, hospital survey and investigation, and their own research dissertation. Most students focus on the hot-spot issues of China's health-

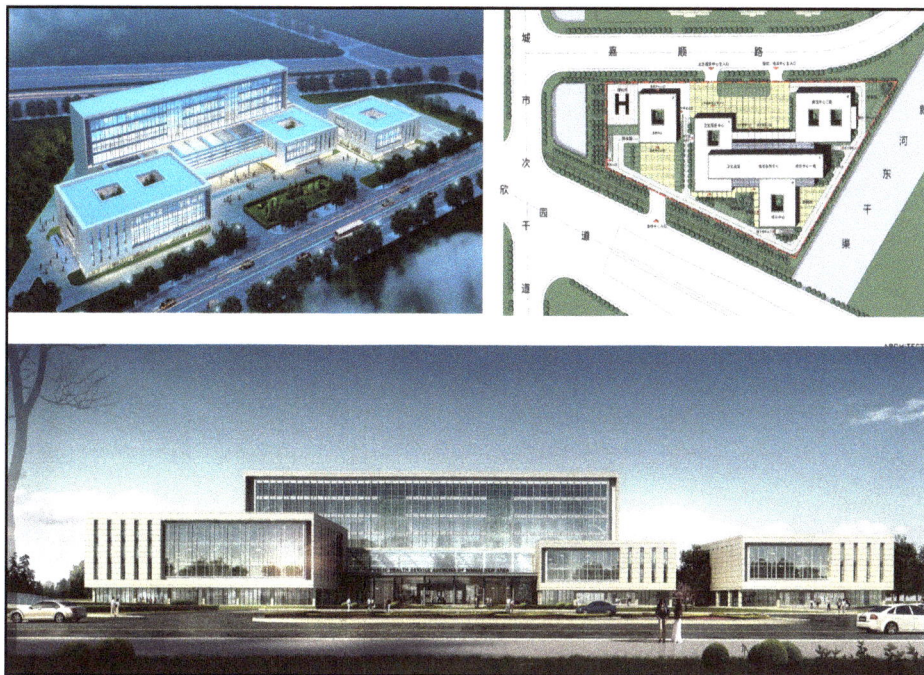

Figure 5. Student Project2: Community Health Service Center of Binhai

care construction problems or combine their research with the National Natural Science Foundation of their instructor. During the past 8 years, our team accomplished two "National Natural Science Foundation of China" focusing on healthcare facilities. One is "City Planning and Architectural Design to deal with Public Health Emergencies", the other is "Construction and Evaluation for Prevention and Control of Infectious Diseases". To sum up, student research topics can be divided into three categories, comprehensive issues of healthcare architecture development, design and research of new hospital function type, and technical measures of hospital construction. Table 2 shows our recent PhD's research topics.

NEW APPROACHES AND TEACHING AT HARBIN INSTITUTE OF TECHNOLOGY

Training about Research Specificity of Healthcare Architecture

Learning about healthcare architecture design must be connected with field experience and research, so we try to instill it in all three stages. Field experience for undergraduate only takes 2 to 3 days for some basic streamlines, functions and atmosphere. For master graduate students it is generally 1 to 3 months connected their dissertation topic while 6 to 12 months for PhD students based on different researches. Different countries take different procedures and strict degrees for survey and investigation. In principle, any research related

338

Figure 6. Student Project3: Pingshan Hospital

to participation of people should takes the procedure of ethical approval, (e.g. IRB or ERB in America), however, the current architecture research in China is in a mixed state of official approval and private communication. Since the behavior and psychology of people in hospital are more sensitive, so the risk of controversial is much higher than other investigations. When it comes to healthcare architecture and environment research, we need to require students to pay more attention to this confused condition. No matter what kind of intervention they take, must attach great importance to the rights and interests involved, in order to protect both sides and avoid causing resentment or even adverse effects. So here we also call for architectural education in China (not just the healthcare architecture education) should be further strengthened on

STUDENT NAME	DISSERTATION TOPIC
JIANG YILIN	DIGITAL TECHNOLOGY-ASSISTED DESIGN OF HOSPITAL BUILDINGS
DANG RUI	STUDY ON DESIGN OF HOSPITAL LANDSCAPE BASED ON NEW MEDICAL MODEL
BAI XIAOXIA	RESEARCH ON FUNCTION EFFICIENCY OF HOSPITAL SPACE SYSTEM
KONG ZHE	THE MATERNITY HOSPITAL DESIGN STRATEGY UNDER NEW HEALTH CONCEPT
HAO FEI	RESEARCH ON FUNCTIONAL CONFIGURATION OF COMMUNITY HEALTH SERVICE CENTERS
LIU TAO	STUDY ON ENERGY SAVING OF HOSPITAL BASED ON GREEN HOSPITAL EVALUATION STANDARDS
SUN LIMING	RESEARCH ON DESIGN OF HOSPITAL UNDER THE INFLUENCE OF HOSPITAL ALLIANCE
ZHANG XIAOMING	THE SECURITY RESEARCH OF IN-PATIENT DEPARTMENTS BASED ON THE CROWD SIMULATION EVACUATION
QI YI	RESEARCH ON DESIGN STRATEGY OF INFECTIOUS DISEASE HOSPITAL IN THE VIEW OF PREVENTION AND CONTROL SYSTEM
WANG ZHAO	RESEARCH ON GENERAL HOSPITAL BUILDING DESIGN BASED ON COST CONTROL
PEI LIDONG	RESEARCH ON MENTAL HEALTH CENTER DESIGN STRATEGY BASED ON THE ANALYSIS OF BEHAVIOR AND PSYCHOLOGY
MA YULIN	RESEARCH ON DESIGN OF REHABILITATION CENTER BASED ON THE RATIONAL ALLOCATION OF MEDICAL RESOURCES
ZHAO XIUJIE	OUTPATIENT SPACE DESIGN COUNTERMEASURES UNDER THE INFLUENCE OF "ONE-STOP" SERVICE MODE
ZHANG YUFEI	STUDY ON DESIGN OF FIRST-AID CENTER IN GENERAL HOSPITALS FOR PUBLIC HEALTH EMERGENCY
HOU CHANGYIN	RESEARCH ON DESIGN OF DISEASE PREVENTION AND CONTROL CENTER
DONG XU	STUDY ON DESIGN OF OLD HEALTH CENTER ACCORDING TO THE EMERGENCY MEDICAL EVENTS
ZHANG JIA	STUDY ON HOSPITAL PUBLIC SPACE BASED ON NEW MEDICAL MODE
TIAN HAO	THE RESEARCH ON BEHAVIOR OF PATIENT IN EMERGENCY SPACE
ZHANG YU	THE RESEARCH OF CHILDREN'S MEDICAL ENVIRONMENT BASED ON NEW MEDICAL MODE

Table 1 Summary of Master's Dissertations of Healthcare Architecture and Environment

339

STUDENT NAME	DISSERTATION TOPIC
LIU NAN	STRUCTURE STUDY ON THE MEDICAL BUILDING NETWORK OF EMERGENT INFECTIOUS DISEASES PREVENTION AND CONTROL
ZHANG HONGZHE	EVALUATION SYSTEM STUDY ON THE MEDICAL ARCHITECTURE NETWORK OF EMERGENT INFECTIOUS DISEASES PREVENTION AND CONTROL
JIANG YILIN	STUDY ON THE SPATIAL PATTERN OF HOSPITAL ARCHITECTURE BASED ON EFFICIENCY OPTIMIZATION
BAI XIAOXIA	ENVIRONMENT RISK OF HEALTHCARE SPACES THROUGH A MEDICAL SAFETY VIEW
PEI LIDONG	DESIGN OF TRANSLATIONAL MEDICINE RESEARCH CENTER
QI YI	APPLICATION OF LIGHT STRUCTURE IN HOSPITAL DESIGN

Table 2 Summary of PhD's Dissertations of Healthcare Architecture and Environment

the student's research ethics knowledge. Chinese society is full of social relations everywhere. Some research is very difficult to continue if there is no "Acquaintances" to help. So in this case, we need to require students pay more attention to some skills of communication, observation, sampling and recording. Training about the specific characteristics of healthcare architecture research is mostly carried out internally in our institute. For example, no matter the research has the official approval or it is just privately communication, the process must avoid adverse interference to healthcare behavior. Students cannot contact the patients without the permission of their doctors. It is not allowed to take pictures on many occasions in hospital, so researchers must choose other way to record instead, such as sketches. Staff interviews must be taken at appropriate time and place even if with acquaintance.

Cultivation of Research-Based Design Consciousness

Healthcare architecture is constantly updated with the development of medicine, medical technology, construction science and technology and also affected by regional culture, healthcare model, etc. At this age of information, education for healthcare architecture design is not only teaching the existing model of hospital, but also help the students to grasp the inherent elements of these differences and changes. So teaching process should cultivate students' ability to keep track with the latest trend of international advanced medical technology, construction technology, and keep a keen academic insight. Only keep the research-based design concept in mind and implement it in their future design, could ensure the forward-looking of healthcare architecture design. During the daily teaching, our program actively promotes interdisciplinary cooperation, so that students can get a more comprehensive knowledge through other relevant professional teaching. China is in the hospital construction peak, learning from the international advanced design concepts must be combined with the local medical system and culture. So it is necessary and urgent to cultivate designers according to local conditions of China.

Link Theory and Practice through University-Enterprise Cooperation

The important significance of university-enterprise cooperation is providing an innovative verification platform for education, and at the same time giving the frontier practice feedback to the colleges and universities. In order to link theory and practice, "Engineering Practice Education Center" for healthcare facilities between HIT (China) and HKS (USA) was established in 2014 which will provide an opportunity for students to learn from architects with practice experience and international perspectives. During the teaching process, designers of HKS will also participate the education in university and discuss their latest healthcare building design projects.

CONCLUSIONS

After 10 years of development, program of "Healthcare Architecture & Environment" at HIT has established a complete teaching and research system. This program is committed to addressing the complex needs of healthcare facilities in China, cultivating local designers, promoting healthcare architecture

education and sharing these approaches in international platform. Healthcare architecture education started late in China, and the number of professional designers is still relatively small right now, so here we hope to have more experts and scholars to pay attention to healthcare architecture education in China.

REFERENCES

Li Yucong, Teaching, *Researching and Practice of Medical Architecture in Katholieke Universiteit Leuven- Rational Design, Chinese Hospitals and Meditex System*, Urbanism And Architecture, 2008. 07PP33-36.

George J. Mann, translated by Guo Yan, Proofread by Zhu Xuemei, T*he Evolution of the "Architecture for health"* Program at Texas A&M University. Urbanism And Architecture, 2008. 07 PP39-40.

David Allison, *Graduate Studies in Architecture + Health of Clemson University.* Urbanism And Architecture, 2009. 07, PP31-34.

Ronald L.S Kaggs, Joseph G. Sprague, George J. Mann, *The Asian Practice of the "Architecture for Health" Program at Texas A&M University in USA*, Urbanism And Architecture, 2009. 07, PP41-45.

342

The Latest New Research & Design Projects at Texas A&M University

George J.Mann

gmann@arch.tamu.edu
RA, AIA, Professor, holder of the Ronald L. Skaggs, FAIA Endowed Professor in Health Facilities Design, Department of Architecture, Center for Health Systems & Design

343

INTRODUCTION

Case studies of collaborative research & design projects were presented, including but not limited to: - "A Hospital for Roatan Island, Honduras" - "Rapidly Deployable Transportable Modular Units for Isolating Patients with Ebola and other Communicable Diseases" - "A Satellite Ambulatory Care Clinic & Sports Medicine Center for TSRHC - Texas Scottish Rite Hospital for Children, Dallas, Texas USA, A collaborative architecture and landscape architecture studio" - The "Architecture for Health" visiting lecture series that supports the research & design efforts were presented and discussed.

DESCRIPTION

Organizing the collaborating team which included the actual client and site, as well as the architects, along with the process for the project results of these projects, were presented.

METHODS

The project scope and design and the project statement was defined. The local culture, religion, climate, materials and methods of construction were analyzed. How the facilities were to be staffed was considered.

This method further defined the project space program and scope. The site was selected and a site analysis developed. Upon completion of the analysis and the space program design concepts were developed.

RESULTS/OUTCOMES

As a practice based collaborative studio, emphasis was placed on the continuous participation and input of the client.

CONCLUSION

Schools of Architecture have a duty and responsibility to extend the frontiers of architectural research and practice by creating research and design studios that are practice based, involve actual architectural firms, clients, and sites. This requires a tremendous amount of coordination and planning, but creates a dynamic development learning environment for the students.

344

DESIGN AND
CONSTRUCTION OF A
RAPIDLY DEPLOYABLE
SUSTAINABLE MODULAR
**ISOLATION UNIT FOR
EBOLA** AND OTHER
COMMUNICABLE
DISEASES
ARCH 607
SEP. 2015

345

346

www.ingramcontent.com/pod-product-compliance
Lightning Source LLC
Chambersburg PA
CBHW061230150426
42812CB00054BA/2552